Wounded Cities

Wounded Cities

Destruction and Reconstruction in a Globalized World

Edited by
Jane Schneider and Ida Susser

BERG

Oxford • New York

First published in 2003 by
Berg
Editorial offices:
1st Floor, Angel Court, 81 St Clements Street, Oxford OX4 1AW, UK
838 Broadway, Third Floor, New York, NY 10003–4812, USA

Berg is an imprint of Oxford International Publishers Ltd.

Library of Congress Cataloging-in-Publication Data
A catalogue record for this book is available from the Library of Congress.

British Library Cataloguing-in-Publication Data
A catalogue record for this book is available from the British Library.

ISBN 1 85973 683 1 (Cloth)
1 85973 688 2 (Paper)

Typeset by JS Typesetting Ltd, Wellingborough, Northants.
Printed in the United Kingdom by Biddles Ltd, Guildford and King's Lynn.

www.bergpublishers.com

Contents

Figures

Contributors

Dominic Bryan

Dr. Dominic Bryan is a lecturer at the Institute of Irish Studies at Queens University in Belfast. He has published widely on the use of symbols and rituals in Irish politics including a book *Orange Parades: The Politics of Ritual, Tradition and Control* (Pluto Press, 2000). His present project, funded by the Economic and Social Research Council, "Representing a new Northern Ireland," looks at the use of political symbols through the peace process.

Suhong Chae

Suhong Chae (recent graduate, Ph.D. Program, C.U.N.Y.) has been studying factory workers' class identity in the developing countries of Asia. In 1990–1, he studied a labor movement in an industrial complex located in a suburban area of Seoul and wrote a thesis, "Poong-Mul (a Korean Traditional Music Genre) and the Formative Process of Working Class Identity". In 1998–2000, he also conducted fieldwork in a multinational textile factory in a suburban area of Ho Chi Minh City. His dissertation is on the Vietnamese factory worker's class consciousness and resistance in the context of reform (*Doi Moi*) policy.

David Harvey

David Harvey is Distinguished Professor of Anthropology at the City University of New York Graduate Center. Previously he was Professor of Geography at the Johns Hopkins University and Halford Mackinder Professor of Geography at Oxford University. He is a recipient of several awards for outstanding work in geography, most recently the Patron's Medal from the Royal Geographical Society, the French Vautrin Lud Prize, and the Centenary Medal from the Royal Scottish Geographical Society. Among his many books exploring themes of importance to urban development are *Social Justice and the City; Consciousness and the Urban Experience; The Urbanization of Capital; The Condition of Postmodernity; and Spaces of Capital: Towards a Critical Geography.*

Caroline Humphrey
Caroline Humphrey is Professor of Asian Anthropology at the University of Cambridge, U.K. and a Fellow King's College, Cambridge. She has worked since 1966 in Asian parts of Russia, Mongolia, Inner Mongolia (China), India and Nepal. Among her publications are *Karl Marx Collective: Economy, Society and Religion in a Siberian Collective Farm* (1983); *Barter, Exchange and Value* (ed., with S. Hugh-Jones, 1992); *The Archetypal Actions of Ritual* (with J. Laidlaw, 1994); *Shamans and Elders* (1996); *Marx Went Away, but Karl Stayed Behind* (1998); *The End of Nomadism? Society, State and the Environment in Inner Asia* (with D. Sneath, 1999); *The Unmaking of Soviet Life* (2002).

Claudio Lomnitz
Claudio Lomnitz is an anthropologist who has worked extensively on culture and politics in Mexico. His areas of theoretical interest include cultural geography, history and anthropology, and political anthropology. Lomnitz is author of several books in English and Spanish, including *Evolución de una sociedad rural* (1982); *Exits from the Labyrinth: Culture and Ideology in Mexican National Space* (1992); and *Deep Mexico, Silent Mexico: An Anthropology of Nationalism* (2001) and is Professor of History and Anthropology at the University of Chicago.

Jeff Maskovsky
Jeff Maskovsky is Assistant Professor of Urban Studies at Queens College, C.U.N.Y. He is editor (with J. Goode) of *New Poverty Studies: The Ethnography of Power, Politics and Impoverished People in the United States* (2001), and is currently at work on a book on poverty and grassroots activism in post-industrial Philadelphia.

Carol Meyers
Carol Meyers has 20 years of research experience in Mexico and the U.S. She has participated in a wide array of projects that include an international comparative study of citizen participation in government, a study of community-based alternative housing construction, a comparative study of the impact of Head Start programs, and studies of home health care, and multi-cultural/bilingual education programs. At present she is writing a doctoral dissertation based on her work in Xalapa, Mexico, and is Coordinator of Program Evaluation and Research at the Women's Housing and Economic Development Corporation in New York.

Leith Mullings
Leith Mullings is Presidential Professor of Anthropology at the Graduate Center of the City University of New York. Her books include *Therapy, Ideology and Social Change: Mental Healing in Urban Ghana* (1984); *Cities of the United States* (ed., 1987); *On Our Own Terms: Race, Class and Gender in the Lives of African American Women* (1997); *Let Nobody Turn Us Around: Voices of Resistance, Reform and Renewal, An African America Anthology* (ed. with M. Marable, 2000); *Stress and Resilience: The Social Context of Reproduction in Central Harlem* (with A. Wali, 2001); *Freedom: A Photohistory of the African American Struggle* (with M. Marable, 2002). In 1993 Professor Mullings was awarded the Chair in American Civilization at the École des Hautes Etudes en Sciences Sociales in Paris, France, and in 1997 she received the Prize for Distinguished Achievement in the Critical Study of North America from the Society for the Anthropology of North America. She is currently working on an ethnographic study of gender and globalization in Central Harlem.

Donald Keith Robotham
Don Robotham is Professor of Anthropology at the City University of New York, Graduate Center. Previously he was Pro Vice Chacellor and Dean of the School for Graduate Studies and Research at the University of the West Indies. He did his first degree in sociology at the University of the West Indies, and his Ph.D. in anthropology at the University of Chicago. He has conducted fieldwork in the gold mines of Ghana and in various countries of the English-Caribbean. He is the author of *Militants or Proletarians? The Economic Culture of Gold Miners in Southern Ghana* (1989), as well as articles on the theory of cultural pluralism, and is currently working on a critique of cultural studies from the point of view of political economy.

Mary Roldan
Mary Roldan is Associate Professor of Latin American History at Cornell University. She is the author of *Blood and Fire: La Violencia in Antioquia, Colombia, 1946–1953* (2002), and articles on Colombian politics, violence, and colonization. Her current projects include works on the social and cultural impact of the drug trade in Medellín, Colombia and the relationship between art and politics in mid-twentieth century Latin America.

Aseel Sawalha
Aseel Sawalha, Assistant Professor of Anthropology at Pace University, is an urban anthropologist who conducted fieldwork for her Ph.D. in the city of Beirut, Lebanon. Her research explores the ways in which various readings of the past inform debates over identity, ethnicity, culture and gender relations in the context of urban reconstruction and recovery in postwar Beirut. She has previously done research among Palestinian refugee women in Amman, Jordan, and in a nomadic Bedouin community in south Jordan.

Jane Schneider
Jane Schneider teaches anthropology at the City University of New York Graduate Center. She is the co-editor with Annette B. Weiner, of *Cloth and Human Experience* (1987), and the author of several essays on cloth and clothing. Her anthropological field research has been in Sicily and has led to three books, co-authored with Peter Schneider: *Culture and Political Economy in Western Sicily* (1976); *Festival of the Poor: Fertility Decline and the Ideology of Class in Sicily* (1996); and *Reversible Destiny: Mafia, Antimafia and the Struggle for Palermo* (2003). In 1998, she edited *Italy's Southern Question; Orientalism in One Country*.

Peter Schneider
Peter Schneider teaches sociology at Fordham University, College at Lincoln Center. He is co-author, with Jane Schneider, of *Culture and Political Economy in Western Sicily* (1976); *Festival of the Poor: Fertility Decline and the Ideology of Class in Sicily* (1996); and *Reversible Destiny: Mafia, Antimafia and the Struggle for Palermo* (2003). He is pursuing his interests in organized crime and criminalization through a new section on these issues at the New York Academy of Sciences.

Ida Susser
Ida Susser is a professor of anthropology at Hunter College and the Graduate Center of the City University of New York. Her research, based on fieldwork in New York City, Puerto Rico and southern Africa, has focused on changing patterns of inequality and poverty, social movements, gender and HIV/AIDS. She was the recipient of the 2001 Award for Distinguished Research in North America from the Society for the Anthropology of North America. Her books include *Norman Street: Poverty and Politics in an Urban Neighborhood*; *Medical Anthropology in the World System* (co-author); *AIDS in Africa and the Caribbean* (co-edited); *Cultural Diversity in the United States* (co-edited); and the *Castells Reader on Cities and Social Theory* (edited).

Ara Wilson

Ara Wilson teaches in the Women's Studies and Anthropology Departments at Ohio State University. Having conducted research on the sex industry in Bangkok and on issues of gender and sexuality, she is the author of a forthcoming book, *Intimate Economies: Markets, Sex, and Gender in Bangkok,* University of California Press. Her 1999 article in *Critique of Anthropology* analyses the cultural context of Thai Entrepreneurship.

Acknowledgments

We want to thank the Wenner-Gren Foundation for its generous support of the workshop that led to this volume, and as well Julian Brash and David Vine for preparing extensive, analytical notes on the proceedings. Besides the authors, Louise Lennihan and Neil Smith made significant contributions to the arguments explored in the workshop for which we are also grateful. Michael Burawoy critically read the introductory essay to our considerable benefit. The anonymous reviewer supplied by Berg Publishers made a number of insightful and useful suggestions; his or her comments are greatly appreciated. We thank, as well, Kathryn Earle, Sara Everett and Anne Hobbs at the press for their support and guidance.

–1–

Wounded Cities: Destruction and Reconstruction in a Globalized World

Ida Susser and *Jane Schneider*

Across the world people who live in, have abandoned or been expelled from cities can testify to the mounting crises of contemporary urban life. Tempestuous "acts of nature," no doubt intensified by global warming, stir up crises as do civil wars and preemptive wars of occupation pursued on urban turf. Increasingly, urban wounds also result from globalization processes, unfolding with few constraints since the 1980s. Whatever the source of the affliction, wounded cities, like all cities, are dynamic entities, replete with the potential to recuperate loss and reconstruct anew for the future. Globalization processes are ever more evident in the rebuilding, too. Implicit in this understanding is a framework of analysis that conceptualizes cities from two contrasting, irreducible points of view. On the one hand is the city as a body politic, capable of being collectively wounded and of responding as such; on the other hand, the city is a site where powerful external forces intersect, intensifying differences and conflicts among local groups.

This framework evolved out of a series of informal exchanges in the late 1990s among urban ethnographers in New York City, several of whom were also engaged with urban researchers elsewhere. It was further elaborated at an April 2000 workshop, sponsored by the Wenner-Gren Foundation for Anthropological Research. There a debate emerged regarding the idea of urban "wounding" which, as an organic metaphor, implies a vision of collective well-being that must be negotiated within an identifiable, bounded place. Participants were concerned that this implication deflects attention from the wider field of forces penetrating cities and transforming their internal relations. It also seduces us into forgetting that cities are nested within regional and national entities, not to mention ringed by suburbs, whose taxing and spending practices can help or harm, at times quite dramatically. And yet the image is crucial and compelling. When we take past histories and external pressures into account, it has the power to evoke collective action, imaginative construction in the face of destruction, creative initiatives in the face of decay.

The decision to refine and publish the workshop papers under the title *Wounded Cities, Destruction and Reconstruction in a Globalized World*, was reinforced on September 11th 2001, when New York City succumbed to a shocking and unforgettable urban wound. Subsequent shocking images from cities in Afghanistan and Iraq, considered in an epilogue, powerfully confirm this direction. New York, and the World Trade Center within it, are, of course, ultimate symbols of global finance and wealth. From the mid-1970s, New York's corporate leaders pioneered the core globalizing processes of privatization, the privileging of markets, the reorientation of government finance away from collective public services, all with the effect of widening the gap between rich and poor. Significantly, we believe, the people who died on September 11th, and the populations that have suffered most from the attack, disproportionately represent immigrant entrepreneurial and working-class groups already at the mercy of globalizing trends. They, too, have a stake in the recovery.

If the word "wounded" requires some explanation, so too does the phrase "globalized world." Although clearly referencing the contemporary ubiquity of globalization, it begs the question what globalization means. Generally, two definitions are asserted: on the one hand a series of cultural, informational, and commodity "flows" in which loci of power are difficult to detect, and, on the other hand, a "neo-liberal," finance-driven form of corporate capitalism that subordinates competing institutions, including nation states, to a "new world order". In urban studies, this second meaning has led to the development of a "global cities" framework, inspired by Saskia Sassen's 1991 book of that title. Her identification of New York, London and Tokyo as standard bearers of the "global city" tempted many to classify urban sites in relation to a hierarchy of global engagement. At one extreme are the great financial centers, which coordinate a series of critical functions for the rest of the world; at the other are cities which, as Manuel Castells might put it (1996), languish "off the grid"—so lacking in electronic and telecommunications sophistication as to be irrelevant to the movement of capital and information driving globalization.

In contrast to this view, we look upon globalization as an integrated phenomenon, bringing all of the world's cities into a single, interconnected web. The roster of cities considered in this volume spans a wide range of both scale and geographical location. Drawn from the "third" and "second," as well as "first" worlds, they include (in alphabetical order) Bangkok, Thailand; Beirut, Lebanon; Belfast, Northern Ireland; Ho Chi

Minh City, Vietnam; Kingston, Jamaica; Medellín, Columbia; Mexico City and Xalapa, Mexico; Philadelphia and New York City (specifically Harlem), U.S.; Palermo, Sicily (Italy); and Ulan Ude, Siberia (Russia). Except for New York, none is a major hub of global capital. Yet all are subject, without exception, to pressures emanating from the core institutions of global capitalism to deregulate markets, privatize services like waterworks and electrical energy, pave the way for corporate control of media airwaves, and cut government funding for health, education, and welfare. Variation among them is hardly attributable to a rank order of "more" or "less" engagement with these globalizing pressures.

Regrettably, no African city is considered; two invitees to our conference, specialists on the South African cities of Johannesburg and Durban, were unable to attend. The lacuna is unfortunate, as it reinforces the tendency to caricature much of Africa as peripheral to globalization. South African cities have long been industrialized, their factories managed by global capital. In the post-apartheid South African state, H.I.V./AIDS is now ravaging the cities, affecting both men and women, albeit differently. The poor are dying while a few of the better off, both black and white, have access to treatment. Contemporary processes of revitalization are being undermined as well as promoted by links to global capital, as is the treatment of disease.

Readers will also find a forceful challenge to the viewpoint that African cities are peripheral to globalization in a recent study of Dakar, Senegal, which uses the lenses of youth culture and youth consumption practices to explore recent urban change. Having grown explosively during the 1960s and 1970s when a post-independence national government invested freely and heavily in infrastructure, housing, and local industry, Dakar was then plunged into debt and the shock of structural adjustment in the 1980s. Government spending collapsed, and with it industrial and infrastructural investment, but there has since emerged a flourishing informal economy, including the artisan-level reworking of many imported commodities. Youth, demographically by far the largest group, work and spend in, borrow and steal from, this economy as they envision their futures. Rendering the city a vibrant and exciting place, they also often leave it, or dream of leaving it, to join diaspora Senegalese communities in France, Italy, and especially the U.S. Just as it has been reinvigorated by their presence, Dakar also risks being undermined by their exodus, even though migration remittances are the bread and butter of the informal economy (see Scheld 2003).

As these examples suggest, there is something misleading about arranging cities in a single, seemingly stateless, hierarchical scheme according to which some are more "global" than others. We have preferred to pursue comparisons based on the effects of, and responses to, the *globalizing processes* of neo-liberalism since the 1970s. Among the most salient processes are the redirection of public investment away from collective services and the transfer of service provisioning to the private sector. In many of the cities described here, neo-liberal economic restructuring has also marginalized poor residents, increased or concretized ethnic and racial divisions, increased the subordination of women in new ways, and opened the door to a burgeoning criminal economy resting heavily on drug traffic.

Perhaps most important, this book envisions globalizing processes in relation not only to urban wounds but also to urban recovery. As will be shown, the necessity or opportunity for reconstruction exposes a city immediately and powerfully to neo-liberal capitalist pressures. Often large-scale corporate developers target damaged locations. Here they can transform the landscape in their own image at relatively low cost, thanks to, among other things, tax advantages, the prior reduction of many buildings to burned out hulks or rubble, and the likely absence of organized political protest. A foremost and often over-riding goal is to generate profits for transnational corporate interests associated with finance, name-brand shopping, and tourism. Although hardly a "wounded city," Rome offers a *leitmotif* for this approach. Having relocated most of its working classes to the outer rim, it presents strolling tourists with boutique-lined streets and, hiding the scaffolding of monumental restoration projects, billboard-scale ads for luxury cars and cosmetics. (The Fascist regime of the 1930s, seeking to identify with Caesar Augustus, also dislocated working classes from the ancient core of the city, but its goal was to create vast spaces for parades and political-military spectacles, not consumption.)

To attract tourist dollars and, in association with this, convention dollars and multimillion dollar sports events, cities must recreate themselves as commodities, investing heavily in representation. Several studies, well summarized by Low (1999: 16–18), note the resulting dislocations of people, whether through legally sanctioned eviction procedures or because of suddenly rising rents and land values. Atlanta, for example, "re-imagined" itself to garner the Olympic games, removing its poor and black population from the central city (Rutheiser 1996). Often, in their effort to create a certain appearance or image, the new projects obliterate spaces where, in the past, a variety of groups and classes crossed each others' paths and interacted. Pristine new tourist- and consumer-friendly zones might well mask a precipitous decline in social solidarity.

At the same time, the commoditization of urban sites requires the creation of a massive underpaid service sector (Harvey this volume, Mollenkopf and Castells 1989). In New York City this sector is comprised largely of recent immigrants, people who would otherwise be working in the sweatshops of the Caribbean, Mexico, China or other parts of the world. Even under planning regimes committed to socialist values, the move toward "cultural consumption" (see Zukin 1995) can lead to the "reification of division and subordination in the city," as Mcdonogh (1999: 369) has described for Barcelona.

Commoditization is sure to spell the bleeding of commerce and commercial values into formerly enclaved locales. Architect and urbanist Rem Koolhaas, writing about successfully commoditized cities, puts it this way: "Shopping is surreptitiously becoming the way in which urban substance is generated" (quoted in Lubow 2000: 42). The U.S. leads a world list, he points out, with 31 square feet of real estate per person devoted to shopping. Many of its cities, like cities across the world, have witnessed the penetration of the "shopping industry" into every category of building: churches, temples, museums, means of transportation, and schools—even now into the hallowed ground of the World Trade Center disaster (see Hurley and Trimarco fc; Tucker fc). Furthering this hegemony is the discovery that people spend more money in spaces they perceive to be not fully commercial—where, in particular, cultural performances are also going on.

Just as the causes of urban destruction are multiple and varied, the forms of reconstruction everywhere reflect a battle over the control of the direction of the urban body politic. As global capital, accompanied by neoliberal policies and privatization, extends its reach, a critical question is whether struggles for humanitarian principles can find expression in rebuilding. By way of an introduction, this essay first lays out the globalization processes that threaten contemporary cities. Subsequent sections frame the chapters in relation to four general themes—urban degradation; crises of crime and criminalization; rapid, inconsistent expansion; and reconstruction and recovery. It should be noted that all of the chapters are based on ethnographic research, some of it rendered difficult by violence and the disruption of tenuous urban services. As ethnographers, the authors have tapped into the lived experiences of people who suffer when cities are wounded, and also into people's changing capacities to respond.

Globalization: an Overview

The power of globalizing processes to wreak havoc in cities around the world is best assessed through an historical lens. As documented by urban anthropologists, in the 1940s through 1960s, working people in cities, whether industrial working classes or participants in informal economies, created vibrant neighborhood organizations, constructed kinship and social networks, and actively bettered their lives through protest and struggle. Working people, in response to the demands of capital (socialist cities were less well studied in this period), fought for space, political power and economic resources, in turn contributing to the ever-changing cityscape of buildings, parks and roadways. Although, as Mumford taught us, the city represented and reflected the structures of power of the era, the ongoing demands of workers and their families also mattered (Mumford 1961).

Following the upheavals of the 1960s, the emergence of volatile social movements directed renewed attention to class inequalities in the centers of industrial capitalism. David Harvey (1973), Manuel Castells (1972) and others described the city as structured by the history of class struggles. Focusing on the U.S., the economist, David Gordon (1978) outlined how, as working-class people coalesced in their neighborhoods and workplaces to demand higher wages, they made the northeastern industrial cities the crucible of labor's power, leading to a historical change in the structuring of these cities. Feeling intimidated and disadvantaged, industry moved to the non-unionized South and, especially, to the sprawling, de-centered settlements of the Southwest, taking advantage of the poor, underemployed populations on both sides of the Mexican border. European and Caribbean immigrants who had been recruited along with African-American migrants from the rural South for manufacturing work in the northeast were left stranded.

As if to crystallize these developments, one American city—New York—pioneered a novel response. Following an abrupt (although engineered) fiscal crisis in 1975, it was saved from bankruptcy by national governmental and financial institutions that dictated unprecedented cutbacks in spending for collective services such as health, education, public transportation and housing (Tabb 1982, Susser 1982, 1998). This was in direct contrast to the reduction of poverty and the enhanced spending on public health and education in the 1960s. In fact, it reversed more than a century of progressive social policies in New York, including the founding of the first free urban university in the U.S., one of the first free city hospitals, and the proliferation of community social services for which the city had become famous.

New York's fiscal crisis represented a watershed, not because the city became poorer but because city government, under the wing of Wall Street and Washington, was forced to reorient its priorities towards business interests and the global economy (Henwood 1998). As part of this transformation, widespread arson was directed against working-class and minority apartments, often precipitated or fostered by landlords, exacerbating the effects of the withdrawal of public funds from low- and middle–income housing, and accelerating the disappearance of the stable working class (Freeman 2000). The numbers of unemployed poor mounted, as did the gap between rich and poor, creating what was soon to be described as the Dual City (Mollenkopf and Castells 1989). By the time that it was named a global city in 1991, New York well represented a model for what we now understand as the pervasive effects of globalization: privatization, investment in monumental construction in place of public housing, and a new population of poor and homeless people, not seen in U.S. cities since the Great Depression (Susser 1996, 2002).

As key discussions by Stiglitz (2001), Grieder (2001) and others, have exhaustively demonstrated, global institutions such as the I.M.F. and the W.T.O. have fostered increased inequality between rich and poor countries and also between the rich and the poor in any particular country. The consequences for the social fabric of cities are substantial. "Urban removal," followed by reconstruction or gentrification and the revaluation of real estate, has for decades relocated poor people as they find themselves surrounded by expensive properties and unaffordable rents. The additional impetus under globalization reflects the changing balance of power within the state. Of crucial importance, this does not mean a decline in the power of state institutions to tax and spend; rather, it highlights a shift in spending priorities. In some countries—the U.S. may be the most obvious and dramatic example—there is an increased allocation of funds to military build-ups, prisons, and corporate bail-outs. Public investment privileges centrally located monumental construction, highways, and parks designed specifically for tourist and elite consumption (for an early discussion of Boston Harbor, see Sieber 1991). Conversely, public investment in housing and, increasingly, health and education, are antique social relics.

Previously, working-class and poor neighborhoods managed to survive in the interstices of major cities, in part by making political trouble. As the balance of power within the state has tipped heavily towards corporate capital, the residents of such neighborhoods have lost their urban foothold. Their access to public services for social reproduction is in jeopardy, their costs to society are separated from those of the wealthy, and, to increase the worth of capital investments, they are screened off from the eyes of real estate investors and tourists. Making them invisible seems almost a precondition of rendering the city attractive to outsiders.

A related effect, evident in most of the cities described here, is the increasing segregation of rich and poor. As the wealthy acquire more, and less is spent on social services, segregation by wealth and, often, by race or ethnicity, becomes more marked. Frequently, divisions of race and ethnicity are complicated in new ways, as a middle class arises within a population previously defined by color or nationality, while the majority of the group remains poor, or becomes even more deprived, in contrast. Where the redevelopment of a city center is predicated upon evicting the less privileged residents, the destinations are increasingly jerrybuilt suburban slums.

Herein lies another powerful relationship, the connection between urban displacement and suburban and ex-urban sprawl. Accustomed as we are to imagining the "flight to the suburbs" as undertaken voluntarily by people with means, hoping to lead a better quality of life on a larger piece of land, today's city leavers include an ever-larger proportion of poor and middle-class people who have no choice in the matter. That the new "edge cities" seem unplanned and blighted, that they are haphazardly obliterating green belts almost overnight, reflects both the build-up of pressure for instant, inexpensive housing and the depressed and disillusioned outlooks of the new residents—people who abandoned cities against their will.

Globalizing processes are of course gendered. As has been the case since the earliest phases of capitalism, women earn less than men worldwide. Women are deprived of education and, in many societies, subordinated to men's decisions in the household, sometimes battered or killed. Women have less access to health care than men and, in poor countries, still commonly die of the complications of childbirth. However under the new paths of globalization, in remarkable contrast to previous practice, women have been the first hired (Nash and Fernandez -Kelly 1983). This seems to have contributed to the reconfiguring of persistently unequal relations between women and men. Dowry murders in India have increased rather than decreased in recent decades (Stone and James 2001). Women in the U.S. have been struggling not to lose rights to abortion and contraception won in the 1970s. Internationally, fundamentalist religions newly repressing the rights of women are being revitalized among Hindu, Catholic, Moslem, Protestant, Jewish and other faiths. Worldwide today, the health gap between men and women may be greater than that between the middle and the working class, necessitating a revision of established understandings in public health that correlate disease with social class, ignoring gender as a category.

Studies of cities worldwide indicate women's difficult engagement with globalization processes. As documented for Thailand and Brazil and even China (Zhen 2001), younger women easily become commodities, selling exotica and sexuality as part of the sensuous image of tourism. They are also sold directly as commodities in the newly systematic traffic in women for sex work, which, along with and intimately tied to drugs and the criminal economy, has constituted the underside of globalization. Today workers from many parts of the world migrate illegally and, if successful, work for many years in servitude to pay their fare. Although women often travel this way, they are increasingly at risk of being bound and forced into sex work. Or, women may simply discover, once in a foreign city, that they have to cooperate with the traffickers to find any work at all.

In another crucial way, the newly globalized industries are producing women as the ultimate consumers. This is especially evident in the proliferating off-shore pink-collar industries. Earning the same or less than their sisters in light industry—and a lot less than men in industrial work—telephone receptionists, programmers, and printshop workers, for example, spend an inordinate proportion of their wages on fashionable clothes, shoes and cosmetics, considered necessary for their work status. A recent study documents how, in the islands of the Caribbean, many working women fly to other islands on their free days using air coupons supplied by their corporate employers, to purchase clothes appropriate to their status (Freeman 1998). In other words, the newly globalized woman is not only at risk of being commoditized for sex work; she is also a shopper, caught up in the circuit of glossy, glittering stores. Many contemporary women must preserve a high-maintenance beauty image in order to find work in pink-collar bureaucratic drudgery. Nevertheless, as recent work among Puerto Rican secretaries indicates, the effort to dress appropriately does not prevent women from also participating actively in union organizing and joining picket lines (Casey 2002).

Perhaps the most destructive of the globalizing processes—and one of significance to several of the cities covered in this volume—is drug trafficking and addiction. Propelled by newly emergent desires affecting all social classes, the narcotics economy is particularly devastating for the urban poor. As a rule preceded by the collapse of economic alternatives for working classes, especially youth, and by the concerted withdrawal of public investment from poor communities, accelerated narcotics trafficking marked the 1980s in North America and Europe. In many New

York neighborhoods, for example, the way was paved by the transformation of the city from an industrial hub to one of the first exemplars of globalization. Working-class neighborhoods, their inter-generational networks of kinship and co-residence and their local political initiatives, fell apart (see Bourgois 1995, Sharff 1998, Susser 1982, 1986, 1992, 1998, 2002). In places such as Johannesburg, South Africa, this shift occurred a decade later in the 1990s. In Russian and Eastern European cities, the sudden and dramatic growth of heroin consumption, also in the 1990s, has led to an alarming increase in the incidence of AIDS.

The globalizing processes outlined above have transformed cities almost everywhere to the point that previous ethnographic work seems practically quaint. And yet, as shown by ethnographic research, these developments have not obliterated urban protest; grassroots movements and coalitions continue to form. But organizing is more difficult now, and the results are meager. In several of the following chapters, it is suggested that the world collapse of communist regimes marked not only the end of the Cold War, but the definitive end of an era in which governments, fearful of communism, met protestors half way, and were forced to acknowledge rights to housing, health and education.

The Degradation of Urban Life

Three chapters, one on the depreciation of everyday urban existence in Mexico City by Claudio Lomnitz; one on the decline of poor peoples' grassroots efficacy in Xalapa, Mexico, by Carol Myers; and one on the collapse of infrastructure in Ulan-Ude in Siberia, by Caroline Humphrey point up how the altered priorities of urban investment have undermined city existence, especially in the wake of the Cold War's end. Lomnitz's discussion of Mexico City introduces a concept with wider application—"the depreciation and degradation of urban life." During the 1970s, a municipal and national government, based to a large degree on patron-client relations, appeased various social movements. In contrast, the 1980s was marked by debt restructuring, the earthquake, and halving the value of labor, with steeply falling wages and rising unemployment. Depreciation and degradation are documented in relation to three domains: citizens' apparent fatalism in the face of risk (from traffic, pollution); the emergence of more predatory and violent forms of crime; and technocratic indifference to people's hopes and aesthetic sensibilities, especially in poor neighborhoods. In official rhetoric, degrading historical processes have no cost that cannot be recouped through subsequent economic growth. In the real world, this is far from the case. Lomnitz uses changing images of death in Mexican political cartoons to expose the onset and rhythm of depreciation.

The chapter on Xalapa, another, much smaller Mexican city, traces the transformation, since the 1970s, of grassroots organizations concerned with low-income housing. It argues that these organizations were more autonomous, oppositional, and efficacious in the past than they are today. Governments of the 1970s—both local and national—responded to their demands (while at the same time repressing their more radical elements); moreover, a viable coffee-exporting economy underwrote economic optimism. That this was the height of the Cold War was also relevant. The carrot-and-stick response to social movements led to a patron-client framework for distributing public resources, but there were real resources (in the form of public housing, for example) to distribute. More recently, grassroots activists have been reduced to interminable paperwork, as resources they once considered rights must now be applied for as grants (from the World Bank and various European-based N.G.O.s as well as the national government). This has resulted in a different tone and leadership in the organizations, and a more pessimistic outlook on the future. Meanwhile, the established oligarchs, with their feet well-planted in coffee haciendas and in urban real estate, continue to define the terms of poor people's access to housing.

The grimmest of corrosive scenarios is evoked by the near-collapse of infrastructure in the cities of Siberia—the deterioration of the transportation and communications grids, and of the heating plants that underpin winter survival. Humphrey offers an ethnographic account of the meaning of the collapse for Siberian urban dwellers who grew up with Soviet understandings of the determinative (and taken-for-granted) role of infrastructure in the social order, and who now face unimaginable insecurities. Her chapter further highlights the importance of national policy for urban development. Historically, nation states assumed at least some responsibility for reliable, safe, and affordable urban amenities—heat, light, roads, water, sanitation—almost as in a moral economy. Over and above the maldistribution of these amenities within cities (also an historic given) is the post-Cold War, seemingly callous, withdrawal of national-level commitment, with consequences for the "degradation of urban life."

Crises of Crime and Criminalization

Four chapters, one on Harlem in New York City (Leith Mullings), one on Philadelphia (Jeffrey Maskovsky), one on Kingston (Donald Robotham), and one on Medellín (Mary Roldan), enable a sharpened analysis of global narcotics trafficking, as it intersects with class, race, and gender inequalities, and as it impacts the most vulnerable urban populations. As a group these cases point up an issue of timing. The heavy penetration of drugs in the 1980s and 1990s coincided with a time when globalization created enormous dislocations worldwide while unleashing new patterns of sexuality, family formation, consumption, recreation and tourism, each of these introducing new desires. Another unifying theme is the difficulty of sorting out which wounds are deeper—those inflicted on poor communities by drugs and their merchants, or those that result from state-authorized "wars on drugs." Real recovery from the first kind of wound depends significantly on a healthy urban economy but, in the absence of substantial public support (such as no-strings grants), reconstituting such an economy in the world of today is daunting. Punitive, militarized approaches and escalated rates of incarceration seem to be the preferred alternative, with further damage to the fabric of urban life.

The chapters on Harlem in New York City and on Philadelphia paint a picture of poor people in contemporary U.S. cities—their struggles for housing and fair treatment from the police and criminal justice system. They examine the penetration of narcotics trafficking into local, racially marked communities and the subsequent repression and incarceration of users as well as dealers, with sentencing stiffened by racism. African American residents, battered first by drugs and then by a war on drugs, find many of their sons in prison, many of their women and children struggling to avoid or survive homelessness as new restrictive welfare laws deny them public assistance. Yet, in the midst of this repression, steps toward gentrification are also occurring. Mullings captures the irony: massive federal and state investments have been allocated to building prisons and maintaining a historically unprecedented prison population just as, in an odd juxtaposition, public funds have assisted major corporations in developing the historic center of Black America at 125th Street. Middle-class people now buy real estate, renovate elegant brownstone homes, and set up block associations that make rules about noise in the street. The fact that many of the new investors in Harlem real estate are themselves better off African Americans reconfigures racial categories without challenging racism against poor black Americans. Descendants of the African Americans who made history in Harlem in the past, many of these poor, now leave in search of lower rents in the outer boroughs of the city or in isolated and segregated poverty-stricken suburbs of Long Island and New Jersey.

Taken as a whole, these processes have sapped the energy of grassroots activism. Community organizers are hampered by the marked absence of young men, who are often dead or in prison, and by the unanticipated attractiveness to local constituents of gentrifiers' projects to expunge "undesirable elements" from the community. Partly as a result of the devastating effects of drug trafficking on poor communities, many of their residents have embraced this rather uncompassionate approach to urban reconstruction.

Maskovsky's account of the tensions between local grassroots organizers and anti-globalization activists adds another dimension. In Philadelphia, these tensions came to a head in the year 2000, when anti-globalization protesters gathered to raise their voices against not only the Republican national convention but also against worldwide environmental degradation and the proliferation of low-paid sweat shop workers hired to produce internationally renowned name-brand goods. Many of the city's grassroots groups concerned with declining social conditions in the city rejected the rowdy street demonstrators and sided with the police who restricted their movements. As Maskovsky shows, the protestors' demands for corporate regulation, and their mockery of the glittering flagship stores, upset community organizers newly concerned with the preservation of housing in Philadelphia.

Both Medellín and Kingston, also cities recently transformed by engagement with narcotics traffic, lost important legal sources of revenue and employment after the 1970s; textiles declined in Medellín; bauxite exports from Kingston dried up. In both cities, this was followed by a widening of the geographical and social distance between better off and poor neighborhoods and the dissolution of an earlier paternalistic moral order in which progressive elites looked out for the poor. In Kingston, these elites, a mixed-race bourgeoisie sympathetic to the British Labour Party, ceased going "downtown" for shopping and entertainment, instead patronizing these services near their "uptown" homes, the so-called "new Kingston". Meanwhile the downtown became an increasingly scary place for its high rate of violent crime, fed by the easy purchase of weapons recycled from the Contra War in Central America.

Both cities further illustrate the positive, if transitory, contributions that a robust traffic in drugs can make to classes of people who otherwise have no employment or possibility of participating in modern consumerism. In spite of the staggering death toll in drug battles, and the use of young boys and even women as "cannon fodder" in the transportation of illegal drugs, in Medellín's northern shanty town neighborhoods, traffickers have also contributed to collective ends: for example, to local churches and community enhancement projects. Beyond the pale of the respectable working class, however, the residents of these neighborhoods have now also been terrorized by the state's war on drugs—a war whose contours are heavily shaped by racial and class discrimination, and by a globalizing tie-in with U.S. drug enforcement and military aid.

Rapid, Inconsistent Expansion

Two Asian cases—Bangkok (chapter by Ara Wilson) and Ho Chi Minh City (chapter by Su Hong Chae) exemplify cities that, in the 1980s and 1990s, became sites of hyper-investment and privatization, with industrial plants, office towers, and shopping centers not only proliferating but looming in huge disproportion to the housing made available for the newly recruited working classes, pouring in from the countryside. As noted above, globalization generates and thrives on a tempting consumption economy, exemplified well in Wilson's description of Bangkok. Here streets are lined with new glass-fronted stores filled with luxury goods. A combination of royal ceremonies, bordello-like sumptuous hotels, and an extraordinary reputation for upscale brothels have furthered the commoditization of the "exotic Asian woman" and sexuality. Temples and palaces are to be consumed, as are stores, markets and splendid meals catering to the wealthy and to foreigners. Even the local commerce, the boats selling fresh fruit and flowers in the mornings, are surrounded by tourist gondolas consuming local style.

On the outskirts of Bangkok, as on the margins of Ho Chi Minh City (described by Su Hong Chae) we find miles of former farmland cemented over by factories. In seemingly endless roads and alleyways lined with small garage-size warehouses, multi-generational families live and work around their machines with the help of even poorer rural migrant labor. Factory workers, often recent rural migrants, live in the very rooms where they work or in shacks and shantytowns. As many analysts have pointed out, while the central cities have become the consumption showrooms of global capital, the heart of cheap global production is the rural migrant labor pouring into the unserviced, informal, and non-unionized industrial outskirts of these same cities. Here urban expansion has been so fast-paced as to raise the question of whether it is mainly creative or destructive in its effects.

These chapters also reiterate the significance of regional and national political contexts to urban development. Policy makers may either open or close the door to private corporations seeking to take over critical domains of urban services and infrastructure, provisioning everything from education to a safe and adequate water supply. As such they either bolster, or undermine, the health, welfare, and educational status of urban residents. Wilson's chapter analyses how a national campaign of "Thais helping Thais" sought to mitigate the consequences of the Asian financial meltdown of 1997–98 for Bangkok, as the city reeled from the effects of an exaggerated boom followed by a devastating bust. Blaming the crisis on global financial institutions, the campaign exonerated a binge of speculative over-building and runaway commercialism in the city's center. Not only had exuberant developers, backed by the national government, obliterated an earlier integration between home and work while channeling newcomers into problematic pursuits (among them the sex industry); they had also generated a vast amount of empty downtown office space.

Ho Chi Minh City exists within a socialist state that, despite its earlier resistance to global markets, has been courting foreign investment and fostering privatization for over a decade. Huge construction projects are transforming the old city; factories now dominate the periphery; immigrants are flooding in from rural areas to live in slums and work in these factories; entrepreneurs in the construction industry are making enormous profits. Workers to date show no signs of attributing their problems to the policies of the state, not only because it is socialist and presumably their ally, but because until circa 1985, when the boom was initiated, they had no possibility of purchasing any of the markers of modernity; indeed their families were often deprived of food. Their present poverty and miserable housing are relative and are mitigated, moreover, through participation in a proliferation of revolving credit associations.

Here as in all of the cities considered, a crisis of social reproduction appears to be in the making evidenced, on the one hand, by the degeneration of life—incarceration, benign neglect, displacement, infrastructural fragility—and, on the other hand, by the lack of a clear path, as yet, to effective political protest. Most recently, cocaine and heroin have rampaged through densely populated areas of poor housing in the center of Ho Chi Minh City, just in the shadow of the high-rise banks and expensive hotels that corporate investors are hastening to build for businessmen and tourists.

Reconstruction and Recovery

As noted above, it is not our point to argue that all of the processes that destroy cities are attributable to globalization. In an epilogue we consider what else may be at stake in the wounding of Baghdad. Certainly, the cities discussed in this volume present us with a number of additional crises to consider and compare. Among these Mexico City's 1985 earthquake can perhaps be considered an "act of God," even though its consequences have reflected both a prior history of relegating some groups to much less solidly constructed residences than others, and the national government's brutal launching of neo-liberal economic policies only two years earlier. In Beirut and Belfast, civil wars took on a life of their own, exacerbated not only by growing poverty and unemployment but by the dynamics of reciprocal injury, at times manipulated by external allies. Palermo is another city wounded by processes that are not directly understood in terms of globalization. Serious damage to its built environment followed upon allied bombing raids at the end of the Second World War and a nearby earthquake in 1968. A municipal and regional government, corrupted through dependence on the Mafia for votes, allowed the historic center to decay as the orchards and vineyards of a beautiful periphery were sacrificed to cement and sprawl. Another era of globalized capitalism, that of the second half of the nineteenth century, was the context for the emergence of the Mafia. But the engagement of contemporary mafiosi in real estate speculation and construction—an engagement that deepened in the late 1970s and 1980s as drug profits began to circulate—is best understood in relation to the intense (and vengeful) rivalry among Mafia factions.

Although Palermo (chapter by Jane and Peter Schneider) could easily be grouped with the cities affected by narcotics traffic, it is instructive to include it with Beirut (chapter by Aseel Sawalha) and Belfast (chapter by Dominic Bryan), in a segment whose emphasis is on processes of reclamation following extraordinary violence. The difficulties of reclaiming a city damaged by widespread killing, and of projecting a new image of healthy restoration, are shown to be considerable, the more so because reclamation processes can themselves have destructive spin-offs. Significantly, all of these cities missed out on large-scale, transforming investments during the 1980s and much of the 1990s but are currently witnessing an investment turn-around. In Beirut, the Lebanese Prime Minister until 1998, nicknamed "Bulldozer," owns majority shares in a property development firm spearheading reconstruction. Diaspora capital is also relevant. Belfast has the attention of the European Union and of various nations hoping to foster peace in Northern Ireland. Its cityscape dotted with lifting cranes, new hotels, and high rises, it has also attracted foreign private investment. In both cities, the enormous hurdles of constituting legitimate policing practices (the self-policing of neighborhoods in the tough-guy paramilitary tradition remains widespread), and of reconstituting claims to residential property (displaced persons abound) are noteworthy. Renewal may well worsen rather than ease these problems, both by provoking debates over whose history will be acknowledged, and whose erased, in the (presumably civil and harmonious) city of the future; and because reconstruction inevitably displaces people, and disrupts their security-enhancing social and political networks.

After nearly two decades of anti-Mafia prosecutions and social activism, Palermo's municipal leaders now promote an image of success in fighting organized crime and building "civil society." With its murder rate having fallen from around 100 per year in the early 1980s to less than 10 per year today, the city has recently been rewarded with a good rating from Moody's. National and European Union capital are available for reclaiming the abandoned and degraded historic center and the overbuilt, chaotic periphery. But the complexities are greater than appears. Following the Second World War, the Palermo economy became heavily weighted toward the construction industry. Highly permeable to the Mafia and to corrupt politicians who protected mafiosi for votes, the unions, workers, and contractors associated with this industry are anathema to the anti-Mafia planners of the reclamation projects who, envisioning a greener, less built-up city for the future, have gone out of their way to engage contractors from northern Italy and abroad. Increasingly without work and unable to sustain either the livelihoods or the respectability they enjoyed during the heyday of the Mafia, many working-class Palermitans now pose a challenge to the continuation of the anti-Mafia process.

The Politics of Reconstruction

Although widely varied in scale and place, most of the cities examined in this volume raise questions about the efficacy of political struggles to shape urban outcomes—an emphasis that perhaps reflects the centrality of ethnography as a research strategy. In an overview essay framing this concern, David Harvey vividly illustrates that, politically speaking, cities are far from the same. In Singapore, for example, the authoritarian city-state thrives on public investment in housing and social services (see Castells et al. 1990). The shifts in public investment characteristic of globalization are clearly evident in London, where the government has partnered with private corporations in projects of monumental proportions. The extensive and historic working class areas of the East End have been destroyed without trace as both public and private funds have contributed to beautifying and expanding the City (the financial center) and opening up the Thames embankment for development. At the same time, decreasing public investment in transit is reflected in the deterioration of the national rail system. And yet, unionized transportation workers have been striking to prevent further plans to privatize the London Underground.

Similarly, in Paris, gentrification and the magnificent reinvention of the central city have not precluded a lesser but continued investment in public housing and the provision of social services, even if the poor have been relegated to the distant outskirts (Wacquant 1996). As Harvey reminds us, the body politic is a product of a specific political history. The globalizing processes that have led to the prison-informational economy in the U.S. may encourage a more variegated reminiscence of the social democratic city in Europe, with a stronger commitment to the social contract and modestly greater constraints on corporate investors. Although the segregation of rich and poor moves on apace in every city examined here, the outcomes are multiple and locally determined.

In cities torn apart by violence and war, globalized processes, far from being the principal or obvious source of devastation, may actually present themselves as part of the solution, a path to the restoration of urban health. Robust reinvestment in a war-torn city will, the developers and their supporters assert, help to heal the wounds. This is explicitly the rhetoric surrounding the redevelopment of central Beirut, it is evident in Belfast, and we can anticipate it in Afghanistan and Iraq. In Palermo, in the 1990s, a local, national and international mobilization against the Mafia went hand in hand with revalorizing the decaying central city and real estate prices have risen. As the drug mafia recedes and the beauty of the ancient city re-emerges, international tourism has begun to expand, but whether employment in this sector can compensate for the considerable decline of the construction industry—earlier the nexus of the Mafia and corrupt politics—is another matter. Construction workers feel alienated by the change.

American cities and neighborhoods harmed by the reorientation of fiscal policies away from middle and low-income housing and public services, then by drugs and the war on drugs, have also looked to urban redevelopment schemes as their salvation—as evidenced by the substantial gentrification projects underway in Harlem and Philadelphia. Here, too, the infliction of new wounds is a concern. Urban dwellers, responding to the destructive processes that they must endure, generate a lively politics of reconstruction.

In order to assess their political potential *vis-à-vis* urban change, it is crucial to know who among a city's residents are affected and in what ways. An earthquake is likely to be particularly devastating for impoverished communities whose jerrybuilt houses and fragile infrastructure cannot resist the impact. Depending on geology and social location, however, the tremors and their aftershocks can create havoc and sow terror in privileged communities, too. The violence and criminal activity associated with narcotics trafficking has been the source of widespread insecurity and malaise among middle class as well as lower class city residents and this is also true of sectarian strife and outright war. Sudden bursts of investment and abrupt withdrawals of support similarly have widespread, cross-group effects as do epidemic diseases.

It is probably safe to say that the poor or less privileged urban constituencies are by far the most vulnerable to swings of political-economic intervention. Their dwellings crumble quickly when employers pull up stakes or the municipal or national government ceases to fund or monitor one or another program. Should their neighborhood be targeted for gentrification, they will surely be pushed out. But these processes—capital flight, government cutbacks of social services, reinvestment through gentrification—also destabilize some middle-class people, sometimes to the point that they cease to be middle class. Conversely, many members of working-class communities may benefit from, and appreciate, the remake of downtowns. In dramatic contrast to decades of neglect, new public and private investment in parks and the built environment may be generally aesthetically pleasing and, with some unhappy exceptions, accessible via public transportation. As noted above, protestors who smash the windows of flagship stores may be disparaged not only by established authorities, but also by neighborhood grassroots organizations. In considering responses, in other words, it is important to eschew easy assumptions about victimization; to consider the varied and complicated stories that inevitably emerge from on-the-ground observation; and to acknowledge the reality, grounded in propinquity, of the wounded city as whole. This book includes accounts of a middle-class reform movement (the anti-Mafia mobilization in Palermo) and of poor communities becoming themselves differentiated and internally divided on the advantages and disadvantages of gentrification.

There is a truth that residents of contemporary cities are coming ever better to appreciate. Globally organized corporations, prompt to pounce on damage and decay, offer the promise of reconstruction and the specter of further destruction at the same time. It has long been true of cities that almost everything—buildings, neighborhoods, communities, people—can be replaced in fairly short order; people can even be made invisible through expulsion to refugee camps, peripheral suburbs or, as happens too often in America, to prison. Intensifying and transcending this uprooting of residents is the push for privatization, not only of real estate but increasingly of other assets. Whether vulnerable parties, their capacity for political action diminished through relocation and dispersal, can continue to defend a sense of the whole, advancing support for collective investment, is among the questions asked in these pages. It is also a question to follow in the real world future of New York City and of cities like Kabul and Baghdad.

Figure 1.1 Trillium Sellers, We Will Not Forget.

References

Bourgois, P. (1995), *In Search of Respect: Selling Crack in El Barrio*, Cambridge, UK: Cambridge University Press.

Castells, M. (1972), *La Question Urbaine*. Paris: Maspero.

—— (1996, 2nd edition 2000) *The Information Age: Economy, Society and Culture*, Oxford: Blackwell.

Castells, M., Lee Goh, and R. Yin-Wang Kwok, R. (1990), *The Shek Kip Mei Syndrome: Economic Development and Public Housing in Hong Kong and Singapore*, London: Pion Limited.

Freedman, L. (2000), Human Rights and Women's Health. In Goldman, M. and Sargent, C. (eds), *Women and Health*. New York: Academic Press, pp. 428–41.

Freedman, L., and Deborah M. (1993), "Women's Mortality: A Legacy of Neglect", in Koblinsky, M., Timyan, J., and Gay, J. (eds), *The Health of Women: A Global Perspective*, Boulder, CO: Westview Press, pp. 147–71.

Freeman, C. (1998), "Femininity and Flexible Labor", *Critique of Anthropology* 18(3): 245–63.

Freeman, J. (2000), *Working Class New York: Life and Labor Since World War II*, New York: The New Press.

Burawoy, M. and Blum, J. et al. (eds) (2000), *Global Ethnography: Forces, Connections, and Imaginations in a Postmodern World,* Berkeley: University of California Press.

Goode, J. and Maskovsky, J. (eds) (2001), *The New Poverty Studies: The Ethnography of Power, Politics, and Impoverished People in the United States*, New York: New York University.

Gordon, D. (1978), "Capitalist Development and the History of American Cities", in Tabb, W. and Sawers, L. (eds), *Marxism and the Metropolis*, New York: Oxford, pp. 25–63.

Greider, W. (2001), "The Right and US Trade Law: Invalidating the 20th Century", *The Nation,* October 15.

Harvey, D. (1973), *Social Justice and the City*, Baltimore, MD: Johns Hopkins Press.

Henwood, D. (1998), *Wall Street*. London: Verso.

Hurley, Molly and James Trimarco, (fc), "Marketing Memory: Vendors, Visitors and Police at New York City's Ground Zero," *Critique of Anthropology*; Special Issue on 9/11, forthcoming.

Lockwood, V. (2001), "The Impact of Development on Women: The Interplay of Material Conditions and Gender Ideology. In Caroline

Brettel and Carolyn Sargent", (eds), *Gender in Cross-Cultural Perspective*, Upper Saddle River NJ: Prentice Hall, pp. 529–44.

Low, S. (1999), "Introduction: Theorizing the City", in Low, S. (ed), *Theorizing the City: The New Urban Anthropology Reader*, New Brunswick, NJ: Rutgers University Press, pp. 1–37.

Lubow, A. (2000), "Rem Koolhaas Builds", *The New York Times Magazine*, 9 July, pp. 29–41.

Mcdonogh, G. (1999), "Discourses of the City: Policy and Response in Post-Transitional Barcelona", in Low, S. (ed), *Theorizing the City: The New Urban Anthropology Reader*, New Brunswick NJ: Rutgers University Press, pp. 342–77.

Mollenkopf, J. and Castells, M. (1989), *The Dual City*, New York: Russell Sage.

Mumford, L. (1961), *The City in History*, New York: Harcourt Brace.

Nash, J. and Fernandez-Kelly, P., (eds) (1983), *Women, Men and the International Division of Labor,* Albany: SUNY Press.

Piot, P. (2001), "A Gendered Epidemic: Women and the Risks and Burdens of HIV", *Journal of the American Medical Women's Association* 56: 90–1.

Rutheiser, C. (1996), *Imagineering Atlanta: The Politics of Place in the City of Dreams*, London: Verso.

Sassen, S. (1991), *The Global City: New York, London, Tokyo*, Princeton NJ: Princeton University Press.

Sharff, J. (1998), *King Kong on 4th Street: Families and the Violence of Poverty on the Lower East Side*, Boulder CO: Westview.

Scheld, S. (2003), *Clothes Talk: Youth Modernities and Clothing Consumption in Dakar, Senegal*. Ph.D. Dissertation. Ph.D. Program in Anthropology. Graduate Center, City University of New York.

Sieber, R. (1991), "Waterfront Revitalization in Postindustrial Port Cities of North America", *City and Society* 5: 120–36.

Smith, N. (1996), *The New Urban Frontier: Gentrification and the Revanchist City*, New York: Routledge.

Stiglitz, J. (2002), *Globalization and Its Discontents*, New York: Norton.

Stone, L. and James, C. (2001), "Dowry, Bride-Burning and Female Power in India", in Brettel, C. and Sargent, C. (eds), *Gender in Cross-Cultural Perspective*, Upper Saddle River NJ: Prentice Hall, pp. 307–17.

Susser, I. (1982), *Norman Street: Poverty and Politics in an Urban Neighborhood*, New York: Oxford.

—— (1996), "The Construction of Poverty and Homelessness in U.S. Cities", *Annual Reviews in Anthropology* 25: 411–25.

—— (1998), "Inequality, Violence and Gender Relations in a Global City: New York", *Identities: Global Studies in Culture and Power* 5(2): 219–47.

—— (1999), "Creating Family Forms: The Exclusion of Men and Teenage Boys from Families in the New York City Shelter System. 1987–91", in Low, S. (ed.), *Theorizing the City: The New Urban Anthropology Reader*, New Brunswick NJ: Rutgers University Press, pp. 67–83.

—— (2002), "Losing Ground/Finding Space: The Changing Experience of Working Class People in New York City", in David Nugent (ed.), *Locating Capitalism in Time and Space: Global Restructurings, Politics, and Identity*, Stanford CA: Stanford University Press, pp. 274–90.

Tabb, W. (1982), *The Long Default: New York City and the Urban Fiscal Crisis*, New York: Monthly Review Press.

Tucker, Jed, (fc), "Making Difference in the Aftermath of the September 11th, 2001 Terrorist Attacks," *Critique of Anthropology*; Special Issue on 9/11, forthcoming.

Wacquant, Loic, (1996), "Red Belt, Black Belt: Racial Division, Class Inequality, and the State in the French Urban Periphery and the American Ghetto," in Mingione, Enzo, (ed.), *Urban Poverty and the "Underclass": A Reader*. Oxford and New York: Basil Blackwell, pp. 234–74.

Zhen, Z. (2001), "Mediating Time: The 'Rice bowl of Youth' in Fin de Siecle Urban China", in Appadurai, A. (ed.), *Globalization,* Durham: Duke University Press, pp. 131–55.

Zukin, S. (1995), *The Culture of Cities*, Oxford: Blackwell.

–2–

The City as a Body Politic

David Harvey

In the history of destructive strikes against a city, September 11th, 2001, in New York will undoubtedly rate a special place. But in what sense and why its claim to fame might last, as its immediacy fades and it enters into the record books and historical memory, is worth considering. In physical terms, the event was equivalent to a moderate earthquake, like that of Northridge (Los Angeles) in 1994. It nowhere near matched the devastation wrought in San Francisco (1905), Mexico City (1995) Kobe/Osaka (1995), and Ahmedabad (2000), to name just a few of many cities afflicted by "natural" disasters (which are often as much humanly as naturally provoked). In this case, however, the wound was inflicted directly by human agency. But here, too, the physical dimensions of the event pale into insignificance compared to Hiroshima and Nagasaki, the fire-bombing of Dresden or Tokyo at the end of the Second World War, the London blitz or the damage wrought by civil wars more recently in Beirut and Sarajevo.

Cities are vulnerable forms of human organization. But, as the examples already mentioned illustrate, they have also proven remarkably resilient, recovering fast from devastation, sometimes (though not always) in a "better state" (however defined) than they were in before. Only in the far distant past did cities sometimes crumble into dust not to rise again. In recent times, the extraordinary growth of cities throughout the world seems set to override catastrophes, losses, indignities and woundings, no matter whether externally visited or self-inflicted. In one century, the proportion of the world's rapidly expanding population judged to be "urban" has grown from less than 10 per cent to more than 50 per cent.

The capacity for contemporary cities to overcome all manner of tribulations must in part be attributed to the fact that cities, in their capitalistic form, are hyper-active sites of "creative destruction." They dance to the capitalist imperative to dismantle the old and give birth to the new as expanding capital accumulation accompanied by new technologies, new forms of organization and rapid influxes of populations (now drawn from all corners of the earth) impose new spatial forms and stresses upon the physical and social landscape. If, in making way for and creating the new, some of the old must first be destroyed, then why does it matter if this destruction is carried out by the wrecker's ball or inflicted by some contingent act of violence? While the former has the advantage of usually avoiding direct human casualties and being organized with due deliberation, the latter has the advantage of immediacy, speed and in some instances completeness, avoiding the tangles and snares that inevitably attach to any deliberative political process. The rapid reconstructions of Japanese and West German cities in the wake of their devastation in the Second World War had much to do with the economic renaissance of those countries during the 1960s. The unseemly haste with which developers and other interests have converged on the possibilities of profitable reconstruction on a prime site in lower Manhattan (which just happens also to have become a graveyard) lie firmly in this capitalist tradition.

The economically, politically and socially driven processes of creative destruction through abandonment and redevelopment are often every bit as destructive as arbitrary acts of war. Much of contemporary Baltimore, with its 40,000 abandoned houses, looks like a war zone to rival Sarajevo. And when Robert Moses "took a meat axe to the Bronx" (to quote one of his more memorable phrases) and rammed highway after highway through the neighborhoods of New York City in the 1950s and 1960s, there were many critics (like Jane Jacobs, Robert Caro and Marshall Berman) who thought he did far more damage to New York City than anyone before or since. Creative destruction (usually disguised as "modernist progress") always goes hand-in-hand with incessant capital accumulation.

The phrase "wounded cities" suggests, however, that cities are susceptible to life-threatening damage in some way over and beyond the chronic habits of creative destruction that capitalism ordinarily produces. The idea attracts because we are drawn to drama, horror, spectacle and shock; events like September 11th, the Kobe-Osaka earthquake, the chemical disaster in Bhopal, or the fire-bombing of Dresden are far more likely to register in our historical memories than the slow and cancerous erosions of political-economic sustainability that created human and physical wastelands in so much of Baltimore, Buffalo, Cleveland, Liverpool, Mumbai, Sao Paulo and far beyond, even in years (such as the 1990s) of general boom and affluence. But any balanced accounting of matters surely requires us to go beyond the spectacular, not to diminish it, but to integrate it with the sad and slow declines that also inflict untold harms on the fabric of urban life. How, then, can we construct ways of thinking that allow of critical engagement with what metaphors like "wounded," "sick," or "ailing" cities might be about?

Such metaphors presume that the city is in some sense an organic form of social life that originates through human action. The city grows, is sustained, or dies out as the case may be. In the process it can assume different states, such as robust or wounded, healthy or sick, elegant or shamefully ugly. Organic metaphors of this sort are beguiling and dangerous as well as useful. These days they usually come dressed in distinctively disciplinary clothing. Some economists, for example, model cities as marvels of self-organizing systems in which efficiencies and economies of scale are realized in the quest to achieve better standards of living and a more civilized life. Others like to assimilate cities to the metaphor of a vast hive of human activity, prompting immediate reflection on Marx's famous question as to what might separate "the worst of architects from the best of bees." Many environmentalists, on the other hand, look upon cities as cancerous blobs that spread onwards and outwards engulfing all that confronts them in a miasma of pollution, environmental degradation, habitat destruction and species (including, in the long run, our own) extinction.

Pride of place among the organic metaphors must be accorded to the idea of the city as a body politic. This has had a long, enduring, and often troubling history. When Karl Popper attacked Plato as an enemy of an open society, it was the ideal of the perfect harmoniously organized city state run by philosopher kings that was the focus of his wrath. Popper may not have been entirely right in this but at least he brought into question much that is problematic about the whole utopian tradition and its frequent reliance upon ideals of an organic and enclosed social harmony. Models of this sort can just as easily be repressive as emancipatory and liberatory. Organic thinking lies at the heart of much authoritarian and even fascist ideology. The desire to purify the body politic, for example, can lead to "cleansing" activities in which unwanted elements are either expelled or repelled as potential pollutants. As the whole history of liberalism and neo-liberalism stridently proclaims, the "road to serfdom" (to use von Hayek's famous title) can all too easily lie in adoption of a political philosophy and system in which individual judgement is surrendered (either through consent or coercion) to the all-embracing will of some larger organic entity (such as the polis or the nation state). We have to look no further than the authoritarian and repressive city-state of Singapore since its independence in 1964 to illustrate the point. But the problem here is that Singapore has also been an economic success story over the past four decades, delivering ever-increasing states of material well-being to its population, in a reasonably well-distributed manner across the class and ethnic spectrum, and suffering from remarkably little internal strife and very few defections abroad. It organized itself not only to survive but to profit handsomely from competing within the capitalist world system. An efficient, clean and very modern city has arisen out of the dismal heritage of colonialism. It is a sobering thought that many examples of major urban transformations of this sort have occurred under conditions of authoritarian control (Haussmann in Second Empire Paris, Niemeyer in Brasilia), overwhelming hegemonic power (Moses in New York) or well-organized political solidarities (Mayor Daley in Chicago or Lee Kuang Yew in Singapore).

The dangers of appeal to the idea of the city as a body politic as a normative goal are many. But if there is to be any kind of alternative to free-market neoliberalism/capitalism (which more often than not entails a great deal of corporate monopoly coupled with state powers) then some sort of collective action organized around the public interest is necessary. For this reason alone, we cannot afford, in spite of all the dangers involved, to turn our back upon the idea of the city as a body politic. The issue is not whether it makes sense to construe the city this way, but what kind of body politic rules and by whom and for what purposes it functions. The body politic is necessarily, therefore, a contested term; what might serve one set of interests (such as capitalist developers) does not necessarily serve another (such as the affected minorities living in unemployed squalor). Malfunctioning of the body politic then depends—at least in the first instance—on who is not being served and what is not being done. What looks like a wounded city to some appears perfectly healthy to someone else. But there is also a rather more transcendent argument to be made; insofar as cities form some roughly bounded contiguous space within which all citizens have their being, then common problems arise (such as those of public health, criminality and violence, education and civility, investments in physical and social infrastructures) that require some commonality of action. Cholera epidemics, to take the classic example, (and the S.A.R.S. epidemic today), do not acknowledge class and ethnic boundaries and require the application of comprehensive city-wide solutions. Failure to act as a body politic under such circumstances can have catastrophic results for everyone. Breakdowns in key mechanisms for exercising collective responsibility in the public interest are one indication of a sick and ailing body politic. Furthermore, a strong case can be made that political failures of this sort are far more serious than physical failings. To take the organic metaphor quite literally, a broken bone is usually far less threatening than a spreading cancer.

The metaphor of the city as a body politic needs unpacking to understand how it might fruitfully be deployed. This I shall do with a little help from history and dialectics. Historically, the idea of the state or the city as a body politic originates in the early modern period. It arose, Kantorowicz (1957) explains, as it became necessary to distinguish between the monarch as a private person and the monarch as an embodiment of territorially bounded state power. An imaginary line was drawn between the private and the public "bodies" of the king. The distinction was meant to protect the public realm from personal arbitrariness, failure, or death (witness the motto "the king is dead: long live the king!"). The monarch was supposed to act in the national interest without regard to personal interests. When Louis XVI most famously proclaimed "L'etat c'est moi" he was simply voicing this elemental truth. The obvious difficulty was how to police this imaginary line. Two things happened over time. Firstly, the question arose as to whose body might best represent the polity and, secondly, the distinction between the private and public realms became democratized and rendered more abstract (as opposed to being embodied in a person).

Consider the case of France. The French Revolution produced a powerful iconography in which the king was portrayed as an impotent figure wearing a Phrygian cap. This was a way of saying that the king had lost his power to rule. Decapitating the king was equivalent to leaving the body politic headless. Revolutionary republicanism and liberty were portrayed, by contrast, as a powerful woman storming the barricades. Agulhon (1981) provides a fascinating account of this iconographic shift from male to female and the struggle it spawned throughout the nineteenth century. The motif of liberty and revolution as woman reappeared very strongly in the revolution of 1830, most effectively symbolized by Delacroix's famous painting of *Liberty Leading the People* (see Figure 2.1). A veritable flood of parallel images arose throughout all France in the immediate aftermath of the 1848 revolution. How the woman was represented was, however, significant. Opponents of republicanism often went along with the representation but portrayed the woman as a simpleton (a "Marianne" from the country) or as an uncontrolled lascivious woman no better than a common prostitute. Those desirous of respectable bourgeois republicanism preferred stately figures in classical dress and demeanor surrounded with the requisite symbols of justice, equality and liberty (an iconographic form that ended up as a French republican donation to adorn New York City's harbor). Revolutionaries expected a bit more fire in the figure. Balzac captured this in his novel *The Peasantry* in the figure of Catherine who:

Figure 2.1 Eugène Delacroix, Liberty Leading the People. Reunion des Musées Nationaux/ Art Resource, New York.

> recalled the models selected by painters and sculptors for figures of Liberty and the ideal Republic. Her beauty, which found favor in the eyes of the youth of the valley, was of the same full-blossomed type, she had the same strong pliant figure, the same muscular lower limbs, the plump arms, the eyes that gleamed with a spark of fire, the proud expression, the hair grasped and twisted in thick handfuls, the masculine forehead, the red mouth, the lips that curled back with a smile that had something almost ferocious in it—such a smile as Delacroix and David (of Angers) caught and rendered to admiration. A glowing brunette, the image of the people, the flames of insurrection seemed to leap forth from her clear tawny eyes . . .

Flaubert took the negative view. In *Sentimental Education* (p. 290) he described a scene witnessed during the invasion of the Tuilleries Palace in 1848: "in the entrance-hall, standing on a pile of clothes, a prostitute was posing as a statue of Liberty, motionless and terrifying, with her eyes wide open." These are very different renditions compared to the figure of liberty in New York harbor.

It is on this contested terrain that Daumier's version (Figure 2.2), painted in response to the Republican government's invitation in 1848 to compete for a prize representation of the republic, is doubly interesting. For not only is the body politic of the republic represented as a woman—indeed, it would have been surprising under the circumstances if it had not been—but it is also given a powerful maternal rendering. Two lusty children

Figure 2.2 Honoré Daumier, The Republic, 1848. Reunion des Musées Nationaux/Art Resource, New York.

suckle at her breasts and another sits at her feet reading a book, echoing Danton's slogan: "after bread, education is the primary need of a people." Daumier depicts a nurturing body politic; an idea common in socialist and communist movements during the 1840s. This was the kind of state and city that the revolutionaries wanted to construct. (As Foucault among others has remarked, an identity was frequently assumed between city and state during these times.) But the revolution and counter-revolution of 1848, followed by the establishment of the Second Empire, crushed the idea of a nurturing body politic. The masculine version was revived: Louis Bonaparte was presented as an embodiment of the spirit and grandeur of the Empire (which was why the novelist Victor Hugo, a critic in exile, always referred to the Emperor in deflating terms as "Napoleon le Petit"). Under this version, the state would engage in grandiose military campaigns and the city would radiate imperial splendor while organizing the internal policing of dissent and the production of space for capital accumulation. But it was not the responsibility of the state or the city to nurture anyone.

These distinctive iconographic models indicate a range of choices for how the body politic might be constructed and understood, and what the ideals and tonalities of its actions might be about. The masculine version could be patriarchal/regal or macho/imperial, deteriorating into flatulent and geriatric impotence, while the feminine version could be youthful and revolutionary (cultivating the flames of insurrection); a stern but benign figure of justice and liberty; a nurturing matriarch for all citizens; or an irresponsible whore (squandering the state's finances on worthless people and projects). Shadowy versions of these iconographic figures are still with us and part of the political battle that has to be waged is to establish an aura of political power that embodies one or other of these virtues while discrediting its rivals and offsetting its own negative connotations.

The democratization of the body politic depended upon a clear distinction between the public and the private spheres (see Kantorowicz 1955, Bratsis 2002). This seemed to make representational and iconographic struggles of the sort that occurred in France superfluous, anachronistic and merely quaint. In its place an imaginary line was drawn between public institutions and private interests. Government within the body politic was supposed to pursue purely public interests through public institutions uncontaminated by private concerns. To police the line, a theory of political corruption was constructed. Accusations and legal proceedings could be taken against officials for betrayal of the public trust, for utilizing the powers of public institutions for private gain. Contamination and corruption of the body politic by private interests must be guarded against at all costs. But, as Bratsis (2002) shows, this distinction is fraught with difficulties; the imaginary line is impossible to police without arbitrary judgements and sometimes debilitating effects upon both governance and private actions. It presupposes individuals with divided bodies and loyalties, individuals who live in an institutionalized schizophrenic state, supposedly able to switch personas as they cross the line into public service and lay aside everything they have learned and know as private citizens. Plainly, this is not how the body politic of the U.S. (or anywhere else for that matter) is organized. Public institutions provide a trough at which many private interests feed while access to the trough depends on political economic power. The body politic in the U.S., though democratized, is organized primarily to serve the interests of aggressive capital accumulation rather than the well-being of the public as a whole (except under the presumption that what is good for capital accumulation is also good for public well-being). But collective interests do get expressed and acted upon. How and why that might happen is an important question. To fashion some sort of answer I turn to dialectical frames of argument.

I have argued elsewhere (Harvey 1996) that process-thing relations lie at the heart of dialectical modes of analysis. Here I define urbanization as the process and the city as the thing that crystallizes out as a relatively permanent structure from the fluidity of that process. The city has no existence outside of the processes that produce, sustain, enhance, undermine, diminish, reshape, or destroy it. Processes are, however, affected and shaped by the things and structures they produce. Circumstances arise in which things, such as organized institutions, acquire power over the processes that sustain them. The organic metaphor of the body politic here has meaning. Organisms cannot exist outside of the environments that sustain them, but all organisms work to transform their environments to better sustain themselves. Beavers, bees and human beings all have that in common. The city is a collective organization to support human life and activities. So what kind of organization is it and by what processes is it produced, sustained, transformed, undermined or even, occasionally, destroyed? And how does it affect and manage the processes that sustain it?

Consider the city first as a humanly constructed resource system, a vast assemblage of heterogeneous physical artifacts and assets, produced through human work and ingenuity, ready for people to use for whatever purposes they wish. These resources support daily life in all of its aspects: symbolic, aesthetic and affective as well as material. Production, exchange, distribution and consumption are collectively organized around them according to certain criteria (such as those structured by the imperatives of capital accumulation). From this perspective, however, the city appears as a set of inanimate objects (roads, buildings, water mains, houses, factories, churches, offices, and so forth) which possess no agency of their own.

Cities are constituted out of the flows of energy, water, food, commodities, money, people and all the other necessities that sustain life. These flows must be maintained as must the capacity to expel wastes effectively so that populations do not die in their own excrement. But such flows are channeled through the fixed things that guide and in some instances even mandate their movements. Any cut-off of the flows or congestion in the channels for even a short period of time can be highly damaging: recall the power grid failure that once blacked out New York City for nearly 24 hours or the terrible consequence of the long drawn-out garbage workers strike where trash mountains fouled the interior environment of the city generating serious public health hazards. It follows that cities can usefully be looked at in material balance, metabolic and ecological terms. The idea of the physical metabolism (a very organic term) of the city, first proposed by Abel Wolman (1966), has now been taken up by many environmentalists who see it as a fundamental tool for analyzing what sustainable cities might look like. Healthy cities may then be defined in terms of ecological sustainability. Cities must also be sustained economically. Flows of commodities, of labor power (migrant streams), of money and finance, must be keyed to economic activities and well-being. Some cities acquire a parasitic status, feeding upon surpluses and inflows from elsewhere without returning much of any material significance (apart from wastes) to the environments which support them. This was the case in older theocratic centers with predominantly symbolic and religious functions. Cities largely given over to administrative and political functions are parasitic rather than productive. Other cities generate powerful economic bases through the production and export of goods and services. "Global cities" as centers of command and control (particularly finance) are in turn to be differentiated from production and industrial centers (like Ciudad Juarez or Dacca). Whatever the structure and however orchestrated, sustaining the economic flows is fundamental to the health and well-being of the city.

These ecological/economic processes together constitute the urban process. Disruptions and failures in the flows that support the city pose serious threats to its existence. If the flows of finance into a city environment diminish significantly then abandonment of factories, offices, housing, and so forth will probably result. If sea levels rise or prolonged droughts occur then the metabolism of the city alters. The spread of plague or epidemics (such as AIDS) changes urban life. If the water supply is contaminated then life becomes extremely difficult. These are all active processes affecting city life. They are the lifeblood of the city as a collective site for living and working. Cities exist in a contingent relationship to these processes and are vulnerable to any shifts that occur in how they are working, how the flows might change direction. Cities do not command these processes in any direct sense and it may be concluded therefore that particular urban fortunes are mere products of, say, the shifting currents of globalization as unleashed under neoliberalism. But far from being passive victims of such shifting flows, we need to examine more carefully how cities organize to initiate, stimulate and influence these flows, while mediating their internal effects upon the urban fabric and city life.

If cities are active rather than passive in relation to their environments and the processes that support and effect them, then how should we conceptualize this role? Human beings transform their environments through labor and in so doing, as Marx puts it, transform themselves. This dialectic has been fundamental to the world's evolving historical geographical condition and it lies at the heart of the urban process and city creation. Robert Park (1967: 3) expresses a similar idea when he writes:

> the city and the urban environment represent man's most consistent and, on the whole, his most successful attempt to remake the world he lives in more after his heart's desire. But if the city is the world that man created, it is the world in which he is henceforth condemned to live. Thus, indirectly, and without any clear sense of the nature of his task, in making the city man has remade himself.

It is exactly at this point that the organic metaphor has both revelatory power and problematic application. The political-economic organization of the city is about the collective management and attempted orchestration of environmental transformations and urban processes not only in the city but far beyond. This entails a conception of the city as a "power container" capable, in some way or other, of unified actions that are meaningful above and beyond what can be gleaned from a study of the activities of the individual elements that constitute it. These individual elements are important in their own right. Traders, financiers, producers, immigrants, laborers, households, bureaucrats, scientists, educators (the list is endless) all work and live their lives and take actions that have implications for urban processes in and beyond the city. The city is, furthermore, in no sense a clearly bounded entity (except administratively). The body politic has porous boundaries (and in some instances no boundaries at all) while it also contains within itself all manner of divergent and potentially conflictual processes. It is more like a porous ecosystem organized across a hierarchy of scales than an individualized body. But, unlike many other ecosystems (including ant-hills and bee hives), it has a fluid and changeable directing authority constituted as territorialized governance. This is what the body politic of the city is all about. Insofar as it is more than the sum of its individual parts, it has an ontological status in human evolution. It has had a pivotal role in how we, as human beings, have "remade ourselves" in the past and how we might "remake ourselves" in our future. And we can either view this urban process as uncontrollable (led by blind forces such as those of the capitalist market, individualism, competition and ecological evolution) or try to get a clearer sense "of the nature of our task" and construct an appropriate politics of interventions in the urban process. How governance of the body politic is constituted and how it construes the nature of its task therefore becomes a crucial element not only for the evolution of human society but also for the evolutionary process more generally.

Here, too, a range of choices exists. The body politic can indeed be constituted on the model of fascism or authoritarian control. It can construe the nature of its task to suppress individualism, egoism and selfishness of the elements that constitute it and organize itself in ways that testify to its own unity, strength and grandeur by assembling vast wealth within its confines. Inevitably, it must then adopt a competitive, even expansionary and belligerent attitude to other entities (late medieval Venice is a great example). It organizes itself for geopolitical struggle, building class alliances and local solidarities to congeal its powers on the world stage. But the body politic can also be organized around the idea that it should either liberate entrepreneurial energies (like late medieval Genoa) or, as many municipal socialists have hoped (not entirely in vain), deliver the conditions for individual enlightenment and emancipation democratically to all, without suppressing individualism. Plainly, in this latter case, conflicts will occur precisely because certain kinds of individualism can be oppressive to others. The latency of the iconographic struggles already described re-emerges and struggles for the "soul" of the body politic ensue; it can be revolutionary, imperial, founded on justice and order, patriarchal, maternal and nurturing, impotent, or profligate and wanton, as the case may be. Cities can become entrepreneurial, managerial, democratic, socialist, neo-fascist, theocratic, authoritarian, or whatever. They can orient themselves and direct their powers towards boosterism, entrepreneurialism, corporatism, competition, innovation, social justice, or simply seek to offer a civilized life and humanistic values. The personality of each city is shaped out of the long history of these choices.

Cities change their qualities and their standing, grow or shrink and differentiate themselves internally according to certain rules of engagement (such as capitalistic markets) and practices of governance. Contemporary cities are deeply implicated in the circulation of capital and a strong case can be made that this is now the primary (though by no means exclusive) process out of which city forms crystallize and have their being. The self-organization of the capitalist city proceeds according to its own rules, such as those given by entrepreneurial activity, private property, market exchange, the commodification of labor and land, and state interventions of various kinds. The commodification of land is particularly important: the extraction of land rent typically forces land uses into some configuration of "highest, best and most remunerative uses," thereby imparting a particular spatial structure to the city form. Individual decisions broadly conform to this logic and therefore play a key role in how the body politic as a whole is constituted. But the system of territorialized governance helps to orchestrate these micro-processes and express them at a variety of sub-national geographical scales.

Bearing this in mind, let us return to the initial question. Did September 11th wound the city as a thing or so intervene in the process of urbanization that New York's existence was threatened in other ways? And how did or could the body politic respond?

The direct physical damage was relatively trivial (the metaphorical equivalent of a broken bone). Confined to a few square blocks, it took out largely surplus office space anyway, and while 3,000 deaths are appalling in themselves, they hardly made a dent in the New York labor market, no matter whether it was for skilled financial operatives and lawyers or waiters, janitors and cleaners. The disruption to the urban process was far more serious and poses long-term problems. The social, psychological and symbolic damage was also serious. The trauma of September 11th necessitated some sort of response. The capacity to do so depended upon how the body politic had been constituted over the previous decades. Two basic points need to be made.

The twin towers symbolized the role of New York financial markets in forcing a certain pattern of political-economic development known as neo-liberalism upon the rest of the world, particularly during the 1990s. But in their early years, the towers had been mired in the problems of serious recession and stagflation, marked by the technical bankruptcy of New York City in 1975. The recovery of New York from those difficulties entailed the de-industrialization of the city's economy and its single-minded devotion to and ultimate dependency upon financial services and ancillary activities (legal services, information processing, the media).

Financial speculation and the invention of new instruments of debt and credit became the life-blood of a city that was proudly global at one level but also increasingly parasitic upon the production of real values in the miserable workshops of Bangladesh, the maquillas along the Mexican border and in the tyrannical factories of South Korea, Indonesia, China and Vietnam. New York's economy rode the neo-liberal tiger in the 1990s. The twin towers marked the transition from fordism to flexible accumulation (see Harvey 1989) and symbolized the new-found dominance of finance capital over nation-state policies and politics. By the time of the Clinton presidency it was clear that even the federal government had to submit to the discipline of New York bond markets. New York extracted vast wealth from the rest of the world to become the richest and the most spectacularly successful of the "global cities" operating as command and control centers for global financial flows. It made itself the center of economic empire. The astounding wealth accumulated in New York City forged a basis for a remarkably rich cultural life and levels of conspicuous consumption beyond belief. It became a tourist mecca. But it became highly vulnerable to international shifts in financial flows.

New York also developed a vast low-wage economy to service its needs in restaurants, in hotels and apartment houses, in shops and workshops, in transportation and in the upkeep of the city. Wave after wave of immigrants crammed into the city to feed on the crumbs from the tables of the wealthy financiers, lawyers and media moguls. This other New York (many of whom died in the twin towers) was perpetually on the brink of total impoverishment, its slowly rising incomes often more than offset by spectacular rises in rents and other living costs in one of the most successful urban economies of all time. Spiralling inequalities were threatening the qualities of urban life. Real incomes plunged for even the lower middle classes, and job and financial insecurity, now attached to neoliberal flexibility, proliferated. Social inequality and the uneven geographical development of the city became much more emphatic. Median income increased by more than 11 per cent in Manhattan but decreased by more than 3 per cent in the other four boroughs of the city between 1990 and 2000 (see Scott 2002). But the vehicles for any kind of collective antidote to escalating inequalities were sidelined. The body politic of the city, traditionally democratic but fragmented and never that coherent, was reduced by the end of the 1990s to a loosely corporatist-entrepreneurial and pro-business structure with an authoritarian mayor, Rudolph Giuliani, who staked his reputation on racially charged savage policing, crime reduction, and the exclusion and expulsion of marginalized and impoverished populations from Manhattan. He construed "the nature of his task" to be to make New York (and Manhattan in particular) as safe as possible for the wealthy and as attractive as possible for financial services, tourism and developers interested in servicing conspicuous consumption.

This was not, on the face of it, the kind of governance needed to respond to the trauma of September 11th. The attack revealed, however, the existence of a different kind of body politic, latent and submerged. Values that had gotten lost under the dominance of the "dot.com" boom, Wall Street greed, Madison Avenue gloss and Giuliani politics, were rediscovered almost overnight. New Yorkers, faced with unspeakable tragedy, for the most part rallied around ideals of community, togetherness, solidarity and altruism as opposed to beggar-thy-neighbor individualism. The outpouring of help, monetary as well as tangible (the lines to donate blood were incredible), from all sources, was extraordinary. An abrasive and divisive mayor was transformed into a ministering angel of the streets. Giuliani became an icon of comfort and common sense for everyone at the same time as he deployed his authoritarian talents to ensure efficient governance. It became possible to talk about the collective good instead of individual interests. Unionized municipal employees became heroes. Government, which had been castigated for the preceding 20 years as all bad, except when it reduced taxes and crime, was suddenly looked to as a source of comfort and good. Its failure to provide security and to fund public health adequately suddenly became a problem. Above all, there were three days of non-commercial television, as if the country and the city were collectively ashamed of their terrible habits of mindless and conspicuous consumption.

For many New Yorkers this was extraordinary. They found themselves in a world where different values of social solidarity were being articulated—values quite at odds with those that prevailed before September 11th. It was almost as if they glimpsed Daumier's vision of nurturing institutions. True, much of this was wrapped up in a troubling jingoism. American flags festooned the city, though it was not always clear with what motivation (immigrants used them to protect against harassment, some used them as signs of local solidarity and others as a sign of patriotic fervor). Dissident views on what provoked the attacks were condemned and civil liberties threatened. There were more than a few signs of U.S. versions of fanaticism and zealotry (initially directed against Muslims). But Giuliani, for one, immediately condemned this: the last thing he needed was intercommunal violence in a multi-ethnic city. And as it became more apparent that a cross-section of the whole of New York's immigrant population and occupations from bond traders to firefighters, waiters and janitors, had died in the twin towers so solidarities briefly congealed. Racial divisions and class hostilities diminished and a sense of collective identity emerged to fuel a different sense of what the body politic was and should be about and what the nature of its task must be.

But then the economy turned sour, powerfully so in New York City as well as nationally. Calls to patriotism did not avert a plunge when stock markets reopened. New-found solidarities did not prevent mass-firings from the airline, travel and "hospitality" industries and close to 100,000 jobs were lost in New York City alone in the wake of September 11th. Unemployment surged in the city. Financial services that had half a foot in New Jersey or Connecticut anyway completed their moves out and surpluses of office space were identifiable in mid-Manhattan even after the losses of lower Manhattan had been compensated for; September 11th increasingly appeared as an excuse for companies and industries to do what they were preparing to do anyway (including moving out of a congested and overpriced Manhattan). Creative destruction mapped into September 11th all too easily.

Consider, then, the urban process side of things. New York is now the quintessential city of finance capital. Capital is a flow of value in search of profits rather than a stock of physical assets. For a few days the flows on which New York depends were seriously interrupted if not closed down (like the airports, the bridges and tunnels, and the Stock Exchange). And when the flows of funds, of people, and of commodities did resume it was often at a diminished rate. Theaters were empty, restaurants half full, hotel rooms unoccupied, even garages left unused, and the reverberations of that were enormous for almost every aspect of life in the city. Tax revenues declined precipitously forcing a newly elected mayor to face up to a severe municipal budget crisis with drastic cuts in public services and spiraling indebtedness the only answer. The body politic was in deep trouble from all angles because the urban process was in trouble if not in free fall.

Capitalism is inevitably a speculative affair; one in which expectations and anticipations (of both consumers and producers) play such a major role that they often become self-fulfilling. It was "the animal spirits" of U.S.-based capitalism (or what Alan Greenspan called the "irrational exuberance" of financial markets) that sustained global capitalism and overrode all manner of problems in the 1990s (the bailouts of Mexico and Russia, the containment of the Asian crisis and the chronically depressed conditions in Japan). And much of this activity was centered in New York with huge local effects (exorbitant year-end bonuses on Wall Street, for example). What bin Laden's strike did so brilliantly was to undermine confidence by hitting hard at the symbolic center of the system and exposing its vulnerability.

Consumer confidence was therefore seized upon as the key to revival. Everyone was urged to reinstate all the old values, to shop until they dropped, to travel the world as if nothing had changed (even though the national guard was patrolling everywhere, traffic was being stopped and arbitrarily searched and the lines at airport security were often chaotic). But it proved difficult to "normalize" lives in abnormal times without losing new-found solidarities. Social inequality in the city became more rather than less emphatic. The financial compensation scheme for those killed in the disaster illustrates the problem. Although much praised for its moderation, the government plan envisaged payments between $350,000 and $4.2 million depending mainly upon the discounted lifetime earnings of those who died, making a mockery of the idea that all human life is sacrosanct and that we are all in this together irrespective of class, race or gender. Proliferating law suits among the beneficiaries signaled declining solidarities. The *New York Times* reported early in December that more than a million people in the metropolitan region were now relying on soup kitchens and charity meals in order to have enough money to pay their rents and avert the fall into homelessness. Homelessness nevertheless surged within six months to its highest level in two decades.

None of this was consistent with the new-found narrative of "American values" or of empathy with the plight of New York. It betokened, in short, a return to that "dog-eat-dog" American way of life and its class-bound privileges that had prevailed before September 11th. But it was now considerably worsened by the onset of a recession that had actually been in the making at least six months before the attack. The flows so vital to the sustenance of the city were already weakening and it is hard now to distinguish between what September 11th distinctively wrought and what was beginning to occur anyway. For more than a decade money had poured into a booming U.S. stock market to cover the huge current account balance of payments deficit that the U.S. was running. But then the boom went bust and the proliferating scandals that beset Wall Street undermined confidence in New York's highly touted financial services industry. The dollar started to weaken in world trade, making investment in dollar-denominated securities even less attractive. As inflows slackened, so New York's primary business began to soften. The New York economy seems to be headed for difficult times; the processes that sustained it so triumphantly in the 1990s are diminishing in vigor.

In response, the body politic seems to be trying to consolidate itself around its corporate-entrepreneurial core in an effort to promote revival, even as it invokes and trades upon the solidarities that emerged in the immediate aftermath of the attack. The complicated process around planning for the reconstruction of the World Trade Center site bears watching because it provides several clues to how this process is working. Political-economic pressures to revive financial functions backed by developer and financial interests are dominating other concerns but key decision makers have to step lightly out of respect for public sentiments and democratic impulses expressed through public forums. The other symbolic event of some significance was the relocation of the elitist World Economic Forum from its habitual (and increasingly contested) location in Davos, Switzerland to the Waldorf Astoria in New York. This was meant as a sign of international solidarity and sought to bring back confidence and to stimulate the flows of people, commerce and money so vital to the sustenance of the city. It also signaled a certain nervousness worldwide at the prospect of serious troubles in New York, the heartland of international and multinational capitalism. But the concerns expressed at the forum suggested a broader nervousness about the stability of global capitalism and its financial base as well as about the need to mollify criticisms of the escalating social and geographical inequalities and environmental degradations that neoliberal policies (including draconian structural adjustment programs administered by the I.M.F.) were producing. The question tacitly posed was whether or not the body politic as presently constituted could reform itself sufficiently both locally and internationally to address these issues.

Half a world away, in Porto Alegre, a southern Brazilian city of some 1.3 million people, the Worker's Party (P.T.) was staging an alternative event called the World Social Forum, bringing together many of the political groups that had been in the forefront of the global protest movement against the ravages of neoliberalism. The contrast is worth examining briefly, by way of conclusion, because the body politic has been reconstituted in Porto Alegre according to quite different principles from those that currently dominate New York City. In Porto Alegre, the P.T. has been in power continuously since 1989 and has in many ways revolutionized the system of municipal governance to create an alternative kind of political body to that which generally prevails under the neoliberal regime of accumulation. The P.T. pursued popular participation and inverted priorities so as to switch resources away from central city power elites and their interests to marginal and peripheral populations hitherto unincorporated, either economically or politically, into the social order. To do this, the P.T.:

> developed an entirely "bottom up" system of participatory governing in which openly elected forums have a great deal of deliberative power over an expanding number of policy arenas. The central participatory policy is the "participatory budget": a system of decision-making that gives power over public resource allocation to forums elected at neighborhood level assemblies and at open "thematic" meetings. This system has grown in scope and power over time, at first largely addressing decisions about community level capital expenditures and eventually gaining decision-making power over major capital investments, service and maintenance programs and personnel issues. (Abers 1999: 70)

The success of this model, Abers argues, was largely due to the process of implementation of the ideas rather than to the cogency or appeal of the ideas themselves. In her analysis, she identifies three major processual shifts: (1) mobilizing the poor (through independent and autonomous neighborhood organization); (2) transforming the bureaucracy (largely from the inside with "ideologically mobilized" personnel); and (3) building political support (through coalitions and alliances that incorporated segments of the middle class, professional organizations and even sectors of business, such as the builders and contractors).

The relative success of the P.T. in Porto Alegre so far, in confronting many of the problems of social and economic exclusion, provides an alternative model for how the body politic might be reconstituted around more democratic practices and with a quite different class content. It is not revolutionary, but it does illustrate how social democratic means coupled with popular mobilization within the body politic can make a significant difference. Interestingly, the immediate aftermath of September 11th in New York City provided more than a few hints of the possibility of such a model working in New York too. Depending upon how the situation evolves, particularly whether finance capitalism drifts into a downward spiral crisis mode to provoke an urban crisis of similar depth to that of the city in the 1970s, it may be that a reconstitution of New York's body politic more along the lines of Porto Alegre will become not only possible but necessary. In this way the city would be able to recover its health and well-being in general as well as confront the appalling levels of social inequality and exclusion that have already been generated.

Viewing the city as a body politic in relationship to urban processes illuminates the various ways in which the health of the city can be evaluated. But it also illuminates the simple fact that there are political choices to be made concerning how the body politic becomes constituted and how, once constituted, it can position itself to confront issues such as social inequality, health and welfare, and environmental degradation. Above all, it illuminates the ways in which the body politic offers a terrain of political contestation worth struggling over precisely because it is the locus of debate and action over what, exactly, might be the "nature of our task" as we seek to transform ourselves by transforming the urban process and the city as a physical and social environment in which we live.

References

Abers, R. (1999), "Practicing Radical Democracy: Lessons from Brazil", *Plurimondi* 1 (2): 67–82.

Agulhon, M. (1981), *Marianne into Battle: Republican Imagery and Symbolism in France, 1789–1880*, Cambridge: Cambridge University Press.

Balzac, H. de (ND), *The Peasantry*, London and New York: Chesterfield Society.

Bratsis, P. (2002), *Everyday Life and the State: a Materialist Revision of State Theory*. Doctoral dissertation, Graduate School and University Center, City University of New York, Political Science.

Eaton, L. (2002), "Looking to Suburbs to Map 9/11's reach", *New York Times*, Section 10, 16 June.

Flaubert, G. (1964 edition), *Sentimental Education*, translated by Baldick, R. Harmondsworth, Middlesex: Penguin Classics.

Foucault, M. (1984), "Space, Knowledge and Power", in Rabinow, P. (ed.), *The Foucault Reader*, Harmondsworth, Middlesex: Peregrine Books.

Harvey, D. (1989), *The Condition of Postmodernity,* Oxford: Basil Blackwell.

—— (1996), *Justice, Nature and the Geography of Difference*, Oxford: Basil Blackwell.

Kantorowicz, E. (1957), *The King's Two Bodies*, Princeton: Princeton University Press.

Scott, J. (2002), "Census Finds Rising Tide, and Many who Missed Boat", *New York Times*, B1 and B8, 17 June.

Steinhauer, J. (2002), "Bloomberg Plans more Housing Aid for the Homeless", *New York Times*, A1, B7, 18 June.

Part I
The Degradation of Urban Life

–3–

The Depreciation of Life During Mexico City's Transition into "the Crisis"[1]

Claudio Lomnitz

Urban Decay in Mexico City

In an effort to communicate the impossibility of comprehending Mexico City, the impossibility of summarizing it, of studying it in any systematic fashion, or even of knowing it in the way that a taxi driver might aspire to know a city, the urban anthropologist Néstor García Canclini reminds us that the size of the population of metropolitan Mexico City "is close to the population of the whole of Central America, and it includes a diversity of ethnic groups, life styles, productive activities and habits of consumption that is comparable to that of the five countries that make up that subcontinent" (García Canclini 1996: 29). Discussing Mexico City's problems, discovering its "wounds" in connection to an event, any event, is made difficult by the city's enormous scale.

It is clear, too, that this scale has been shaped in an historical process that begins before the epoch that concerns us in this collective effort. In fact, at a very general level of analysis, Mexico City presents one of the few "success stories" that doomsday futurologists can tout: predictions written in the early 1970s regarding population size, scarcity of water, and pollution, based largely on lineal extrapolations, have been borne out to an annoying degree. Moreover, the destruction and construction of Mexico City is a story that could be told in the *longue durée* (beginning, perhaps, with the centuries-old process of draining the basin of Mexico), or as modern history (beginning with industrialization and the extension of the city beyond its colonial limits under Porfirio Díaz). The twentieth-century history of Mexico, in any case, is a story of constant, and accelerating, destruction, construction and reconstruction.

It is tough, in this context, to ask a more narrowly focused question, like "what were the effects of the epochal shift in the political economy that began with the 1982 debt crisis on the texture of the city?" And harder yet when you try, as I aim to do in this essay, to deal with an especially diffuse kind of issue, which is the depreciation of life. Nonetheless, it is clear, too, that this sort of specificity can be achieved, even if at an imperfect level. My hope is to make a few in-roads on this topic, which in my view as a former *vecino* of Mexico City, is widely perceived and deeply felt, even if it may be difficult to express with tangible referents.

However, the lack of value placed on life is something that needs to be unpacked a little before our discussion of this question in a specific historical moment, *la crisis* (1982–9) can proceed.[2] I shall be concerned with four ways of disparaging life. The first occurs at the level of representation. It is the playful use of death as a way of carnivalizing life. The second form is the experience of violence, and the fear, guilt, and impurity that are associated with it. The third form is to do with the depreciation of people's time; and the fourth with a low opinion and degradation of the human sensibility of people. I will explore these issues in a loose way, in order to propose a general idea regarding the processes of depreciation and appreciation of life that characterized Mexico City during the crisis.

I begin with a general discussion of representations of death in Mexico and move from there to the representation of impoverishment in the 1970s and 1980s. This section is followed by a discussion of crime and of the rise of a particular form of democratic politics in the 1980s, and then by a discussion of the degradation of the human sensibility of the popular classes that was displayed by the reigning technocracy in that period. Throughout these discussions I highlight the cultural transformation of Mexico City from the 1970s to the 1980s.

An Overview of the Crisis in Mexico City

An analysis of the crisis of the 1980s in Mexico City needs, at a minimum, to recognize the relationship between the brutal deterioration of social conditions in that period and the developments in the 1970s. I want briefly to provide some general parameters here.

In the 1970s and 1980s Mexico was still ruled by a single party (the P.R.I.). State power was disproportionately centered in the executive branch, and the mayors of Mexico City were directly appointed by the president (mayor Sentíes by Luis Echeverría, Hank González by José López Portillo, Aguirre by Miguel De la Madrid, and Camacho by Carlos Salinas). The first popular election for a Mexico City mayor in the contemporary period was in 1997. Since that time the Mexico City government has been in the hands of the center-left party P.R.D.

(mayors Cuauhtémoc Cárdenas, Rosario Robles, and now Manuel López Obrador).

Like in most parts of the world, the effects of the reorganization of capitalist production that is now often referred to as flexible accumulation were first felt in Mexico City in the early 1970s. At that point, as Diane Davis (1994: 220) has shown, the position of Mexico City in the national economy began to decline, while its political volatility grew.

Up until that time, Mexico's economic model had been predicated on import substitution industrialization, and it had Mexico City as the central location for this industrialization. President Echeverría (1970–6) attempted in the early portion of his period to implement a balanced, regionally based export substitution policy; however the weakening of the peso and of Mexico's position in the international economy got in the way of this, and the president continued to funnel resources into expensive Mexico City projects like the subway, new projects for urban governance, and public housing, despite the fact that the economic model was failing.

The governments of Luis Echeverría (1970–6) and José López Portillo (1976–82) confronted Mexico City's growing fiscal crisis, the city's relative decline in the national economy, and its mushrooming social problems by bolstering public investment that was financed by foreign credits. Investments in the Mexico City subway, in streets, water, drainage, housing, education and urban development were enormous, hugely ambitious and often inefficient. Although I cannot elaborate on the successes and failures of these many programs, there are two elements that are pertinent to the discussion. First, the fact that urban social movements, which multiplied in this period, were often met with government programs and subsidies; and second, that the political aims of government expenditure were complemented by the economic interests of corrupt politicians and developers, as well as by the larger propaganda concerns of the presidency, which sought to shore up the popularity of the P.R.I. in the aftermath of 1968.

For example, urban social movements' demands for cheap and efficient public transport were met under mayor Carlos Hank González (1977–82) with investments in subway and road construction that benefited his own companies and those of his allies. The symbiotic relationship between tending social demand and tending the private interests of the political elite was elegantly summarized by Hank himself in a saying that would become famous: *un político pobre es un pobre político* (a politician who is poor is a poor politician).[3]

José López Portillo's educational policies illustrate the relationship between state expenditure, social movements and state propaganda. In his final state of the union address (1982) president López Portillo remarked that "As we promised, we have provided primary education to every Mexican child, and Junior High Schools for 90 per cent of the graduates of the primary schools . . . [In my term] we have quadrupled the enrolment in basic education, and doubled enrolment in higher education." However, in an analysis of educational problems of the period, Jaime Castrejón Diez, who was closely associated with educational policies at the time, remarked that "[The growth in social demand for education] has meant that one of the characteristics of our educational system is that it centers its attention on growth, but not necessarily on the quality of education. Under these circumstances educational planning focuses on the demands of admission to the system . . . We might say that in Mexico the system is completely dominated by the growth in enrolments."[4]

From a very broad perspective, the 1970s can be characterized as a period in which urban problems grew dramatically, while the city's fiscal health deteriorated badly. Between 1966–76 family income spent on transport went from roughly 9 per cent to 13 per cent, overtaking expenditure in rent. The number of cars tripled between 1970–80 (Davis 1994: 231–2). Meanwhile, although in 1970 "Mexico City still financed 60.26 percent of its budget from tax revenues, the figure dropped to 22.14 percent in 1980, and by 1982, at the end of Hank González's term as mayor, it fell to 9.66 percent." Municipal debt went from being 15 per cent of its total budget in 1970 to 44 per cent of the budget in 1982 (Paris 1994: 250–1).

And all of this debt and expenditure seems to have been driven by the twin motors of social appeasement (Mexico City's votes for opposition parties in 1979, which was during the oil boom, was as high as 41 per cent), and favoring the allied interests of urban developers and politicians.

In this context, the transition into a neo-liberal economy was brutal. From 1983 to 1988 Mexico's per capita income fell at a rate of 5 per cent per year; the value of workers' real wages fell between 40 per cent and 50 per cent; inflation, which had oscillated between 3 per cent and 4 per cent per year in the 1960s, had gone up to the mid-teens after 1976, and surpassed 100 per cent in several of those years (Lustig 1998: 2, 40, 67). At the same time, due to the government's fiscal problems and the reorientation of the country's governing economic model, state expenditure on public goods declined. Food subsidies were restricted to the poorest segments of the population, and the quality of public education and health care stagnated or declined. As the primary center of an industry that was geared to the domestic market, conditions in Mexico City deteriorated dramatically, while Mexico's northern and border areas prospered in

relative terms. The proportion of Mexico City's contribution to the national tax based dropped 18 per cent between 1980 and 1983 (Davis 1994: 276).
Davis summarizes the situation as follows:

> Squeezed both locally and nationally, in 1985 alone resources for Mexico City were so scarce that expenditures on critical urban services in the capital plummeted 12 percent on transport, 25 percent on potable water, 18 percent on health services, 26 percent on trash collection, and 56 percent on land regularization. . . . In the three-year period starting in 1984, prices of dietary staples in Mexico city rose at phenomenal rates—757 percent for beans, 480 percent for eggs, 454 percent for fish, 340 percent for milk, and 276 percent for cornmeal . . . In 1985, the Mexico City government even closed over two thousand commercial establishments in Mexico City for price gouging. (Davis 1994: 277)

Thus, the early crisis period is one of vertiginous insecurity and collapsing buying capacity (middle-class neighborhoods in 1983 organized strikes over property tax payments, for instance).[5] Attempts by labor to mitigate falling wages were by and large unsuccessful, or else were countered with layoffs. It is also a time that is marked politically by three major events, the devastating earthquake of September 1985, the student movement of 1986, and the mass mobilization around the presidential campaign of Cuauhtémoc Cárdenas of 1987–8, with its aftermath of electoral fraud and changing strategies of legitimation under president Carlos Salinas. This is the general context of my discussion.

La Vida no Vale Nada?

The lack of value placed on human life in Mexico has long been a staple in the stock and trade of national stereotypes. Alongside the sentimental Russian, the Italian gigolo, the Brazilian mulatta and the ugly American, is the Mexican dancing with death.

The stereotype is in part, as Stanley Brandes has remarked, fostered by the commercialization of Mexico's Day of the Dead, a commercialization that begins in Mexico itself, with the sale of sugar skulls, paper offerings and *pan de muertos*, but that also captured the attention of artists, film makers and, ultimately, of the tourist bureaus (1997: 273). In recent decades, the Mexican ritual elaboration of death has also found a place in the voracious American appetite for identity.[6]

Curiously, the scholarship on the historical development of the Day of the Dead in Mexico is only beginning to develop. This is because the earlier explosion of writing and fascination with this subject was concerned principally with describing the contemporaneous phenomenon, and then providing it with the historical pedigree that was required to make popular attitudes towards death, and the Day of the Dead in particular, into national attributes. Lugo Olín's extensive bibliographical study of Mexican writings on death (1994) reveals that studies of Mexican practices toward death do not emerge before the 1920s, and the literature on the subject does not really consolidate before the 1940s. In this sense one could tackle Mexican elaboration of death as a social formation that is parallel to Brazilian carnival, since both of these cultural practices were picked up for the construction of a national art and a national consciousness in the critical decades of the 1920s and 1930s. The coincidence is not a fluke, since sex and death are the great levelers, and both Brazil and Mexico were engaged in forging national societies based on the idea of *mestizaje* at that time.

This does not mean, however, that there was not a rich cultural elaboration of death in Mexico before the 1920s and 1930s, or that nationalists such as Diego Rivera or Octavio Paz invented Mexican attitudes towards death in their work. Elaborate mortuary rituals, funerary pyres, homilies, processions, days of the dead festivities and crafts can be traced back at least to the seventeenth century. Among the various dimensions of the fusion of indigenous and baroque imagery and traditions surrounding death, the subversive dimension of the Day of the Dead was also present in the colonial period, and this was recognized by Enlightened reformers in Mexico City in the eighteenth and early nineteenth centuries (see Viqueira Albán 1981: 27–62; 1994: 14). Indeed, there are still today a number of villages and towns where masques and dances associated with carnival are also associated with the Dia de Muertos. Moreover, there was also an elite cultural tradition, close to the morality of the baroque church of the Hapsburgs, that elaborated the carnivalizing potential of death, a tradition that is evident in the prominence of the *vanitas* painting motifs in baroque Mexican art, and in the use of the skull as a prop in the *mundo al revés* sensibilities of popular artists in the nineteenth and twentieth centuries.

With the advent of freedom of the press (beginning in 1812, and especially after 1821), death begins to be used as a device for satire, and especially for political satire, a genre that continues into the present day, but that was made most famous in the engravings of José Guadalupe Posada in the years prior to the Mexican revolution. Posada used his famous *calaveras* to portray the whole of Mexican society, from high to low, from the equalizing vantage point of death. This tradition was used amply since the time of independence, when writers as prominent as José Joaquín Fernández de Lizardi, Mexico's first novelist and premier journalist, constructed satirical dialogues between the dead as an instrument of political criticism.[7]

The transition from Posada, who was still using *calaveras* as a form of social satire, to Rivera or Octavio Paz, who use Mexican familiarity with death as a national attribute, is quite subtle. In the earlier usage, the proximity and familiarity with death is a reminder of the vanities of life and its idle pursuits. It is fair to say that this strategy of diminution of life is "carnivalizing," in so far as death provides the ironic distance from which to criticize the hierarchies and pretensions of the living. However, this form of carnivalizing becomes essentialized in the twentieth century as a Mexican characteristic, and hence commercialized as an icon of national identity (see Figure 3.1: Posada).

Given this rich cultural elaboration of death, and especially the successful incorporation of these practices into notions of national identity, the depreciation of life is easily naturalized and assimilated to a long tradition.

CHISPEANTE Y DIVERTIDA CALAVERA DE DOÑA TOMASA Y SIMON EL AGUADOΓ

Figure 3.1 Posada, Carnivalized death as an icon of national identity.

Although this gesture is not entirely illegitimate, as there is a high degree of elaboration of death in Mexican folk and popular culture, the gesture always proceeds at the expense of closer inspection of the specificity of various practices and phenomena.

An example is the question of the low level of safety precautions in Mexico City. Construction workers without hard hats, drivers ignoring seat belts, or pedestrians preferring dangerous street crossings to using overhead passes. All of these attitudes can be chalked up to the "fatalism" of the Mexican without any further challenge. However, if we inspect these practices more closely, we often find that very general cultural attitudes are mingling with a specific set of conditions: the perception, for instance, that daily risks in the city are so high that worrying too much itself becomes a hazard. Thus, García Canclini and Rosas Mantecón (1996: 95) present their informants' attitudes towards the hazards and risks of the city, and especially of pollution: "We shouldn't think about it so much because in the end our body adapts to it," or another voice: "you cannot be constantly thinking that 'this is going to do me harm' because soon you will find yourself dead in the middle of the street." Neither of these informants is claiming that risk is unimportant or meaningless; what they are saying is that they would be worse off worrying about risk than coexisting with it.

In short, it is useful to dispense with the temptation to place practices of life depreciation in a broad cultural framework, even though such a system of categories can be shown to be relevant, if we wish to understand the process of life depreciation at a specific juncture. Which brings us to our point: what occurs with the carnivalizing form of "depreciation of life" in the Mexico City crisis of the 1980s? What is the difference between the 1970s and the 1980s on this issue?

A look at the media provides a useful perspective on these questions. Because this essay is part of a broader study, I proceed directly to key examples. The image of the regime's relationship to popular classes in the 1970s was perhaps best (and most popularly) captured by Abel Quesada's representations of the propped-up popular groups alongside the bourgeois politico, Don Gastón Billetes.

In Quesada's caricatures we find a portrayal of impoverished urban groups and peasants that have three characteristics: they are shown with very human, personal perspectives on events that surround them; they are flattened out, as if they were made of cardboard; and they are propped up, Salvador Dalí fashion, with a hodge-podge of crutches. These three characteristics are related to the relationship between the state and popular groups at this time, when individual rights were systematically trampled (or at least went unattended) while the state legitimized itself by appealing to its defense of social rights, hence the flattening of characters who are thereby susceptible to being appropriated as representatives of corporate sectors. At the same time, the characters' reliance on a very improvised set of crutches would appear to index a set of *ad hoc* solutions to the real situation of the individual, and if we look at the ethnography of the period we find that those "crutches" indeed included some government investments and public goods (see Figure 3.2: Quesada).

Figure 3.2 Quesada, Caricatures of disrespected citizens.

Death imagery and the sort of carnivalization carried out by Posada was not an especially popular form of lampooning in Mexico in the 1960s and 1970s, and we do not find it often either in Quesada or in Rius, who were the most outstanding political cartoonists of the time. In part, no doubt, this is because this is an era of intense Americanization, in which the Day of the Dead was increasingly seen as a rural thing, and Halloween was making inroads in the city's middle classes. Official appropriation of Mexican crafts under new institutions such as FONART (Fondo Nacional Para Artes Populares) and the under-ministry of popular culture fomented Día de Muertos imagery, so we do not see this used quite so prominently as an instrument of political satire and critique. But there is more to it than this.

Posada's images used death as a site from which social pretensions could be showed up in their vanity. Death provided a distance from the everyday that allowed for the development of an egalitarian critique. In Quesada's day, on the contrary, demonstrating that we are all, at bottom, equal was not so pressing or transgressive. Instead, social criticism focused on the ways in which Mexico's corporate state "flattened out" the needs and aspirations of the people, and then used these two-dimensional images as characters in a kind of allegory of social justice that fell far short of the state's actual efficacy in that terrain.

The 1982 crisis, and the 1985 Mexico City earthquake, which in some respects marked its nadir, changed all of this. As the edifice of the corporate state began to crumble, the popularity of Mexican skull imagery and of macabre humor had its renaissance. Black humor played on the disasters that befell the city during the early years of the crisis, from the fall of the peso, to the economic difficulties of the crisis, to the spectacle of the corruption of the oil boom era that was finally exposed, to the horrors of the San Juanico gas explosion and of the 1985 earthquake.

In this context, significantly, skull imagery and play with death no longer focused on death's role as a leveler, but rather on the differentiated distribution of the social costs of the crisis. I now turn to these representations by focusing on the tensions between forms of depreciation of life that were "democratic," in that they affected everyone, and forms that brought out inequality most keenly.

Urban Violence

There are forms of urban decay that we can think of in some respects as "democratic." This is because, like death itself, they are perceived as levelers, in that they include and affect all inhabitants of the city equally. Perhaps the best example of such an inclusive form of depreciation is air pollution, which is seen as affecting everyone (even though it is not caused by everyone equally). Another example of a democratic form of urban decay is petty corruption. The city, with its exasperating urban congestion (inhabitants travel between two and four hours per day on average), becomes an obstacle course in which laws must routinely be bent or broken. To cite once again from Canclini's study of urban imaginaries (García Canclini and Rosas Mantecón 1996: 94):

> Taxi drivers run red lights and policemen extract quotas from them. If a car or a street-business finds no place in the street, it will invade the sidewalk. If the pedestrian is in a hurry, he does not bother to go around and use the pedestrian bridge when crossing the highway . . . We believe that with the routine succession of these small tactics, a particular kind of citizen is shaped. That citizen contributes to the reproduction of systemic inequality and to the legitimation of corruption.

In this comment, Canclini and Mantecón identify what is in fact a general property of "democratic" forms of degradation such as pollution, corruption, and urban violence, which is that they contribute to the construction of an idea of citizenship through the identification of common problems and an identity of shared practices, while at the same time they tend to distribute the blame evenly, tending either to pit "society" against "the state" or to make the whole of society equally culpable. Because these forms of decay are employed to shape ideas of citizenship, I believe that it is appropriate to call them "democratic," in the loosest sense of this term, and the role of these forms of degradation in the construction of democratic processes in Mexico, which has not yet been studied, may be large indeed.

Random violence and revolutionary violence are often themselves archtypal images of Mexican proximity with death (in a most famous ballad, Rosita Elvírez's spurned dance partner "only shot her three times," and she was in fact lucky because of these three shots "only one was fatal"); this procrustean bed of violence is widely recognized, and is often referred to in the press as a kind of sleeping ogre (*el México bronco*). Yet the transformation of urban violence in the past years is universally acknowledged and has become a central political concern. In 2000 all three presidential and mayoral candidates ran their campaigns with fighting crime and corruption as their top issue. What is this transformation? How does it relate to the transformation of Mexico City's position in the world economy?

During the Mexican Revolution, Mexico City was a conservative bastion, and a place of refuge for people fleeing the violence of the surrounding countryside. A space akin to a balcony, it was full of spectators who were gripped by the horrors of the revolution. It also became the prize that was taken by revolutionary captains. As a result, the fear of armed confrontation was just under the surface for decades after the Revolution, and the notion that a banal argument could end with someone pulling out a gun was well recognized in the collective imaginary.[8]

On the other hand, Mexico City's murder rate which, like that of the whole country, was always comparatively high, was dominated by conjugal violence and rivalries between friends. As a Mexican émigré explained to me when I moved to the U.S. in the late 1970s and found myself perplexed by my first (news) encounter with an American random serial killer: "Here in the United States people are so lonely that they shoot complete strangers." This perception pretty much summed up people's general impression of violence in Mexico City: you might be killed by your *compadre*, your lover or your husband, or you might get killed in an argument in a bar or over a fender-bender, but not by a total stranger. Thieves were interested in money, they had no desire to hurt you.

This is what changed so radically with the crisis, and although the process of transformation has been ongoing and complex, some details are enlightening. The first of the new crime waves occurred immediately after President De la Madrid took office (December 1982), in the midst of the shock of the crisis and in the face of the free-falling peso. De la Madrid, who had run his campaign with an anti-corruption slogan, "The Moral Renovation of Society,"[9] began his term with a two-pronged effort: first, to implement I.M.F. conditions while trying to keep a modicum of stability, second, to modernize and democratize the bureaucracy. This second idea had a political rationale behind it. Whereas P.R.I. politics of the 1970s held forth both the large carrot of state subsidy and the big stick of state terror, De la Madrid's motto could have been "no carrot, no stick."

Although he was unable to follow through on either side of this motto (there was both repression and cooptation under President De la Madrid), the impulse to balance state disinvestment in the national economy with democratic concessions was clear. For instance, De la Madrid moved to democratize the Mexico City government shortly after taking office. The movement was blocked initially by the P.R.I., but a transition into a system of elected officers (first an assembly, and with time a popularly elected mayor) was eventually set in motion. Similarly, there were a number of attempts simultaneously to professionalize and to shrink the size of state bureaucracies: salaries of certain sectors of the bureaucracy were raised or protected in the face of galloping inflation and plummeting real wages, while workers and bureaucrats in other sectors were fired and state agencies were closed.

De la Madrid's initial policy toward the police was of a piece with these tendencies. He tried to professionalize and train a sector of the police, while disbanding another sector. Thus, the first crime wave of the crisis period, which as a whole is an era in which Mexico City went from being a relatively safe city to a very unsafe city, immediately followed the closing of the Dirección de Investigaciones para la Prevención de la Delincuencia (D.I.P.D.), and the placement of an army general at the head of a project to modernize the Mexico City police. *Proceso* magazine described the effects of these changes in the following terms:

> Inside the police department work was reduced to a minimum. No one dared to do anything under the gaze of the agents of the General Inspection. . . . The city was left without protection.

And then they explain the problem further:

> The presidential decree and agreement was meant to establish a baseline for the moral renovation of the police corps by way of technical improvement and training. . . . However, the measures that have been adopted face a hidden reality: the police until now had to a large degree financed itself out of the pockets of the policemen themselves, whose income came to a large extent from gifts, extortion and bribes that they extracted. Policemen worried about maintaining their vehicles in good repair. With the change in the administration the cars began to stall. . . . Little by little, the surveillance of the city diminished, and with it crime rates grew remarkably.[10]

In addition to this, the 3,000 policemen who were let go from the D.I.P.D. participated actively in the new crime wave.

Several key characteristics of the Mexico City crisis of the 1980s are evident in the case. First, there is an attempt to jump start bureaucratic reform by intervening in the continuing operation of what had been to a large degree a prebendal system; second, this was done as an ideological measure ("moral renovation of society" and "modernization"), but it had a hidden economic incentive as a subtext (balancing the budget); third, the costs of this brutally orchestrated transition were very unevenly distributed (3,000 policemen were thrown out of work, the city was left in the hands of criminals, while a "technically correct" bureaucracy was maintained and, as *Proceso* remarked in another article, rich neighborhoods began hiring private forces).[11] Because the older system was easily assailable as corrupt, which of course it was to its very core, it could be altered and reformed without too much discussion of social costs. And this despite the fact that the older system was, in a number of key respects, essentially the system of policing that had been in place since the colonial period.[12]

Like De la Madrid's attempt to democratize Mexico City, the chaotic effect of this early police reform led the city to return to its earlier policing practices for a while but, also like the case of democratization, the engine for modernizing the police bureaucracy and severing the older forms of policing had been set in motion. Although we have no good study of this process as of yet, it seems clear that the fractured old police system, compounded with the sharp decline in employment and wages in the mid 1980s, and especially after the third peso crisis of late 1994, brought Mexico City down from being a relatively safe city to a situation comparable to that of cities like Sao Paulo, Caracas, Rio and Lima.

In the social imaginary, this new form of depreciation of life looms large and is transmitted in conversation and rumor, but these forms of transmission began to be multiplied in the late 1990s by the media. Since Mexico City's first mayoral elections in 1997, the city's mayors have been from the left-of-center P.R.D., so the two television networks, both of which have debts with the old P.R.I. establishment, felt no need to restrain their exposés of urban crime and scandal, the way they had in the past.

In this new imaginary, the violence that is exerted against innocent victims is the source of outrage and fear. Kidnappers who sever ears or fingers and send them to the victims' families, only to end up killing their victims once they have received their recompense, is a common theme, as are assault, battery, mayhem, and the abasement of victims. The growing popularity of people who take justice in their own hands is also worth mentioning; cases such as the one of the passengers of a *pesero* minibus who lynched an assailant and silently dropped his body at a terminal, or the popularity of a former television comic who was witness to a stick-up, drew his gun, and killed the assailant.

In an essay (1992) on the history of Mexico's crime pages (*nota roja*), writer Carlos Monsiváis identified this genre as one of the earliest forms of popular literature of Mexican mass society, and he compared the horrors that were told in them with other forms of morality tales. Husbands killing wives, children murdering their parents, the model student running amuck and murdering young women . . .

We don't yet know much about the sorts of stories that are being popularized today, and we know even less about the ways these stories are incorporated into processes of self fashioning amongst the citizenry.[13] However, we can at least advance a general hypothesis. The new crime stories generally do not feature crimes of passion, but are instead about predators, victims, and justice. Not divine justice, but procedural justice. Their consumption is related to morality tales about what constitutes proper precaution, the daily heroism of the navigator in Mexico City's urban maze, the production of a new idea regarding policing, justice and democracy, and the affirmation of the urban community. These four aspects are visible in the city today.

On the topic of what constitutes proper precautions in the city, we have everything from the rise of vigilantism, to the emigration of people from the middle classes out of the city, to the exponential growth in the numbers of gated communities, multiplication of private police forces, depreciation of real estate in locations that are considered unsafe, increased height of walls, growing use of alarms, dogs, armed guards, and a range of security devices, decline in the use of taxis, and the growing importance of well-patrolled malls for the social life of teenagers.

The exponential growth of urban violence in Mexico City has heightened the pattern of settlement and movement that has been described by García Canclini's research team. Because of the city's growth, it was already a multi-polar metropolis by the time the crisis began in 1982, with a declining city center, and a highly uneven distribution of cultural offerings. Bookstores, museums, movie theaters, cafés and public parks were and are disproportionately concentrated in a triangle that has its base in central Mexico City and its apex in the city's southern area. Industrial and working-class areas in the city's east and north have very little of this. The combination of high transport costs, the wear and tear of increasing daily commutes to and from work, the growing insecurity of public places, and the expense of socializing in the malls means that social life is centered in the workplace, at home, and on public and private transportation. The propagation of violence has made the city even more addicted to television and the Internet (see García Canclini 1996).

On the other hand, like all "democratic" forms of life-depreciation, increased violence has also shaped new forms of appreciating life, which are visible in a blossoming human rights discourse, the craze with polls and poling, and the multiplication of demands based on refurbished ideas of citizenship. There is undoubtedly a process of appreciation of life that has also come with what I am calling democratic forms of degradation. I will turn to this in my final section.

Technocratic Depreciation of Life

One of the central contradictions of Mexico's crisis period was the relationship between economic and political reform. The liberalization of the economy undermined a one-party regime that was built on import substitution industrialization and a "mixed economy." It is not coincidental that the Mexican state did not undertake trade and investment reforms willingly. The Mexican government's first reaction to the process of globalization in the 1970s was to try to create a cordoned free-trade zone on the border, while absorbing an ever greater number of failing private firms into what was later described by neo-liberal president De la Madrid as "an obese state." The Mexican government did not turn to full reform until it was bankrupt, and so when it did transform, it did so under extreme duress and in a brutal manner.

As a result of the violence of the transformation that Mexican society faced, the transition required the kind of authoritarian structures that the P.R.I. had acquired over its history. Thus, there emerged a contradiction between reliance on an authoritarian state to make liberalizing reforms, and the fact that those reforms undermined the authoritarian state. This is well known, and the practice of the regime of this transition was aptly characterized as "liberal authoritarianism" (Meyer 1995). In fact, we have already discussed instances of this contradiction in Miguel De la Madrid's stops and starts in democratizing the city government and in professionalizing the police force.

What has gone by with less systematic attention is the effect that this contradiction had on the practices of the country's technocrats, and the ways in which the new situation led to a systematic depreciation of life in their hands.

Tensions between an enlightened leadership and an ignorant people have been a staple in Latin American history from the mid-eighteenth century forward, and indeed every era of intense modernization has sponsored its technocracy: *ilustrados* under the Bourbons, *científicos* under Díaz, *profesionistas* under Miguel Alemán, and *tecnócratas* in the period I am considering. All were apprehensive about popular culture and all sought to use the instruments of the state to reform the people.

The low opinion that these various generations entertained toward the people, toward their ignorance, gullibility, unreliability and lack of hygiene has been amply documented. François Xavier Guerra has reminded us of the example of Jovellanos, Spain's most influential *ilustrado* of the late eighteenth century, who blocked the publication of a book that he deemed to be "perfect" because criticism of the state should not be put in the hands of people who lack instruction. Similarly, Mexico's liberals of the Juárez era tried to ban blood sports such as bullfights because they allegedly brought out the violence and ungoverned passions of the so-called *clase ínfima* (Lomnitz 2001). The post-revolutionary state also staked an educational mission out for itself, a mission that framed its hostile relation to Catholicism and its politics of assimilation for Indians, for example.

The lack of regard that these enlightened elites displayed toward the popular classes can also be seen in their low estimation of popular needs. In his ethnography of a squatter settlement in southern Mexico City, Miguel Díaz Barriga (1996) described a discourse regarding needs (*necesidad*) among the urban poor. In a number of formulations referring to their connections to politicians and administrators, inhabitants of Ajusco complained that they were taken advantage of because administrators could "see their *necesidad*," because they could not hide their needs. The exhibition of necessity is embarrassing because it reveals a person's vulnerability. The salience and visibility of *necesidad*, of popular needs, contrasts with the callousness of a government that has abruptly abandoned its prior paternal duties and left its people exposed to the inclemency of the market.

It is in this context that skull and death imagery re-emerge as useful tropes. So, for example, in his scathing cartoons of the 1980s and 1990s, Naranjo consistently pairs off technocrats and members of popular groups. However, instead of using death and the skull imagery to show up the vanity of the technocrat, as Posada might have done, Naranjo uses it to show the radical *disparity* between them. In Naranjo's cartoons, the skull is simply the most extreme form of poverty and emaciation (see Figure 3.3: Naranjo).

Moreover, there is a kind of perverse need for the technocrat to produce a public display of *necesidad* in order to justify even the most meager form of state beneficence. Because governments of this period could only justify subsidies in the most dire circumstances (or when they were needed to retain political control), they demanded the public exhibition of *necesidad* in order to produce assistance. There is, in fact, a sort of aesthetics of the presentation of *necesidad* that developed in tandem with state assistance that deserves to be studied.

The Mexican crisis of 1982 required technocratic leadership on a scale that no previous government ever had. Thrusting economists upon the presidency was the most secure and expedient way to accomplish the globalizing reforms that were required by finance, and indeed they presided over a long, eighteen-year, economic and political transition.

Figure 3.3 Naranjo, Skull representing extreme poverty and emaciation.

Today they are no longer in the presidency and they have gone back to having a more specialized role. In the meanwhile, however, the liberalizing transition required a state that was both authoritarian and technocratic. This gave a special accent to the quandary of the technocracy, for most technocrats are meritocratic at heart, and as such they would like to be democratic. The trouble was that people did not behave properly, and so national reforms had to be imposed, instead of being discussed and willingly adopted.

In the Mexico City of the 1980s, a privileged site of this particular conflict was the university. This institution, which in the 1970s and earlier was touted as the principal engine of instruction and mobility, was now portrayed by government officials as a behemoth that was comparable in many ways to any other wasteful, bloated and inefficient government program of the previous decade. The city's public universities struck once, and sometimes even twice, per year for the first couple of years of the crisis but like the workers' strikes at government-owned plants in these same years, these strikes failed miserably. This was one of the exemplary areas of De la Madrid's "no carrot, no stick" policy. Strikes were allowed to drag on free of repression, but no significant monetary concessions were made. In the process, the prestige of the public university was compromised and private institutions began to grow, to the extent that today the combined campuses of the Instituto Tecnológico de Monterrey have more students than the National University.

However, there was no real popular outburst in Mexico City's streets until the university reforms of 1986, which produced a student movement that was in some ways as significant as the Mexico City earthquake of the previous year. Just as the earthquake dramatized injustice, state ineptitude and the communitarian strength of civil society, so the student movement dramatized the problem of the construction of an idea of the future, the problem of expectation and of hope, which had been an area that the technocracy had abandoned or degraded.

The events of 1982 were in the strongest sense a crisis of historicity. The ways in which people had framed the past and the future in the present were no longer operative for large segments of the population. While Mexican revolutionary ideology slipped away as official ideology and was adopted by a new rising left, others told a story in which the bankruptcy that forced the crisis was caused by the corruption and over-extension of the state. These people placed the mythical origins of Mexico's future not in the Revolution, but rather in nineteenth century liberalism (the Restored Republic and the early Porfiriato), and they charged the regime of the Revolution with ultimate responsibility for the Mexican crisis. Thus they built an idea of the future that highlighted democracy and private enterprise (Krauze 1982).

Although this second group would be more successful in framing a dominant version of the future than the first, neither was well-suited to the actual circumstances of that long process which came to be known as *la crisis*. This was true to such a degree that when the journal *Este País* carried out a poll on nationalism in Mexico in 1991, it was surprised to find that 59 per cent of their sample (which was meant to be nationally representative) had no objection to Mexico being incorporated into the U.S. if this meant an improvement in living conditions.[14] The mismatch between the vague expectations built around the contention for the Mexican state and people's difficult day-to-day reality for this extended period has been so strong that Mexico City, like many other great Latin

American cities today, has a palpable crisis of the future or, as Brazilian cultural critic Beatriz Jaguaribe has recently put it, a "nostalgia for the future," which in the Mexico City of the 1980s was manifested in a flourishing and dramatic nostalgia for the past, and particularly for the bygone 1940s, 1950s and 1960s.

The technocrats' disregard for people's expectations, and their utter incapacity to shape alternative futures, became painfully visible in the student movement of 1986, when a series of eminently "reasonable" reforms, like limiting enrolment in bachelors degree programs to a ten-year period, for instance, met with the first massive demonstrations in Mexico City since the start of the crisis. Technocratic disregard for the people's need to nurse a vision of the future proved to be more politically combustible even than their budget cuts.

Technocratic depreciation of life is visible in the popularity of languages of hope, even when these do not develop particularly convincing programs, as has been evident in the popularity of Zapatismo in Mexico City in the 1990s and especially in the year long student strike of 1998, when the distance between students and university authorities, and even between students and their teachers, became painfully obvious.

Conclusion

The degradation of people and of life appears at first to be an impossible topic to study during a short period, such as the Mexico City crisis of the 1980s. Most of the practices involved are very old. On the other hand, this is an important subject because it counters the technocratic fiction that systematically erases the social costs of historical processes. Technocrats would like people's lives to carry on as they were as soon as the economy grows at an acceptable rate. Their ways of measuring the economy and society elide the suffering, the wear and tear of crisis: the sacrifice of generations or of disproportionate members of one sex or class, or the transformations in forms of amiability, sociability and social peace.

I argued that although the depreciation of life has a long story, once can track new practices and new issues in the crisis period. At a certain level, these claims would appear to be banal. We know that the value of labor power was halved in Mexico City between 1982 and 1987; do we need to elaborate on the social significance of such a substantial statistic? In my view we do, because the social relations of production and reproduction have been transformed in ways that cannot be deduced or understood by figures alone.

In Mexico City the crisis produced a rift between technocrats and the general populace, it allowed for forms of democratic identity to emerge, but often around "democratic" forms of degradation, such as the damage caused by pollution, crime or the earthquake, damages that were suffered by all, but that were caused disproportionately by some. The crisis also changed the relationship between state agencies and local society, producing, in the case of the police, waves of terror and a growing concern with citizens' rights. More generally, the state's abandonment of social rights in this period changed the forms of collective mobilization.

I have argued that these transformations are visible in the ways in which attitudes toward death, toward corruption, and toward the past are mobilized. The death figures drawn by cartoonist Naranjo in the 1980s, for instance, are rather like the rotting corpses in the *danza macabra* paintings of the fourteenth century; both dead and alive, they are the embodiment of a struggle for life. This way of figuring death, as opposed to the "clean" skeleton of Posada, is always more disturbing, because it does not signify equality. In Naranjo's cartoons it is the worker's uniform or the Armani suit that determines whether the figures drawn are healthy or deathlike. The poor of the 1980s are no longer propped up as they were in Abel Quesada's cartoons, and their emaciated figures find little solace in the shade of the technocracy.

Notes

1. I am grateful to Jane Schneider for her invitation to the "Wounded Cities" conference, and for her comments and encouragement.
2. In this chapter I will be focusing especially on the depths of Mexico's crisis in the 1980s. However, because we are speaking here of a major structural transformation, I will at times refer to developments in the 1990s and into the present.
3. It is interesting to note that the neoliberal reforms implemented by De la Madrid in Mexico city hurt Hank's businesses immediately. See Pinchetti, F.O. (1983), "Con el gobierno creció y sin él se marchita el emporio económico de Hank González (pérdidas millonarias, cierre de fábricas, despidos masivos)", Pinchetti. *Proceso*, 25 April: 6–10.
4. Masa, E. (1983), "La mexicana, una sociedad de tercer año de primaria", *Proceso*, 17 January: 23.

5. D.F. IMPUESTOS (1983), "Huelga de pagos y manisfestaciones contra la Ley de hacienda del D.F.," *Proceso*, 31 March: 31–2; see also D.F. (1983), "El DDF intenta recuperarse con más impuestos y servicios caros", *Proceso*, 14 November: 6–9.
6. This initiates in the early Chicano movement itself. So, for instance, U.C. Berkeley's first Chicano cultural magazine (1973), whose mission statement declared that it was dedicated to "la busqueda de nuestro auténtico ser así como el rescate de nuestro pasado y nuestra cultura" (the search for our authentic being as well as for the recuperation of our past and our culture) was titled *La Calavera Chicana*.
7. For example, in "Los diálogos de los muertos. Hidalgo e Iturbide" (1825). For a partial list of publications of this genre in this time period, see Lugo Olín (1994: 111–17).
8. The prominence of this imagery is discussed in Stern (1995: 51–6).
9. For a discussion of the cyclical importance of anti-corruption campaigns in Mexico, and of De la Madrid's anti-corruption campaign in particular, see Morris 1991.
10. "Policía Capitalina, ante el auge de delincuentes el presidente decreta la reorganización", *Proceso*, 17 January: 25–6. The best and most useful study of the traditional form of operation of the Mexico City police is Martínez Murguía (1999).
11. D.F. (1983), "Ante la ineficiencia de la policía surge una firma privada que vende protección en Las Lomas", *Proceso*, 12 September: 17.
12. It is probably this continuity that accounts for the situation that perplexed Paul Chevigny (1995) in his comparative study of police violence in the Americas: the Mexico City police appeared to be capable of reigning in criminality with less display of organized violence than the police of Kingston, Rio de Janeiro or even Los Angeles, because policing was "socially embedded".
13. For a recent incursion in this topic, see Hallin (2000).
14. "Hacia la integración económica", *Este Poís*, April 1991: 7.

References

Brandes, S. (1997), "Sugar, Colonialism and Death: On the Origin of Mexico's Day of the Dead", *Comparative Studies in Society and History*, 39(2): 270–99.

Chevigny, P. (1995), *Edge of the Knife: Police Violence in the Americas*, New York: New Press.

Davis, D. (1994), *Urban Leviathan: Mexico City in the Twentieth Century*, Philadelphia: Temple University Press.
Díaz Barriga, M. (1996), "Necesidad: Notes on the Discourses of Urban Politics in the Ajusco Foothills of Mexico City", *American Ethnologist*, 23: 291–311.
Fernández de Lizardi (1825), *Los diálogos de los muertos. Hidalgo e Iturbide*, Mexico: Oficina del finado Ontiveros.
García Canclini, N. (1996), "Los viajes metropolitanos", in García Canclini, N., Castellanos, A. and Montecón, A.R. (eds), *La ciudad del los viajeros: travesías e imaginarios urbanos: Mexico, 1940–2000*, Mexico City: Grijalbo.
—— and Rosas Montecón, A. (1996), "Las múltiples ciudades de los viaheros", in García Canclini, N., Castellanos, A. and Rosas Montecón, A. (eds), *La ciudad del los viajeros: travesías e imaginarios urbanos: Mexico, 1940–2000*, Mexico City: Grijalbo, pp. 61–107.
Hallin, D.C. (2000), "La Nota Roja: Popular Journalism and the Transition to Democracy in Mexico", *Communication Abstracts*, 23(5): 267–84.
Krauze, E. (1982), "México: el timón y la tormenta", *Vuelta*, 71: 14–22.
Lomnitz, C. (2001), *Deep Mexico, Silent Mexico: an Anthropology of Nationalism*, Minneapolis: University of Minnesota Press.
Lugo Olín, M.C. (1994), *En torno a la muerte: Una bibliografía*, Mexico City: INAH.
Lustig, N. (1998), *Mexico: The Remaking of an Economy*, Washington DC: Brookings Institution.
Meyer, L. (1995), *Liberalismo autoritoario: las contradicciones del sistema político mexicano*, Mexico City: Océano.
Monsivais, C. (1992), "La Nota Roja en Mexico", *Nexos* 176 (August): 1–20.
Morris, S. (1991), *Corruption and Politics in Contemporary Mexico*, Tuscaloosa: University of Alabama Press.
Martínez Murguía, B. (1999), *La policía en México ¿orden social ó criminal?* Mexico City: Planeta.
Stern, S. (1995), *The Secret History of Gender: Women, Men and Power in Late Colonial Mexico*, Chapel Hill: University of North Carolina Press.
Viqueira Albán, J.P. (1981), "El sentimiento de la muerte en el México Ilustrado del siglo XVIII a través de dos textos de la época", *Relaciones* 5(2): 27–62.
—— (1994), "La Ilustración y las fiestas religiosas populares en la Ciudad de México (1730–1821)", *Cuicuilco*, 14–15: 14.

–4–

International Commodity Markets, Local Land Markets and Class Conflict in a Provincial Mexican City

Carol J. Meyers

Xalapa, the capital of the central gulf state of Veracruz, represents one of a hundred or so medium-sized cities throughout Mexico. Together these cities have come to play a central role within a restructured system of capital flows that has resulted from the country's program of neoliberal economic reform. This process, as the introduction to this volume notes, inflicts economic and social violence on populations wrought by reform. Within Mexico, the vast majority of the population has suffered an agonizing process of pauperization due to increasing job insecurity, disruption of rural production, plummeting of real wages, and drastic cuts in social expenditures. This wounding process has also taken a specific spatial form as the geographic restructuring of public and private capital flows has led to the rapid expansion of the medium-sized cities noted above and, with this, an increasing polarization in development between regions as well as within them.

Within this system of regions and cities, Xalapa has functioned primarily as a regional administrative, commercial and financial center. Nationally, the city has taken on a secondary role to much more important urban centers like the maquiladora cities to the north and the petroleum-processing cities along the coast. From an historical perspective, Xalapa's role within this system represents simply the most recent form of the city's incorporation into wider circuits of mercantile and capital flows. Since the colonial period, and even before, the city's relationship with regional and subsequently international and national circuits of exchange has been determinant in its development, with trade and transport routes being critical. This is due to Xalapa's strategic location midway between the country's principal eastern port of Veracruz and the nation's capital on the one hand, and on the other to Xalapa's competition with the cities of Orizaba and Córdoba, equally advantaged by their geographical position.

The nature of Xalapa's specific wounds and the process of its wounding are directly related to the possibilities that have emerged from the city's historical development and the consequent form of its incorporation within the present system. The most acute problems center around speculation in land and the consequent differential constraints and opportunities for access, control, and usage. Those who have suffered the greatest and deepest casualties are Xalapa's working classes with a precipitous decline in living standards that reached crisis levels with Mexico's financial bust in 1994, leading to the emergence of a level of hunger usually seen only in rural communities. However, even the city's middle-class professionals and local business sector have suffered as living standards and business opportunities once apparently secured, have dissipated. Only the region's hegemonic elite, whose members control the city's land and economy, has been able to maintain position as it has benefited from the increasing emphasis on exports and the privatization of the state sector.

In this essay, I will examine the specific impact that economic restructuring has had on Xalapa. Of particular concern will be the way in which the global forces of restructuring have been refracted through the city's and region's economic and political configuration. I will begin by giving a brief outline of Xalapa's basic economic, demographic and urban characteristics. I will then focus on the impact of economic reform on the city, paying particular attention to the economy, the population and the built environment. Finally, I will conclude by examining the creation of Xalapa's land reserve, a large tract of land purchased by the state allegedly to provide access to low-cost land and housing for the city's working population. The process of the creation of this reserve clearly illustrates the economic and political forces at work that produced Xalapa's specific wounds as well as the differential ability to recover among the city's social classes.

Xalapa: Economy and City

As of 1995, the city of Xalapa covered an area of approximately fifteen square miles and had a population of 336,000. Since the mid-twentieth century, its economy has been based on commerce and services, which employ 72 per cent of the city's workforce. Within the service sector, real estate as a source of accumulation and government bureaucracy as a source of employment are particularly significant. Xalapa's manufacturing sector accounts for only 20 per cent of employment, having suffered a process of continual decline that is not a recent development, but rather began in the early decades of the twentieth century. What has remained of the manufacturing sector is primarily the construction industry, due to its association with real estate and the critical role it has played in the production and spatial expansion of the urban habitat. While economic activities are carried out primarily through small and medium-sized firms, economic power is concentrated in a few oligarchic families whose capital is invested primarily in real estate and commerce (INEGI 1989, 1991).

Overall wage labor is the predominant form of insertion within the labor market, accounting for 74 per cent of the labor force. However, the structure of Xalapa's economy has given rise to a split labor market. On the one hand the city's need for a large number of public sector employees along with the establishment of a number of local colleges has led to the influx of middle-class professionals from other urban areas. Together with other upper level white-collar workers in commerce and services, they enjoy stable employment with benefits. Their situation contrasts with that of the majority of Xalapa's working class employed in unskilled and semi-skilled jobs where they barely earn subsistence level wages. In 1990, nearly 62 per cent of Xalapa's workforce earned less than twice the minimum wage, an amount that was insufficient to meet even their most basic needs (INEGI 1991, Rodríguez 1996).

The process of decreasing economic diversification, especially in the manufacturing sector, can be traced back to the latter half of the nineteenth century. At that time conflicts over rights to water for agriculture and the city's nacent textile mills prevented Xalapa's hegemonic *hacendado* class and its emergent industrial bourgeoisie from uniting to construct a railroad line (Leon 1987). As a result, Orizaba and Córdoba obtained the railroad several decades in advance, stimulating their industrial growth due to greater access to markets. Unable to compete, Xalapa's incipient industry began a lengthy and irreversible process of decline. With industrial profitability diminishing, the principal source of investment in Xalapa became urban real estate and commerce.

As Xalapa's dominant economic group, real-estate developers have impressed a speculative logic onto the city's spatial expansion. The cityscape reflects this speculative growth, being characterized by a pattern of social and spatial segregation typical of capitalist urbanization. Xalapa's real-estate elite own much of the land in the downtown area, obtaining windfall profits through monopoly control; one family alone, the Fernández, is believed to own approximately 50 per cent. Surrounding this central area are middle-income properties and rental units of modest size. Another of Xalapa's elite families, the Grayeb, has cornered much of this middle-income rental market through control of over 6,000 rental units (Rodríguez and Bozzano 1985). To the east and south respectively are two luxurious residential neighborhoods for the highest income groups. One of these, *Las Animas*, is a gated community replete with its own water and electrical supply, a lake and artificial landscaping. By far the most exclusive area of the city, it was developed by the Fernández family in the early 1970s on what had once been part of the family's coffee hacienda. In general, much of the land in the eastern and southeastern zones is controlled by Xalapa's urban latifundista families who, for several decades, have exerted influence over urban policy. Not surprisingly, most public investment in infrastructure has been directed toward these zones, thus increasing their market value.

In contrast to these luxurious residential neighborhoods are the northern and western areas of the city where most of the working classes live. Poverty-level incomes along with monopoly control and speculative pricing in the city's land and housing markets have greatly limited the options for shelter open to these strata. Their lodgings are of two sorts. The city's older working-class neighborhoods have seen the proliferation of a number of makeshift squalid tenements where families live in single rooms lacking ventilation and adequate drainage, sharing with other tenants a common washbasin, bathroom and shower stall. However, due to the saturation of and speculation on even this housing stock, large sectors of the working classes have been displaced to the barren lands of the urban periphery. Here as elsewhere in Mexico, settlements have been created through the illegal but *de facto* occupation of land, or more commonly through purchase from illegal land developers. Without infrastructure services or security of tenure, these lands are sold at way below the formal market rate and even run cheaper than a monthly rent in some of the city's tenements (Rodríguez and Bozzano 1985). Creation of these settlements represents a highly lucrative market for changing land use where petty speculators profit from the need of the poor for shelter.

Once there, these urban homesteaders have built makeshift homes from wood, cardboard, corrugated tin, sacks and plastic bags, gradually constructing more permanent structures over a period of many years as finances permit. Much of the land where these settlements are located is inappropriate for habitation, greatly increasing the cost of urbanization and leaving families vulnerable to flooding, landslides and other potential *natural* disasters. In contrast to the public investments from which the real-estate developers have benefited, homesteaders have waited between ten and twenty years for the introduction of basic urban services and infrastructure. As of 1990, 50 per cent of the city's inhabitants lived in these areas; 39 per cent of households were without water directly in their homes, and 37 per cent of households were not connected to the municipal sewage system but depended on self-constructed, rudimentary septic tanks or simply left their waste out in the open air (INEGI 1991).

The Mexican state has clearly tolerated this form of irregular settlement and even actually promoted it at times. In lieu of a program of low-income public housing, benign neglect of this form of urban growth in effect has constituted the fundamental feature of the state's housing policy and relations with the urban poor. The illegality of land holdings has formed part of a political structure of mediation and control, functioning as a safety valve for the housing crisis and social discontent, and as a source of political support. Given the illegality of these settlements, residents' vulnerability has involved greater dependence on state largesse; and the government has used this vulnerability to mobilize settlers for political rallies and elections. This process of social control has been organized within a patron-client structure where self-designated community leaders affiliated with what, until quite recently, had been Mexico's permanent governing party exercised power over residents. Their power rested in direct control of key resources such as access to the land, and as political brokers between community residents and high level officials in government who could deliver the goods.

Ultimately, the nature of Xalapa's economy and the spatial expansion of the city can only be understood in terms of its relation to coffee production. As one of the most dynamic productive activities in the region, coffee cultivation and processing has fueled the local economy. It has also functioned as an attraction pole for migratory flows, and given the seasonal nature of work on coffee farms and plantations, many of these migrants depend on work within the urban economy during the rest of the year (López and Borja 1990, Rodríguez 1996). The coffee economy has also had an impact on the nature of land development in Xalapa and on the rate of the city's spatial growth. This is due primarily to the fact that the same oligarchic families who control much of the urban real estate market also have extensive investments and are the predominant players in the region's coffee economy. The Fernández family, for example, derived its original capital from coffee, having built a coffee empire during the early part of the twentieth century that vertically integrated production, processing and marketing. The family's investments in urban real estate began with the diversification of its agro-industrial surplus as a way of consolidating both economic and political power within the region, a process that accelerated in the period of agrarian reform and then during the subsequent period of the city's growth (León 1983).

What is significant about these dual interests is that the variable relation between the land's potential agrarian and urban values has, to a great extent, structured these oligarchic families' investment decisions. The key element in this variable relation is that Xalapa's regional coffee production is primarily for export. As such, it is subject to the booms and busts in the international coffee market. By establishing the profitability of coffee or the lack thereof, these pendular swings in international prices have shaped Xalapa's economy and spatial growth, influencing the flow of labor to the city, the overall health of the urban economy and the relative value of the agrarian land *vìs-à-vìs* its potential urban use.

The effect of these international market forces is pervasive. In the period following the mid 1970s, in particular, when the international price of coffee increased 300 per cent over a three year period (between 1975 and 1977), all the statistical information on Xalapa and the region indicated an unequivocal impact: a 130 per cent increase in the volume of coffee production between 1975 and 1982; an average annual increase of 5.3 per cent in the city's population between 1970 and 1980; an even more rapid increase, 7.3 per cent, in the urban labor force attributable to the coffee boom; and, perhaps most important, stagnation in the city's speculative spatial expansion (INEGI 1981, López and Borja 1990, Rodríguez 1996).

In 1982, when Mexico embarked on a dramatic restructuring of the economy, the coffee-based dynamic of Xalapa's form of urban growth was already in existence. Critical to understanding how the national reform has played out in this city are the dual interests of the elite within both the urban and agrarian economy. As the following sections show, the forces of economic reform have been filtered through Xalapa's specific conditions. Rather than creating contradictions in and of themselves, the effect has been to accelerate the development of existing tensions and to accentuate their impact.

Destabilization of the Local Economy, Informalization and Pauperization

While Xalapa formed part of the emerging system of urban centers within Mexico's economic and geographic restructuring, it did not receive the large injections of capital investment characteristic of more privileged cities within the system. At the same time, during the early years of restructuring, Xalapa's economy was somewhat cushioned by a highly favorable international coffee market. Nevertheless, overall the impact of economic and state reform was to undermine the local economy and populace. Shrinking of the state apparatus meant that public sector employment, critical to the local labor market, declined, while fluctuating prices, high interest rates and government austerity measures to curb these all greatly affected the commercial and service sectors. With little capital to weather the storm, the small and medium size firms that employed much of the urban workforce were especially hard hit.

Xalapa's economy and labor market were further shaken by disruptions in its agrarian hinterland resulting from the national program of economic reform. The sudden opening of markets to foreign goods and capital left peasants vulnerable to foreign competition. Only large landowners integrated into the agro-industrial sector were able to compete, leading in turn to increasing polarization within the countryside. The precipitous privatization and dismantling of two key parastatal institutions in the region led to increasing vertical integration and the consolidation of agro-industrial intermediation and control (Arias and Nuñez 1992). Then, in 1989, the international price of coffee plummeted 50 per cent. Together these changes severely disrupted peasant communities, leading to the expulsion of an ever greater percentage of their inhabitants (Hoffman, Portilla and Almeida 1994). The level of disruption was so pronounced that by 1990 and for the first time in its history, the population of Xalapa's hinterland experienced not only a relative decline, but an absolute decline as well (Rodríguez 1996).

Xalapa was the recipient of many of the rural refugees of economic reform. Between 1980 and 1995, its population increased from 205,000 to 336,000, 50 per cent of which was due to migration (Ayuntamiento de Xalapa 1995). A 1994 study by Angélica Simon (1994) of the recent migrant population indicates that the majority came precisely from rural communities most disrupted by market forces. Ironically, as the international coffee market went from boom to bust, Xalapa was no longer able to absorb the increasing number of migrants into the urban labor force.

The conjuncture of economic reform and fluctuating coffee prices led to profound changes in this labor force. Rodríguez (1996) argues that there were two significant developments. First was the feminization of labor as increasing numbers of women began to work in an effort to offset falling household incomes; second was an increasing informalization of the economy indicated by a doubling of the number of self-employed. Despite the coffee boom that continued through most of the 1980s, the proportion of people unable to find full time employment increased from 32 per cent to 41 per cent between 1980 and 1990 (INEGI 1981, 1991).

Mexico's financial crash of December 1994 transformed Xalapa's economic stagnation into a full-blown crisis. The local Chamber of Commerce calculated that in 1995, 20 per cent of local businesses went bankrupt and were forced to shut down, while another 30 per cent laid off some of their employees. In the previous decade, the city's middle class had been able to maintain a degree of job stability despite contracting public sector jobs (Rodríguez 1996); but by 1995, the rate of unemployment among white collar professionals had risen to 11 per cent.[1] With a rapid loss of purchasing power and an uncertain economic future, middle-class families increasingly decided to forego the use of domestic services. This, in turn, left women who depended on domestic work with a greatly reduced work week or without a job at all.

However, the sector of the local economy most affected was the construction industry, as public investment in infrastructure was drastically reduced and private housing construction came to a near standstill. Unable to compete with larger national contractors for the few projects available, local businesses went under and employment collapsed. Within the formal sector of the construction industry alone,[2] between January 1994 and August 1996, 25 per cent of permanent workers and 57 per cent of temporary workers lost their job. Added to that was an even larger pool of workers in the informal sector of the construction industry not included in the statistics. When one considers that 10 per cent of Xalapa's working population was employed in construction at the time, the full magnitude of the problem becomes quite evident.

The impact of these economic changes on people's social conditions was dramatic as the problem of employment was compounded by the precipitous decline in real wages. By 1995, the value of a minimum wage had declined to 29 per cent of its 1980 level.[3] The consequences of this decline were clearly reflected in increasing levels of overcrowding in existing housing, the mushrooming of slums on the city's periphery, and the rapidly declining health of the majority of the population. A 1995 health survey of children under five in several working class neighborhoods, conducted by the grassroots organization UCISV-Ver, with which I worked in Xalapa, found that 40 per cent of the children suffered from malnutrition and 20 per cent could be classified as suffering from conditions of extreme malnutrition.[4]

In conjunction with and as a complement of this survey, my study of UCISV-Ver provides some of the ethnographic details underlying these results. In the face of declining incomes, families had reduced the amount of food being purchased on any given day and often reduced the number of meals being served. In addition, they had reduced or eliminated certain items such as meat and other dairy products from their diet, becoming, as many stated, *vegetarians* or depending exclusively on beans and tortillas. As the crisis deepened, an increasing number of families were unable to purchase even these basic staples on a regular basis, as the cost of two kilograms of tortillas and one kilogram of beans was the equivalent of a daily minimum wage. This was especially the case at the end of each pay period as money ran out or when fluctuating daily incomes were insufficient. On such occasions, strategies for food provision broke down, and families would be forced to choose who would eat and who would go without. In some cases, families would send children off to relatives to be fed; in other cases this option was not available, either because relatives were not around or because they faced similar circumstances, preferring to keep what little they had within their own nuclear family or household. In fact several families noted with emotion how, in contrast to the past, family members had turned them away, indicating the limits of local networks of mutual support during an acute social and economic crisis.

Accumulation, Speculative Urban Growth and Deepening Segregation

The geographic restructuring of capital that came with economic reform accentuated the speculative expansion of Xalapa's built environment, increasing the social and spatial segregation within the city. While the rise in coffee prices had temporarily constrained this expansion in the latter part of the 1970s, in the 1980s it regained momentum. Between 1981 and 1987, Xalapa grew from 7.8 to 10.1 square miles and by 1990, only three years later, to 15 square miles (Rodríguez 1996). Real-estate magnates and large construction companies continued to profit from the formal land market, investing in a series of highly lucrative private projects which included exclusive residential developments and social clubs, high-rise, luxury office buildings and commercial centers. As in the past, the state added value to land through its own investments. Towards the east, where the undeveloped lands of elite families were located, the state invested in infrastructure and services and opened up extensive tracts for development with the construction of several new public buildings. In the downtown area, where the elite controlled many properties, the municipal government authorized permits for commercial development and invested in a multi-million peso downtown renovation project with federal funds.

In contrast to, and partly as a consequence of, the local oligarchy's sustained accumulation in land and construction was the growing misery of Xalapa's working population and the continued mushrooming of squalid slums. The decline in other sources of accumulation along with the pressures on urban land led to a dramatic increase in the level of speculation in both land and housing. By 1984, the cost of rent even in the city's tenements could run as high as a monthly minimum wage, fueling migration to the periphery. Rodríguez (1996) calculates that by 1990, 86,000 people had followed this path. Meanwhile, the state sought to incorporate irregular settlements into the formal land market to expand the local tax base of property holders. This was because Xalapa, like all municipalities in Mexico, is highly dependent on federal contributions to its municipal budget.[5]

Economic crises and the shrinking of the state sector that came with neoliberal economic reform greatly reduced the flow of federal money to the municipality; indeed, the percentage of the municipal budget that came from federal contributions declined from 78.2 per cent to 54 per cent between 1988 and 1996. This in turn added to the importance of locally generated income, of which property taxes were the most significant, accounting for approximately 50 per cent of locally generated funds.

In other words, regularization of Xalapa's irregular settlements and their incorporation into the city's tax base became critical. Rather than simply promising regularization, however, the state increasingly put pressure on impoverished urban homesteaders to regularize their lots themselves, refusing even to discuss the introduction of urban services until such regularization was under way. Interested in filling the public coffers, the state frequently placed the cost of regularization beyond people's ability to pay. This had the multiple effect of accentuating the rate of speculation in urban land and producing a growing number of people who defaulted on their regularization payments, while providing the state with a justification for denying the urban poor access to the basic services that they needed.

Social Polarization, State Reform and its Political Impact

The deteriorating living conditions of the majority of Xalapa's population following economic restructuring brought both the level of discontent in general and the housing problem in particular to an explosive level that quickly became politicized. Several grassroots community-based organizations emerged in the tenements and mushrooming slums independent of the governing party's structure of political control. The most significant of these organizations was the Union of Homesteaders, Tenants, and

Housing Seekers of Veracruz or UCISV-Ver. Founded in 1984 by a group of tenement dwellers demanding adequate shelter, the organization sought not only to resolve this need but also to create an alternative type of settlement and an oppositional political force. In the first two years of its existence, UCISV-Ver created six new settlements in Xalapa's periphery for 1500 families, based on the collective purchase and control over the land rather than vertically structured patronage relations. Within the context of economic reform and the precipitous deterioration in people's living conditions, the organization rapidly expanded its following into forty of Xalapa's existing working-class neighborhoods.

The subsequent deepening of the economic crisis led to other forms of protest as well. For example, the proliferation of street vendors produced conflicts with the established commercial sector, provoking the vendors to organize to defend their rights to public space. As banks sought to sustain their rate of profit, middle-class families saw their monthly mortgage payments increase nearly 400 per cent. With the banks' policies of raising interest rates and capitalizing interest, they found that despite years of payment their total debt was increasing, leaving them owing more than what their home or business was actually worth. Threatened with foreclosure, many joined a national organization, El Barzón, which defended people's rights against the banks. Local branches of national civic organizations such as Alianza Cívica and CESEM emerged as government watchdogs and to promote citizen rights.

Finally, and perhaps most importantly, opposition was also expressed in party politics. As elsewhere in Mexico, during the 1988 presidential elections, Xalapa saw a groundswell of support for the opposition candidate, Cuauhtemoc Cárdenas. Son of Mexico's most famous president, in 1987 Cárdenas broke ranks with the nation's hegemonic party, the P.R.I., over the neoliberal turn in economic policy and the lack of internal party democracy and decided to run for president on an independent ticket formed by a coalition of political forces. In the aftermath of the election, in Xalapa as elsewhere in the country, individual activists and representatives from labor and community organizations along with the traditional left-wing political parties worked together to build the new center-left Revolutionary Democratic Party (P.R.D.).

The state responded to the growing contradictions of Xalapa's urban expansion and to the growing opposition in the streets and at the polls with the disbursement of funds on the one hand, and increased government regulation and control on the other. Funds from the federal government's recently created anti-poverty program, PRONASOL, were politically distributed to regain legitimacy among key sectors of the population and to wrest support from opposition groups. While allegedly earmarked for low-income families, in fact much of the funding went to improve conditions in middle class neighborhoods. As elsewhere in Mexico, funding was allocated primarily to organizations affiliated with the P.R.I.

The government's traditional practice of patronage politics had its effect. By the mid 1990s, Xalapa's upsurge in organized protest and oppositional coalition building had effectively been contained. However, the decline in the level of protest was not due simply to government tactics. Two additional causes are important to note. First, many of the city's activists became increasingly involved in party politics at the expense of grassroots organizing. Second the devastating impact of economic restructuring greatly curtailed people's ability to participate in collective action. With the dramatic decline in real wages, working-class families were forced to dedicate an increasing amount of time simply to make ends meet, thus leaving less time available for political participation. This was especially the case for women who formed the backbone of the city's community-based organizations. In addition, many people lacked the extra money necessary to travel to meetings in other neighborhoods. When it was a choice between purchasing a kilogram of tortillas and paying the roundtrip bus fare, the former usually took priority.

The introduction of a process of urban planning was also important in the state's response to the city's economic and political crises. In the past, the state had regulated land usage through its control over zoning, building permits, regularization of land tenure and its extensive yet selective investments in infrastructure and services. However, beginning in the 1980s three new mechanisms became especially significant: the creation of urban development plans, the enactment of legislation to regulate the expansion of the irregular land market and the creation of a land reserve for the city. Central to all three was the state's control over land. As the physical foundation for all other activities, it constituted the key element for regulating urban development. Rather than serving as instruments of long-term planning, however, these three mechanisms have functioned primarily to control the city's chaotic expansion and its political fallout while protecting the interests of the real-estate elite.

The importance of planning to urban policy was not simply an outgrowth of internal contradictions accentuated and produced by the process of economic reform. Rather it was also a product of World Bank mandates that have sought to enhance capital investment in cities. These mandates have emphasized the need to go beyond government investment in housing and infrastructure, focusing more on the urban economy and productivity overall; here urban planning and management are seen to play a strategic role (Casa y Ciudad 1994, World Bank 1991). At the same time, however, the neo-liberal program of economic reform, which emphasizes privatization and export-led production, not only renders urban development vulnerable to international market forces; it also greatly curtails the possibility *to plan*. A telling example is the creation of Xalapa's land reserve, to which I now turn.

Xalapa's Land Reserve

The creation of Xalapa's land reserve, as elsewhere in Mexico, formed part of the federal government's effort to support the geographic redistribution of economic activities to medium-sized cities and the consequent need to control the form of urban expansion. Part of the World Bank's urban policy for developing countries, the program required that national governments acquire extensive tracts of land to regulate the direction of urban growth. The stated purpose of the reserves was to provide access to land at a reasonable cost for low-income families, thereby functioning as an alternative land market to the unplanned, illegal one that had led to the chaotic, speculative expansion onto agrarian lands. Most important, the land reserve program shifted control over urban expansion from the agrarian authorities responsible for regularizing the illegal occupation of peasant lands to urban policy managers.

The need for a land reserve in Xalapa was already contemplated in the city's first municipal plan, published in 1982. It was not, however, until 1989 that a reserve was actually constituted. In the interim, two developments had emerged that gave added impetus to its creation. First, the onset of economic reform greatly accelerated the rate of speculative land development in both the formal and informal land markets such that by 1988, the government was forced to revise its plan to incorporate the city's immensely expanded spatial configuration. Given the economic and environmental cost of the existing rate of expansion, of particular concern was the political feasibility of using land already within the city's limits as part of the reserve. To do so would be to increase the level of population density primarily in the areas of illegal growth. Second, increased speculation had also accentuated conflicts over land. According to government declarations at the time, by 1989 there were over 8,000 families affiliated with nineteen grassroots organizations demanding access to a piece of land (Pacheco 1988). Many of these organizations formed part of the government's patronage structure. However, the independent opposition groups that had been growing in strength throughout the 1980s had begun to take a more militant stance, pressing for their demands through continuous mobilizations in the streets while at the same time implementing a strategy of large-scale land occupations within the city.

The most successful of these occupations took place in March of 1988 in the Colonia Revolución, a regularized settlement located in the northwestern part of the city. Within the settlement, the government itself had calculated that there were about 2,500 empty lots that qualified for repossession for low-income families. To pressure the government to take action on repossessing the land, the UCISV-Ver staged a massive land recuperation effort. On the eve of a campaign visit to Xalapa by the governing party's presidential candidate, one thousand people occupied empty lots in the Colonia Revolución. The UCISV-Ver's initial success led other existing urban organizations (both independent and affiliated with the governing party) to take over additional empty lots, and a year long process of negotiation ensued. Only two months after the occupation, the government publicly declared the need to create a land reserve to resolve the growing housing crisis.

The significance of this growing level of conflict was also reflected in discussions by the government commission responsible for planning the reserve. In the minutes from the commission's 27 March 1989 meeting, for example, it is explicitly noted that,

> The Coordinator of the Urban Development Commission, upon taking the floor, states that the most conflictive area in the state [of Veracruz] is Xalapa, [and] that organized and coordinated action amongst the various state, municipal and federal agencies is absolutely necessary to ensure that this situation does not grow.

One of the "organized and coordinated actions" agreed upon at the meeting was the decision not to provide any services or infrastructure in the existing irregular settlements. This decision in fact represented at least in part a response to the independent organizations' critique of the proposed reserve. The UCISV-Ver, for example, while not against the creation of a land reserve *per se*, took a strong position against the coercive nature of the state's control over land use. They argued that, rather than opening up new areas for development, the government should give priority to extending services to the existing irregular settlements where 50 per cent of the city's population already lived.

Creation of the reserve, however, was not simply a response to grassroots pressure. Also at stake were the interests of Xalapa's urban *latifundista* families who sought to protect their investments. Of particular concern to them was the location of the reserve and how it might affect their holdings. In the original planning, the government identified two areas in the eastern zone as potential sites. The first alternative was toward the northeast where basic urban infrastructure already existed, thus reducing the cost of urbanization for the reserve. The area's soils and topography, moreover, made it the most appropriate for urban development and the least destructive to the environment. The affected land was dedicated primarily to sugar production on small holdings. The area, however, had some drawbacks. At the time, sugar producers still benefited from a guaranteed price in the national market and thus were reticent to sell. Moreover, unlike many other peasants in the region, those occupying this land had a long history of active struggle for their rights. Even more important, the lands in question were adjacent to, and could affect, the holdings of Xalapa's principal real estate magnate, the Fernández family, along with those of two lesser urban *latifundistas*.

The second site, located towards the southeast, was an area primarily dedicated to coffee production. While lacking much of the necessary infrastructure, it did have several unpaved roads constructed to get cash crops to market that could serve as a basis for urbanization. In addition, there were already plans for major public works in the area such as a water treatment center and a new water pipeline that would benefit development. Finally several low-income settlements already existed so that creation of a reserve for low- and medium-income housing would simply consolidate existing patterns of urban growth.

The major problem with this second option was that the vast majority of the targeted land was private property, 70 per cent of it belonging to the city's major latifundistas including the Fernández. Almost all of this land had been purchased between 1975 and 1981 when international coffee prices had skyrocketed, encouraging investment in production. Indeed, to protect the elite's coffee investments, during the mid-1980s the government had designated the area a *productive, ecological reserve*. Thus coffee production served the dual function of maintaining an extensive protected area while providing income to the agro-industrial elite whose interests lay in both agrarian and urban land.

Given the physical and social characteristics of the two areas, the first alternative to the northeast had been chosen when planning for the reserve began, a choice that in fact followed the original plans for urban growth as set out in 1982. However, only a few months before the reserve was actually created in 1989, the site was suddenly switched to the second option to the southeast. According to the government's 1993 *ex-post facto* development plan, the reason for the change "lay fundamentally in the availability for acquisition and incorporation of the area with respect to the other options, motivating a shift in proposals from the one set out in the 1988 program" (Secretaría de Desarrollo Urbano 1993). According to one of the officials most directly involved in the process, the determining factor was the landowners' eagerness to sell.

The question, of course, is why the urban latifundistas who owned the land had a change of heart. Simply put, in the interim the international price of coffee had plummeted 50 per cent and with it the value of their coffee investments. Through the expropriation and indemnification of their land by the state, these latifundista families were able to recuperate their investment in its money form. In fact, they obtained highly advantageous terms of indemnification: 50 per cent upon signing the settlement agreement and the remaining 50 per cent within a month, while at the same time maintaining usufruct rights up until the land was put to use. Whether they actually made a profit on the transaction, however, or simply made good on losses is not altogether clear.

In the end, not all the land owned by the latifundista families was expropriated. Indeed, the Fernández family used its power to ensure that its holdings remained intact, while two more of Xalapa's most prominent real-estate magnates retained part of their land. They did so, however, not to maintain the land's agrarian use, but rather to obtain windfall profits derived from the land's potential urban rent. As the urban infrastructure necessary for the reserve would pass through their holdings, their value for future development increased immensely. To make up for this area lost to the reserve, the state expropriated adjacent peasant holdings.[6] Whereas the real-estate magnates recovered their capital, the peasants lost their means of livelihood; and while the real-estate magnates received immediate indemnification, the peasants had to prove their rights, waiting several months and even years for payment.

Conclusion

In this essay I have tried to show how Mexico's general program of economic and state reform has wounded Xalapa: its economy, its population and the built environment. As elsewhere in Mexico, the city's wounds have been dramatic and all-encompassing. Restructuring has greatly disrupted the regional economy and pauperized the vast majority of Xalapa's population, while at the same time accelerating an ongoing process of elite-propelled real-estate speculation. Much of what is described here is not unique to Xalapa; most if not all of Mexico's medium-sized cities, along with the country's major metropolitan areas, have been similarly affected by the geographic restructuring of capital that has accentuated uneven development regionally.

At the same time, the nature of Xalapa's integration into the international commodity markets has influenced the specific way that global economic processes have unfolded at the local level and the specific form of the city's wounds. While the booms and busts of Mexico's financial markets have greatly affected the city, as elsewhere in the country, equally important has been Xalapa's dependence on international commodity markets. To be specific, the cycles of the international coffee market have not directly coincided with Mexico's program of economic reform and financial crises, at times cushioning and at other times accentuating their impact. Similarly, the local configuration of political and class forces, itself a product of Xalapa's historical development, has influenced the nature of conflict within the city, affecting the way in which international and national policy dictates have been implemented. With little to no industry to speak of and with real estate the dominant form of accumulation, the principal manifestation of class conflict in Xalapa has been around issues of access to land and housing. The city's oligarchic families, whose interests lie in both coffee production and urban real estate, have played a determinant role in the nature, timing and location of the city's land markets, including those for housing the impoverished population. Within the context of economic reform, the state has sought to revitalize Xalapa's urban structure as set out by World Bank urban policy. It has done so, however, while attempting to control the political fallout of restructuring and at the same time leveraging the investments of the city's hegemonic group.

The creation of Xalapa's land reserve clearly illustrates the impact of the overall constellation of class forces and interests in urban planning. Mexico's land-reserve program has been framed by World Bank policy. However, the nature of the reserve's creation in Xalapa was determined by the complex interaction of local class and international, capitalist, market forces. On the one hand, increasing pressure from below in the form of collective political action forced the state to act upon the city's increasing housing crisis. Equally, and even more important, were the interests of Xalapa's urban *latifundista* elite. In the actual creation of the reserve they actively sought to impose their will as they had always done in the past. However, they did so not only as they exercised their power locally, but also as they were subjected to the imperatives of wider economic forces.

Notes

1. Secretaría del Trabajo y Previsión Social. Veracruz: Capacitación y Trabajo. *Boletín Informativeo del Servicio Estatal de Empleo*. Julio-Septiembre de 1995.
2. The analysis is based on statistical information provided by the Federal Social Security Office. By law in Mexico, all companies with six or more employees are required to register their employees with the social security system, which primarily provides health benefits to members. The Social Security database automatically records all new members and discharges on a monthly basis. Information is classified by geographic zones and type of occupation and it probably represents one of the most objective sources regarding employment trends.
3. According to the 1990 census, 62 per cent of the population earned less than two times the minimum wage, which in real terms represented only about 50 per cent of what they earned a decade before; and by 1995 it was worth even less. According to Boltvinik (1995), for a family of five to live above the poverty level in 1995, it would require 6.7 times the minimum wage. Considering that the average number of workers per household was 1.6, less than two minimum wages each, in 1995, these households could not even cover half of their basic needs, placing them in conditions of extreme poverty.
4. The survey was based on internationally accepted criteria of the relation between height and weight to age.
5. In Mexico, the federal government collects all income and sales taxes, subsequently redistributing a small percentage to state and local governments.
6. I note in passing that this probably was no accident as this land in fact had been the only land expropriated from the Fernández family during the period of agrarian reform.

References

Alonso, J. (ed.) (1980), *Lucha urbana y acumulación de capital*, Mexico: Ediciones de la Casa Chata.

Amezcua Cardiel, H. (1990), *Veracruz: sociedad, economía, política y cultura*, Mexico: Universidad Nacional Autónoma de México.

Arias Lovillo, R. and Nuñez Madrazo, C. (eds) (1992), *Veracruz: la difícil transición a la modernidad*, Jalapa, Veracruz: Centro de Estudios Agrarios, A.C.

Ayuntamiento de Xalapa (1995), *Plan municipal de desarrollo 1995–1997*, Versión Abreviada. Xalapa: H. Ayuntamiento de Xalapa.

Casa y Ciudad (1994), *¿...Y quién hace la ciudad?* Mexico: Casa y Ciudad, A.C.

Castells, M. (1977), *The Urban Question*, Cambridge MA: The Massachusetts Institute of Technology Press.

CENVI (1991), *Plan parcial de mejoramiento urbano de las colonias populares de la periferia de Xalapa*, Mexico: CENVI, A.C.

Duhau, E. (1990), "Planeación institucionalizada y modernización económica", *Ciudades* (3)9: 9–14.

Esteve Díaz, H. (ed.) (1992), *Los movimientos sociales urbanos*, Mexico: Instituto de Proposiciones Estratégicas, A.C.

González Casanova, P. and Jorge Cadena Roa (1988), *Primer informe sobre la democracia: México 1988*, Mexico: Centro de Investigaciones Interdisciplinarias en Humanidades, UNAM.

Hoffman, O., Portilla Viveros, B., and Almeida Monterde, E. (1994), "Urbanizarse o migrar: ¿Cuáles opciones frente a la crisis? El devenir de las comunidades cafetaleras en el centro de Veracruz, Mexico", *Revista de Historia*, 30: 166–185.

Instituto Nacional de Estadística, Geografía e Informática (1981), *X Censo general de población y vivienda*, Mexico: Instituto Nacional de Estadística, Geografía e Informática.

—— (1989), *Resultados oportunos del estado de Veracruz, censos económicos*, Mexico: Instituto Nacional de Estadística, Geografía e Informática.

—— (1991), *XI Censo general de población y vivienda*, Mexico: Instituto Nacional de Estadística, Geografía e Informática.

Gobierno del Estado de Veracruz-Llave (1988), *Programa de ordenamiento de la zona conurbada Xalapa-Banderilla. H. Ayuntamiento de Xalapa 1985–1988*, Xalapa: Gobierno del Estado de Veracruz-Llave.

León Fuentes, N. (1983), *Conformación de un capital en torno a la cafeticultura en la región de Xalapa-Coatepec 1890–1940*. Thesis for Maestra en Historia degree. Universidad Veracruzana.

—— (1987), "Los antagonismos empresariales de Xalapa en el siglo XIX", *Anuario del Centro de Investigaciones Históricas*, 9: 79–97.

López Decuir, V. and Borja Castañeda, E. (1990), El proceso histórico de desarrollo capitalista en la región de Coatepec. Cuadernos del IIESES No. 13:1-56. Xalapa, Veracruz: Instituto de Investigaciones y Estudios Superiores Económicos y Sociales de la Universidad Veracruzana.

Martínez Rodríguez, R. (1989), Análisis de la encuesta de empleo e ingresos en Xalapa. Cuadernos del IIESES No. 29. Xalapa, Ver: Instituto de Investigaciones y Estudios Superiores Económicos y Sociales de la Universdiad Veracruzana.

Navarro, B. and Moctezuma, P. (1989), *La urbanización popular en la ciudad de México*, Mexico: Instituto de Investigaciones Económicas, U.N.A.M./Editorial Nuestro Tiempo.

Pacheco García, V. (1988), "Crean el programa de reserva territorial en el estado", *Diario de Xalapa*, 23 December: pp. 1 and 6.

Rodríguez, G. and Bozzano, J. (1985), Mi colonia, mi ciudad. Manuscript.

Rodríguez Herrero, H. (1996), Movilidad social y espacio urbano en dos ciudades del Golfo de México. Tesis de Doctorado en Ciencias Sociales. Centro de Investigaciones y Estudios Superiores en Antropología Social-Universidad de Guadalajara.

Secretaría de Desarrollo Urbano/Gobierno del Estado de Veracruz-Llave (1993), Programa de ordenamiento urbano de zona Conurbada Xalapa-Banderilla-Coatepec-Emiliano Zapata-San Andrés Tlalnelhuayocan. H. Ayuntamientos de Banderilla-Coatepec-Emiliano Zapata-San Andrés Tlalnelhuayocan-Xalapa.

Simón, A. (1994), Persistencia y cambio cultural en un contexto urbano: Xalapa. Thesis for Licenciado en Sociología degree. Facultad de Sociología de la Universidad.

Ward, P. (1986), *Welfare Politics in Mexico; Papering over the Cracks*, London: Allen & Unwin.

World Bank (1991), *Urban Policy and Economic Development. An Agenda for the 1990s*. A World Bank Policy Paper. Washington DC: World Bank.

–5–

Rethinking Infrastructure: Siberian Cities and the Great Freeze of January 2001

Caroline Humphrey

During the winter of 2000–1 a series of "accidents" at thermo-electric power stations revealed the precariousness of life in Siberian cities. As infrastructural systems cut out and broke down, desperate measures had to be taken, thus exposing to the population the social conditions of existence of technologies they had taken for granted. This essay reveals the fundamental role of infrastructure in the character of urban life. It shows how cities may be wounded from their very depths and how people respond as citizens—within familiar urban landscapes suddenly turned unfamiliar and scary. At the same time, the essay suggests that the politics of infrastructure reveal a dimension in which "the city" is not in fact a bounded and integrated entity (see introduction). For a given urban infrastructure is often dependent on external and distant resources and decisions. Finally, the chapter addresses the "taken-for-granted" character of infrastructure, and the way this has been embedded in mid-twentieth-century ideologies of state provision that are now destabilized and (in their strong form) virtually defunct.

In Russian, as in English, *infrastruktura* can be seen as the basic equipment, facilities and services necessary for the functioning of a community and also as the Marxist category of the foundational structure of a social formation. The relation between the two is metonymic, in that the word *infrastruktura* in the former sense imaginatively evokes the latter.

I suggest that because the Marxist idea was deeply inculcated in the thinking of people brought up in Russia, the realization that the urban infrastructure is literally cracking and eroding under the ground one walks on has had a particularly devastating effect. More is at stake, it seems, than just the unreliability of essential services. For one thing, technologies are revealed to imply a relation between time and risk. But more than this, people are now talking about social upheaval and "moral loss." I argue that an important factor lying behind such statements is the perception that politics is now "interfering" in the functioning of the infrastructure, thus overturning the accustomed understanding of how society works. The city now appears as something like a community, unified by common dependence on its infrastructure. Yet suddenly it has been revealed that its very foundations may not be foundational at all, but rather appear as terrifying threats, and as malign instruments in the hands of unreliable particular interests.

The Infrastructure

The simple variant of the Marxist concept of the infrastructure is that it constitutes the economic basis for the reproduction of the social formation. Politics, religion and culture are superstructural elements that rise above the foundational base of the infrastructure and are ultimately determined by its character. As we know, Marx himself and subsequent neo-Marxist theorists revised and latterly greatly elaborated this idea (Althusser 1976), and indeed anthropology in the 1970s turned it inside out and on its head (Terray 1969, Godelier 1978, Bloch, 1975). But the simple variant is the idea all Soviet citizens grew up with. No alternative theoretical perspective on the infrastructure has been produced in post-Soviet times, at least none that has spread to the mass of the people.

But there is something a little unexpected in the way the Marxist ideas came over to Soviet subjects, for example schoolchildren. The fundamental idea was that material life determines consciousness (*byt'ye opredelyaet soznanie*). *Byt'ye* was the entire material structure of society, including productive forces, production organization, and of course the physical and technical infrastructure, while everything that pertained to the life of the mind was the superstructure (*nadstroika*). People educated in the Soviet system have told me, however, that their lessons focused almost entirely on *production* and *class relations*, while infrastructure was hardly mentioned. It was depicted as a mere support for production (factories, industrial complexes, and so forth). Never was it mentioned that infrastructure might be constructed to benefit the everyday life of *people*. The ruling idea was that production must be increased and modernized, and the industrial city would be the site of the transformation of consciousness. Production as the vanguard would be followed by infrastructure (as the boss is trailed by his well-muscled but largely ignored side-kicks, as one might imagine it) and sooner or later fully developed socialism would follow.

Physical and technical infrastructure had been more ideologically prominent in the first years of Soviet rule. Lenin said, "The Soviet State is Soviet power plus the electrification of the whole country." I mention this because Russians have pointed out to me that ordinary people were taught to identify both infrastructure in general and its individual elements with the Soviet state, as if they had not existed before the Revolution. For example, country people were encouraged "naively" to call electric light bulbs "Illych lamps"—Illych being the patronymic of Lenin and Lenin being the personification of the state.

Following the production obsession, the Soviet Union did indeed make massive investments in physical infrastructure. Even the most distant settlements of Russia were supplied with water, electricity, gas, central heating and transport far more thoroughly and extensively than in comparable rural and underdeveloped countries.[1] These extraordinary Soviet achievements, however, could only have been attained through the distorted and unacknowledged manipulation of the "productive forces" (the mass use of convicts, forced labor drafts, and prisoners of war, as well as orchestrated allocations of "free" labor). The built result was remarkable, indeed in some ways bizarre and ultimately irrational. The absolute assumption that the infrastructure, however expensive, would be provided by the state allowed the construction of whole cities in barely habitable places, such as in the extreme north of Siberia. In other words, just as in the taught ideology, in actuality physical infrastructure was *taken for granted.*

Specifically germane to this chapter is the fact that even in "ordinary" cities the infrastructure was subordinated to production whims, and hence extraordinarily geographically extenuated. This affected the whole character of the given city. What happened was that a Ministry in Moscow would decide to site a factory somewhere suitably close to a natural resource. Even the presence of a population was not absolutely necessary for such a decision, as labor could be drafted in. In most cases, industry was established near a city, so as to make use of certain services already present, such as a railway line. The Ministry would then recruit labor, and build apartment blocks, schools, and shops, etc, and would simultaneously negotiate with the state authorities for infrastructural utilities to be extended to the new site. Often these "work settlements" would be several miles from the city center. Eventually networks of cables, central heating pipes, bus services, and so forth, would wind their way to each settlement. Zhimbiev, in his interesting book on the Siberian city of Ulan-Ude (2001), has called this kind of town a "departmental city", referring to the priority of departmental central Ministries over town planning. Even the latter often took little account of local conditions; (the general plans [*genplan*] of Siberian cities were worked out in Moscow or Leningrad). These plans were frequently over-ridden by the whims of powerful Ministries. Thus the unfortunate city authorities (the soviets) were left to juggle with mismatches in provision by two different kinds of centralized juggernaut. Sometimes, as we shall see, the general plan had priority, and infrastructure was provided in advance, way out in the country, for an industrial development that never took place.

To summarize so far: I have argued that there was a significant relation between the infrastructure as ideologically formulated in the Soviet Union and its actual manifestation as material construction. In both cases, it was regarded as so basic as to be treated as a matter of course, and it trailed behind the more exciting and competitive "vanguard" of production. The result was that Siberian cities were developed as though the infrastructure had no cost. In fact, of course, this very attitude meant that services turned out to be gigantically expensive and difficult to maintain. And this is where the paradox of the relation between the two senses of "infrastructure" lies. For although in practice provision of material infrastructure was often almost an afterthought, ideologically it remained a crucial "determining" (*opredelyayushchii*) factor. It was not only identified with the Soviet state, which provided it and owned it, but its modernity was also regarded as indexical to, and determinant of, the level of the development of society, and hence of the consciousness of the people in that society. In brief, a lot was at stake with the infrastructure so conceived. Now let us see what happens when its tendency to breakdown is revealed. In the following section I consider the case of the East-Siberian city of Ulan-Ude, capital of the Buryat republic, where the main thermo-electric plant exploded during the coldest part of the winter of 2001.

The City of Ulan-Ude

The city, with a population of 369,700,[2] has two thermo-electric stations, called TETs-1 and TETs-2.[3] These stations make both electricity and hot water for central heating but their main function is heating. Built in the 1960s from central government funds, TETs-1 is located near the center of the city in the Railway District and is the main provider.[4] TETs-1 provides heating to government buildings, institutions, shops and apartment blocks in the central area, but not to the districts of wooden housing, which are heated by log stoves, nor to the more distant industrial settlements. The latter, such as Aviazavod (aircraft manufacture township), have their own boilers, still supplied on a ministerial basis, and these provide only central heating but no electricity.

TETs-2 was built at the end of the 1990s, again with money from Moscow. It was set 13 km out of town at a place now called Energetik. It was planned long ago, in the 1980s, when the authorities thought they would develop industry in that area. But this never happened, and now TETs-2 is marooned in the countryside. It heats only a small surrounding area and therefore does not work at full strength. In effect, it is irrelevant to the heating of the city.

TETs-1's combined operation works as follows. It has several large boilers heated by coal, which comes from open-cast mining in a rural district some 100 km to the south. The boilers heat water to make steam, and this turns massive turbines, which make some electricity, about 5 per cent of the total used in the city. The great majority of the city's electricity comes from outside the Buryat Republic, from Irkutsk and Bratsk, while a smaller amount comes from the Gusinoozersk electricity station (GRES) located in the south of the Buryat Republic. The external suppliers charge Ulan-Ude residents double the price per kilowatt paid by their own local users. Meanwhile, the coal used to fire the TETs-1 boilers is of ever lower quality. Thus, although the Gusinoozerk GRES was built to use this local coal, it operates with constant breakdowns. Furthermore, one of the major mines has been closed down, and the other runs at a loss but is kept open for the sole reason that it supplies the city heating stations. Labor unrest at this mine constantly threatens the operation of the stations.

The steam from the TETs-1 turbines enters huge central heating pipes, most of which are laid underground. Reaching a group of buildings, the steam encounters a heat-exchange mechanism at very high pressure. Here it is turned into hot water, which is mixed with cool water to circulate through the heating system of the buildings at low pressure. Part of the hot water is not used in this local circulation and returns back to the station via a different set of pipes to supply the next shift. In theory this system should work all year round, delivering hot water for domestic use during the summer when central heating is not required. But in fact, the system needs regular and constant repair, and pipes have to be completely replaced after ten years of service. So for this reason, the entire system closes down seasonally for maintenance, and this means that the city does not have hot water during the summer. During the winter, the pipes often crack under the combination of high pressure steam and sharp frosts. The frozen ground makes underground repairs difficult and expensive.

It was an explosion in one of the TETs-1 boilers that caused the crisis in the winter of 2001. As the outside temperature dropped to an almost unprecedented –50 degrees, the boiler workers should have reduced the pressure. Instead, they allowed it to increase. When the boiler exploded, thousands of square meters of windows were blown out at the station, freezing air rushed in, and this threatened the rest of the boilers with similar explosions. In extreme danger, emergency workers used mountaineering techniques to scale the walls of the station, working through the night amid steam and ashes to cover the empty windows with heavy felt. High winds kept blowing the coverings away, and a cloud of dirty blackish steam rolled out of the station over the town. The temperature dropped quickly in people's houses. People telephoned in alarm to find out what was happening, and one women even said to the emergency team leader who was trying to explain the situation to her, "Well, yes, you are warming yourselves at the boilers over there, but we are freezing in our flat!" Apparently the emergency workers laughed when they heard this. When many hours later they finally fixed the coverings, soaked to the skin, shivering, and covered in soot, the city authorities sent a representative to shake each of them by the hand. He said, as reported in the local paper, "Thank you, lads. You saved the city" (Borkhodoeva 2001: 13).

This kind of near-catastrophe, as well as complete shutdowns, occurred in central heating plants all over Siberia during the winter of 2001 (Gentleman 2001). The electricity systems were equally vulnerable, as extreme cold causes the wires to snap. The two technologies are linked, for many cities have combined stations, as in Ulan-Ude, and even if this is not the case, when the central heating is lowered people turn on all their electric heaters and this overloads the electrical system causing a blow-out. The supply of water can also be affected, as several cities use electric pumps to circulate water. In other words, there are places that experienced the simultaneous shut-off of all three major supplies, water, electricity and heating, and this in temperatures that reached as low as –60 degrees in some areas. Major cities mostly only suffered for a few days, but even in such a short time deaths and amputations of frost-bitten limbs occurred (Savchenkova 2001). Some small towns and rural settlements were completely cut off, without heat or electricity right through the winter since October 2000 (Gentleman 2001).

Living with the Crisis

I would now like to describe residents' reactions to the crisis in Ulan-Ude, as seen through the eyes of one Buryat woman. She said:

The cold came from Krasnoyarsk—we saw on T.V. that it was coming, there were 1-2 weeks to prepare. They should have given instructions. We were frightened—what will happen to us?

In Krasnoyarsk we saw houses totally covered in ice, all the walls and windows. Even the inner walls were frozen up. It will be terrible here, we thought. Our house is recently built, so we thought we would suffer from the low building standards these days. We were also convinced there would be an epidemic of flu. The central heating was on minimum in Krasnoyarsk, and we heard how the people put on all their electric heating, and then whole districts went dark as the electricity cut out. They started to light with candles and kerosine lamps, and heat with *burzhuiki* [portable stoves].[5] Our relatives rushed over and said, "Buy *burzhuiki*! The cold will be coming to us soon!" We were all scared. We wondered: should we buy a *burzhuika* or a Western heater of the latest model? We couldn't think what to do! We didn't know which one would work best in our conditions. So we did nothing. We just knew something terrible was coming our way. We thought we would have to hang the walls of the flat with wool blankets. In fact, we didn't have to do that. We were thinking in a Buryat way, about how they used to hang felt blankets inside the yurt in winter.

The city authorities did nothing, even though the people were in a panic. The cold soon came, the boilers were old, they couldn't take it. I heard the explosion at 7 in the morning, a huge noise and the house shook like in an earthquake. Was it military exercises? I looked out of the window and saw a huge thick cloud—it was steam. I live across the river, maybe about 2 km from the TETs.

The temperature fell in the house, from 20 degrees to about 8. Then the powers [*vlasti*] gave us to know on TV that we must not turn on our electric heaters. We put on all our clothes, huddled in the flat. We even wore felt boots [*valenki*] and fur boots [*unty*] in the house! Even hats!

The authorities said nothing about why it had happened, but rumours were flying round the town. At first people said it was a "*diversia*" and the Chechens had blown the station up. But soon I began to wonder: why do the Chechens need our city, why, when we are so far away from them? There's no logic to it. Then I thought it must be our own people, just carelessness,—or someone fell asleep at his post, drunk. That's what I thought. Then we found out that the TETs people simply had not followed the instructions—in deep cold you have to lower the temperature, but they put it up. My husband went over there and talked to the people. He has a way of getting them to converse. They finally admitted: "It was our negligence." But none of this was made public, and no-one was punished.

In public they didn't want to recognize their fault. The city officials said things like, "We had Caucasians come to visit us, the situation is being monitored," or, "a provocation is not excluded." Then there was silence. After a while people came to realise that all these stories about "diversions" could not be right.

Here we see how the crisis spread from city to city across Siberia with the wave of cold, and how fear *preceded* it, and was ignited and sustained by TV images. The narrative highlights the role of rumor and lays bare the deep uncertainty about the cause of the crisis. We see that the city authorities were looked to "to provide instructions", but their habit of secrecy and refusal to take responsibility only exacerbated the people's anxiety.

The Sense of Space in Siberian Cities

As soon as the explosion happened, money was sent in. All the windows in TETs-1 were replaced. The city and Buryat Republic budgets, both in debt, were supplemented by money from Moscow and other Siberian cities. Local firms also contributed. Suddenly everyone rushed to give, as the taken-for-granted infrastructure was brought to people's attention. But the intense cold continued.

Now, living through deep cold can bring many different urban systems to a standstill, but because of the extraordinarily spread-out nature of Siberian cities, they are particularly vulnerable. Trams and trolley-buses no longer run, buses become irregular, the new *marshrut* taxis refuse to take people to distant suburbs, the antifreeze runs out and the people with private cars have to use primus stoves to try to get them started. People stand waiting at bus stops, but soon give up the idea of going to work, as it is far too far to walk. Schools close down. In general, all this is born with equanimity, but even so people are forced to notice distances, the more so in the wake of the economic crisis with its price rises and shortages of gas. Before this crisis, residents were more likely to take the voids of Siberian cities for granted. I was told, for example, that Ulan-Ude is counted as a very compact city, because it requires only 40 minutes to drive from one side to the other in a car. Ulan-Ude is nothing compared to a city like Novosibirsk, people said. There, you have to drive for 45 km to get to the suburb of Akademgorodok, and that is not the edge of the city.

Reflecting on the winter crisis, one woman who grew up as a child in Irkutsk recalled being troubled by living in such a spread-out city. She remembered the expanses between built areas as mostly dark forested areas of *taiga*. Even if they had been cleared for future development, they were threatening from a human point of view. She said that her father worked in the academic suburb (Akademgorodok) attached to Irkutsk, which was 13 km distant from the nearest housing area. Everyone always went there by bus. But one day, she and her brothers and sisters had a row with the family in town. They had no money and decided to walk to their father. This was a terrifying experience. There were hardly any houses, and as soon as they emerged from the forest, they met encampments of "wild Gypsies", who tried to snatch the youngest brother. Then they came across a cleared wilderness where a settlement of rough workers had been placed. Now, she says, this whole road has been built up, so one could hardly recognize it any more. The terror of emptiness has gone, but the sense that the city's edges are peopled by settlements of unknown, threatening "others" has intensified. My respondent called these settlements *sloboda* (colony) and characterized their inhabitants as *lyumpen*, an insulting term she probably would not have used in Soviet times for the working-class. The post-Soviet city, which is also developing elite gated communities for the rich (Humphrey 2002: 175–201), is thus coming to be more like the Western city with its separated enclaves of class and ethnicity, such as the protected spaces of the suburbs and the zones of low-income housing for the poor described by David Harvey for Baltimore (2000: 133–56) or the "fortified enclaves" discussed by Caldeira for Sao Paulo (1999 : 83–107).

One has to imagine the situation in Russia without widespread car ownership. The message with regard to infrastructure is clear. Ordinary life for the vast majority of people in this kind of city, that is the life that keeps a city functioning and psychologically secure, and which provides pathways between one's accustomed sites of activity, is utterly dependent on there being an infrastructure of public transport, as well as other now threatened services such as street lighting and policing. Russians are accustomed to walking far greater distances than citizens in European or American towns, but even they give up at some point. Confined to their apartments they are vulnerable to cut-outs of heating, electricity and water. During the freeze, as one resident of Ulan-Ude said, our apartments became like "icy coffins" (Anosov 2001: 5). A crisis like the explosion at TETs-1 may briefly unite the citizens, but the slow and lingering collapse of infrastructure tends to isolate them.[6]

The Politics of Infrastructure

If the above picture has echoes in many other cities of the world, the politics of post-Soviet infrastructure is both analogous to and starkly different from situations elsewhere. Perhaps in most places, including the U.S., infrastructure is backgrounded and thus separated in public discussion from social policy. Yet the political economy of infrastructure comprises a whole set of physical structures and social relations that are necessary for a city to function. It is surely not only in Russia that this is a pawn in political games.

The TETs-1 thermo-power station belongs to Buryatenergo, which is part of the vast electricity monopoly RAO YES[7] run from Moscow by the well-known politician Anatoly Chubais. This is a state organization, not so far privatized. Liberal political advisors wanted to privatize RAO YES, along with the railways and Gasprom. But this has so far been blocked by the Communists and others in the Duma, who have always argued that basic services, like gas, electricity, and transport should remain in the hands of the state. As elsewhere in the world (London Transport is just one example), a crucial issue of the 1990s has been who should fund infrastructure like the Ulan-Ude TETs,—the Moscow center, the local municipal budget, or a combination of these with private capital?

This question is already a clue as to why state ownership does not preserve institutions from the vagaries of politics. But in Russia confrontations over policies pale before the clash of personalities over naked power. Everyone knows about the battle between President Vladimir Putin and Yevgeny Nazdratenko, the Mayor of Vladivostok, who was forced to resign earlier in 2001, ostensibly because of the crisis in his region, where hundreds of thousands of people were stranded without heating or electricity. In the end, not just Nazdratenko but swathes of his subordinates, as well as the Energy Minister in Moscow, resigned. I shall not dwell further on this history, which has been widely reported in the Western press, but I do wish to comment on how it was regarded locally in Siberia. I have been told by Buryats that the energy crisis in Vladivostok was not fundamentally caused by local negligence but orchestrated by Chubais, as part of his long-standing vendetta against Nazdratenko. People say it is naïve to imagine that such crises happen only because of small things like slip ups over coal supplies, the embezzling of heating oil funds, and so forth. Rather, great politicians are using the supply of current as personal weapons of war.

Much evidence is produced to support this view. In Vladivostok, it is said, Nazdratenko first stumbled onto the idea a couple of years ago, when he switched off the current in order to embarrass his rival for the mayorship, Chepekov. Now Chubais had not supported Nazdratenko for mayor, and the political battle between the two of them was continued when Chubais was later appointed to run the electricity monopoly. In this position he was able to discredit Nazdratenko by cutting off the supplies to Vladivostok that came from outside the mayor's fiefdom.

I was able to understand the logic of this only when more local Buryat examples were given to me. I was told by a middle-aged woman, a long-standing inhabitant of Ulan-Ude, that people in Buryatia are now saying, "We don't need election campaigns, they are too expensive. All they have to do is turn off and turn on the electricity." They were referring to the fact that the current is being used directly as a demonstration of political power.

How does this work? These days few citizens pay for electricity. So a whole district may be cut off on that pretext. Everyone understands that this is a matter of local politics. But still, how does the practice relate to how people vote? This was explained to me as follows. The candidate wanting electoral support will have made vague threats, not in newspapers, but through rumors. You might go out to put out the rubbish and you'd meet a neighbor and ask "Why don't we have light?" She'd reply, "Don't you know? X is loosing ground in the election campaign, he's had the current turned off" (she knows about the election campaign through newspapers publishing polls of voters' intentions). So these days, people say, there's no need to set up a "diversion" or reveal *kropromat* (compromising materials about rivals). All X has to do is get the heat/electricity/water turned off before the big freeze. The deputy then has his agitators on the doorsteps, or distributes leaflets, to let people know that he was responsible.

This works electorally because turning off the electricity is a demonstration of power (*sil*).[8] People understand that "This man can do everything," I was told. In more established democracies, the townspeople[9] would almost certainly not vote for the person who turned off the electricity; would consider him irresponsible, and at least a bad manager. In Buryatia, they vote *for him*, because they are afraid he'll do it again if they do not. People vote this way "on the level of instinct," said one woman academic in Ulan-Ude. Hardly anyone would vote against him for doing this. After all, such a person can also restore the current and keep it on. To manage such things the politician would have to be "strong, connected to Moscow."

Yet the townspeople are not resigned to such methods. The same woman academic said, "It is difficult for us also to understand. I have the feeling I am standing on my head when I come across these things."

"Moral Harm" and its Implications

Amid the revelations of sheer power, the infrastructure crisis also reveals a titanic battle of values. Essentially this relates to the question: how do people view services, as a right or a commodity? This is an important question throughout the world with the decline of the welfare state. Here I outline the Buryat situation.

The director of Buryatenergo, Lystsev, was interviewed by a newspaper and congratulated for reducing the debts of the company and bringing some order to its management (Anosov 2001). Lystsev replied that he had two main aims, and when we see what they are it is apparent that he is pursuing the idea of market value. The first is to reduce barter and payment in kind. In 1999, only 9 per cent of electricity payments in Buryatia were in money as opposed to goods of all kinds. Lystsev's second task is to get people to pay at all. As of early 2001, only about 40 per cent of electricity bills were paid. "Our goal," said Lystsev, "is to destroy the stereotype that 'Illych's Lamp' is some gift of God, like the sun, air or water. Electricity is a commodity, and it must be paid for." The correspondent asked how he would change people's attitudes. "By switching off the current," was the reply. "We'll work out technology so that it can be done by the individual apartment." But the fact is, it is still illegal to turn off the current to private citizens who do not pay their bills. In other words, the Russian state itself has not come to a definite decision as to whether electricity should be regarded as a commodity or not.

This can be seen from two recent court cases, in one of which a woman sued Buryatenergo for turning off her electricity because she had not paid her bills, while in another a women sued her local housing authority for not keeping her apartment warm. Both women sued for compensation for the "moral harm" (*moral'nyi vred*) they had experienced (Angotkin 2001). These were complex cases, in which the citizens were found to be at fault in various ways, so the sums they had spent on repairs, alternative sources of energy and so forth were not repaid. But the charges of "moral harm" were upheld. It is not quite clear what "moral harm" is as a legal category. But it was evidenced by things like being unable to take a shower for months because the flat was too cold, being unable to provide a cooked breakfast for one's son, and the pain of seeing an aged relative fall ill in barely heated rooms. Basically, we can conclude that "moral harm" implies the impossibility of leading a normal life, and the courts upheld the idea that the infrastructure authorities are responsible for providing this for all citizens, whether they pay their bills or not.

In this context, the citizens are seen as the receivers of morality, but not the providers of it. Paying bills is not regarded as "moral", only something you do if you absolutely have to. Thus Lystsev, the head of Buryatenergo, observed that he knows people *can* pay because his best-paying customers for electricity are pensioners, the poorest sector of the population. Other people have confirmed this picture. The pensioners pay because they are scared the bills will mount up and they will have nothing to fall back on if their current is switched off. But almost no other private person pays, even if they easily could. The explanation some people give is: we will not pay if others do not. But a considerable number continue to think that if electricity is not a gift from God, then it is at least given by the state. Why should we pay for it, they argue, if we work and the state does not pay us? One must remember here that wages to state employees are widely in arrears, paid in kind, or even not paid at all. In this reasoning value is still created by labor, and the state appears as the Great Employer, who is not keeping his side of the bargain.

So in fact, in a place like Ulan-Ude the infrastructure continues to exist more or less in the old Soviet framework whereby it was provided virtually free. But what is new is that its existence is seen as a right that *individuals* should fight for, as is suggested by the idea of suing for "moral harm". "Snow Man: you may become one if you don't know your rights," was the headline in a Buryat newspaper this winter.[10]

Furthermore, politicians seem now to be regarded as somehow separable from "the state". Instead of being faceless, invulnerable representatives, they are now seen as individuals, almost like malign children, who can in principle be battled against. So one sign of hope is that in some cities, people are getting together to form social organizations to become more informed about their rights, as well as to check the budgets of infrastructure companies, verify that repairs have been carried out, and so forth. Such citizens' groups are quite active in large cities like Moscow or Irkutsk.

But why is this *not* so in provincial towns like Ulan-Ude? In metropolitan cities with their varied and competing authorities, citizen activists can get access to certain sympathetic politicians, and they also find it easier to get funding for campaigns, usually from Western sources. But in a city like Ulan-Ude, this is not the case. The infrastructure authorities are linked with other political leaders in a small, tight-knit network. They resist the formation of citizens' groups. For example, the chief architect of Ulan-Ude, who is responsible for all official construction projects, told a colleague of mine, "We don't need those groups to check us. We have already appointed our own control organizations. These citizens' groups just raise scandals and disturb social opinion. They are full of all sorts of unreliable, weird people. No, we don't want them."

Conclusion

The advance of actual and ideological capitalism, squeezing out and discrediting state funded projects, has meant that city infrastructure has become a serious problem all over the world. Coinciding with the end of the Cold War, we can see parallel—though different—processes under way: in the U.S. the dismantling of the Great Society programs, in distant parts of Russia the withering of what had been total state responsibility for basic services. Each region is no longer as concerned as before with certain human investments and is constructing new categories of the expendable.

I have argued that this process has taken a peculiarly acute and disturbing form in Russia. On the one hand the economic crisis has combined with partial privatization in a disastrous mixture, such that expenditure on maintenance of infrastructure has "inevitably" been much reduced. This leaves the physical plant liable to collapse at any time. On the other hand, there is the psychological-ideological landscape, which has specific post-Soviet contours. Here, the infrastructure was regarded as socially foundational, that is, as constitutive of the level of civilization achieved by society. But now, from being a taken-for-granted support, it has become a source of anxiety and destabilization. Rather than being an index of modernity, it has become a sign of decay.

What this does is to reveal the relation between technology and its timespan, throwing accustomed understandings of social time reckoning into doubt. "What does it mean," writes one correspondent to a newspaper in Buryatia

> to say that a central heating pipe is 90% worn out? Either it will break tomorrow or it will last for another ten years. Or let's take the towns built for the workers on the B.A.M. railway. Economists told us they were built to last 5–7 years, but people are still living there 25 years later, contrary to all common sense. So we are living on tenterhooks, just waiting for the next breakdown. Half of Russia, including Buryatia, is supported on the basis of potential ruins. (Anosov 2001)

A related upheaval in the citizens' sense of space occurs when the "bus-journey of half an hour" one dozes through every day is suddenly revealed to consist of the 15 km of frozen pitted roadway one might have to walk to work. The city on its own is revealed as unable to cope with disasters, and this undermines the idea of it as a bounded spatial unit, let alone a safe place to live. Perhaps Soviet cities, particularly those most subject to the production decisions of central Ministries, were never felt to be such independent self-governed wholes as many old European towns. But even so—and even today—people feel a strong sense of belonging to their city and anxiously compare the cost of electricity, and so forth, in their town as opposed to others. Thus the recent conviction among the citizens that distant politicians might cut off one's essential services *at whim* is highly destabilizing to the understanding that "we are supported by 'our' resources."

Russia has not been isolated from the "time—space compression" of the modernist project, nor from some of its postmodern effects (Harvey 1990), and what I have described for Siberia could be seen perhaps as a distant consequence of globalization, if that elastic concept is to include the ending of Russia's global super-power status. One correlative of that was the inability of the Russian state fully to meet its national responsibilities with regard to basic services—that is, the particular configuration of rights and expectations of its citizens in the post-Soviet context. Ulan-Ude, seemingly, must be one of the less "global" towns on earth. Strangers are rare and notable people on its streets. It does not produce for international markets. But even so, we see here processes of de-industrialization, retraction of state support, and the growth of unstable micro-services and petty trade that are parallel to those happening elsewhere in the world. In this post-socialist context, the foundering of infrastructure has the opposite effect of "time-space compression." We see instead an unraveling and disintegration, and a lengthening of times and spaces. Immobility, dependency, and waiting—for the incalculable "accident"—starkly interpose themselves, cutting flows and disconnecting sites of sociality. People are ready psychologically to accept what the local newspapers shout. "Unless measures are taken in the immediate future to stabilize the situation, Russia will sink into pre-industrial darkness, lit by the flashes of the explosions of the last working factories," and even more starkly, "Technology has declared war on humanity" (Bagdaev and Anosov 2001).

The status of the infrastructure as a "determinant of consciousness" is, not surprisingly, up in the air. On the one hand, it now evident that the actual physical infrastructure must *itself* be controlled, looked after, maintained and invested in. Furthermore, how determining can it be if politicians can *play* with it? On the other hand, many people perhaps still really fear that the infrastructure *is* determinant, and that the harsh and volatile state of society—including the politicians' games—is a reflection of the perilous decay beneath the city.

Notes

1. China, for example, which experienced a much shorter period of ideologically driven communist development, has a less sound infrastructure in rural areas to this day.
2. Demograficheskaya (2000: 1). The data are for 1 Jan 2000.
3. TETs: Teplo-Elektro Tsentral
4. Before that, each multi-apartment block had its own boiler-house (*kotelnaya*), which was supplied through funding from the Ministries that ran the factory to which the given block was attached.
5. The *burzhuika* can be fuelled by coal or wood. It is put near a window, and a hole has to be made for the pipe to go out. Gas cylinder stoves are also available, but most people find them too expensive to run.
6. For a brilliant discussion of the social effects of household isolation in Armenia brought about by "cataclysmic paralysis of urban and industrial infrastructure" in the early 1990s, see Stephanie Platz (2000).
7. RAO YES: Rossisskoe aktsionernoe obshchestvo yedinaya enegticheskaya sistema Rossii
8. The technique is not, it seems, confined to internal Russian politics. Gazprom has been accused of trying to control much of Eastern Europe by threatening to cut off the gas supply (Boyes 2001).
9. This ploy is just as, if not more, common in rural townships and villages as in the city, I was told.
10. *Nomer Odin*, no. 17, January 2001.

References

Althusser, L. (1976), *Marxisme et Luttes des Classes*, Paris: Maspéro.

Angotkin, A. (2001), "Sud, svet i moral'nyi vred", ("The Court, Electricity and Moral Harm"), *Inform Polis*, 11 (114): 8.

Anosov, A. (2001), "Buryatiya igraet v russkuyu ruletku" ("Buryatia is Playing Russian Roulette"), *Nomer Odin*, 7, 15–21 February: 5.

Bagdaev, B. and Anosov, A. (2001), "Tekhnika ob'yavila voinu lyudyam", ("Technology has Declared War on People"), *Nomer Odin*, 3, 18–24 January: 6.

Bloch, M. (ed.) (1975), *Marxist Analyses and Social Anthropology* (ASA Monograph no. 2), London: Malaby.

Borkhodoeva, E. (2001), "Kak spasali TETs-1," ("How they Saved TETs-1"), *Inform Polis*, 7(437): 13.

Boyes, R. (2001), "Russia's New Power Game", *The Times 2*, 26 March: 2–3.

Caldeira, T. (1999), "Fortified Enclaves: the New Urban Segregation", in Low, S.M. (ed.), *Theorizing the City: The New Urban Anthropology Reader*, New Brunswick: Rutgers University Press, pp 83–107.

Demograficheskaya situatsiya v g. Ulan-Ude (2000), Ulan-Ude: Goskomstat Respubliki Buryatiya.

Gentleman, A. (2001), "It's minus 60, there's no heating and no electricity. Welcome to Vladivostok", *Guardian*, 16 February: 3.

Godelier, M. (1978), "Infrastructures, Societies and History", *Current Anthropology* 19(4): 763–71.

Harvey, D. (1990), *The Condition of Postmodernity,* London: Blackwell.

—— (2000), *Spaces of Hope*, Edinburgh: Edinburgh University Press.

Humphrey, C. (2002), *The Unmaking of Soviet Life: Everyday Economies After Socialism,* Ithaca and London: Cornell University Press.

Platz, S. (2000), "The Shape of National Time: Daily Life, History and Identity during Armenia's Transition to Independence, 1991–1994", in Berdahl, D., Bunzl, M. and Lampland, M. (eds), *Altering States: Ethnographies of Transition in Eastern Europe and the Former Soviet Union,* Ann Arbor: University of Michigan Press, pp. 114–38

Savchenkova, I. (2001), "Moroz rvet provoda", ("Frost Breaks the Wire"), *Nomer Odin*, 3, 18–24 January: 4.

Terray, E. (1969), *Le Marxisme Devant les Sociétés Primitives*, Paris: Maspéro.

Zhimbiev, B. (2001), *The Urbanisation of a Siberian City: Ulan-Ude*, Cambridge: White Horse Press.

Part II
Crises of Crime and Criminalization

–6–

How Kingston was Wounded[1]

Don Robotham

How was Kingston wounded and how can these wounds be healed? In this chapter I want to discuss some of the current social and cultural processes fracturing a Third World urban center and to examine some of the forces underlying these processes. How has it come about that this medium-sized Caribbean city has developed one of the highest homicide rates in the world? Between 1977 and 1996, the rate of crimes against property fell from 1,446 to 342 per 100,000. Over the same period, the rate of violent crime increased by 30 per cent, from 758 to 985 per 100,000 (Harriott 2000: 11). Kingston, to quote one researcher, became "the most murderous city in the Caribbean" with one of the highest murder rates in the world (Harriott 2000a).[2] At the same time, it became the source of one of the most globally influential and politically progressive expressions of popular culture emanating from the Third World (Stoltzoff 2000). I am particularly concerned with exploring the fracture Uptown/Downtown, which, along with others, I regard as one of the main sources of social and political division in Kingston and the wider Jamaica, typical of the Third World.

I identify five moments in this process of the wounding of Kingston: first, there was the flight from the countryside and the growth of the urban colonial ghettos from the 1880s onwards; second there was the residential exodus of the upper and especially the middle classes; third, there was the construction of the New Kingston business district; fourth there was the establishment of the so-called "garrison communities;" and presently, there is the phase of the rise of the black bourgeoisie. I shall briefly discuss each of these in turn.

Background: Uptown and Downtown

As has been pointed out elsewhere, the Caribbean represents an especially interesting case for attempting to unravel contemporary social, economic, political and cultural processes in the Third World (Robotham 1998). This is because the region is one of the original sites of globalization—small societies and cultures cobbled together on the basis of the most predatory of colonial economic interests and struggling in this inhospitable neo-liberal "now" to establish themselves as nation-states. With their traditional agricultural/mining and now tourism-based economies these Caribbean societies were prototypical export-led development models, centuries before export-led development became the mantra of neo-liberal development.

What is more, Caribbean societies with a long history of plantation slavery such as Jamaica have always had an oppressive economic, social, ethnic and political structure which, thankfully, makes impossible the construction of a romanticized pre-colonial imaginary. These societies, while subordinated as a whole to global capitalism, are sharply divided internally along class and ethnic lines, not just between, but, most importantly, within ethnic groups. Characteristic of the Caribbean and Latin America, the racial or ethnic system generally divides groups along a number of distinctions—white, brown, black, Indian, African and sometimes more—rather than simply white and black. Ethnic and racial groups are ranked socially but no ethnic group is socially homogeneous; each—especially brown, black and Indian—is riven with class distinctions.

In this paper I wish to consider the case of Kingston, the capital of Jamaica—a city whose very origins as a colonial entrepot and capital in the nineteenth century deeply inserts it within processes of globalization. Today, this city has a population of about 700,000 persons of a total island population of 2.6 million persons and in a country that was about 65 per cent urban in the year 2001. Although a process of secondary urbanization is proceeding in Jamaica, mainly in connection with the expansion of the tourist industry on the northern side of the island, Kingston is overwhelmingly the primate city, with about 80 per cent of the island's total urban population residing in this town and with about seven times the population of its nearest rival—the north coast resort town of Montego Bay (Gordon et al. 1997).

Kingston proper is a smaller area within the old municipal boundaries on the southern coastal end of the present city, itself on the south coast of Jamaica, 70 miles and more away from the tourist beaches and cruise ship ports on the north coast. Geographically and administratively as well as in everyday usage by Jamaicans, the name "Kingston" actually refers to a larger area that includes the parishes of Kingston and the adjacent northern parish of St. Andrew (the larger part of the population), which demographers sometimes designate with the initials KMR—the Kingston

Metropolitan Region. In this chapter, the name "Kingston" refers to this larger region (formally Kingston and St. Andrew) which includes the old city proper, the "New Kingston" business district, the inner city and its "outer city" suburbs where the middle and upper classes live.

More than any other site in the Caribbean, this city exhibits all the contradictions and divisions of Caribbean history before and after political independence from Britain in 1962. For example, a commonplace distinction used widely in everyday discourse and in academic analysis of life in Kingston is the distinction Uptown/Downtown. Uptown is where the tiny light-skinned postcolonial bourgeoisie, the brown upper middle class, the growing black bourgeoisie and upper middle class, the large black middle class and some more fortunate members of the black working class live. Downtown is the inner city, the home of about one-third of Kingston's population, with high levels of unemployment, poverty and violent crime. Downtown Kingston is also the cultural capital of the English-speaking Caribbean, the *fons et origo* of the Rastafari religion and way of life, a place of thousands of small traders and scores of small recording studios where hundreds of young men dream of becoming the next Bob Marley. Like many other urban centers in the Third World, it is a hotbed of social contestation and political radicalism as well as of postcolonial disillusionment.

Characteristic of this division of Kingston is a feeling of abandonment of Downtown by Uptown. During fieldwork in a well-known Downtown community in 1998, a young female resident presented her views of the attitude of Uptown to Downtowners:

> And those who 'have it' now, dem just wind up dem car glass and you don't even see who a drive and them just, bups! Pass we! Because is only thieves dem see here so. Dem a run from robbers!
>
> Dem naw stop and even say [puts on her imitation of a mincing Uptown accent], 'Youngsters, why so much of you people sit down here so? You don't have a job? What do you plan to do?' Let me see if I can go in as a top class person then . . . and say something then and really help a few and make you all know what's going on.
>
> No, everybody just full up inna themself, because them no inna fi we class—them a "Tops", so them just go through! So them alright. Them better than everybody else. Them better than we! (Robotham 1998a)

"Those who have it *now*" refers, above all, to the upwardly mobile black middle class and the emergent black bourgeoisie—the leadership of the nationalist movement presently (2001) holding political power.

In a similar vein a young man from the same community related his experiences in the labor market:

> But it come in like you gi dem the Kingston 12 address, dem a look 'pon you a way as a . . . you know? Say you a top "shotta" or you a tief or you a something, you understand? And many time I and I go out there and get a work and them start lay off all Kingston 12 man, you understand? And when me check de program, it come in like dem a fire youth and youth foundation. Where you live inna de society, you understand? (Robotham 1998b)[3]

Globalization in the Nineteenth Century: Free Trade and the Rise of the Colonial Ghettos

Often modern Third World economic history appears to be a saga of how the global economy creates a configuration which, for a brief period, generates a limited prosperity for some, then moves on, consigning the previous political economy to stagnation and even collapse. From this viewpoint, the defining moment in the development of Kingston was the creation of what I call the colonial ghettos where urban poverty remains concentrated to this day (Stolberg 1990).[4] When slavery ended in 1834, only approximately 8 per cent of the slave population was resident in towns; their descendants would be urban (Higman 1973). It was only in 1872 that Kingston became the capital of Jamaica and its growth in the last part of the nineteenth century was the expression of broader political and economic changes at the global level. The population had fallen to about 27,000 in 1861 (after the cholera epidemic of 1850–2), but by 1911 it had increased by about 80 per cent, to 48,504 persons.

Between 1881–91 there was a large Jamaican migration to Panama and later to Cuba, yet Kingston's population increased at the rate of 2.3 per cent annually, with the overwhelming majority of the increase due to rural-urban migration. After 1921, it was the turn of the St. Andrew part of the city to grow rapidly, with an annual increase of 4 per cent per annum over 1921–43 (Roberts and Nam 1989).[5] By 1943, the population of Kingston had already reached 202,000 persons, largely as a result of the operation of the forces outlined below (Norton 1978). In fact, the striking thing was that the large majority of "Kingstonians" were not from Kingston at all but were deracinated peasants compelled by economic pressures to migrate to the city or abroad in order to escape the deadly pressures of rural life.

The immediate cause of the rural collapse was the passage of the Sugar Duties Act in Britain in 1846 and the Free Trade era which then ensued until Imperial Preference was restored after 1932. As a consequence, between 1873 and 1900 sugar prices fell by 56 per cent, from 25 shillings and sixpence to 11 shillings and three pence per hundredweight. There was an equally catastrophic collapse in the number of sugar estates. In 1839, there had been 664 but by 1900 these had been reduced to 122. Sugar production declined 72 per cent between 1838 and 1900, from 1,053,000 hundredweight to 295,000 hundredweight. Given the land monopoly maintained by the British—45 per cent of the land in holdings exceeding 500 acres were in the hands of less than 3 per cent of all landholders, while 78 per cent of landholders were relegated to 15 per cent of the land in holdings of less than 5 acres each—widespread rural immiseration was the inevitable outcome. After 1880 a massive rural outmigration unfolded, to Panama and other parts of Central America, to Cuba and New York and, of course, to Kingston.

The first colonial ghetto was established by these rural migrants to Kingston who built informal communities near the large open market on the western end of the city where rural traders had been bringing their produce for sale for decades. This is the origin of the present West Kingston district and the famous Trench Town—immortalized in song by Bob Marley. To this day the general area of western Kingston remains the most impoverished part of the city, in which most political violence and homicides are concentrated and at the same time the source of the apparently endless musical creativity. It is at the core of where Jamaicans have in mind when they speak of Downtown.

Fortunately, we have many good newspaper descriptions of these early colonial ghettos. Here, for example, is an account of conditions in Kingston Pen (West Kingston) in 1911:

> Kingston Pen is the name this village is known by, and how people manage to live and move, and have their being amid such surroundings, is more than one can tell. The whole place was years ago a swamp, but the land has been gradually reclaimed by depositing the city's refuse over it. And amid litter that is indescribably unsightly, a village of remarkable shacks constructed of tin sheets, wattle and mud, and covered with thatch in some cases, old zinc sheets in others, pieces of kerosene boxes and in fact anything that be laid hold of, has grown up and is increasing every day. (Moore and Johnson 2000: 91)

The failure of the society to cope with the Free Trade policies of the British Empire spelt economic disaster for the small open, trade-dependent economies of the West Indies, recently emerging from plantation slavery. But despite appointing a West Indian Royal Commission in 1897, these problems of the by now marginal Caribbean islands were little more than an annoyance for the British. Free Trade was too profitable for the dominant economic and political interests in the Empire who had long moved on from plantation slavery to greener pastures—in Asia, Africa, Latin America and the U.S.

But not all the urban masses in Kingston were small-scale artisans and petty traders or unemployed and semi-employed hustlers. Although significant manufacturing was restricted by the legislation of the colonial state, the light-skinned planter-merchant bourgeoisie had developed extensive docking facilities, public transportation and public utilities. In addition, the colonial state employed a small army of workers in the lower levels of the civil service, including the postal service. Thus there arose a union organized proletariat in Kingston from the turn of the century and especially after the uprisings of 1938. They were to play a critical role in the formation of political parties, the growth of the anti-colonial movement and the struggle for political independence. Kingston was and remains the center of the agency of this group from which it developed and directed its union and political activities.

This working class shaded upwards into a lower middle class of clerks and salespersons who enjoyed a somewhat better standard of living. In addition, a critical group had begun to emerge in Kingston—the professional middle class. Usually but not exclusively drawn from the brown group (many were black in Caribbean terms), they were lawyers ("barristers" rather than solicitors), teachers, doctors and ministers of religion and lower civil servants—that fortunate few who had managed to secure tertiary education in the colonial period. This group found its social advancement blocked by the color bar of the colonial state which reserved positions of seniority to whites from Britain or to local so-called "Jamaica whites." A very small number of them were also involved in light manufacturing and found their expansion limited by colonial legislation which restricted the colonies to the status of a raw materials appendage of the metropolitan economy. The emergent black and brown middle classes thus opposed colonial rule and became in fact the group that, in alliance with the working class and better-off sections of the peasantry, formed and led the anti-colonial movement against the British in the period after 1938.

One of the peculiar features of this important group in Kingston was its contradictory cultural character. On the one hand, it was anti-colonial and opposed British rule. On the other it was steeped in British colonial and metropolitan values and attitudes. Profoundly color conscious, anti-colonial but also often anti-black, its members too built modest colonial-style houses not too far from the core commercial district of the city and adjacent to the homes of the colonial oligarchy—usually on the eastern side. They avoided the west where the impoverished rural migrants congregated, preferring to live in East Kingston, in the areas known as Bournemouth, Vineyard Town or Rollington Town (Austin 1974). If they lived in the west they would move a bit north, closer to the Cross Roads and Half Way Tree areas, with some distance however small between themselves and the masses of people whom they considered their social and cultural inferiors, even as they sought their political support.

Thus a physical shaping of the city developed in a rather small area with the different class and ethnic groups defining residential and commercial spaces for themselves which reflected their relative standing in the political economy. I write "in a rather small area" since one of the features of Kingston of this period was its relative compactness. The city was beginning to expand into the adjacent parish of St. Andrew and was no longer confined to what would today be called "Kingston proper". But, apart from scattered residences of very wealthy members of the planter-merchant class in the hills of St. Andrew, this expansion was largely into St. Andrew's south and center, areas that were adjacent to the neighborhoods of the urban poor. The different social and ethnic groups by and large lived and worked side-by-side in adjacent communities, while maintaining their social and cultural distinctions. The distances—from East Kingston where the middle and lower middle classes lived to Kingston Gardens and Hope Road to which the planter-merchant group had begun to move, to West Kingston where the colonial ghettos had been established, to the main commercial business districts—were not large. There was certainly spatial segregation by social class and ethnicity but not of the dimensions of today. The fatal border—Uptown/Downtown had not yet been erected.

The Restoration of Imperial Preference and the Rise of Uptown (1946–99)

Unlike the colonial ghettos, responsibility for the development of the Uptown/Downtown boundary cannot be laid at the door of the British. It is really a product of the rise of the middle and upper middle classes and the postcolonial bourgeoisie, and ultimately of the development model pursued by the anti-colonial movement within the global political economy prevailing at that time. The restoration of Imperial Preference after the Ottawa Conference in 1932 provided subsidized prices for sugar produced in the British Empire. This is turn led to a revival of the Caribbean sugar industry after 1936. The victory of the Labour Party in Britain after the end of the Second World War, their construction of a welfare state, and their ideas of a British Commonwealth of Nations protected from the global economy and to which all ex-colonies would belong, provided the accepted framework for policymaking.[6] Such ideas shaped the entire thinking and economic and social policies of the leadership of the anti-colonial movement right into the recent postcolonial period, not only in the Caribbean but in Africa and India as well. Beginning in 1949 during the time of the second popularly elected Jamaican regime, a program of so-called "industrialization by invitation"—the Puerto Rican Model of import substitution industrialization—was launched. This was accompanied by huge American and Canadian investments in the bauxite-alumina mining sector, connected with the American military build up during the years of the Korean and Vietnam Wars, and in the emergent large-scale tourist sector.

This policy rested locally on the establishment of urban industrial estates of small industrial plants which enjoyed a virtual monopoly of the local market, ten-year tax holidays as well as other incentives for local and foreign investors in both manufacturing and tourism, and protection of local markets from foreign competition. It is also depended on the control of foreign capital and currency markets by the state, on the general body of international economic agreements collectively known as Bretton Woods, as well as on preferential access to British colonial markets. The economy was firmly based on private property driven by a market but this market was regulated by the state utilizing indicative planning and Keynesian macroeconomic tools. The state was responsible for providing opportunities for upward social mobility and subsidized social goods to the mass of the population, especially the poor.

In the years up until 1974, these policies resulted in a high rate of G.D.P. growth for the Jamaican economy, at a level similar and even higher than that of East Asia, for example higher than Singapore's, not to mention Malaysia's. There were large social investments made in public health and education as well as in public transportation and housing. Nevertheless, the economic and social outcome would be very different from that of Singapore and the Asian Tigers. In Kingston, the planter-merchant and the newly industrializing groups fused into a postcolonial bourgeoisie and prospered. The middle classes who had formed the anti-colonial and trade union movements and led the fight against the British, experienced dramatic improvements in their social and economic circumstances. A rapid exodus from Downtown to live "above the clock"[7] ensued, leading to the expansion of Upper St. Andrew.

This was the really first step in the emergence of Uptown as a distinct physical and socio-cultural space. It was critical because it involved the movement away, not only of the postcolonial bourgeoisie but of the emergent black middle class as well. From 1957, the nationalist government embarked on a subsidized project with closely allied construction interests—providing choice public lands Uptown and access to easy credit—to transform the residential location of the black and brown middle classes. Beginning with the first such project—Mona Heights—the middle classes, who had hitherto lived in physical proximity with the urban masses whom they had mobilized for anti-colonial political purposes, began their fateful move away. Rightly hailed at the time as an unprecedented opportunity for social mobility and home ownership for what was, after all, one of the classes oppressed and confined under colonialism, nevertheless it was also a move *away*. Instead of concentrating on improving the quite good housing stock already occupied by these emergent middle classes and located close to the communities of the urban poor, the nationalists pursued a different policy. They decided to open up the city to the north and the east in the Upper St. Andrew area, embarking on a program of urban road building, drainage and industrial house construction basically aimed at benefiting the middle-class section of their following.[8]

Over time the postwar import substitution policies were sufficient to raise up the black and brown middle class, to enrich a postcolonial bourgeoisie and even to improve the conditions of significant sections of the unionized working class. But this approach failed to transform the productive base of the society. The conditions of life of the urban poor concentrated in the old colonial ghettos and of the poor in the countryside continued to deteriorate. A sense that the anti-colonial movement was failing socially and economically began to take hold on the eve of political independence in 1962, as the growing inequalities of Jamaican society were documented.[9]

But, this was only one of the critical moments in the creation of Uptown. It only involved the movement of middle-, upper- and some working-class residences. The main business district and shopping area was still very much Downtown—there being no suburban shopping centers in Kingston at this time. The middle and upper classes had made their social point, but still had to go downtown on a daily basis because this was where their places of work were located. Nor was there as yet that segregation of cinemas and nightclubs and even forms of popular culture that have subsequently occurred, although, as one might expect, it is in the area of sports, public recreation and popular culture that social and spatial segregation least occurs today. Thus there was still considerable mixing in daily life across class and ethnic borders, especially in the crucial relationships between the urban black middle class and the urban black poor.

The development of New Kingston—the third moment in the wounding of Kingston—changed the situation for the worse. This was the development of a new business district in the 1960s, under the aegis of the same nationalist regime, but conceived and executed by other wealthy families, some of them economically and politically at the very heart of the nationalist anti-colonial movement. With the assistance of the state, they and their associates constructed an entirely new business district for Kingston, built Uptown on a previous racetrack, adjacent to the areas where the middle and upper class had been moving. Over a ten-year period, the main business operations in Kingston—banks, insurance companies, hotels, diplomatic missions, shopping and retail establishments, and the government itself constructed and/or occupied a nest of office buildings—scaled-down models of the business district of a medium-sized American city. Concurrent with this was the construction of a series of Uptown "plazas", new American-style shopping malls into which the leading retail establishments re-located. A whole new stratum of "developers" emerged in Kingston, drawn from the brown upper middle class and the bourgeoisie, many of whom had long-standing ties with the nationalist movement.

In addition to moving the offices of the white collar strata into a new locale relatively insulated from the neighborhoods of the urban poor, shopping too was moved Uptown. In a familiar pattern, it has continued to move further and further up with the construction of new malls. In other words, having first moved their places of residence away from the urban poor, the middle and upper social strata now moved their places of work and shopping to join their residences. An almost self-contained area "above the clock" began to be delimited in which Uptowners could live, work, play, shop, go to school, get private health care and "have their being" as Uptowners.

But there can be no "Uptown" without a "Downtown." To understand the dynamics of the present division fully, one has to understand what I have called the "fourth moment" in the fracturing of Kingston. This was the process by means of which low-income housing for the urban poor began to be used as a tool of political mobilization and as a central part of the struggle for hegemony between the rising black middle classes and the postcolonial bourgeoisie. This struggle provided the context for the creation of what are called "garrison communities" in Jamaica—one-party constituencies formed by dense concentrations of low-income public housing, packed with the political supporters of the government of the day, and dominated by armed political gangs. This was a process by means of which the urban poor were divided and politically apportioned to one or the other of the alliances of classes struggling for political power.

As with manipulation of the police, some of this political allocation of public housing was pioneered in the late colonial period, especially after the political upheaval of 1938. Then the British were seeking to divide the nationalist movement and the corruption of the delivery of social services was one way to achieve this. This was the origin of one of the best known of the Kingston "garrisons"—Denham Town (formerly the colonial ghetto of Smith Village but renamed for a deceased colonial Governor), adjacent to Kingston Pen and politically allied with the Right to this day. One of the worst colonial ghettos in West Kingston, it became the earliest beneficiary of a colonial housing project after 1938 and into the early 1940s. The same applies to the already-mentioned Trench Town: this too was a colonial ghetto—the site of public "hurricane" housing built by the first conservative Jamaican "self-governing" regime which shared state power with the British during the transitional period preceding political independence. After 1949 and 1951 a number of such relatively small colonial housing projects were built in Western Kingston and the adjacent South St. Andrew areas, after major hurricanes created widespread homelessness for the urban poor. Neglected for over 50 years, broken down and overcrowded, these projects were still inhabited at the time of my fieldwork—notorious for their absence of any sanitary or kitchen facilities, with predictable consequences.

It was at the point of political independence in 1962 that the usefulness of public housing as a device for building the mass base of political parties began to dawn. If this housing was allocated to carefully selected members of the poorest urban strata—some petty traders, some unemployed, in many cases, the *lumpen*—then they would provide a captive constituency as well as a reliable strike force for their benefactors. It was with this in mind—to build an urban mass base to rival that of the Left which historically dominated the urban working class areas—that the Right audaciously established the first garrison communities in Kingston.

The first—"Tivoli Gardens" (after an old cinema named Tivoli located nearby)—was built on the site of Kingston Pen in 1963–4. After the bulldozing of squatters from the "Dungle," this oldest and worst site of urban degradation and squalor in West Kingston was erased.[10] Military force was needed to displace many of the original inhabitants of different political allegiances (who fled to other squatter communities) and to ensure that the future allocation of housing would be limited to members of the governing political party—that of the Right. This political innovation from the Right was rapidly copied and expanded on by the Left when the nationalists returned to government in 1972. They completed the construction of already-started low-income housing and later named the new community Arnett Gardens. This became the garrison of "Jungle;" face-to-face with the Right-affiliated Tivoli and the Denham Town garrisons, it was controlled by the Left.[11] Thus was the political division of the urban poor in the city consolidated along spatial lines—literally set in concrete.

Globalization and the Present

Finally, one must come to the present "fifth" moment which is that of the rise of the black bourgeoisie under the conditions of deregulation and neoliberalism. Through a series of stages, this class developed out of the black middle classes in the 1980s. Initially, they were senior managers in the large state-owned enterprises that dominated the economy during the "socialist" period of the 1970s. After socialism fell, in 1980, these state enterprises were privatized and this group moved fairly smoothly to becoming salaried professional managers of large private sector firms in Kingston. However, as they accumulated business experience, capital and contacts, and when the nationalists recovered control of the state in 1989, this nascent bourgeois group moved decisively to expand their own medium-sized business enterprises. Using the state to displace the postcolonial elite, they attempted to achieve a position of economic dominance, in effect as a new ruling class (Robotham 2000).

The difficulty was that, because of their background in trading, finance, private management and the state bureaucracy, this feat was attempted mainly by financial and political means. Seldom was there significant investment in the real sectors of the economy—little attempt being made to generate new wealth by the transformation of the productive base of the society to meet the challenges of the era. But in the new situation these old political and speculative techniques would hardly suffice. The entire global political economy had begun to undergo radical change—to move on yet again from the postwar Keynesian era. In this emergent deregulated global market environment, the power of a small postcolonial state to influence economic policy was minimal and not likely to have much of an impact. In fact the state was forced by global market forces to place the reduction of inflation at the very center of its economic policy. Interest rates were raised astronomically to the point where the reverse repurchase rates of the Bank of Jamaica (the mechanism for setting interest rates for the entire economy) reached 33 per cent in November 1996. A financial crisis ensued in which the largest financial enterprises of the nascent black bourgeoisie were ruined.

At the same time, in order to finance the budget without going to the I.M.F., this government of the black bourgeoisie was compelled to embark on a large-scale program of domestic borrowing. In other words, here was pioneered the policy later adopted in South Africa whereby the Third World country pre-emptively develops "its own" I.M.F. program, before the global market (in the form of massive capital flight) compels it to accept an actual I.M.F. program.[12] The total public debt increased from 104 per cent of G.D.P. in 1995/6 to 144 per cent in 1999/00. By 2000, domestic debt had shot past foreign debt to become 57 per cent of the total debt burden of Jamaica. Charges on the total debt (domestic and foreign) now absorb about 60 cents of every dollar of the national Budget (Gordon 2001).

Four consequences followed from this failed attempt of the black bourgeoisie to capture the "commanding heights" of the economy by speculative means during this era of deregulation, globalization and downsizing of the state. First, was the further enrichment of the post-colonial bourgeoisie—the main holders of the public debt. Second, was the colonization of large areas of Kingston that had hitherto been residential areas by the businesses of the black bourgeoisie. Most of these were areas in which they or the older middle and upper classes had once lived but out of which they had moved in their journey Uptown. An astonishing proliferation of medium and small enterprises of all kinds, as well as the construction of small, and rather ugly, "plazas", spread in areas that had once been residential, in an orgy of haphazard, unregulated "development."

The third result was the drying up of any resources for social programs and for public employment or assistance. Public works construction vanished from Kingston overnight, even as taxes increased and user fees for health and education were introduced. The black bourgeois state, its very existence threatened, struggled with its fiscal and foreign exchange crisis, garnering resources from any quarter in a life-and-death struggle for survival. A powerful sense of social abandonment took hold of the urban poor and the precarious middle classes, especially as one of the consequences of the crisis was the contraction of the formal sectors of the economy and a significant decline in formal sector employment. This takes us to the fourth consequence.

As the formal sectors of the economy were experiencing sharp contraction, the urban and rural poor and the weaker sections of the bourgeoisie and the middle classes in Kingston confronted mounting insecurity. Those who could, migrated, creating new Jamaican communities in the North Bronx and in areas of South Florida. An obvious answer for the others was the age-old one of expanding the informal sector, one branch of which was the underground, illegal drug economy. Some moved into this sector, especially the trans-shipment of cocaine to the U.S., Canada and the U.K., forming alliances with Colombian drug interests for this purpose. The leaders of the resulting political gangs, sheltered from the police in their garrison communities, became far wealthier than the politicians who nominally controlled them and whose state was now in a profound fiscal crisis. As other scholars have demonstrated convincingly, the expansion of the drug trade and the brutal disputes which inevitably accompanied it, was the chief source of the growth of homicides and violent crime in Kingston and these have grown in direct proportion to the growth of the informal sector (Harriott 2000).

"Own account" employment in the Kingston Metropolitan Area (KMA) increased from 27.6 per cent to 38.9 per cent of the employed labor force between 1991 and 1998. In 1998, the official unemployment rate for the 14–29 age group was 26.5 per cent (Anderson 2000). The growth in the informal and illegal sector is best captured statistically by the growth of the category "not in the labor force." We have no data for Kingston, but for Jamaica as a whole, the population 14 years and over who were classified as not in the labor force, *increased* by 114,500 people, to 592,700 between 1991 and 1998 (Anderson 2001). As has been pointed out in the same work by Anderson, "the most pronounced changes in participation rates were found among persons under 25 years"—in other words in the group most involved in violent crime (Anderson 2001). In the 14–19 age group, labor force participation rates for young males *declined* from 34.3 per cent to 25 per cent between 1991 and 1998. For males of the 20–4 age group, participation rates declined also, from 92.1 per cent to 84.6 per cent over the same period.

As was the case with the old light-skinned elite and the postcolonial bourgeoisie in earlier periods, the emergent black bourgeoisie of the most recent period has also failed to transform the productive base of the society to meet the new global conditions. I offer this as an observation, deliberately not venturing a judgment on whether and how such severe global challenges can be met in a small open economy. One thing seems certain: how these issues are resolved will have major consequences for the healing or otherwise of the wounds of Kingston.

Notes

1. I am extremely grateful for the comments on this paper by my colleagues at the Graduate Center, City University of New York. I am also indebted to the many, only too patient, informants in Kingston, Downtown as well as Uptown. The Honourable Mayer Matalon, one of the major business architects of Kingston's destiny throughout this entire period, graciously gave up time to discuss some of the issues reviewed in this paper. My access to inner city communities as well as some Uptown informants would probably have been impossible without the kind assistance of the Honourable Dr. Omar Davies, Minister of Finance of Jamaica and Member of Parliament for a well-known Downtown constituency. I also benefited greatly from his many insightful and penetrating criticisms, robustly delivered as usual. Finally Dr. Patricia Anderson of the University of the West Indies allowed me to benefit from her invaluable labor market studies as well as her unrivalled knowledge of Jamaican society.
2. The murder rate for Jamaica as a whole in 1997 was 40 per 100,000. As more than 85 per cent of these murders occur in the "Downtown" sections of the Kingston Metropolitan Region, the rate is horrendous indeed when concentrated over this much smaller population.
3. "Kingston 12" is a Downtown postal code. "Shotta" is Kingston slang for "shooters" or young gunmen. "Tief" is "thief" The phrase "dem a fire youth and youth foundation" translates roughly as "They are trying to destroy young people at their very root."
4. It is worth emphasizing that rural poverty, often concealed, remains much more widespread and intense than the poverty in the cities. It is the social and political volatility of the cities that tends to create a different impression.
5. This increase refers to "Kingston proper", that is within the parish boundaries of Kingston which today is only the Downtown area of a much larger city; Kingston today includes the Uptown St. Andrew area.
6. It is worth noting that this concept—shared in different ways across both the Left and Right in Britain and France—was transferred to the European Union. It survives today in the very important Lome Agreements with the African, Caribbean and Pacific countries, which offer these countries limited protection from some of the worst effects of globalization.
7. That is, above the clock in the center of Half Way Tree in St. Andrew, seen as a public spatial marker of the border between Uptown and Downtown.

8. In fairness, they followed with large subsidized housing projects for the lower middle and better-off sections of the working class that without doubt significantly improved their living conditions as pointed out to me by Mayer Matalon. However, these were built some distance away across town, with the effect of further aggravating the isolation of the poor in the colonial ghettos of Western Kingston. The housing projects there contributed to the emergence of a Downtown in the sense in which it is used in this essay.
9. Interestingly, this is also the period of the emergence of the plural society theories of M. G. Smith.
10. "Dungle," as in Standard English "dunghill." The name speaks for itself. This is the same area as Kingston Pen, the colonial ghetto so vividly described by the journalist in 1911.
11. "Jungle" is of course, "Concrete Jungle." This is by analogy with the Sidney Poitier and Glenn Ford film on urban youth violence in the U.S. from an earlier period—*Blackboard Jungle*. Those interested in tracing transnational cultural "mediascapes" may want to note that this Jamaican urban "Jungle" is, in turn, the source of the term "Jungle Music" which developed in London in the 1990s, influenced by Jamaican immigrants who had ties back home to Arnett Gardens. For these connections, I have to thank Raymond Codrington, who recently completed his anthropology doctoral dissertation on hip-hop in London, at the Graduate Center, City University of New York.
12. Of course, this was with the silent approval of the International Monetary Fund, with very good reason. It is of some interest that Stanley Fisher, the recently retired managing director of the I.M.F., ranked Omar Davies—the Jamaican Finance Minister, and Trevor Manuel—his South African counterpart, as among the ten top finance Ministers in the world in this period. This is by no means to suggest that these finance Ministers and the I.M.F. share the same goals: these are tactical alliances often with as much mutual deception as agreement. How and why the policies that created the financial collapse were pursued is explained in Robotham (2001).

References

Anderson, P. (2000), *Work in the Nineties: A Study of the Jamaican Labor Market: Context, Conditions and Trends*, Washington DC: World Bank.

—— (2001), Social Risk Management, Poverty and the Labour Market in Jamaica. Paper presented at the Conference Reinventing Jamaica,

Institute for Research in African American Studies, Columbia University, New York City, 2 February.

Austin, D. (1974), *Kingston*, London: Croom Helm.

Gordon, D., Anderson, P. and Robotham. D. (1997), "Jamaica: Urbanization during the Years of Crisis". in Portes, A., Dore-Cabral, C. and Landholt, P. (eds), *Urbanization in the Caribbean: the Urban Transition to the New Global Economy*, Baltimore: Johns Hopkins University Press.

Gordon, P. (2001), Reinventing the Jamaican Economy. Paper presented at the Conference Reinventing Jamaica. Institute for Research in African American Studies, Columbia University, New York City, 2 February.

Harriott, A. (2000), *Police and Crime Control in Jamaica*, Kingston: University of the West Indies Press.

Harriott, A. (2000a), *Controlling the Jamaican Crime Problem: Peace Building and Community Action*, Washington DC: The World Bank. Caribbean Group for Cooperation and Economic Development.

Higman, B.W. (1973), *Slave Population and Economy in Jamaica*, Cambridge: Cambridge University Press.

Moore, B.L. and Johnson, M.A. (eds), (2000), *Squalid Kingston, 1890–1920: How the Poor Lived, Moved and Had Their Being*, The Social History Project, Department of History, University of the West Indies, Kingston: University of the West Indies Press.

Norton, A. (1978), *Shanties and Skyscrapers: Growth and Structure of Modern Kingston*. Working Paper No. 13, Kingston: Institute of Social and Economic Research.

Roberts, G.W. and Nam, V.E. (1989), *Study of Internal Migration in Jamaica: A Demographic Analysis*. UNFPA Project No: TRI/84/PO2, Georgetown, Guyana: Caricom Secretariat.

Robotham, D. (1998), "Transnationalism in the Caribbean: Formal and Informal", *American Ethnologist* 25: 307–21.

—— (1998a), Interview with Sonia and Miss Cherry. Field Notes, Kingston.

—— (1998b), Interview with a Group of Youths. Field Notes, Kingston.

—— (2000), "Blackening the Jamaican Nation: the Travails of a Black Bourgeoisie in a Globalized World", *Identities: Global Studies of Culture and Power* 7: 1–37.

—— (2001), Analyzing the Jamaican Crisis. Paper presented at the Conference Reinventing Jamaica, Institute for Research in African American Studies, Columbia University, New York City, 2 February.

Stolberg, C.F. (1990), *Jamaica 1938: The Living Conditions of the Urban and Rural Poor: Two Social Surveys*. The Social History Project,

Department of History, University of the West Indies, Kingston: University of the West Indies Publishers Association.
Stoltzoff, N. (2000), *Wake the Town and Tell the People*, Durham, NC: Duke University Press.

–7–

Wounded Medellín: Narcotics Traffic against a Background of Industrial Decline

Mary Roldán

Understanding the sources of Medellín's "wounding" requires peeling back numerous layers of urban history over several decades. It has become commonplace to only view the city and its troubles through the narrow lens of the international narcotics trade and the actions of now defunct epic figures such as the drug lord, Pablo Escobar. But violence, economic dislocation/transformation, skewed urban development and an uneasy relationship between the lower classes and the city's authorities predates the emergence of the narcotics business *per se*. Medellín represents a microcosm of many of the opportunities and ills that have characterized urban areas in both industrialized and developing nations over the course of the twentieth century. The city has been a major industrial hub, a financial nexus, and the center of a booming legal export trade in coffee, gold and textiles (Toro 1988). Many an ambitious rural migrant once fulfilled the dream of social and economic mobility in Medellín. But like rust belt cities in the U.S. where traditional manufacturing became obsolete or gave way to the imperatives of a "new economy", Medellín ultimately left its inhabitants bewildered and hopeless as the blue-collar jobs they had once relied upon to scale the ladder to a better future withered away.

Medellín is a city, moreover, where paternalism, civic duty, a tradition of non-partisan public service, and ascent based on merit have always coexisted with exclusion, discrimination, parochialism and selective repression. The following essay does not pretend to offer a systematic measure of the material impact of the narcotics trade on Medellín, but rather, constitutes a tentative attempt at unraveling the complex skein of convoluted histories that have shaped the specific contours of Medellín's urban crisis. Many Colombian cities were directly affected by the emergence of the global phenomenon of narcotics trafficking, but each responded to the challenges posed by the narcotics trade in different ways. An underlying assumption of this chapter is that each city's individual history of constantly shifting and renegotiated systems of authority, production, social relations, cultural expectations, values and norms ultimately determined the impact of the drug trade on urban life.

The narcotics boom vastly inflated prices for urban real estate, redefined the stylistic taste and even the character of particular urban neighborhoods and architecture, and modified the possibilities of lower class urban employment in cities as diverse as Cali, Bogotá and Medellín. In Cali, for instance, the penetration of the Rodriguez Orejuela narcotics clan's monies in construction was so vast within licit sectors of the local economy that when the cartel's leaders were finally jailed and the cartel was broken up in the mid-1990s, the city's real estate market nearly collapsed. Among the "victims" of the narcotics bust in urban real estate was the public Universidad del Valle. The university had undertaken an ambitious building campaign and expanded its campus during the heady days of narcotics-fueled economic growth, but when the degree to which the finances and curricular expansion of this public entity had been underwritten by narcotics support became evident, the university was forced to dismiss professors, renege on salaries and auction off properties.

Although half-completed shopping malls and abandoned high-rise building projects bankrolled by narcotics money also dot Medellín's landscape and the break up of the Medellín cartel certainly depressed urban real estate prices, the city's public entities and manufacturing sector have proved far more impervious to narcotics penetration than Cali's. Early on members of the city's major manufacturing and financial concerns formed a "syndicate" (known as the Sindicato Antioqueño) to actively block the purchase of shares or the penetration of decision-making boards by men linked to the narcotics industry. The regionally autonomous Empresas Públicas de Medellín (Medellín's Public Works Department), moreover, has historically pursued a policy of hiring strictly on merit—actively eschewing the influence of patronage-based interests, particularly those linked to Colombia's two traditional political parties. A long history of technocratic management and commitment to non-partisan economic development coupled with an unprecedented degree of regional autonomy from the central state have been peculiar to Medellín and Antioquia since the turn of the twentieth century. The particular structure of the regional economy and its social relations thus enabled some sectors of the city to limit the direct consequences of the drug trade in ways that proved impossible for cities such as Cali or Bogotá. The impact of the narcotics trade in particular areas of the urban economy seems to be directly proportional to the degree to which those areas are controlled or influenced by clientelist political machines. Since the existence of the latter clearly predates the emergence of the narcotics trade, the symbiotic relationship that has developed between narcotics trafficking and specific political sectors represents the accommodation of the narcotics trade to pre-existing structures of corruption, nepotism and collusion, rather than a transformation of the political system by the narcotics trade per se.

This is not to say that Medellín has been immune to the narcotics trade. A national recession since 1998, in part touched off by the reorganization of the narcotics trade and the escalation of internal civil conflict associated with, but not solely determined by narcotics trafficking, has had a profound effect on the quality and standard of urban life and public services. Yet the ability of Medellín's Empresas Publicas and Sindicato Antioqueño to remain aloof from narcotics influence is the direct consequence of exactly the specific convoluted urban histories to which I made allusion in the introduction of this essay.

Periodizing the Impact of the Narcotics Trade

For the purpose of analyzing how the narcotics trade has affected Medellín over the last several decades, it is useful to think in stages (always keeping in mind that these are loose approximations, not fixed or discrete temporal units). A first stage would encompass the years between 1940 and 1965 ("Medellín before cocaine"). This was when the city enjoyed a reputation as a manufacturing center (Latin America's largest textile exporter) and when it became the point of refuge for victims of Colombia's decades long conflict in the countryside known as *la Violencia* (Farnsworth-Alvear 2000, Roldán 2002). Traditional working-class neighborhoods were transformed during this period into sites of intense competition for housing, resources, jobs and political primacy. In some neighborhoods—such as the Barrio Antioquia or the Comuna Nororiental—Liberal/Conservative conflict even evolved into opposing bands of local patronage distribution and influence that eventually dovetailed with emergent petty criminal organizations devoted to robbery, racketeering, and incipient drug (marijuana) and prostitution rings (Riaño Acalá 2001).

A second stage might encompass the period between 1965 and the mid-1970s. Growing urban unemployment in the wake of a serious decline in textile manufacturing spurred both the expansion of local criminality and a massive outmigration from Medellín's lower class urban neighborhoods with established criminal rings to cities such as New York (especially Queens), Miami and Chicago. Immigrants to the U.S. continued to maintain close ties to the working class neighborhoods they left behind in Medellín, creating a complex system of exchange and mutual support that would later also serve the narcotics industry as a distribution and laundering vehicle. As the marijuana trade centered in the northwestern Caribbean coastal region waned, moreover, and demand increased for cocaine, incipient organizations schooled in the smuggling and robbery networks that connected Medellín with the Caribbean via the Pacific coast began gradually to restructure Medellín's labor and capital markets (Betancourt and Garcia 1994).

By the third stage (1972–82), Colombia had solidified its position as the international center of the cocaine trade. Medellín emerged as the industry's financial and processing hub, but the tangible material effects of the narcotics industry on the city were just beginning to be felt, most notably in the massive purchase and technological modernization of moribund cattle and commercial agricultural land (whose production was destined for sale in Medellín), the incipient explosion of luxurious urban residential and commercial construction, and a growing retail and service industry tailored to the taste and demands of a newly minted narcotics aristocracy. The fourth stage (1983–93) represents the most violent phase of the narcotics industry and that in which the state and the narcotics traffickers engaged in an open struggle for political control that converted selective areas of Medellín into something resembling a war zone. The city's lower class neighborhoods and in particular its poorer young men emerged as the primary targets of prolonged bloodshed, altering in dramatic fashion the configuration of urban spaces of sociability, communal interaction, and memory.

Finally, in the period since the death of Pablo Escobar in 1993 Medellín has experienced several concurrent crises linked to or spurred by, but not limited to, developments in the narcotics industry. The break up of the centralized "cartel" structure that had dominated the industry since at least the mid-1980s produced a critical reorganization in which some 220 smaller, loosely linked and scattered criminal organizations took over the drug industry and expanded increasingly into heroin production and export. The new narcotics "capos" lacked the charisma, tribal/kinship relations, links/loyalties, or constitutive power of Medellín's former cartel leaders. The absence of organizational leadership coupled with the economic effect of the cartel's demise on small businesses, construction, retailers, and the local labor market, spurred both a spike in urban unemployment and the proliferation of gangs, self-defense groups, and guerrilla cells within the city's lower class neighborhoods. Diffuse kidnapping, extortion, robbery, smuggling and "social cleansing" operations mushroomed as unemployed youths struggled to find substitutes for now defunct cartel jobs (Riaño Alcala 2001). The proliferation of competing armed groups within neighborhoods coupled with a rise in territorial struggles in rural areas outside Medellín, contributed in turn to the emergence and/or expansion of paramilitary and vigilante security forces that operated both in and around Medellín (Salazar and Jaramillo 1994, Alternativa 1996: 11–14).

A brief respite between 1994 and 1996 when both the central and regional governments embarked on a last-ditch strategy of negotiation with armed groups produced a short-lived period of "relative peace" in Medellín. But the last four years (1998–2002) have been ones of unremitting difficulty for urban inhabitants of all social strata. Right-wing terrorist groups have grown and spread and enjoy the overt support of members of the city's economic elite including a former regional governor, Alvaro Uribe Vélez (winner of the Colombian presidential election in May 2002). Calls for the "restoration" of law and order and appeals to rule "with a firm hand" are embraced not only by the city's well off, but voiced increasingly by many lower class inhabitants, especially young people in Medellín's most violent and poorest neighborhoods (Roldán, Interviews 2001). Neo-liberal economic policies intended to "open" Colombia's economy to international investment and trade have effectively killed local manufacturing, while the declining market in legal agricultural export commodities such as coffee and cutbacks in public spending mandated by I.M.F.-sponsored economic restructuring have put thousands out of work. A severe economic recession has eliminated funding for the "communal action" plans implemented to reduce tensions between the state and Medellín's lower class neighborhoods while a precariously balanced middle class of professionals and civil servants has been hard hit by cutbacks in state employment and the recession's effect on salaries, prices and job security. Finally, the combined effect of Plan Colombia's military aid program to combat narcotics trafficking and violent confrontations between the left, the state and right-wing groups have pushed tens of thousands of poor people from marginalized "peripheral" zones in Urabá and the Chocó into Medellín's already overwhelmed urban shantytowns (CODHES and UNICEF 1999).

The narcotics industry has played an extraordinarily important role in shaping many of the conflicts that characterize urban life in Medellín and has fundamentally altered the cultural parameters of style and consumption in the city as well as erased or reconfigured social and ethnic boundaries of citizen interaction. However, the current crisis in Medellín is ultimately the result of the intersection of drugs *and* other unresolved and complex structural issues whose origins predate the presence of the narcotics industry *per se*.

Medellín: Politics, Society and the Economy Pre-Cocaine

Antioqueños have historically thought of themselves as a culturally distinct group of no-nonsense, driven, industrious, devout and efficient individualists and of Medellín, the region's capital, as the urban embodiment of regional identity and pride. The city's better-off inhabitants boast of the efficient and non-corrupt management of municipal services; of sewage, water and electricity coverage for 95 per cent of the urban population; a 24-hour number for pothole repair; the most successful municipal tax assessment and collection system in Latin America; an excellent telephone service; and Colombia's only Metro (*Financial Times*, 23 July 1993). These public services are complemented by a kind of civic consciousness much less evident in other parts of Colombia. Shopkeepers and domestic help scrub the sidewalks outside stores and homes every day in Medellín; the city's inhabitants queue up in orderly lines to board buses throughout the city, and there is rarely to be found the accumulated refuse or private vehicles inconsiderately parked on public sidewalks that were (until recently) common sights in Colombia's capital, Bogotá. The perception that Medellín is a much better run city than any other in Colombia and a more pleasant place to live is widespread: in a 1997 poll conducted by the Bogotá-based daily *El Tiempo* Colombians were asked which city they would prefer to live in, and Medellín won by a considerable margin.

Mining, commerce, coffee production, and manufacturing formed the basis for a diversified economy in Antioquia, the region of which Medellín is the capital. The cultivation of coffee on small to medium-sized family-owned farms in particular ensured a modest but significant distribution of wealth among a broad sector of the region's inhabitants before 1945. In addition to a diversified economy Antioquia also developed several distinctive political and cultural features that distinguished it from other areas of Colombia and which came to form an integral part of an emergent regional identity. Economic, political and social power was concentrated in the hands of a broad network of extended families with diversified fortunes in coffee, mining, commerce, finance and ranching. Partisan differences notable in other parts of Colombia as a source of strife played a secondary role to bonds defined by shared economic interests, kinship ties and regional residence in the determination of political power and participation. In addition, social peace was secured through the complex exercise of a combination of access to economic opportunity and the assertion of paternalistic philanthropy.

Antioquia emerged as the premier center of industrial production in Colombia by the early twentieth century. The region also boasted more private charities and joint public/private philanthropic or mutual aid societies than Colombia's capital, Bogotá (a far more densely populated city), but far fewer labor unions or autonomous popular organizations. Despite a large working-class population, Medellín experienced fewer strikes than other Colombian industrial cities and fewer outbreaks of violent social protest or unrest. In the 1930s and 1940s when lower class voters in other Colombian cities were drawn to socialist political appeals or to the dissident campaigns of candidates such as Jorge Eliécer Gaitán, Medellín's popular classes refrained from openly expressing an explicitly confrontational or class-based political stance. The seemingly low level of popular urban mobilization in Medellín (or the reluctance to give open expression to it) was due in part to the extraordinary level of cohesion among the region's elite, a level that enabled it to shift with relative ease from the private sector to the public, and to integrate the interests of these two spheres in a way that distinguishes the exercise of authority in Antioquia from that in other regions of Colombia to this day. But the absence of significant, overt popular radicalism was also a product of the complicated and overlapping bonds of shared religious belief, regional loyalty and extended kinship connections that bound various Antioqueño social sectors together. Economic opportunity and the real possibility of social mobility coupled with appeals to regional identity and pride created a discourse and point of contact between divergent sectors of Antioqueño society that often eclipsed appeals to class solidarity or confrontation.

Very early on Antioquia's elite identified "good government" with regional economic development and tended to shy away from the intrusion of partisan politics in the day to day management of municipal and regional administration (Roldán 2002). In effect this meant that while the process by which decisions regarding investment and development were made was hardly democratic, Antioqueño legislators and authorities did spend considerably more than other regional leaders on education, public infrastructure, health and other public services. These expenditures expanded avenues of economic mobility, contributed to the emergence of a middle class of professionals (especially engineers and doctors) and fomented a relatively widespread notion of an Antioqueño equivalent of the "American Dream". Like the latter, achievement of the regional dream was predicated upon conformity to a series of bourgeois values and a kind of apoliticism that discouraged open class conflict or recourse to radical movements of any kind (Roldán 1992 and 2002).

By the decade of the 1950s, however, the careful balance of elite hegemony and economic access that had made class mobilization an unappealing route for the expression of popular ambitions in Medellín began to fall apart. Like other Colombian urban centers, Medellín received an influx of migrants and refugees escaping the effects of *la Violencia* (1946–58) that permanently transformed the character of urban life, particularly for the poor. The majority of *la Violencia's* refugees arrived with little or no property at a time when a once flourishing industrial economy had exhausted its ability to absorb additional workers. Fierce competition for a reduced number of employment possibilities coupled with turf wars over control of established working-class neighborhoods and shantytown invasions made for an increasingly violent and precarious existence for a majority of the city's poor.

Medellín: A Study in Socio-Economic Contrasts

A study by the National Planning Department (Departamento Nacional de Planeación) commissioned in 1991 in response to a special Presidential Program created to address Medellín's alarmingly high rates of violence found that by the 1960s "two cities" had developed and that Medellín as a whole was characterized by a high level of "social, spatial and economic inequality among its residents" (Departamento de Planeación Nacional 1991: 8). Most of the rural migrants to Medellín in the 1950s had had to settle on the geologically perilous hillsides along the perimeter of the valley in which Medellín was nestled (the Valle del Aburrá). Medellín's valley location, moreover, meant that there was little available flatland on which to expand. In addition, 80 per cent of the housing settlements established twenty years earlier were still illegal in 1990; these amounted to 30 per cent of all the city's housing (or 100,000 settlements) (Departamento de Planeación Nacional 1991: 20). The distribution of income in Medellín also contrasted sharply with tendencies in other Colombian cities during the same decades. Whereas income inequality in the rest of Colombia had tended to decrease, in Medellín income inequality had increased to such a degree that the distribution of wealth was worse in 1989 than it had been in 1967. Of Colombia's four major urban centers, Medellín exhibited the highest concentration of wealth (Departamento de Planeación Nacional 1991: 10).

Indeed, the data collected by the National Planning Department only confirmed the results of an earlier study published by IDEA (a regional economic think tank) in 1969. The IDEA study noted that Medellín and the industrial satellite towns that surrounded it (Itagui, Envigado, Bello, Caldas) had become home to 48 per cent of Antioquia's population in less than two decades. The 1964 census showed moreover that 45 per cent of Medellín's then population of 772,882 had not been born in Medellín itself, but were migrants from other parts of Antioquia (IDEA 1969: 3). Most of those migrating to the city were drawn by the promise of jobs, better public services and educational opportunities for their children, but Medellín's economic reality was already quite bleak by the mid-1960s. Antioquia's Economic Development Institute estimated that between 1957 and 1966 industrial jobs had grown by only 4.1 per cent a year and that the paucity of employment possibilities had made Medellín the city with the highest unemployment rate in the country (14.5 per cent in 1967) (IDEA 1969).

The gulf separating lower class inhabitants from the city's wealthy has historically been spatially, morally and politically defined. Poor neighborhoods cling precariously to the slopes that ring the city while the principal administrative, commercial, political and cultural establishments are located in the city's valley. Until the decades of the 1950s and 1960s, Medellín's upper class inhabited large, art deco mansions in Prado or apartment buildings they constructed to house themselves and their kin near the Metropolitan Cathedral in the Parque de Bolívar in the heart of Medellín's commercial and banking district. As working-class neighborhoods spilled down the slopes of the city and bled into the downtown commercial area, begging and petty thievery made the downtown streets unsafe in the eyes of the city's better off. In the 1960s and early 1970s, Medellín's rich relocated to what had once been semi-rural estates and have since been converted into luxurious apartment complexes and villas in the sector of El Poblado. The middle class built it's own tree-lined, park-like suburban enclave in Laureles, while recently arrived migrants erected precarious shacks further and further away from the center of the city or in the polluted, rat-infested settlement of Iguaná along the shores of the Medellín River.

Medellín's wealthy fled to country clubs or nearby estates on weekends leaving the city's central district to be appropriated by the poor. Downtown streets and squares became sites of transient sociability populated by black washerwomen and maids from the Chocó, informal vendors, itinerant picture takers and snake oil salesmen who eeked out a meager living from the sale of trinkets among the servant class during the latter's one day of weekly rest. In the neighborhoods of Antioquia, Manrique, Lovaina, Santo Domingo, and Villatina, unemployed or barely employed young men played billiards, drank, smoked joints and conspired to run numbers, pull a heist or deploy a pick-pocketing ring (Riaño Alcala 2001). These were the *malandrines* and *maleantes* modeled on the petty criminals of Argentine tango lyrics and immortalized in Rubén Blades' salsa tribute to the neighborhood thug, Pedro Navaja ("Switchblade Peter"). Pablo Escobar and his "lieutenants" emerged out of the lower class neighborhoods and working-class suburbs of Medellín and Envigado. Here respectable houses had been built and maintained by an older generation of factory and public-sector workers who, managing to secure a pension and a modicum of protection from the National Security Institute, struggled desperately to remain afloat amidst a rising tide of unemployment and social malaise (Salazar 2001).

The inequitable distribution of power and the location and use of public space in Medellín also reflect broader political, economic and cultural changes affecting not only Medellín but Colombia and the world as a whole since the 1960s. While the dissonances of urban life in Medellín may not exclusively or simplistically be attributed to a generalized metropolitan crisis experienced throughout areas of the less developed world as a result of debt, economic restructuring and declining public investment in the 1980s, the decline of manufacturing in what was once Colombia's premier industrial center, rising unemployment and the explosion of the city's informal sector are certainly linked to recent global trends in downsizing and de-industrialization. When Medellín's industrial base experienced a profound crisis in the decade of the 1970s, the city's already high unemployment rate soared, and the number of unemployed or "inactive" male youths between the ages of 12 and 29 rose to become the highest in the nation (Departamento de Planeación Nacional 1991: 15). These young men formed the pool from which the narcotics cartel would actively recruit its most loyal henchmen.

The Wages of Political Exclusion

The problem of violence in Medellín, however, is not simply a matter of material wealth or its absence. Unlike the shantytowns in many other areas of Latin America, in Medellín's *tugurios* the streets are often paved and the homes—except for those built by the most recent and poorest migrants at the apex of the valley's slopes—are permanent structures of brick and cement. A sewage system and electricity reach most of the city's inhabitants. The percentage of unsatisfied basic needs among Medellín's population, for instance, is considerably lower than the national urban average (23.6 per cent versus 32.3 per cent) (Departamento de Planeación Nacional 1991: 10). As is true in other parts of Colombia, moreover, the cost of public services is indexed to income. Until a few years ago when subsidies were eliminated as part of neo-liberal economic restructuring, the lowest two strata paid but nominal fees for access to water and electricity. In contrast to what is true of other cities in Colombia, moreover, in Medellín public services actually *do* work and are accessible not simply to the well off, but to the poor too. Aside from the serious problem of declining employment opportunities then, what troubled *comuna* dwellers even before the advent of the narcotics trade was not so much the absence of basic services but the fact that even when the city provided necessary services, it did not take into account the wishes or needs of the urban poor. Public works projects might raze neighborhood dwellings with no advance notice while curfews and states of siege were used to justify unwarranted searches and arrests.

The tendency to impose from above rather than consult and negotiate ensured that sullen hostility and mutual distrust characterized the relations between the city's authorities and shantytown inhabitants. Policemen, public works officials, the army, and politicians seeking election were the only contact between lower class inhabitants and the formal mechanisms of power based in Medellín. The poor's alienation from state and official institutions was neatly summarized in a poll conducted by the mayor's office in 1991 among the city's *comuna* residents: it found that 84 per cent of the respondents distrusted the police, 69.5 per cent extended that sense of mistrust to the army, and 89.5 per cent distrusted political parties. The only institution that enjoyed any credibility among Medellín's poor was the Catholic Church. *Comuna* dwellers also revealed an atomized and parochial sense of identity; community was defined as the neighborhood whereas "the rest of the city did not count" (*El Espectador*, February 13, 1994).

The narcotics trade and the upper echelons of those who organized the cultivation, processing, and distribution of cocaine in Medellín altered the balance of power between rich and poor, and the state and its citizens in fundamental ways. First, the cocaine trade created employment: mules who could transport cocaine back and forth between Colombia and the U.S. and Europe; accountants who could "cook the books" and find legitimate sectors or complicit financial institutions to launder the fabulous profits of cocaine; drivers; bodyguards; overseers on newly acquired ranches; chemists and technicians to monitor the delicate alchemy of converting coca paste into pure *postre de ñatas* (nose candy); recruits to man the growing army of youth assassins and enforcers that protected the criminal organization from desultory government penetration or competition. Unemployment did not disappear in Medellín, but it certainly improved. Second, there were the indirect beneficiaries of cocaine—what we might term the "trickle down" effect. Suddenly flush young men fresh from successfully seeing off a shipment of drugs or having completed *un trabajito* (a little job—a contract killing) spread their new found wealth in their own neighborhoods. They bought their mothers refrigerators and stoves, construction materials to finish off the second or third floor of an incomplete illegal invasion, food and beer at the local corner store to keep their comrades in crime happy, clothing, jewelry and make up for their girlfriends. As a result, even businesses not directly connected to the narcotics trade nonetheless felt the immediate impact of cocaine profitability.

The middle ranks of the narcotics trade bought houses in stable, old middle-class neighborhoods such as Boston, imposing striking new facades on the staid one story, turn of the century houses that lined streets like Caracas, Bolivia, Argentina and Peru. The cartel "capos" moved in among the old elite in El Poblado, horrifying and thrilling Medellín's stodgy bourgeoisie with their marble encrusted luxury apartment buildings, their hi-rise pools, gold faucets, and *capodimonte* light fixtures. Art galleries and antique dealerships driven to the edge of bankruptcy by the frugal customs and nickel and dime haggling of Medellín's traditional elite sprang back to life and reinvented themselves as purveyors of soft-porn nudes and wall-sized tropical fruit still-lifes to fill the cavernous palaces of the cocaine barons. The drug lords, moreover, were not snobs. They never forgot their humble origins or the neighborhoods where they had grown up. They recruited their support staff from their old neighborhoods and rewarded local loyalty with the donation of parks, athletic equipment and contributions to the local churches and schools. They celebrated their good fortune by sponsoring public festivities accompanied by abundant food and drink. The *patrones* became heroes. Little wonder that men such as Pablo Escobar and Carlos Lehder should have ventured to turn their popularity into legitimate (if ultimately unsuccessful) political careers; they were after all, Colombia's new *gamonales* (political bosses).

For a while a kind of truce existed in Medellín: the lives of the poor improved and their access to the possibility of accumulating wealth no longer depended upon deference to a moralistic, patronizing and indifferent elite. Violence continued to characterize lower class neighborhood life, but the police became more hesitant to pin any unsolved crime on unemployed *comuna* males whose sole crime was to lounge on street corners (this was true in part because the police were now also in the pay of the cartel). Indeed, cocaine turned out to have an added benefit in the eyes of Medellín's poor: it revealed that state officials either did not care about the drug traffickers and their illicit activities, or were downright afraid of them. The boon to lower class inhabitants accustomed to having their privacy continually violated, to submitting to street searches, shake downs and general abuse, was that with the backing of the narcotics industry, the poor now represented a threat, one most policemen and government agents were reluctant to provoke.

Transgressing the Boundaries of Propriety and Power

As the poor lost their awe or terror of the state and Medellín's authorities, and as their employment in the cartel's organization gave them greater opportunities to consistently transgress the invisible but powerful boundaries that separated people in the "poor" part of town from those secluded in their upper and middle class suburbs, the mental and cultural "cartography" of the city changed. High-end bars and discotheques expanded where both "proper" and shady figures mingled and interacted. Medellín's *hijos de papi* (children of the rich), moreover, loved the sensation of flirting with danger and adopted the narco or "gangsta" style of clothing and adornment imported by low end *traquetos* (drug dealers) from their frequent back and forth travels between Queens and Medellín. Proper young ladies who by day attended expensive, all-girls' schools could be seen prowling Medellín's recently constructed shopping malls by night, attired in the tight jeans, urban hip attire and woven wrist amulets of religious medals popularized by drug dealers to ward off evil spirits. The wealthy parents of youngsters who turned up their noses at the narcos' vulgar ways and derided the nouveau ostentation that characterized the latter's building and consumption habits, nonetheless capitalized on the enormous profits to be made by selling their unproductive, quasi-feudal lands to men anxious to launder their illicit gains through the purchase of state-of-the-art farm machinery, pedigree cows and the latest in chemical technology. It was possible through the early part of the 1980s to maintain the fiction that the narcos were but a marginal breed, one whose presence flooded society with unprecedented cash and affluence, and that Medellín's licit society and economic sectors were immune from the cocaine industry and not dependent upon its survival (Roldán 1999).

The illusory buffer between the violent world of narcotics traffickers and Colombia's *gente de bien* (upstanding citizens) dissolved, however, when the Constitutional Assembly of 1990–1 re-wrote Colombia's hundred-year-old Constitution and considered the possibility of extradition to the U.S. for narcotics traffickers. Suddenly, the degree of inter-penetration between licit and illicit spheres and the real power of the narcotics cartels became completely evident. The cartel set off bombs that destroyed not only the lowly vendors that populated the downtown San Antonio Park where Fernando Botero's "Peace Dove" sat, but the houses, cars and bodies of the wealthy in El Poblado. The wealthy's new found vulnerability and the cartel's absolute lack of respect for the rich came as a complete surprise to Medellín's (and Colombia's) elite. There existed no historical precedent for a "war" in which the elite was also a target—neither the civil wars of the nineteenth century nor the *Violencia* that took more than 200,000 lives in the space of 15 years between 1948 and 1963 had been directed against the elite.

A brief phenomenal change occurred in Medellín: the rich were suddenly afraid of venturing into the city. The places they had considered their own—the financial district, El Poblado, the shopping malls, the restaurants and bars along the Las Palmas highway—were now colonized and controlled by the cartel and sites of danger. Buying real estate in Medellín became an impossible proposition for those hoping to escape the range of the cartel—many of the apartments, commercial and residential properties, automobiles and farms—proved to be owned by a dense web of straw men and cartel-related interests. The cartel leaders' fearsome power of violence meant that no title was safe, no building immune from a shoot out or sudden bombing (particularly once the Medellín and Cali cartels broke off relations and began to attack one another over the wisdom of using violence to pressure the state to withdraw the legislation on extradition). The elite and Medellín's authorities were now on the defensive and they increasingly viewed the source of all disruption in Medellín as the cartel, and more specifically, the lower class inhabitants who formed the cartel's loyal support network.

The Geography of Violence

In the early 1990s, the "war" took on a distinctly "take no prisoners" quality to it. The state parried the cartel's firepower by repressing and conducting massive (indiscriminate in many cases) massacres against the young male inhabitants of the *comunas*. Perhaps not surprisingly, the San Pedro Cemetery emerged as Medellín's new social gathering place. Young widows, sisters, girlfriends, babies, grandparents and the remaining comrades of the deceased flooded the cemetery every weekend, bringing food and drink with them, playing the dead cartel soldier's favorite heavy metal music on imposing loudspeakers, writing notes and leaving offerings before the graves of their disappeared *parches* (buddies) (see Figure 7.1). Outside the cemetery's gates a lively business in flowers, candy,

Figure 7.1 San Pedro Cemetery, Medellín. Tombs of youth killed in the 1990s, covered with notes from girlfriends and family members, soccer stickers, and other offerings. Photograph by Mary Roldán.

trinkets and soccer club stickers grew up creating a perversely festive air akin to that of a country fair each Sunday (Aricapa 1998: 148–55). The Medellín metro was completed around the same period and one of its most popular stops was the San Pedro Cemetery leading Medellínenses to joke in characteristic gallows humor about the "backwards and forwards linkages" and "assembly line integration" of the local death industry: as the *comunas* bordered on the cemetery it was possible to arrange "non-stop" service for a potential victim, from massacre to burial in one fell swoop. The number of young men killed was so high that crypt builders could barely keep up with the demand for spaces to bury the casualties of the war (between thirty and forty young men every weekend would end up dead) and contracting for the more ostentatious mausoleums dedicated to the cartel's deceased lieutenants became a flourishing business.

By the time Pablo Escobar was killed on a rooftop in a middle class Medellín "safe" house in December 1993, the lines of conflict in Medellín were so complex and confusing that it was difficult to say with exactitude who was fighting whom. The elite sector and the state declared that the "war" was against drug traffickers in general, but they concentrated their force against the Medellín cartel and left Cali's to largely grow undisturbed. The police who had once been in Escobar's pay were now the most frequent targets of the increasingly decimated cartel's actions. Meanwhile, lower class neighborhoods became sites of continual struggle in which "orphaned" criminal groups formed competing armed bands to monopolize control of the remaining sources of illicit activity now abandoned or no longer absolutely controlled by the cartel. In turn, armed "self defense" groups sprang up within Medellín's lower class neighborhoods to defend local businesses and neighbors from victimization by constantly shifting bands of armed assassins and extortionists (Jaramillo 1993, 1994). The state, moreover, stepped up its repression of the *comunas* in an attempt to "impose order" and destroy the remaining vestiges of Escobar's organization. Massacres perpetrated by masked, heavily armed men travelling in unmarked jeeps and commanded by "rogue" or off-duty policemen and emergent death squads paid for by associates of the Cali cartel (among them Fidel Castaño's forces, which later developed into the Autodefensas Unidas de Colombia or AUC, a paramilitary army now led by Fidel's brother, Carlos Castaño) became ordinary events.

For a brief period (between 1993 and 1995) violence rose to such unprecedented levels that Medellín's economic elite and the city's authorities (with the support of the central government) agreed to negotiate with lower class dwellers on the latter's terms. The proliferation of community organizations created and staffed by comuna inhabitants (often with the backing of the neighborhood clergy) and a history of mutual aid independent of government or elite funded philanthropy surprised the government's representatives and the city's businessmen. The urban authorities and elite had always assumed that Medellín's lower class inhabitants were incapable of organizing among themselves and dependent upon outside interlocutors for their day to day survival.

In its effort to promote a dialogue with its opponents, the state pursued a strategy quite similar to that which it has currently adopted with regard to coca producers in areas where leftist guerrillas and the narcotics industry are powerful. Offers were made to give public credits, promote alternative small businesses, fund community development projects and build educational centers in the shantytown communities perceived to be most violent in order to lure youth away from participation in gangs and criminal organizations. But just as current attempts to promote crop substitution in southern Colombia among small producers have failed because the state has ultimately proved unable to actually deliver promised credits, technical support and needed monies to make substitution worthwhile to hungry peasants, so the state ultimately failed to live up to its promise to create jobs, educate and support community activism among Medellín's *comuna* dwellers. Many within neighborhoods such as Barrio Antioquia believe that the "peace accords" hammered out between neighborhood representatives and the authorities were but a ruse. Indeed some poor urban inhabitants firmly believe that peace initiatives were concocted with the support of cartel "bosses" who hoped the disarmament of local youth groups would preclude any possibility that these would turn state's evidence against the cartel or pose a challenge to the restructuring of the narcotics trade (Riaño Alcala 2001). Whether the state acted in conjunction with paramilitary death squads or with newly reorganized narcotics groups to eliminate community leaders between 1995 and 1997, the fact is that all of the young men who gave up their arms and participated in "peace accords" with the regional government have been killed.

By Way of Some Conclusions

I want to conclude this telescopic overview of the impact of the narcotics trade on Medellín with a brief reflection on what I consider to be have been its most enduring effects. The re-structuring of the cocaine cartels into multiple independent small operations and the proliferation of criminal bands with no ideological or fixed association or loyalty gave rise to a situation of unparalleled terror. These constantly shifting criminal groups may be hired to kill a state agent, kidnap a wealthy businessman or conduct a massacre against elite children at a local bar to "send a message." They may also hire themselves out as security forces for the narcotics operations of right-wing paramilitary groups engaged in an all-out war against leftist guerrillas and a struggle to dominate the resources and property of sparsely populated but rich peripheral zones. They also simultaneously oversee prostitution, smuggling, and urban larceny rings. In short, the new modality is one of guns for hire organized on an increasingly transnational scale. *La Terraza*, one of Medellín's most fearsome terrorist and criminal organizations, is rumored to have an office in Madrid and to coordinate criminal activities in Colombia and elsewhere.

The state's sheer inability to maintain public order on the one hand, and its failure to make good on its promises of social development and political inclusion to beleaguered lower class inhabitants in chronically violent neighborhoods, on the other, has deepened a sense of the state's illegitimacy among broad sectors of Medellín's society. Otherwise "respectable" economic and social actors put their faith and money in right-wing paramilitaries who now have cells that operate not only in the countryside where many Medellín businessmen have investments, but in the city itself. A new era of migration and colonization has emerged as the inhabitants of entire rural villages are forcibly displaced or migrate to Medellín and are compelled to compete for livelihoods and survival in an already depressed and saturated labor market. It is harder and harder to divorce urban from rural conflict—the two are inextricably intertwined.

Future studies of the narcotics trade and its relationship to urban life will have to take a broad perspective that defies the distinctions between rural and urban and national and international arenas of exchange and struggle. Latent, unresolved issues of land concentration, resource exploitation, ideological struggle and the impact of neo-liberal economic policies have fundamentally altered the character of urban life and its possibilities in multiple and complex ways. The spatial dimensions of urban exchange, memory, identity and interaction no longer obey fixed territorial limits. Medellín's history has long been part of a broad, multinational, almost virtual community that stretches from New York and Europe to Colombia. The exchange and distribution requirements of the narcotics industry accelerate and energize the globalization of cultural influences in multiple directions: food, clothes, slang, music, money and fads jet from the lower class barrios of Medellín to the urban hipster in Manhattan and back again with dizzying speed. The narcotics trade exploded neat "nationalist" conceptions of geography and historical contingency while de-industrialization and "free trade" have reconfigured urban life and the possibilities for individual survival in contemporary Medellín in unimaginable ways.

References

Alternativa (1996), Mano dura o tenaza militar? *Alternativa*, 5: 11–14.
Instituto de Desarrollo Economico de Antioquia
—— (1969), *IDEA II: August 11*, Medellín: Imprenta Oficial.
Aricapa, R. (1998), *Medellín es así: Crónicas y reportajes*, Medellín: Editorial Universidad de Antioquia.
Betancourt, D. and García, M.L. (1994), *Contrabandistas, marimberos y mafiosos. Historia social de la mafia colombiana (1965–1992)*, Bogotá: Tercer Mundo.
CODHES (Consultoría para el Desplazamiento Forzado y los Derechos Humanos) and UNICEF (1999), *Un país que huye. Desplazamiento y violencia en una nación fragmentada*, Bogotá: Editorial Guadalupe.
Departamento de Planeación Nacional, Colombia (1991), *Medellín: Reencuentro con el futuro*, Bogotá: Presidencia de la Rebablica.
Farnsworth-Alvear, A. (2000), *Dulcinea in the Factory: Myths, Morals, Men, and Women in Colombia's Industrial Experiment, 1905–1960*, Durham NC: Duke University Press.
Jaramillo, A.M. (1993), "Milicias populares en Medellín: entre lo privado y lo público", *Revista Foro*, 22: 25–37.
—— (1994), *Marginalidad y delincuencia en el Medellín reciente: entre lo imaginario y lo real*. In Memorias del Seminario Medellín: actores urbanos y proyectos de ciudad. Medellín: Corporación Región.
Riaño Alcala, P. (1993), "'Por qué a pesar de tanta mierda este barrio es poder?' Historias locales a la luz nacional", *Revista Colombiana de Antropología*, 36: 50–83.
Roldán, M. (1992), *Genesis and Evolution of La Violencia in Antioquia, Colombia (1900–1953)*. Ph.D. Dissertation, Harvard University.
—— (1999), "Cocaine and the 'miracle' of modernity in Medellín", in Paul Gootenberg (ed.), *Cocaine: Global Histories*, London and New York: Routledge, pp. 165–82.
—— (2001), Interviews with shantytown youths at the Universidad de Antioquia, Medellín.
—— (2002), *Blood and Fire: La Violencia in Antioquia, Colombia, 1946–1953*, Durham NC: Duke University Press.
Salazar, A. (1994), *La parábola de Pablo: Auge y caída de un gran capo del narcotrafico*, Bogotá: Planeta.

Salazar, A. and Jaramillo, A.M. (1994), *Las culturas del narcotrafico*, Bogotá: Cinep.
Toro, C. (1988), "Medellín: desarrollo urbano", in Melo, J.O. (ed.), *Historia de Antioquia*, Bogotá: Editorial Presencia Ltda, pp. 299–305.

–8–

Global Justice in the Postindustrial City: Urban Activism Beyond the Global-local Split

Jeff Maskovsky

The summer of 2000 was not an easy one for the city of Philadelphia. After years of image enhancement, downtown redevelopment, and high-profile politicking by the municipal elite, the city was poised to gain a significant political and economic boost by hosting the Republican National Convention. But the same convention that brought throngs of Party delegates, political operatives and media pundits to the city also attracted thousands of protestors intent on disrupting the highly orchestrated political spectacle that U.S. party conventions have become. Building on earlier protests in Seattle and Washington DC, the R2K coalition brought together activists from around the globe to demonstrate at the convention. During a week of marches, rallies, and direct action protests in July, demonstrators advanced a range of demands, including calls for economic justice, improved environmental regulations, universal health care, greater union democracy, the dismantling of the prison industry, the end of the death penalty, and justice for the political prisoner and then-death-row inmate Mumia Abu Jamal.[1] From the point of view of global justice activists, the convention constituted another opportunity to protest downsizing, deregulation, privatization, welfare state retrenchment, unfair trade and other neo-liberal austerity measures that are the hallmarks of economic globalization. From the point of view of the city government and its corporate backers, however, the protests threatened Philadelphia's growing but ever-fragile reputation as a tourist and conference destination.

This organizing effort, and the tensions it produced in Philadelphia, exemplifies a dynamic at the heart of grassroots political action occurring across the U.S., particularly in its cities. In recent years, "growth" politics has come to dominate cites like Philadelphia. In the context of declining federal and state revenue, an eroding tax base and capital flight, image enhancement has been elevated to new heights as cities compete with each other to transform themselves into productive sites in the post-industrial landscape.[2] Yet the conventional wisdom on urban activist movements, the global justice movement in particular, tends to endorse an overly simplistic assessment of the nature and scope of activism occurring in this context. The conventional wisdom among scholars, politicians and policy makers is that global justice activism is separate from—even unintelligible to—neighborhood movements, union drives, anti-racist movements and other putatively traditional forms of grassroots engagement because of their respective "global" and "local" orientations. Global justice activism, the story goes, must be distinguished from political action involving neighborhood-based civic activists and others, who concern themselves with exclusively local, place-based issues that remain unarticulated to the broader democratizing politics being forged across global space. Conventional wisdom also tells us that global justice is separated from other activist movements along lines of race and class, with new global justice movements presumed to be overwhelmingly white and middle-class, and more traditional movements presumed to be racially diverse and overwhelmingly working class. In short, we are told that the emerging movement for global justice, in order to keep pace with the global economy that it seeks to oppose (or at least "democratize"), has unhinged itself in every way from local forms of grassroots engagement.[3]

As is usually the case with conventional wisdom, this story of global-local disconnection contains just enough truth to be misleading. The relationship between global justice activism and other forms of urban activism is a complicated one characterized by multiple convergences and divergences. Broadly speaking, different forms of urban activism today typically share the common political context of "growth" politics, they share the common economic context of uneven development, and, as I shall explain below, they share a pattern of traversing multiple scales of political identification and practice from "local" to "global" and back. At the same time, movements develop multiple, often contradictory responses to the common political and economic dynamics they oppose.[4] By invoking the local/global divide, academics and activists alike risk overlooking important points of commonality and divergence across activist groups. Within this broader set of issues, this chapter focuses specifically on the importance of the urban growth agenda in constraining political deliberation and dissent and in shaping the nature and scope of grassroots alliances and divisions. Through an ethnographically informed analysis of global justice activism in Philadelphia, I hope to trace the political contradictions that strain relations between global justice and other activist groups, and to problematize the conventional wisdom on the global-local split.

Beyond the Global-local Split

The workings of locality are not any more opaque to global justice activists than they are to other activists, just as the workings of global capitalism are no less intelligible to neighborhood-based, civil rights, and union activists than they are to global justice activists. Many activists routinely demonstrate a complex understanding of political and economic realities in the course of waging struggles that policy makers and the news media invariably label as local. For example, a multi-racial coalition of residents in a neighborhood bordering on downtown Philadelphia has since 1999 fought the activation of a cell tower located next to several residential houses. Coalition members view the tower, which was established to provide cell phone service to downtown residents, as an environmental health threat and an eyesore that depresses their property values. They worry that it will blow down onto one of their houses during a storm, creating a threat to their safety and property. In their fight to remove the tower, they have made contact with an international set of health care activists who have published reports linking cancer and childhood learning disabilities with prolonged exposure to cell phone radio waves; they have negotiated with two multinationals who subcontract work to each other; and they have investigated telecommunications and zoning laws at federal, state and city levels. All of this has led the activists to realize exactly how the elite proponents of corporate globalization view their neighborhood, and has led them beyond local patterns of analysis and agency. LeAnn Smith,[5] a white working-class resident who lives next door to the cell tower, understands the struggle as fundamentally a struggle of a poor black neighborhood against a corporate giant: "These things tend to happen in neighborhoods like this. It's a marginal neighborhood, a black neighborhood, and they thought they could come in and no one would have the wherewithal to stop it." LeAnn and her allies possess a "global" understanding of the politics of the situation, rejecting their opponent's efforts to label them as passive, indifferent, and backward. In other words, they reject being labeled as "local." The localist assumption certainly threatened to disempower the residents, but it also made the cell phone company complacent, as it believed there would be no resistance to its tower activation.[6]

For their part, global justice activists are concerned with locality in ways not often noted in journalistic and ethnographic accounts. As the movement has grown since late 1999, activists have become attuned to criticisms that their politics do not take into account local political and economic considerations. An interesting leader in this regard is Laila Cottman, an African American woman who works as deputy director in a non-profit youth health promotion program in Philadelphia. Active in anti-racist and global justice politics for years, she has attended protests in many cities, and has given considerable thought to the question of locality:

> I'm concerned about pollution in my neighborhood and in the neighboring town in Chester. I'm concerned about the quality of the schools in my community, which are not prioritized by our government. The Republican convention protest was just an opportunity where we might be able to draw some attention. It's just one singular event, it's not the movement. The one thing that's clear is that high profile militant street tactics are just that, just tactics, not what a movement is built from. And when high profile events come to town they are great opportunities to raise issues, but what we have learned is that day to day outreach and organizing among local forces for social change is the most important work we have in order to draw out how the economic realities on the local level relate to what is happening globally.

It is worth noting that the activist mobilization in Philadelphia represented the first real attempt in this emerging movement to thoroughly integrate the specificity of locality into the broader agenda of the emergent movement for global justice. The criticism that protestors do not have a unified message can in part be attributed to the challenge posed by this expansion of the protest agenda.[7] In the weeks leading up to the Republican convention, activists held teach-ins and training sessions in Philadelphia, all designed to disseminate information about inequality and poverty in the city, and to show how these manifestations connect with "imperialist globalization." In particular, a number of activists worked hard to draw connections between Right-wing social and economic policies on the one hand, and uneven development in the city on the other. A major focus was the rise of the convention/tourist industry in Philadelphia, which has polarized local wages and holds the city's neighborhoods hostage to corporate out-of-towners. With the collaboration of leaders from the Brown Collective, a local affinity group led by people of color, the fight against police violence and "criminal injustice" became a major focus of the protests, adding a third component to the economic and environmental concerns that had dominated the Seattle and

Washington protests. Protestors spotlighted the case of Thomas Jones, a black Philadelphian who was beaten the week before the convention by twenty-two police officers, and they organized a daylong training in nonviolent civil disobedience specifically for people of color. Sponsored by the Ruckus Society, a California-based group that lends support to environmental and human rights organizers, this was the first training of its kind in the movement. As Cottman said:

> I think that there was a core of activists from Philadelphia who were involved in planning, who were involved in doing teach-ins. Part of the struggle to localize globalization is that too often local community activists who are working on quality of life issues feel, like, too busy to look at the larger picture and so the challenge of this new anti-imperialist movement is to work hard at articulating what globalization means on the local level.

Cottman shares with many of her comrades a nuanced understanding of the relationship of her political work not only to a larger global justice movement, but also to other forms of activism in the city.[8]

Urban Growth Politics: A Common Target

As these examples indicate, the patterns and politics of urban economic development constitute the locus of concern and protest for many activists in the global justice movement. In order to understand why and how urban growth has become the focus of this activist movement, it is necessary to review the recent history of urban political economy, with particular focus on Philadelphia.

Philadelphia is a city that has undergone a post-industrial transformation that differs significantly from that of well-known, oft-studied "global cities" like New York, Miami, Tokyo, Los Angeles and Rio.[9] If Philadelphia ever were a "global" city, it had lost that status by the early nineteenth century, with political power shifting to Washington, DC, and commercial and financial supremacy belonging to New York. Until the early twentieth century, Philadelphia did achieve significant economic success and global integration as a port and nondurable manufacturing center, but this did not give the city world-class status, as industrial development was accompanied by such extreme political cronyism that the city's image remained notoriously backward, provincial, and "privatist."[10]

Deindustrialization and the transition from a manufacturing to a service economy only exacerbated the city's woes and further enforced its backward, second-class reputation. Manufacturing employment never rebounded fully from the effects of the Great Depression, and continued to decline after the Second World War as industry migrated to the suburbs, the southwest and overseas. This decline occurred well in advance of and more thoroughly than in many other Northeastern cities.[11] White flight, encouraged by government-sponsored suburbanization, and the precipitous withdrawal of federal funding for cities eroded Philadelphia's tax base, inducing recurrent fiscal crises throughout the 1980s and early 1990s.[12] The white middle class and its planning-driven urban reform agenda of the 1950s and 1960s were largely destroyed by these developments, and the regimes that cropped up to replace them made dramatic cuts in city services and employment while paradoxically trying to maintain racial and ethnic patronage arrangements. Not surprisingly, this was a rather frustrating and divisive time in Philadelphia's history, replete with racial and ethnic conflict and repression.

In the 1990s, Mayor Edward G. Rendell and the city's corporate elite imposed an economic model of commercialization and privatization designed to redevelop the city as a "growth machine" (Logan and Molotch 1987; see also Ruben 2002). Exploiting its regional advantage as a center for academic research, higher education, and health care (by the 1990s, the University of Pennsylvania, with its giant hospital system, had become the city's largest private employer), the municipal elite consciously sought to transform the city from a decaying postindustrial backwater into a globally integrated regional economic hub, "knowledge center," and world-class conference and hospitality destination. This strategy for postindustrial economic growth was self-consciously framed in terms of the "challenges of globalization" (Peirce and Johnson 1995: 12) for a city such as Philadelphia that is not a haven for international investment. Central to this endeavor has been an attempt to improve the image of the city. A report issued by the Metropolitan Philadelphia Policy Center entitled "Fight (or) Flight: Metropolitan Philadelphia and Its Future," declares, "Philadelphia is not a second-class place. We've got too much going for us. We've got to do better, to grow in the right way" (M.P.P.C. 2001: 6). Growing "the right way" requires better regional governmental coordination, reduced suburban sprawl and redirected infrastructural spending in "existing communities." It also includes reducing the city wage tax to attract residents and businesses back to the urban center. In effect, this plan de-centers the city, valorizing the region as the main protagonist of economic development, and downplaying the role of the city's residents, nearly a third of whom are living close to or below the poverty line, in the reworking of the city's identity.

Given these development priorities, it is no surprise that the selection of Philadelphia to host the Republican National Convention (R.N.C.) in the summer of 2000 represented a significant commercial and symbolic achievement, despite the overwhelming dominance of the Democratic Party in every area of the city's politics. "I guess its fair to say we're no longer a footnote between New York and Washington, D.C.," Rendell declared (quoted in Todt 1998). The non-partisan embrace of the R.N.C. was part of a pragmatic politics of economic development and urban restructuring that Rendell and others had cultivated, signaling that the city had made the difficult and unlikely transition into a world-class destination.

It is in the context of this admixture of economic development policy and urban image enhancement that we may understand global justice activism as urban activism. Pursuing world leaders, political party conventioneers, and trade negotiators around the nation and the globe is not commonly understood as part of the movement to transform the urban landscape. Yet through its strategies and tactics, the global justice movement has pitted itself against the "growth" politics of municipal elites, who see the staging of large meetings such as the R.N.C. (and the W.T.C. meetings in Seattle in 1999) as a cornerstone to their economic development strategy. Indeed, the disruptive actions of global justice protests call into question the image of the city as an orderly, clean, and safe place for tourists and conventioneers. They thus create a representational crisis for cities like Philadelphia that are trying to sell their images to compete in the global economy.

Activist Divergences and Divisions

It was precisely this threat to the city's image—and the strategy for economic "growth" that it indexes—that posed the greatest challenge for global justice activists to form alliances with other constituencies rooted in Philadelphia politics. On the surface, global justice groups and local political constituencies (labor unions, civil rights organizations, neighborhood activists) share a litany of complaints that would make them natural allies in a struggle against "growth" politics and its consequences. For example, neighborhood groups in Philadelphia, as elsewhere, have exerted their own form of pressure on "growth" politics, contesting the discriminatory patterns of investment and disinvestment that have transformed city centers. These new "zones of consumption," to borrow Sharon Zukin's label (1991), are economically and geographically attuned to the needs of developers, professionals, suburbanites and visitors at the expense of poor, working class and nonwhite neighborhoods outside the city center.

Yet the results of coalition-building attempts in the run-up to the convention were mixed, with scattered endorsements from labor leadership, little rank-and-file support, and minimal support—and even some opposition—from civil rights leaders. The reluctance of individuals and groups to support global justice politics indexes deep contradictions in the way residents in poor and working-class areas understand their neighborhoods and their politics in relation to the urban growth agenda. The failure, by and large, of the global justice movement to fully understand the nature and power of these contradictions also made the alliances that did come about rather tenuous and ambivalent, as local organizations perceived themselves as subject to an agenda imposed upon them from "above," as it were.[13]

Despite their many potential affinities, then, global justice activism and the kinds of political action that tend to engage the city's poor and working-class residents did not (and have not) coalesced into a larger movement. The contradictions within which city-based activists operate give them a fundamentally different relationship to the state, and to urban politics in general, than that of global justice activists. The roots of these contradictions lie in the changing dynamics of urban activism in Philadelphia since the 1980s.

Philadelphia has famously been called the "city of neighborhoods," owing to its exceptionally low number of tenement apartments and its correspondingly high proportion of home ownership via small, cheap row houses. From urban renewal in the 1950s to enterprise zones and empowerment zones in the 1980s and 1990s, "slum clearance" and "blight removal" have been the order of the day for neighborhoods outside the downtown business district, while gentrification (and its concomitant displacement of local residents) has been the rule for neighborhoods in the city center. As in other cities across the U.S., a vibrant neighborhoods movement in Philadelphia emerged in the 1960s, in opposition to the mass displacement associated with urban renewal, highway development and gentrification. This movement was linked in many ways to the civil rights movement, and from the beginning focused on issues of racial and class justice.[14]

Since the close of the 1980s, however, new urban conditions have transformed the politics of gentrification and have reconfigured neighborhood alliances within and across lines of race and class. As nationwide recession caused Philadelphia's real estate market to collapse in the late 1980s, developers and speculators delayed their investment plans, choosing instead to land bank properties they had already acquired. At the same time, the rate of property abandonment accelerated as households struggled to survive the consequences of economic recession. With gentrification effectively stalled, the neighborhood movement shifted direction and a new politics of neighborhood stabilization emerged. Whereas the older model opposed the growth coalition associated with urban renewal and was oriented instead around the construction of low-income housing as a source of stability for inner-city neighborhoods, a new pro-growth politics of property ownership has in the 1990s come to define neighborhood stability almost exclusively in terms of the rehabilitation of decayed housing stock by the creation of new, moderate-income housing units.

The politics of neighborhood stabilization has emerged in the context where marketization has become the dominant model of urban redevelopment and revitalization. Akin to privatization, inner-city neighborhoods themselves are now expected to be marketized. This provides a powerful rationale for poor communities to adopt the privatist priorities of capital in their quest to save their neighborhoods from decline. Indeed, poor neighborhoods, once thought of as pathological, isolated and unproductive places, are now being recast in urban policy circles as potentially productive spaces, as investment frontiers that can be integrated into the technological flow of information and investment that is now circulating at a global scale (cf. Porter 1995, 1997). Residents who have watched their neighborhoods decline for decades can now tap into this marketization model as a means of gaining access not only to sparse public resources, services and funding but also to the arena of political deliberation itself.

Accordingly, a new vision of the role of the state has emerged as an aspect of neighborhood stabilization. Residents who have become accustomed to a climate of fiscal austerity, who have been forced to abandon the New Deal/Great Society notion of public expenditure as a means of guaranteeing social welfare and economic growth, and who know that they can expect only a bare minimum of public resources, services and funding now call upon the state to restore some abandoned residences and help with neighborhood clean-up in order to stimulate the housing market and make the neighborhood into a more attractive site for capital investment; they also demand novel forms of policing and other governmental strategies to rid their neighborhoods of low-income renters and homeless people who pose not just a threat to the quality of life of property-owning residents, but also to the creation of that market and, thus, to the neighborhood's prospects for revitalization.[15]

The politics of neighborhood stabilization has brought concrete concessions to neighborhoods across Philadelphia and elsewhere and cannot, therefore, be dismissed merely as an expression of false consciousness—as the misapprehension of resident's material/class interests—as some might be inclined to argue. Rather, concessions such as city-funded trash disposal, the removal of abandoned cars, the fencing off of empty properties, and the removal of abandoned housing yield concrete quality-of-life improvements. Moreover, neighborhood activists tend to exhibit a nuanced understanding of the ways absentee landlords, speculators and other less than salutary but very powerful interest groups have done damage to their neighborhoods. Indeed, the politics of neighborhood stabilization is not pro-gentrification politics. And, despite their disdain for rental properties for low-income residents, activists are often careful to avoid the overt vilification of the poor and homeless as pathological and deviant categories of individuals. Rather, what these activists are interested in is the sanitization of the landscape of its bad qualities, which just happen to include the poor and homeless. Indeed, in the cosmology of neighborhood revitalization, the removal of these groups is the equivalent of the removal of abandoned cars, dilapidated housing and other symptoms of "blight." Not vilified as immoral or pathological *per se*, they are instead seen simply as impediments to growth—they are an expression of the decadent, unproductive built environment and, as such, must be cleared. What we see here encoded in the politics of neighborhood stabilization is, thus, the post-civil rights era redefinition of the boundary between the "deserving" and the "undeserving" poor, which is no longer defined around race alone, but rather in the current conjuncture around market efficiency and productivity as well.

The post-gentrification politics of stabilization goes a long way toward explaining why civic activists in poor neighborhoods may not only feel politically disconnected from global justice activists, but may actually oppose them and, in doing so, may condone and excuse the state repression against the global justice movement. After weeks of pre-convention surveillance and potentially illegal infiltration by undercover police, hundreds of "outside" activists and bystanders were arrested during the convention. Virtually all were held illegally without arraignment until the convention had ended, and were charged with misdemeanors and felonies for crimes legally equivalent to jaywalking. Many were beaten, tormented and denied medical treatment while in custody. Some were held on six and seven-figure bails and paraded before the media as "ringleaders" and "terrorists". One first amendment specialist termed the situation "a civil rights disaster"—an assessment thus far borne out by the fact that after more than 300 trials the city has obtained only a handful of convictions on minor summary offenses and misdemeanors. And yet, grassroots leaders in Philadelphia's poor neighborhoods have not spoken out.

Many civic activists I have interviewed framed their criticism of the anti-R.N.C. protestors in terms of their potential impact on the city's reputation as a tourist/entertainment/convention site. For example, the same resident quoted earlier who so eloquently diagnosed the potential effects of the predations of capital on her neighborhood had this to say about the protestors:

> I was very pleased with how the police handled the situation. It prevented the protestors from getting out of hand and hurting the city. We had a lot at stake in that convention, in showing the world that we are first rate. I'm glad that the police did such a good job. They made Philadelphia look good.

Implicit in this statement are all of the ideological trappings of growth politics. The link is made between the city's images and its economic fortune. Moreover, this statement also legitimates and excuses coercive police practices in the name of preserving the city's image. Indeed, many anti-R.N.C. activists were perplexed by residents' seemingly indifferent responses to widespread police abuses. Many assumed that this indifference can be attributed primarily to bad media coverage of state atrocities. This is certainly true enough. The media did downplay the extent of police brutality, activist profiling and illegal arrests and therefore did much to cultivate public indifference. However, it is also true that for many neighborhood residents, the desire to speak up for the civil rights of the protestors was far less important in the current conjuncture than the need to project an orderly image of Philadelphia to the world. It was thus not that the excessive use of force by the police was unintelligible to many residents. Worse, it is that it was condoned, even encouraged, as a cornerstone of the city's growth strategy. Here we see how coercion meets consent in the construction of neo-liberal political subjects.

There is, of course, no unitary perspective on the boundary between legitimate and illegitimate protest. Residents have complex and sometimes contradictory political viewpoints covering a wide ideological spectrum. Many had fairly conciliatory things to say about the anti-R.N.C. protestors. One example is Bernadette Jackson, an elderly African American woman who has lived in South Philadelphia for all of her life. She is active in ward politics and works part-time for a publicly funded program, housed in a Catholic church, that provides referrals to the elderly. In an interview I conducted with her shortly after the Republican National Convention, she defended the rights of protestors:

> I don't see where it hurt anything . . . this is America; you supposed to have freedom of speech. You know if you want to protest as long as you not out there shooting and, and wrecking other people's property, you know. A peaceful demonstration, I don't see no harm in that. Just like I said, I like all the, uh, [sports] teams. I always pull for them, because I was born and raised here. But I hate to see them win because when they do, they tear up South Philly. They tear up people's cars, innocent people that got stores; they bust windows. And that's no way to celebrate a victory, tearing up other people's property.

This resident is not alone in defining the limits of "legitimate" protest around the issue of property damage, the practice of which is equated here with the antics of out-of-control sports fans. It is important to understand that this resident's value-neutral comparison between protestors and sports fans is a statement of support for the protestors precisely because it is value-neutral. Popular and political rhetoric in Philadelphia tends to vilify protestors while it apologizes for the antisocial practices of the city's notoriously rowdy sports fans. By equating them here, this resident is actually defending the rights of protestors who tend to receive unequal treatment in the press and by local politicians.

However much residents believe in the right to protest, this did not stop many of them, particularly the most civic-minded among them, from viewing the protestors as a threat to the city. This was in part because of the close alliance that locally based civic activists have developed with city bureaucrats. These relations have contributed to the rise of revanchist politics in neighborhoods across the city, and they serve as a major vector for the dissemination of official, hegemonic ideologies down to the grassroots. To demonstrate this point, here is an example of the hegemonic practices through which anti-R.N.C. activists are vilified and dehumanized as dangerous and inauthentic "outsiders" while neighborhood activists are constructed as respectable, legitimate and "local" political subjects.

The Eastern Philadelphia Organizing Project (EPOP) is a vibrant and successful community organization of churches, schools and civic groups from the poor and working-class neighborhoods of north Philadelphia. For several years, EPOP has organized against a range of "quality of life" threats affecting residents in immiserated neighborhoods. It is a non-partisan group whose organizational core is comprised of professional organizers and clergy, a mixed-race, largely middle class group that exerts no small influence on the organization's "working-class" politics. The organization operates outside of formal city patronage routes and across the boundaries of race and faith. A member of the Pacific Institute for Community Organization, a national network of faith based community organizations, it is an example of the kind of Alinsky-style "place"-based community organizing that has flourished in formerly industrialized cities like Philadelphia. In the spring of 2000, the organization spearheaded an anti-"blight" campaign to jumpstart neighborhood revitalization in North Philadelphia. Three months before the Republican Convention, EPOP invited John F. Street, the city's newly elected mayor, to a public meeting to listen to residents' concerns about blight. As the mayor told the large meeting of neighborhood activists prior to the convention:

> We expect 45,000 people to come to this city for the Republican National Convention. They are going to spend $100 million. This is the premier convention in the last 25 years. We've never had that many people before. We have to prepare for a dramatic influx of people. Did anyone see the confusion that took place in Seattle? We are devoted to the idea that everyone should have a constitutional right to free speech and expression, but on the other hand we have to make sure people, most of whom are not from our city, don't tear up our city and the neighborhoods. (John Street address to the Eastern Philadelphia Organizing Project, May 15, 2000)

This is one example of the hegemonic strategies public officials like the mayor use to manage political deliberation and dissent. In this statement, the mayor defines protestors as non-citizens of the city. In the context of this community meeting, what is asserted here is a divide between the respectable civic activists who have met with the mayor to discuss the problem of blight and "outsiders" whose presence in Philadelphia might tarnish the city's image and thereby threaten the city and its neighborhoods' chances for economic growth. We can see in this comment both the "localization" of neighborhood politics and the "de-localization" of the global justice movement.

The ideological implications of this division cannot be overstated. The "othering" of the protestors as outsiders has a long history in U.S. nation-building ideology. In the post-Cold War period, the coherency of the body politic and the American Way, formerly consolidated through constant comparison with the faults and deficiencies of the communist bloc, is now maintained in large measure through the constant invocation of an internal "other"—an unproductive "underclass" that is prone to drugs and crime and that is unwilling or unable to accommodate itself to the flexible labor demands of the new economy. And like the Soviet Union, this internal villain, this dangerous "other" of the market, must be either converted to what Paul Smith (1997) calls a "subject of value" or destroyed. The ideology of private investment and economic growth seeks to accomplish the former. The law-and-order state, with its prison system, brutality, and invocations of safety and community hygiene, seeks to do the latter. For protestors, the logic is the same. They were consistently mocked by the police, politicians and the mainstream media as laggards, lazy, over-privileged kids with no jobs and no productive function in society. Much like the Cold War-era vilification of hippies and the New Left as "bums" (Nixon, April 1970), today's very similar political logic of othering accomplishes the same kind of vilification of activists and protestors, linking them at the ideological level to representations of the pathologized and criminalized urban poor.[16]

The Rise of the New Coalition?

Although the ideological and material imperatives of growth politics go far in explaining why many civic-minded neighborhood residents and activists were disconnected from, or even opposed, the anti-R.N.C. protestors, contradictions implicit in the growth model have nevertheless created the possibility for the emergence of a political alliance across race and class within the movement for global justice. I have already detailed the strategies anti-R.N.C. activists used in conducting outreach to neighborhood groups, and the meager results of their efforts in that regard. It is worth noting, however, that they enjoyed considerably more success organizing those groups that can be glossed as the "undeserving" or "unproductive" poor. In fact, the protestors' message was remarkably well received among those people who have been cast out of "respectable" community life. Anti-R.N.C. organizers successfully recruited recovering addicts from detox programs and recovery houses, black gay teens, young single mothers and even the homeless. These groups, whose connection to the place-based politics of neighborhood activism, the civil rights establishment and unions is precarious at best, tended to express a good deal of political identification with the protestors. An African American woman encountered many protestors at the jailhouse where she waited for over three hours to bail out her daughter, who had been arrested the night before after what her mother described as a violent altercation with an ex-boyfriend near their north Philadelphia home. She expressed enthusiastic support for the protestors:

> You were really tearing it up down there. All right, all right. Made things easier for us up here in North Philly, with all the cops down there. It was almost like a holiday out here.

This view must be differentiated from that of more "respectable" neighborhood activists and others. Indeed, although civic activists were largely appalled by what were described (somewhat inaccurately) in the press as violent acts of property destruction by the protestors, this was not so for many disenfranchised African Americans whose relationship to the police and whose valuations of private property are more ambivalent. Curiously, what we saw forming in Philadelphia was a nascent cross-race, cross-class coalition comprised of anarchists, sectarian leftists, queers, puppeteers, drug users, homeless men and women, the chronically unemployed, and the super-exploited in certain devalued sectors of the informal economy.

I do not wish to exaggerate the political importance of this grouping. There is a wide gulf between strong political identification and alliance on the one hand and the long-term coherence of an effective oppositional political coalition on the other. Yet it is equally important not to trivialize these developments. In the pro-growth environment so adept at channeling race and class resentments into very narrow, oft-times politically disabling directions, the poorest of the poor represent an important—and growing—constituency whose political agency should not be overlooked. This is especially the case given the predilection in popular, political and academic discourse to treat the middle class as the only true and legitimate subjects of contemporary social movements, and to treat inner-city residents—again, the so-called "underclass"—as socially pathological and politically backward and apathetic. The possibility that such residents might seek to struggle for a stake in the urban future is a political reality that both global justice activists and academics need to consider.

Conclusion

This chapter has argued that the alliances and divisions between global justice and other forms of activism are not based on the capacity of activists to make proper political distinctions between the local and the global, but rather on the capacity of different groups to accept or reject growth politics and the neo-liberal development model in the course of their political action. As we have seen, hegemonic practices that manage dissent by dividing activists are embodied in growth politics, legitimating the uneven development affecting U.S. cities and fortifying the race and class divisions within them.

The ethnographic approach I have employed here also deliberately complicates our assessment of race and class relations in the global justice movement. Academics and established progressives in particular need to be more attuned to these complications lest we uncritically reproduce historic splits such as that between the student-led New Left and much of organized labor that occurred during the Vietnam War years. At the level of the grassroots, these divisions were never quite as rigid as conventional wisdom would have us believe. It would be a mistake to give them theoretical and empirical preeminence again now, in the commentaries we construct about emergent mobilizations.

The history of Philadelphia and other U.S. cities also shows that there are alternatives to the politics of neighborhood stabilization, with its punishing implications for the poorest of the poor, even if civic activists are not considering those alternatives currently. Moreover, racial and class injustice remains at the forefront of consciousness for many neighborhood residents, reminding us of the ever-present potential for more radical forms of civic action that directly challenge the power relations and ideological principles of growth politics. The problem, from the vantage point of many of Philadelphia's residents, is the absence of alternative visions and models. This is, of course, exactly what global justice activists are trying to articulate. Since November 1999, many progressive activists and thinkers have become excited at the prospect of a new movement for global justice. The case of Philadelphia makes clear that achieving a real connection with neighborhood-based civic activism and others is an important challenge and opportunity for this emergent movement to become truly global and to pursue a rich, truly inclusive vision of social justice.

Acknowledgments

Earlier versions of this chapter were presented at "Off the Grid: Urban Ethnography and Radical Politics" on the panel "Public Policy, Activism, and Ethnography" at New York University, 31 March 2001 and at the Wenner Gren-funded conference on "Wounded Cities," organized by Jane Schneider, Tarrytown, NY, 20–22 April 2001. I wish to thank Matthew Ruben for his incisive and detailed comments on several drafts of this paper. I am also deeply indebted to Micaela di Leonardo and Stephen Steinberg for suggestions that helped to shape this essay into its current form. I also thank Kathy Walker, Ara Wilson, Molly Doane, Sarah Hill, Hilary Cunningham, Catherine Kingfisher, Jane Schneider and Ida Susser for their helpful comments and editorial suggestions. The research on which this paper was based was conducted with funds from the National Science Foundation as part of a collaborative ethnographic project on grassroots activism in Philadelphia. I wish to thank my collaborators Judith Goode and Susan Hyatt at Temple University.

Notes

1. Mumia Abu-Jamal is an African American journalist and former Black Panther Party member who was sentenced to death row in 1982 for the alleged murder of a Philadelphia police officer. His case has generated considerably controversy, and many anti-death penalty activists view his murder conviction and death row sentence as an unjust consequence of racial bias in Philadelphia's court system. The campaign to free Mumia Abu-Jamal has become an important case of international anti-racist and anti-death penalty organizing. Williams (2001) offers an analysis of the case that side-steps the question of Mumia Abu-Jamal's guilt or innocence and focuses instead on the pattern of racial injustice in the criminal justice system that led to his conviction.
2. On the politics of growth in U.S. cities, see, for example, Eisinger (2000), Logan and Molotch (1987), Harvey (1985, 1989) and Zukin (1991).
3. The local/global split and the distinctions based on race and class that are presumed to correlate with it are apparent in mainstream media coverage of the global justice movement. A *Philadelphia Inquirer* editorial, for example, ponders why the anti-R.N.C. demonstrators received so little sympathy and support from "Philadelphians." The editorial characterizes the protestors as "annoying out-of-towners with a holier-than-thou attitude." Although the city, particularly its black and working-class communities, has been traumatized by the "post-industrial globalization" that the protestors denounce, the editorial continues, Philadelphians "know that a blanket, cynical rejection of government . . . cuts you off from the very entities you need to work the changes needed *on the scale needed*" (Editorial, *Philadelphia Inquirer*, 20 August 2000: D06, emphasis mine). The academic correlate to these categorizations is longstanding as well. In anthropology and other disciplines, ethnographic work has until quite recently

tended to treat poor and working-class neighborhoods in the U.S. as encapsulated worlds, trapped eternally in locality, bounded and isolated from mass mobilizations and other forms of grassroots activism, and from history and wider political economic developments (see, for example, Liebow 1967, 1993; Valentine 1978; Anderson 1991, 2000; but see di Leonardo 1998; Hyatt 1995; Maxwell 1988; Reed 1999; Susser 1996; Williams 1992; Goode and Maskovsky 2001; Maskovsky and Kingfisher 2001 for a critique of these positions).

4. On the diversity, nature and scope of urban activism and community politics, see, for example, Fainsten and Fainstein (1974, 1991); Shepard and Hayduk (2002); Reed (1999) and, of course, Castells (1974).
5. To protect informant identities, all names, with the exception of those of politicians and public figures, are fictitious.
6. For a more thorough discussion of globalization and the politics of place, see Steven Gregory's important article (Gregory 1999).
7. Mainstream media coverage criticized anti-R.N.C. protestors for lacking a coherent message and for engaging in violence and other disruptive tactics that obscured their message. See, for example, "Was Their Message Heard", *Philadelphia Inquirer* (2000b).
8. On a related point, activists have also debated how the "global" itself is constituted and this debate has contributed to a degree of division within the movement, as some demonstrators stayed away from summer 2000 convention protests in Philadelphia and Los Angeles (the site of the Democratic National Convention) because they felt those events offered no explicitly "global" anti-free trade targets. As one activist who did come to Philadelphia said of the absentees: "It's like some people in this movement don't want to go after the U.S. government or something, like they actually think that the I.M.F. makes decisions on its own."
9. Sassen (1991); Castells and Hall (1994); Portes and Stepik (1993); Soja (1996); Mollenkopf and Castells (1991).
10. Philadelphia has a long history of cronyism and corruption. At the onset of the twentieth century, investigative reporter Lincoln Steffens called the city "the worst governed city in the country" (quoted in Abernethy 1982: 539). This reputation persisted well beyond the early decades of the twentieth century. The wave of progressive municipal reform that spread across the US at the turn of the century arrived late to Philadelphia and did not break the hold of private monopoly control of the city's economy or government. Although

Philadelphia experienced a significant industrial boom in the early decades of the twentieth century, political cronyism persisted to such a degree that the city government allowed Philadelphia's docks to decay and its downtown area to be abandoned even as manufacturing flourished and the economy grew. Sam Bass Warner (1968) calls Philadelphia a "privatist" city. He traces an historical pattern of economic growth for Philadelphia that is based on the triumph of private interests over nearly all forms of public accommodation (see also Abernethy 1982; Adams et al., 1991; Goode and Schneider 1994; Hodos 2002).

11. The city's economy was disproportionately weighted toward manufacturing, and within manufacturing toward non-durables like textiles. In the twentieth century, non-durable manufacturing has been much easier to relocate than durable manufacturing due to its relative independence of natural resources and topography (unlike, say, mining) (see Adams et al 1991; Summers and Luce 1995).
12. The GI Bill and other forms of government funding from the 1940s and 1950s was targeted for suburban construction and not for development projects in urban areas. See Jackson 1995 for a national history of suburbanization. See Adams et al. (1991) for the impact of suburbanization on Philadelphia.
13. Space limitations prevent full comparison of neighborhood, labor and civil rights movements, each of which has its own internal dynamics, history of coalition-building and trans-locational collaboration and history of opposition and accommodation with city government and politics. With respect to city politics, the large municipal and building-trade unions depend on the growth agenda for employment of their members. The municipal unions signed a no-strike pledge before the Republican convention, despite the fact that they were in the midst of heated contract negotiations. For their part, the city's civil rights establishment has since the 1980s been tied up in mayoral patronage and therefore has had a major political disincentive to break ranks and join global justice activists. In fact, Jerry Mondesire, leader of the Philadelphia chapter of the N.A.A.C.P., chastised the anti-R.N.C. protestors for being unconcerned with the issues affecting his constituency. His organization scheduled a small march to compete directly with a rally held by global justice protestors. Conversely, civil rights groups such as the Black Radical Congress, with an active chapter in Philadelphia since the 1990s, are an important part of the U.S.-based global justice movement. Black radical Congress members were active in anti-R.N.C. protests and have participated in other

significant global justice activities such as the 2001 Worldwide Conference Against Racism in Durban, South Africa and the World Social Forum at Porto Alegre in 2002. Some union activists involved with the local chapter of the Labor Party and with District 1199c also participated in the protests around the Republican National Convention.

14. A brief history of urban renewal, the redevelopment process, and the neighborhoods movement in Philadelphia can be found in Adams et al. (1991: 100–25); see also Ruben (2000). See Ley (1996) for an interesting discussion of the neighborhoods movements as an aspect of the New Urbanism in Canada.
15. For a more detailed ethnographic account of these dynamics, see Maskovsky (2001).
16. Since 11 September 2002, this ideological offensive has widened, as an even more dangerous and disabling ideological connection is now made between terrorists, protestors, and the urban poor. Indeed, a neo-McCarthyite politics can be seen in the surveillance and incarceration of Muslims, Arabs, Arab-Americans and others who are viewed as terrorist threats to the wounded U.S. nation. These groups join protestors, undocumented workers and the inner city poor, all of whom have been forgotten in the mainstream press in the months following the World Trade Center and Pentagon attacks, but remain objects of state coercion and persecution for their resistance, both active and passive, to free enterprise and U.S.-style capitalism.

References

Abernethy, L.M. (1982), "Progressivism, 1895–1919", in Russell F. Weigley (ed.), *Philadelphia: A 300 Year History*, New York: Norton & Co.

Adams, C.T., Bartelt, D., Elesh, D., Goldstein, I., Kleniewski, N. and Yancey, W. (1991), *Philadelphia: Neighborhoods, Divisions and Conflict in a Post-Industrial City*, Philadelphia PA: Temple University Press.

Alinsky, S.P. (1971), *Rules for Radicals; a Practical Primer for Realistic Radicals*, New York: Random House.

Anderson, E. (1991), *Streetwise: Race, Class and Change in an Urban Community*, Chicago: University of Chicago Press.

—— (1999), *Code of the Street: Decency, Violence and the Moral Life of the Inner City*, New York: Norton, Inc.

Appadurai, A. (1996), *Modernity at Large: Cultural Dimensions of Globalization*, Minneapolis MN: University of Minnesota Press.
—— (2000), "Grassroots Globalization and the Research Imagination", *Public Culture*, 12(1): 1–19.
—— (2002), "Deep Democracy: Urban Governmentality and the Horizon of Politics", *Public Culture* 14(1): 21–47.
Brecher, J., Costello, T. and Smith, B. (2000), *Globalization from Below: The Power of Solidarity*, New York: South End Press.
Castells, M. (1985 [1974]), *The City and the Grassroots*, Berkeley CA: University of California Press.
Castells, M. and Hall, P. (1994), *Technopoles of the World : the Making of 21st-Century Industrial Complexes*, London, New York: Routledge.
Cunningham, H. (2000), "The Ethnography of Transnational Social Activism: Understanding the Global as Local Practice", *American Ethnologist*, 26(3): 583–604.
Dean, M.M. (2000), "Queen of Civil Protest. Cheri Honkala is Untarnished by Convention Violence", in *Philadelphia Daily News*, 9 August: 5.
Eisinger, P. (2000), "The Politics of Bread and Circuses", *Urban Affairs Review*, 35(3): 316–33.
Fainstein, N. and Fainstein, S. (1974), *Urban Political Movements*, Englewood Cliffs NJ: Prentice Hall.
—— (1991), "The Changing Character of Community Politics in New York City: 1968–1988", in Mollenkopf, J. and Castells, M. (eds), *Dual City: Restructuring New York*, New York: Russell Sage Foundation.
Gills, B.K. (ed.) (2000), *Globalization and the Politics of Resistance*, New York: St. Martin's Press.
Goode, J. and Maskovsky, J. (2001), "Introduction", in Goode, J. and Maskovsky, J. (eds), *New Poverty Studies: The Ethnography of Power, Politics and Impoverished People in the United States*, New York: New York University Press.
Goode, J. and Schneider, J. (1994), *Reshaping Ethnic and Racial Communities in Philadelphia*, Philadelphia PA: Temple University Press.
Gregory, S. (1994), "Race, Identity, and Political Activism: The Shifting Contours of the African American Public Sphere", *Public Culture* 7: 147–64.
—— (1999), "Globalization and the 'Place' of Politics in Contemporary Theory: A Commentary", *City and Society, Annual Review*, 47–64.
Harvey, D. (1985), *Consciousness and the Urban Experience: Studies in the History and Theory of Capitalist Urbanization*, Baltimore MD: John Hopkins University Press.

—— (1989), *The Condition of Post-Modernity*, Cambridge MA: Basil Blackwell.

—— (1996), *Justice, Nature and the Geography of Difference*, Cambridge MA: Blackwell Press.

Hotos, J.I. (2002), "Globalization, Regionalism and Urban Restructuring: The Case of Philadelphia", *Urban Affairs Review*, 37(3): 358–79.

Hyatt, S.B. (1995), "Poverty and Difference: Ethnographic Representations of 'Race' and the Crisis of 'The Social'", in Shenk, D. (ed.), *Gender and Race Through Education and Political Activism: The Legacy of Sylvia Forman*, Arlington VA: American Anthropological Association/Association for Feminist Anthropology, pp. 185–206.

Katz, M. (1989), *The Undeserving Poor: From the War on Poverty to the War on Welfare*, New York: Pantheon Books.

Keck, M.E. and Sikkink, K. (1998), *Activists Beyond Borders*, Ithaca: Cornell University Press.

Kromer, J. (2000), *Neighborhood Recovery: Reinvestment Policy for the New Hometown*, New Brunswick NJ: Rutgers University Press.

Jackson, K. (1995), *Crabgrass Frontier: The Suburbanization of the United States*, New York: Oxford University Press.

Liebow, E. (1967), *Tally's Corner: A Study of Negro Streetcorner Men*, Boston: Little, Brown.

—— (1993), *Tell Them Who I Am: The Lives of Homeless Women*, New York: Free Press.

Logan, J.R. and Molotch, H.L. (1987), *Urban Fortunes: the Political Economy of Place*, Berkeley CA: University of California Press.

Maskovsky, J. (2001), "The Other War at Home: The Geopolitics of U.S. Poverty", in Kingfisher, C. and Maskovsky, J. (eds), "Globalization, Neoliberalism and Poverty in Mexico and the United States", *Urban Anthropology and Studies of Cultural Systems and World Economy*, 30(2–3): 215–38.

Maskovsky, J. and Kingfisher, C. (2001), "Introduction: Global Capitalism, Neoliberal Policy and Poverty", *Urban Anthropology*, (special issue) 30(2–3): 105–22.

Maxwell, A. (1988), "The Anthropology of Poverty in Black Communities: A Critique and Systems Alternative", *Urban Anthropology*, 17 (2–3): 171–91.

Marx, K. (1997), "The Eighteenth Brumaire of Louis Bonaparte", in McLallan, D. (ed.), *Karl Marx: Selected Writing*, New York: Oxford University Press, pp. 300–26.

Metropolitan Philadelphia Policy Center (MPPC) (2001), "Fight (or) Flight: Metropolitan Philadelphia and Its Future", report. http://www.metropolicy.org (15 April 2002).

Mollenkopf, J.H. and Castells, M. (eds), (1991), *Dual City: Restructuring New York*, New York: Russell Sage Foundation.

Nederveen Pieterse, J. (1997), "Globalisation and Emancipation: From Local Empowerment to Global Reform", *New Political Economy*, 2(1): 79–92.

Peirce, N.R. and Johnson, C.W. (1995), "Reinventing The Region: The Peirce Report", *Philadelphia Inquirer*, 26 March, H1–H12.

Philadelphia Inquirer (2000a), Unsigned editorial, *Philadelphia Inquirer*, 20 August 2000: D06.

—— (2000b), "Was Their Message Heard", *Philadelphia Inquirer*, 6 August 2000: A1.

Porter, M. (1995), "The Competitive Advantage of the Inner City", *Harvard Business Review*, 73(3): 55–72.

—— (1997), "New Strategies for Inner-City Economic Development", *Economic Development Quarterly*, 11(1): 11–27.

Portes, A. and Stepik, A. (1993), *City on the Edge: the Transformation of Miami*, Berkeley: University of California Press.

Reed, A. (1999), *Stirrings in the Jug*, Minneapolis MN: University of Minnesota Press.

Ruben, M. (2000), "Penn and Inc: Incorporating the University of Pennsylvania", in White, G.D. with Hauck, F.C. (eds), *Campus, Inc.: Corporate Power in the Ivory Tower*, Amherst, NY: Prometheus Books, pp. 190–217.

—— (2001), "Suburbanization and Urban Poverty under Neoliberalism", in Goode, J. and Maskovsky, J. (eds), *New Poverty Studies: The Ethnography of Power, Politics and Impoverished People in the United States*, New York: New York University Press.

Sassen, S. (1991), *The Global City: New York, London, Tokyo*, Princeton NJ: Princeton University Press.

Shepard, B. and Hayduk, R. (eds) (2002), *From ACT UP to the WTO: Urban Protest and Community Building in the Era of Globalization*, London: Verso.

Smith, M.P. (1994), "Can You Imagine?: Transnational Migration and the Globalization of Grassroots Politics", *Social Text*, 39: 15–33.

Smith, N. (1991), *Uneven Development*, Cambridge MA: Basil Blackwell, Inc.

—— (1996), *The New Urban Frontier*, New York: Routledge.

Smith, P. (1997), *Millennial Dreams; Contemporary Culture and Capital*, London: Verso.

Soja, E. (1996), *The City: Los Angeles and Urban Theory at the End of the Twentieth Century*, Berkeley CA: University of California Press.

Summers A. and Luce, T. (1985), *Economic Report on the Philadelphia Metropolitan Region*, Philadelphia: University of Pennsylvania Press.
Susser, I. (1996), "The Construction of Poverty and Homelessness in U.S. Cities", *Annual Review of Anthropology*, Vol. 25: 411–35.
Valentine, B.L. (1978), *Hustling and Other Hard Work: Life Styles in the Ghetto*, New York: The Free Press.
Warner, S.B. (1968), *The Private City: Philadelphia in Three Periods of its Growth*, Philadelphia, PA: Pennsylvania University Press.
Williams, B. (1992), "Poverty Among African Americans in the Urban United States", *Human Organization*, 51: 164–74.
Williams, D.R. (2001), *Executing Justice: An Insider Account of the Case of Mumia Abu-Jamal*, New York: St. Martin's Press.
Zukin, S. (1991), *Landscapes of Power: From Detroit to Disneyland*, Berkeley: University of California Press.

–9–

After Drugs and the "War on Drugs": Reclaiming the Power to Make History in Harlem, New York[1]

Leith Mullings

Throughout much of the twentieth century, Harlem was unquestionably the symbolic capital of black America. Though it has been half a century since Harlem lost its designation as the largest black urban center in terms of its population, for much of the world Harlem remains the quintessential expression of the black cultural experience. However, the significance of Harlem goes beyond the musicians, poets and artists of the Harlem Renaissance. Harlem also anchored a unique political history. It was not only a place to which people of African descent from all over the world were drawn. It was also a space where people made history through political struggle. This chapter will explore some of the processes that constrained Harlem's history-making capacity in the 1980s and 1990s when the community was whipsawed by both a drug "epidemic" and the so-called "war on drugs." Together these episodes are dramatic testimony to the local, national and global forces that came to bear on a predominantly African American New York community. How, we ask, will Harlem continue to sustain a political movement in light of these events? In what ways will it once again make history?

Harlem Past

When I began my most recent phase of research in Harlem in 1994,[2] I was struck by the widespread nostalgia for a "Harlem Past" that came across in interviews. Residents we interviewed spoke movingly of a past characterized by a sense of community. For example, one of our study participants described her childhood in Harlem as follows:

> I knew I was poor . . . I didn't have what like a lot of people had, but I never knew about like being poverty-stricken . . . You know, we lived in a very family oriented-building. Everybody knew everybody. Everybody had each other's key. You know, people used to get robbed later on when drugs got bad, but I never wanted for anything. And I always had some place to go and eat if I was hungry or if I didn't want to eat at my mother's house like I didn't like what was dinner, I could go next door and eat. I used to love going to my cousin's Barbara's house and eat 'cause they use to always have a lot of food.

Many residents continue to feel that Harlem retains an egalitarian spirit of community; indeed, some middle income African Americans have returned for that very reason: ". . . the warm sense of your neighbors. Harlem is like . . . it's a little town. You know the people in a block. They . . . see me everyday I go to work and come home and I feel more comfortable." And yet, most residents we interviewed felt that Harlem had changed for the worse.

Other researchers working in Harlem have also been confronted with this "Tale of Two Cities." Mindy Fullilove et al. (1999: 842) contrast "Harlem Lost" and "Harlem Present" as "the fractured landscape representing the conjunction of the grim present and the deeply mourned past." The feeling of mourning is reflected in the description of their study participants' views of "Harlem Lost":

> They spoke of Harlem with a mixture of pride in what the community once was and sadness for what existed today. In the past, they noted, there was a cohesiveness that created a sense of stability and belonging. One focus group participant explained, "There was moral pride and moral dignity. It was something that moved around to everyone who was living here. It was electric. The network, it was a spiritual network . . ." (Fullilove et al., 1999: 842)

Why such a deep sense of loss? Though people speak of a changing community, inherent in these nostalgic memories is a sense of loss of history, and hence of agency. Perhaps African political theorist Amilcar Cabral's (1973) description of colonialism has something to tell us. He illuminates how the imposition of colonial rule disrupted the organic evolution and institutional integrity of society. As people became disconnected from their past, they left their own history and entered someone else's. While Harlem was not a colony in the traditional sense, it has been subjected to a series of assaults that have devastated its historical agency.

Harlem has historically been a focus of black political activism. Over three generations, major protest movements and personalities have found a base in Harlem. It was in Harlem that in response to the epidemic of lynching following the First World War, Marcus Garvey developed a mass movement for black empowerment and African American liberation that involved as many as two million people at its height. During the Depression years, Unemployment Councils in Harlem demanded jobs and, when marshals evicted renters for failure to pay rent, the Councils organized community residents to move their possessions back into their homes. In 1945 Harlem residents were the first to elect a Communist, Benjamin Davis, to represent them in the City Council. In 1947 William Patterson and Paul Robeson, reflecting the internationalist consciousness of Harlem residents, presented a petition to the United Nations charging the U.S. with genocide against African Americans.

In Harlem, as in other parts of the country, the civil rights movement spawned militant urban protests. In the 1960s and 1970s, Harlem was the home base of Malcolm X and the New York Branch of the Nation of Islam, the Black Panthers, and various other movements. Perhaps, more than any other black community, Harlem has produced a variety of black leaders including David Dinkins, the former mayor of New York City, Charles Rangel, one of the most powerful Democrats in Congress and Carl McCall, New York State Comptroller and recent candidate for governor of the state of New York.

Harlem's social protest movements reflected the broader African American political struggle that has often been in the forefront of the expansion of rights in the U.S., and therefore central to the construction of American democracy. In the 1960s and 1970s, the civil rights movement stimulated reforms for minority rights, women's equality, democratization of immigration laws and health care for the elderly. It quickly gave birth to such radical anti-capitalist movements as the Panthers. The accumulated lived experience of nine generations of African Americans produced a logic of political participation that emphasizes the redistributive state, the public sphere and the responsibility of government to its citizens. Such a perspective is fundamentally at odds with the decline of the welfare state and the rise of neo-liberal ideology, characteristic of the postindustrial, globalized capitalism of today.

In assessing the consequences of neo-liberal, global capitalism for Harlem, two issues are particularly important. First, the core elements of this political-economic system—the movement of jobs overseas, significant cuts in social services, privatization of publicly funded institutions, repeal of agreements with organized labor about benefits and conditions of work and the abandonment of the state's responsibility to assist the truly disadvantaged—have had a significant adverse effect on many Harlem residents. So much so that in analyzing the consequences of globalization for urban areas in the U.S., progressive theorists often depict racialized minorities, and African Americans in particular, as "marginal," their labor having become economically redundant (Sassen 1991, Castells 1996). While this is accurate as far as it goes, marginality as a descriptor misses a significant process involving both black agency and the response to the black liberation struggle.

In particular, analyses of black marginality fail to incorporate the second, and perhaps most important, issue: that the imposition of global transformations requires new measures for establishing and maintaining order and control. African Americans, who have a history of protest against structures of inequality, pose a particular threat. Their dissent has often been criminalized, the boundaries between protest and crime shifting as the occasion demands. As far back as 1680, the Slave Codes of the Commonwealth of Virginia made public assemblies, bearing arms, traveling without a master's permission, or threatening whites, a crime for black slaves. Marc Mauer dates the triumph of the "Tough on Crime" movement to the 1960s and Richard Nixon's 1968 campaign call for "law and order" in the wake of the civil rights movement and urban rebellions protesting the assassination of Martin Luther King, Jr., and to continuing structures of discrimination (Mauer 1999). Gilmore (1998–9), too, argues that contemporary notions of disorder grew out of the "spontaneous and organized activism" of the 1960s and the need to interpret the turmoil as containable crime, rather than dissent.

Harlem's location in upper Manhattan is also important. In the context of globalization, New York City has been described as a world city by virtue of its role as a preeminent financial capital (Sassen 1991). A world city requires world-class order. As New York's fiscal default of 1973–4 began to be resolved through the championing of neo-liberal and finance capitalism, the city became an important testing ground for enforcing a global order "that reduces the power of individuals and peoples to shape their destinies through participation in democratic processes" (Brecher et al. 2000: 2). In the 1960s and 1970s certain forms of dissent were managed through the welfare state. Subsequently there has been a very different response—incarceration. Today there are two million U.S. citizens in prison or jails, more than half of them for non-violent offenses (Ziedenberg and Schiraldi 1999). With 5 per cent of the world's population, the U.S. has 25 per cent of the world's prisoners. It is in this context that we explore the emergence of the prison-industrial complex and its consequences for communities such as Harlem.

Harlem Present

Central Harlem, occupying an area of Manhattan between Central Park and the Harlem River, west of Fifth Avenue, with an eastern border of Morningside, St. Nicholas and Edgecomb Avenues, is a complex, diverse community, populated by residents of all socioeconomic classes (Greenberg 1991, Huggins 1995, Jackson 2001, Johnson 1990 [1930], Mullings and Wali 2001, Taylor 2002). Predominantly African American, it has a significant minority of Latinos and, since the 1980s, a growing number of foreign-born people. Harlem's complexity and heterogeneity stem from a history of settlement and economic change dating from its emergence as an African American community in the 1800s. In the past quarter century Harlem, along with the rest of New York City, has been deeply affected by global economic restructuring reflected in the shift from an industrial economy to an economy based on information and service (Mollenkopf and Castells 1991, Sassen 1991, Smith 1997).

Marked by the financial and economic crisis of the mid-1970s, the shift intensified an already initiated process of disinvestment. Across America, national government investment in cities, their public transportation and infrastructure, social services and housing declined. National and international corporations pulled up stakes to pursue manufacturing on other continents, eliminating tens of thousands of manufacturing jobs and undermining the unionized sector of the labor force. The result was a drop in wages and benefits for workers. From the early 1980s to the mid-1990s, wages stagnated. In the late 1990s, wages rose slightly as a result of high employment, low inflation, and a small increase in the minimum wage. Still, "the income gap between rich and poor remains wide and the ratio of black to white median family incomes (0.56) was as low in 1996 as in 1972" (Conrad and Lindquist 1998: 1). In New York State, the poorest families earned an average of $10,770, down $1,970 from 1988; by 2000, the state had the largest gap between rich and poor in the nation (CBS 2000). This is in part attributable to the types of occupations fostered by the postindustrial economy: a two-tiered structure with high-wages, information-based, highly skilled jobs at one end and low-wage, service sector, part-time and shift-work jobs at the other end. Downsizing by private industry further reduced the pool of jobs available for people with little postsecondary education or with moderate skills—a loss exacerbated by simultaneous cuts in job training programs.

During the 1980s, New York City, although losing 33 per cent of its manufacturing jobs, began to emerge from the economic recession through a boom driven by the growth of the financial sector. Ironically, compared with previous economic booms, this one did not lead to a narrowing of the gap between rich and poor. In fact, the poverty rate increased from 16 per cent of all households in 1950 (when it was below the national average of 22 per cent) to 23.2 per cent in 1989. The number of children living in poverty grew from one in five to two in five (see Susser 1991: 209). Within the city, race and gender intersected with these socioeconomic transformations in new ways. The civil rights and feminist movements of the 1960s and 1970s increased the opportunities available to African Americans and women, leading to a significant expansion of the black middle class overall. For example, nationally, black-owned businesses experienced a 46 per cent growth from 1987 to 1992 (U.S. Census Bureau, 1997b). However, the distribution of occupations of the black middle class is disproportionately concentrated in the public sphere and the social service sector—precisely the areas most affected by government disinvestment. The fastest-growing sector, the financial sector, is still dominated by white men.

The economic changes wrought by the transition to a postindustrial global economy have brought about troubling social and demographic changes in Harlem, at the same time visibly affecting its built environment. Blight spread after 1974 as public investment in housing collapsed, city-owned buildings and parks were abandoned, and fires, often attributable to private landlords, broke out. Not surprisingly, the population fell. Numbering around 160,000 people in 1970, Central Harlem had barely over 97,000 in 1989. Damage to the housing stock meant that many of these people lived under ever more crowded and deteriorating conditions. Meanwhile, job losses were reflected in an official unemployment rate of 15.8 per cent by 1990, twice that of New York City, and twice again as high if we take into account those who dropped out of the labor force and joblessness among teens. Schools, over-crowded and under-funded, hardly counteracted these damaging trends. Meanwhile, male unemployment, as happened in so many other places, contributed to a high rate of women-headed households in poverty, precisely at a time when welfare benefits were being cut (see Mullings 1995, Mullings and Wali 2001, Sullivan 1991, Susser 1991).

In 1989, a narrow majority of voters coalesced across racial lines to elect Democrat David Dinkins, an African American, as mayor of the city. The Dinkins Administration allocated relatively greater resources to improving conditions for poor and low-income New Yorkers. This took the form of some extension of social services (particularly health care) and expansion of entrepreneurial opportunities through awarding set aside contracts to businesses owned by women or people of color. In Harlem, these policies encouraged a mini-revitalization: a small growth in retail and commercial outlets and services, construction of new housing and renovation of abandoned buildings, and moderate growth in social services.

In 1993, Mayor Dinkins was not reelected, and Republican Rudolph Giuliani became mayor of New York on a platform that pledged to cut the city's budget (because of a projected deficit) and to improve the "quality of life." Soon after he took office, Mayor Giuliani decreased the budget for public education by $1 billion, initiated efforts to privatize public hospitals and public housing, and increased the budget for the police force. The Giuliani administration approved a citywide campaign to arrest "petty criminals" (subway turnstile violators, unlicensed street vendors, and others engaged in the informal economy) and street-level drug dealers and encouraged random stop-and-frisk searches of tens of thousands of minorities. Those years marked the beginning of a significant transition in Harlem, characterized on the one hand by renewed neglect on the part of city and state governments and, on the other hand, by an increase in private sector investments in high-end housing and new retail establishments.[3] Economic transformations were accompanied by political interventions, above all aggressive policing, designed to create an environment in which the "global city" could flourish.

Drugs: A War of Pacification?

The decline of economic opportunities and withdrawal of support for social services after the mid-1970s created a context for a rapid growth of the informal sector, including the illegal distribution and sale of drugs. In some instances the sale of illegal substances became an important source of family income. The many abandoned and deteriorated buildings provided an optimal setting for dealers to set up "crack houses"—24-hour centers for crack consumption, sale and distribution. "Open air drug markets" benefited from empty lots.

Initially, the significant drugs were marijuana and heroin. By 1985, however, the crack epidemic, which had begun in Los Angeles, San Diego and Houston, reached New York. The following year, *Newsweek* declared crack "an authentic national crisis," comparable to the civil rights movement (sic), the Vietnam War, and Watergate (cited in Watkins and Fullilove 1999: 39). All of the hard drugs, but especially crack, had devastating local effects, the most pronounced of which was an increase in violence. Harlem, along with other minority communities in New York, became a retailing center where a non-resident clientele—much of it white and middle class—could purchase narcotics. As the conflict for markets took on a dialectic of its own, youth who were not involved with drugs felt increasingly compelled to protect themselves with guns. The deadly effects of the increased presence of firearms contributed to Central Harlem's rising death rate in the late 1980s. For 15 to 24 year olds, the rate climbed by 45 per cent from 1985 to 1988 (Health and Hospitals Corporation 1991). Urban memorials—walls decorated with flowers and the names of young victims—came to dot the Harlem landscape. A neighborhood resident told one of our ethnographers in the mid-1990s that the pink and white wreaths across the street from her apartment commemorated victims "not even a quarter of a century old." The owner of a card shop on 125th Street informed us that the wholesalers had congratulated her on selling more sympathy cards than any other card shop in New York City. In the course of research, one could encounter 14-year-old children planning their own funerals. In a focus group discussion, one resident, describing the consequences of disinvestment in public education, noted that now when young men refer to "survival," which they "talk about more than anything else," they are

> talking about being able to live an everyday life and not being . . . and not be shot at . . . And they don't care about dying. They're not afraid. Because they don't have anything to live for. They don't think that they have anything to live for.

As Harlem became a contested terrain upon which drug wars were fought, there were concerted, although often unsuccessful, community attempts to confront this intrusion. Residents attempted to intervene in a number of ways that included patrolling neighborhoods, blocks and buildings. At one point in the fieldwork we noticed a large banner hung across St. Nicholas Avenue near 155 Street. It read: "Drug dealers and buyers get out—this is a drug watch neighborhood." In one well-organized building, run by a city program, the young people formed a "junior tenant association" to try to keep drugs off the premises. They designed their own community room in the basement and initiated activities to help young people stay in school and avoid drugs.

Yet the residents felt that they were up against overwhelming odds. This essay cannot fully do justice to how and why communities like Harlem were so massively invaded by narcotics trafficking in the 1980s, or the relationship of these communities to the global markets in drugs, arms, hot money and criminal cartels. However Harlem residents had well-developed analyses of the role of forces beyond their community in making Harlem a center for the international traffic in drugs. In comments to ethnographers, for example, residents noted the frequent presence of outsiders with license plates from Connecticut, New Jersey, and other areas, speculating that their mission was to buy illegal drugs. Many residents attributed the proliferation of sale and use of drugs in Harlem to a hostility towards its residents. In the early 1990s, the director of a drug treatment center expressed this view as follows:

> Drugs were placed in the community as a conscious, political decision. The influx of drugs in the 1950s did not do the job so the effort expanded and became more sinister. The government can do anything except solve the drug problem. Drugs are allowed to proliferate in certain communities. A national emergency would be declared if white communities were experiencing what is happening here.

Another resident stated more mildly: "Years ago racism and capitalism allowed drugs to take hold and now it's out of control."

During our research, a nurse practitioner/midwife asserted that for the first time women had been enticed into the use of illegal drugs "by the tobacco companies," which, she noted, had recently begun to target women through advertising. To her there was a direct relationship between the rise of cigarette smoking by women and their use of illegal drugs. Similarly, Geoffrey Canada, director of the Rheedlan Foundation, a youth organization that serves Harlem, discussed his frustration and "horror" upon learning that guns were being specifically marketed to youth by the firearms industry, which reported a campaign to "expand the market beyond white males . . . A niche marketing plan was undertaken similar to that employed by cigarette and alcohol manufacturers" (Canada 1995: 123).[4] Analyses along these lines are not inconsistent with the discovery by several mainstream journalists and researchers that during the Cold War, sectors of the U.S. government formed strategic alliances with drug dealers throughout the world as a way to protect U.S. corporate interests and contain communism (see Cockburn and St. Clair 1998). For several years, the impact of these relationships on inner city populations has been cause for speculation in the African American popular media.

In other words, to many in Harlem, there appeared to be a government orchestrated conspiracy to expand illegal drugs in inner city communities, either through neglect or with the intended consequence of destabilizing social institutions and political struggle. Hence the popularity among some Harlem residents of the 1995 movie, *Panther*, starring Mario Van Peebles.

Set in the San Francisco Bay Area during the late 1960s, the movie sympathetically portrays the rise of the Black Panther Party for Self Defense under the leadership of Huey Newton and Bobby Seale as a response to the harassment of the black community by the police. The movie documents the "neutralization" of the movement through internal struggles, often instigated by the presence of police informants and exacerbated by the sudden overabundance of heroin in the ghettos of Oakland. The influx of illegal drugs is portrayed as organized by the FBI in collaboration with organized crime. The movie was released in Spring, 1995, accompanied by a series of vitriolic attacks by David Horowitz and other conservative and mainstream media, then quickly removed from mass distribution in American movie theaters.

In 1996, some of these issues were aired in a mainstream source. The *San Jose Mercury News* Pulitzer prize-winning investigative reporter, Gary Webb, reported that money had been raised for the illegal U.S.-sponsored Contra war against Nicaragua by the sale of cocaine. Most important to the black community, he implicated the C.I.A. in the importation of powdered cocaine, and in protecting its transport to south central Los Angeles from where it spread to other inner cities in the 1980s (Webb 1996:1). Webb's three-part series was published in August 1996 and also posted on the Internet with supporting evidence. In response to mounting pressure, *The Mercury News* soon published a partial retraction (Ceppos 1997).[5] Major newspapers such as *The New York Times* and *The Los Angeles Times* discounted Webb's account. Subsequently, Webb wrote a book, *Dark Alliance* (1998), detailing his research and the events surrounding the publication of the articles.

Congresswoman Maxine Waters, whose district includes south central Los Angeles, investigated Webb's allegations and held Congressional hearings. In a foreword to *Dark Alliance*, she concludes:

> The time I spent investigating the allegations of the 'Dark Alliance' series led me to the undeniable conclusion that the CIA, DEA, DIA and FBI knew about drug trafficking in South Central Los Angeles. They were either part of the trafficking or turned a blind eye to it, in an effort to fund the Contra war. (Webb 1998: ix–x)

These findings are not contradicted by C.I.A. testimony.[6] In 1999 a class action suit alleging C.I.A. harm to African Americans and others because of narcotics trading was filed in United States District Court in the Central District of California. Redress was sought for both personal injuries (emotional, psychological, economic) and community injuries: "lack of safety, overburdened social services, loss of local businesses and damage to the tax base" (*Warren et al. vs. C.I.A. et al. 1999*. Case number 99-02603. United States District Court in the District of California.)

But if the crack epidemic, which lasted ten years from 1985–1995, had a devastating effect on Harlem, the "cure" has been worse than the disease.

The War on Drugs

> The War on Drugs forseeably and unnecessarily blighted the lives of hundreds of thousands of young disadvantaged black Americans and undermined decades of effort to improve the life chances of members of the urban, black underclass. (Tonry 1995: 82)

There is a strange disconnect between the drug epidemic and the war on drugs. In 1973, when Nelson Rockefeller, the governor of New York State, declared that every illegal drug dealer should be punished with mandatory minimum prison sentences, the prison population in New York State had fallen to its lowest level since 1950 (Schlosser 1998: 6). Later that year the legislature enacted the Rockefeller Drug Laws which imposed a mandatory minimum sentence of 15 years to life for anyone possessing four ounces, or selling two ounces, of an illegal substance. By 1983, the Organized Crime Drug Enforcement Task Force of New York State had slackened its surveillance of traffickers and distribution networks, turning its attention to criminalizing the users (Parenti 1999a: 47). Cocaine had begun to decline. The appearance of crack cocaine two years later, however, and a few celebrity deaths from cocaine overdosing, generated a national panic about drugs, resulting in a nationally announced "war on drugs" and the appointment of a national "drug czar."

The war on drugs has been the single most important cause of increasing the prison population. Whereas New York State opened thirty-three state prisons between 1817 and 1981, between 1982 and 1999, another thirty-eight were constructed. In 1971 the state's prison population was about 12,500; by 1999 it was over 71,000 (City Project 2000: 1). By this time African Americans and Latinos, who comprise 25 per cent of the state population, represented 83 per cent of state prisoners and 94 per cent of all individuals convicted on drug offenses (City Project 2000: 6–7). Nationally, African Americans who are 13 per cent of the U.S. population are approximately half of the 1.2 million state and federal prisoners (Mauer et al. 1999). As Michael Tonry argues,

> . . . the rising levels of black incarceration did not just happen; they were the foreseeable effects of deliberate policies spearheaded by the Reagan and Bush administrations and implemented by many states . . . Blacks in particular are arrested and imprisoned for drug crimes in numbers far out of line with their proportions of the general population, of drug users, and of drug traffickers. (Tonry 1995: 4)

Tonry (1995: 108) further points out that "arrest percentages by race bear no relationship to drug use percentages". Based on Justice Department data, a study by the Sentencing Project found that while African Americans use drugs at approximately the same rate as Euro-Americans and thus constitute only 13 per cent of all monthly drug users, they are 35 per cent of those arrested, 55 per cent of those convicted, and 74 per cent of those incarcerated for drug possession (Mauer 1997). This discriminatory pattern is evident at every level of the criminal justice system (see also Miller 1996). In April 2000, using data compiled by the F.B.I., the Justice Department and six leading foundations issued a study documenting racial discrimination throughout the juvenile justice process. After entering the justice system, among youth who are arrested and charged with a crime, African American youth are six times more likely to be assigned to prison than white youth offenders and for youth charged with drug offenses, African Americans are forty-eight times more likely than white offenders to be sentenced to juvenile prison (Youth Law Center 1999).

Communities such as Harlem have borne the brunt of this phase of the attempt to control public spaces. Goldberg and Evans (2000: 4) refer to the war on drugs as a "preemptive strike . . . What drugs don't damage (in terms of intact communities, the ability to take actions to organize) the war on drugs and mass imprisonment will surely destroy". The focus on users and the failure to provide treatment means that inner-city areas are targeted for sweeps and searches. In New York City, with the zero tolerance campaign instituted by Police Commissioner Bratton under Mayor Giuliani in 1994, "quality of life" offenses such as panhandling, loitering, squeegee operators, graffiti, and prostitution were actively prosecuted. In the 1990s, there was a dramatic decline in crime but many investigators attribute this to a neighborhood policing program first instituted under the Dinkins administration rather than to the police tactics of the Giuliani regime (Mauer 1999: 95).

Most serious were the rising rates of police brutality and police murders. Between 1992 and 1996, the number of citizen complaints filed with the city's Civilian Complaint Review Board rose more than 60 per cent. In

1996 African Americans, who are 29 per cent of New York City's population, filed 53 per cent of the complaints (Mauer 1999: 98). Police actions focused on communities such as Harlem. Between 1993 and 1996, complaints about police brutality in Manhattan north of 59th Street rose 38 per cent, as compared to 8 per cent south of 59th Street (Maurer 1999: 46). The well publicized murder of unarmed immigrant Amadou Diallo was only one of several lethal police actions that year.

Harlem residents did their best to negotiate between the need for protection on the one hand, and skepticism about police intent and corruption and fear of police harassment and brutality, on the other. We attended several meetings of the local police precincts with community members where such concerns were expressed. For example, at one meeting, the residents berated the police for spending time arresting people suspected of petty gambling—playing dice or "the numbers," an underground lottery especially prevalent among older residents. When the police captain defended these types of arrests, one woman commented, "gambling don't kill nobody" and asked why the police are not spending time on more serious crimes. At the same meeting several people complained that the police were arbitrarily detaining and searching people on the streets. The officers defended this as a tactic to find illegal weapons, but community members remained skeptical.

As we carried out research in Harlem we began to note how many of our informants, across socioeconomic strata, were involved in the criminal justice system, either through their own experience or that of a family member, partner or close friend. Several of the workers we interviewed, middle stratum as well as low income, had been imprisoned for narcotics possession (see also Hamid 1992) and were in work release programs or on parole. Some of the women who participated in our longitudinal case studies who had been in stable relationships at the beginning of the study period were visiting their partners and/or the fathers of their children in prison by the time we completed the research.

The effect of this level of incarceration on individuals, families and the local community has been enormous and the full consequences will not become evident for some time. For the incarcerated individuals, the experience is increasingly inhuman. A recent prison innovation known as "special housing units" (S.H.U.), which prisoners generally call "The Box", consists of solitary confinement cells in which inmates are locked down for 23 hours a day for months and years. The two-person units are electronically monitored structures about 14 feet long and 8½ feet wide, with approximately 60 square feet of usable space. All meals are served through a slot in the steel door and all toilet facilities are located in the cell.

Although Amnesty International and U.S. human rights groups have widely condemned S.H.U.s, claiming that such forms of imprisonment constitute torture under international law, several states including New York State have adopted them (Marable 2001). One man from Harlem imprisoned in upstate New York and confined to an S.H.U. wrote in 2001:[7]

> My confinement is "the functional equivalent of a dungeon." There is minimal outside contact and no educational programs, no psychiatric counseling or other opportunities for rehabilitation. As an SHU prisoner, if I complain, or don't follow the rules, I get additional time in The Box. As inmates in SHU we are treated as if we are less than human and our punishment of being kept in SHU for years on end borders on vengeance . . . Once correctional officers put us, mostly blacks and Hispanics, into SHU we are locked away so tightly that we have no voice. "Out of sight, out of mind" is politically attractive they believe.

When ex-prisoners are released, they face serious obstacles in their attempt to find work and to reconstruct relationships. Furthermore, the demands of parole often interfere with the ability to reconstitute a normal life, and parolees return to prison more often for technical violations of parole than for new crimes (Moore 1996: 4; see also Sharff 1998).

The incarceration of large numbers of men affects not only the individuals, but also entire families and communities. One of the starkest features of the war on drugs and the prison-industrial complex is the shortage of what William Julius Wilson (1987) calls "marriageable males"[8] and the increase of women raising children alone. Although not a new phenomenon (see above), by 1999, 57 per cent of households in Central Harlem were headed by women[9] (New York City Housing and Vacancy Survey 1999).

For women raising children alone, the absence of economic support from partners is made even more difficult by both the lack of jobs and the declining redistributive functions of the state. The investment in prisons comes at the cost of disinvestment in programs and institutions directed toward human needs as money is shifted into the corrections budget. In a particularly cynical example of this, New York State governor Mario Cuomo, in 1982, decided to use the Urban Development Corporation, a public agency created in 1968 to build low-income housing, to build prisons. Between 1988 and 1998, New York State decreased its support for public higher education (SUNY and CUNY) by $615 million while in the same period, the Department of Correctional Services received a budget increase of $761 million (Gangi et al. 1998; see also Sullivan and Miller 1999). In the words of Elliot Currie, "We were, in effect, using the prisons to contain a growing social crisis concentrated in the bottom quarter of our population . . . The prison *became* our employment policy, our drug policy, our mental health policy, in the vacuum left by the absence of more constructive efforts" (Currie 1998: 32–3).

Community residents frequently expressed their concerns about the effects of excessive incarceration on children. Ever inventive, prison "widows" told of child-rearing strategies revolving around women-centered networks already familiar to women heads of households. One of the participants in a male focus group, held in May, 1995, remarked:

> . . . these kids are hungry for positive males . . . and they won't come out and say it, but . . . when I was in (a) school, I had four or five guys follow me around . . . they are starving for something . . .

Men also use (male focused) networks to help care for their relatives, partners and children while they are incarcerated. Some of our research participants reported that friends of their incarcerated partner or relative periodically stopped by to give them money.

Perhaps most disturbing are the long-term consequences for children. Human rights lawyer Dorothy Roberts points out that the incarceration of parents places children at risk for foster care, and placement in foster care puts children at risk of being committed to juvenile detention, as evidenced by the higher percentage of children leaving foster care who end up convicted: "the prison system supplies children to the child welfare system when it incarcerates their parents . . . the child welfare system supplies young adults to the prison system when it abandons them after languishing in foster care" (Roberts 2001).

The Prison-Industrial Complex: Beyond Harlem

As we have seen, many Harlem residents, and others, analyze the penetration of their community by narcotics trafficking in terms that direct attention to a wider field of forces, including: racism, economic restructuring, and the attempt to contain movements for social change. In a 1994 *Wall Street Journal* article, Paulette Thomas (1994: A1) compared the prison situation to the military-industrial complex. Angela Davis (1998: 1) has since suggested that the term "prison-industrial complex" is a useful way to "take account of the structural similarities and profitability of business-government linkages in military production and public punishment". Profit, employment and increased political representation for special interests are consequences of these linkages. Private corporations win contracts for building prisons and supplying prison services; they exploit prison labor; stagnant rural communities pursue development strategies through prisons; black and Latino voters are disfranchised as conservative voting blocks are enhanced.

Although still accounting for only 5 per cent of prison beds, increasingly private, for-profit companies build and administer prisons. During the mid-1990s the largest among them, the Corrections Corporation of America, ranked among the top five performing companies on the New York Stock Exchange (Bates 1998: 2) and is now expanding beyond the border of the U.S. to become the largest multinational prison corporation in the world. In addition, private companies, including AT&T, Sprint and M.C.I. contract to supply food and telephone services to inmates—phone services at approximately six times the average long distance rate (Goldberg and Evans 2000). Use of prison labor is not extensive but it is growing. In addition to government agencies, such companies as T.W.A., Chevron, Starbucks, I.B.M., Motorola, Honeywell, Boeing, and Microsoft employ inmates.[10] A March 2002 *New York Times* article reports on the expanding use of state prison inmates by small towns for jobs once held by public employees: "tending cemeteries, cleaning courthouse restrooms, moving furniture, renovating municipal buildings and even running errands for the police" (Kilborn 2002: A1). As a labor force that works for a fraction of the minimum wage, does not demand benefits and cannot organize, prison labor is ideal for maximizing profits or lowering costs. The issue is complicated by the fact that work is often a privilege for prisoners who otherwise lack access to income and the opportunity to leave their prison cells.

But the capacity of prisons to employ local people outweighs the importance of prison labor (see for example, Gardner 1995). One consequence of flexible accumulation, so integral to the current phase of global capitalism, has been the loss of jobs and livelihood in many rural areas of the U.S. In New York State, as traditional industries such as mining, logging, farming and manufacturing have declined, the prison boom has become a source of jobs in construction, vending, and as correctional personnel, as well as a source of tax revenue. Transforming the economy of an entire region (see Schlosser 1998), recently built prisons have been referred to as the "leading rural growth industry" (Goldberg and Evans 2000).[11]

The dialectic of benefit and deficit has a clear racial and political character. In 48 states incarcerated individuals cannot vote; in 10 states (not including New York) ex-felons lose their right to vote after they are released. Currently 13 per cent of black adult males have lost the right to vote and in some states the number is as high as 40 per cent (Fellner and Mauer 1998). Incredibly, for purposes of political representation, prisoners add to the population of the counties where the prisons are located. Between 1973 and 2000, 70 per cent of New York State inmates came from New York City and its suburbs, but of the 29 correctional facilities authorized by Governor Cuomo, 28 were built in upstate districts —largely Republican, white, and conservative. Currently 93 per cent of state penal institutions are located in Republican senate districts. In some cases, it is the addition of the incarcerated to an otherwise declining population that produces the number needed to create a legislative district (Wagner 2002: 6–7) (see City Project, 2000).

Although black and Latino Americans are disproportionately victims of the prison-industrial complex, and clearly some groups have benefitted from the growth of prisons, in the long run, the effects of mass incarceration extend beyond the populations and communities primarily affected. Prison labor can replace workers who are not imprisoned and control and depress their wages. Public money spent on the corrections system is shifted away from social services that have the potential to enhance the lives of all residents. Furthermore, once order is achieved by force rather than consent, the rights of all citizens are curtailed. Warfare metaphors such as "war on crime" and "war on drugs" rationalize abuses and the suspension of rights for those who are demonized as the "enemy." But they also pave the way for the militarization of civil society—the suspension of constitutional safeguards protecting civil liberties and the constitutional rights of all citizens—a rationale clearly reflected in the U.S.A. Patriot Act.

But perhaps the most important issue is the way the prison-industrial complex with its disproportionate incarceration of black and Latino Americans impedes a critical analysis of society. As Reiman notes, society's treatment of crime "nudges middle Americans toward a *conservative* defense of . . . large disparities of wealth, power and opportunity." By funneling discontent toward the poor, it obscures how the middle class is injured by "acts of the affluent," deflecting a "progressive demand for . . . an equitable distribution of wealth and power" (1998: 152). Race, racism and the racialization[12] of crime play a central role, "undermining our ability to create a popular critical discourse to contest" the prison-industrial complex (Davis 1998). Particularly insidious is the racialization of protest, and the blurring of the boundaries between dissent and disorder. It is within this broader context that we broach the question of Harlem's return to making history.

Harlem Found

The war on drugs and the associated growth of the prison-industrial complex has stifled critical discourse in the larger society and dampened the ability of local communities such as Harlem to continue and extend their protest stance. In addition to the disappearance—as a result of addiction, illness, death, murder and incarceration—of untold numbers of young people who are often the vanguard of protest movements, both the drug epidemic and the war on drugs have severely disrupted the social relationships and networks that form the basis of social movements. Throughout the turmoil associated with postindustrial capitalism, the withdrawal of state support for the community, and the intensification of policing, grassroots organizations and movements for empowerment have continued to emerge, but their ability to organize effectively has been seriously weakened. Meanwhile, another, and quite different process, has begun to unfold.

As the economy recovered in the 1990s, through fits and starts, Harlem entered a gentrification process in which the black middle class has played an active, although ambivalent, role (see Smith 1996, Taylor 1997). Today, largely through an "Empowerment Zone" strategy of private-public investment, major concerns such as Chase Bank, Modell's Sporting Goods, Magic Johnson Theatres, Old Navy, HMV Records, The Disney Store, Starbucks, The Body Shop and The Sports Club have set up shop on 125th Street and Harlem has become a major tourist destination. As is true in other areas of the city (for example, the Lower East Side), it is almost as if the way had been paved by the prior devastation and excessive policing which created "landscapes of . . . abandonment" (Soja 1991: 369).

The rapidity with which these changes have occurred evokes another "Tale of two Cities" subtly different from the tale of nostalgia with which this essay began. In September 1994, a three part series appeared on the front page of *The New York Times* describing a block in Central Harlem that coincidentally was one of our field sites. Entitled "Another America," it portrayed the residents of the block as "a world apart" from mainstream America, caught up in the hopelessness, dependency and destitution of "the underclass" (Lee 1994: A1). It is important to note that the residents of the block publicly protested the article, citing egregious inaccuracies and distortions. A year later, *The Times* reported the changes on the same block—including the rehabilitation of seventeen of its thirty-five buildings through privatization—as "extraordinary" (Waldman 2001).

Shortly after this article was published, we returned to the block to locate some of the women who had participated in our research but were told they had moved. While gentrification will benefit some residents, and will perhaps bring about the long-awaited cultural renaissance of "Harlem Lost," it does not replace political mobilization. For although civil rights and political activists may number among the new settlers, displacing working-class and low-income residents might well impede political struggle. At the same time, how extensively working class Harlemites will be displaced lies partly in their ability to reclaim the "Harlem Lost" of grassroots protest. At present, three overlapping levels of activity are worthy of note.

On the level of individual empowerment, there is the rise of what we might term "revitalization movements," a process of cultural and religious change that often, but not always, involves charismatic leaders, whether Christian or Muslim. The participation of Harlem residents in the "Million Marches"—the Million Man March, the Million Woman March, the Million Youth March—reflects this direction, and the role played in it by religious institutions. In Harlem, some of the major Churches have been especially active in social services and real estate development and the faith-based initiatives of the current Bush administration may strengthen this trend. While such strategies may be important for individual recovery and sustenance, they are not likely to effectively address the ravages discussed above.

On the household level, livelihood struggles through personal networks and individual actions are a major form of ensuring survival. People construct and utilize support systems, primarily women-centered, for garnering and redistributing material and social resources. For example, women spend an extraordinary amount of time attempting to retain shelter for themselves and their families. In 1996, I carried out participant observation in Housing Court, located in downtown Manhattan, where many Harlem women represent themselves, confronting the *lawyers* of the landlords who own the buildings in which they reside. Over one-third of the respondents to our survey had taken their landlords to court, and two-thirds of those had represented themselves without the benefit of a lawyer. Among respondents to the survey, 39 per cent participated in tenants' organizations and 33 per cent in block associations. These household level struggles shade into movements for community empowerment as people link individual problems in schools and housing to larger issues of the neglect of education and housing in Harlem.

On a community level, there are actions around specific contradictions or events. With neo-liberalism and the decline of the welfare state, community organizations that once may have taken a more transformative approach have been forced to concern themselves with ensuring survival. There is a myriad of such organizations concerned with housing, health, education and police brutality. Large-scale mobilizations center on specific issues such as individual acts of police brutality, hospital closings and school privatization efforts. Recent demonstrations against gentrification and displacement have drawn hundreds of people.

Although this activity is currently directed at specific events and issues, it contains the seeds for a wider analysis. We might cite the recent protest of the Giuliani administration's attempt to privatize five of the worst-performing public schools in New York by turning over their management to the Edison Project, a private, for-profit company. In each of the five schools, all of which were in minority neighborhoods, the parents voted against this proposal. The most decisive defeat was in Central Harlem where a significant majority of parents courageously resisted what were perhaps their short-term interests in order to preserve their rights as residents and citizens to quality public education; their actions demonstrated recognition of the necessity to restructure democratic options in the face of an ideology of unfettered markets.

While overarching themes around citizens' rights, unifying sites of resistance, and mobilizing networks of interlocking organizations do not yet exist to the extent they were present during the civil rights era, there are important signs that the movements of today may quickly incorporate broader concerns. In the six months between the end of 2000 and Spring of 2001, there were at least three major gatherings in Harlem, attracting hundreds of people to strategize around the slogan: "education not incarceration"—linking the struggle to defend public education with that against mass imprisonment and mandatory sentencing. In addition, the East Coast Critical Resistance Conference held at Columbia University attracted 3,000 young people, many of whom described the prison-industrial complex as their generation's Vietnam War. Since 2001, there have been annual rallies in Albany, the capital of New York State, to protest the draconian Rockefeller drug laws under the slogan, "Drop the Rock", and these have likewise attracted thousands of young people, including hundreds of Harlemites. In August 2001, Harlem residents participated in the U.N. World Conference Against Racism in Durban, South Africa. Speaking with delegates from all over the world, they and others organized workshops, presented petitions, and distributed information underscoring the global impact of the war on drugs and the prison-industrial complex on people of color, urging the U.N. to include these issues in the conference concerns.

As a result of such actions, a critical discussion of the prison-industrial complex has begun. In a recent op-ed for the *New York Times* former New York State senator John Dunne, wrote:

> I regret that as chairman of the State Senate Committee on Crime and Corrections, I was one of the original sponsors of these laws when they were proposed by Gov. Nelson Rockefeller . . . I particularly regret the disproportionate impact the enforcement of these laws has had on minority communities . . . I regret my own lack of foresight three decades ago, but surely there can be no excuse for not understanding the grim consequences of the drug laws now. (Dunne 2002: A35)

Even in the era of globalization, politics are ultimately local. As Cabral (1973) reminds us in *Return to the Source,* by finding a way back, not to the past, but to the future of their *own* history, people reclaim the capacity to make history for themselves. One cannot predict that as Harlem goes, so go the possibilities for successful resistance to global inequality. Nevertheless, Harlem residents are fully aware that they have made history before and expect to do so again.

Notes

1. A slightly expanded version of this analysis appeared in "Losing Ground: Harlem, the War on Drugs and the Prison-Industrial Complex," *Souls: A Critical Journal of Black Politics, Culture and Society* 5(2). I would like to thank Santa Hughes, Andrea Queeley and Beverly Thompson for their research assistance and the editors for their helpful suggestions.
2. The Harlem Birth Right Project, carried out between 1993 and 1996, was directed toward exploring the social context of health and reproduction. Methodological approaches included participation observation, focus groups, longitudinal case studies and a random sample survey. A discussion of the methods can be found in Mullings et al. (2001); the findings on health are reported in Mullings and Wali (2001).
3. This section is adapted from Mullings and Wali (2001).
4. Sullivan and Miller note that despite the "moral panic" over youth violence, the proportion of young people engaged in violence has not

changed. What has changed is the level of serious injury or death, a major cause of which is the possession and use of firearms (1999: 263). See also Reiman (1998: 31–2) for a discussion of the increase in firearms.

5. *The San Jose Mercury News* also transferred Gary Webb from Sacramento to Cupertino, eventually leading to his resignation.
6. In testimony to a Congressional Committee Frederick Hitz, Inspector General of the C.I.A. from 1990–8, reported ". . . during the 1980s, CIA was aware of drug trafficking allegations or information involving one Contra organization, 30 Contra-related individuals, and 21 other individuals supporting the Contra program . . . there were instances when CIA continued contact with Contra-related individuals after becoming aware of drug trafficking information or allegations" (p. 9). In defense of the CIA, he notes that the agency is not legally required "to report narcotics allegations regarding non-employees" (p. 19). "In the end, the objective of unseating the Sandinistas obscured the importance of properly dealing with potentially serious allegations against those with whom the CIA was necessarily working" (p. 19).
7. This letter was received by the Director of the Institute in African American Research at Columbia University who receives three to five such letters a month. For the protection of the prisoner I have removed identifiers.
8. For example among whites, the number of employed men per 100 women has been stable or increasing for every age group. Among nonwhites, on the other hand, the number has been declining since 1960 for every age group, with the sharpest declines among those under twenty-five (Tonry 1995: 6).
9. Of these households, female householders with no other household members comprised 23 per cent; female householders with children under 18 only, 11 per cent; female householders with no children under 18, 11.2 per cent; female householders with other adults and children under 18, 11.8 per cent.
10. See Parenti 1999b and various Internet sources for an expanded list of companies involved in building and administering prisons.
11. In depressed urban areas, prisons can also be a growth industry. According to U.S. Census Bureau County Business Patterns, in 1957 the greater Youngstown, Ohio area employed approximately 60,000 steelworkers. By 1997, it employed 15,000—a decrease of 45,000. As Phinney notes, to revitalize the area in 1997, Youngstown officials turned to the Corrections Corporation of America and today

Youngstown's biggest business is incarceration, with approximately 48,000 prisoners in correctional facilities in and around the city.

12. Omi and Winant define racialization as a historically specific ideological process involving the extension of racial meaning to a previously unracialized category. While crime and punishment have not been unmarked by notions of race, the events of the last decades solidified the relationship between crime and race. Tonry, for example, reminds us that the conscious manipulation of racial imagery and crime has been a national Republican strategy since the presidential campaigns of Richard Nixon. A particularly egregious example was Lee Atwater's conscious manipulation of Willie Horton during the 1988 election. Tonry provides an analysis of the success of this strategy in polarizing the population along racial lines, ensuring a Republican victory and Lee Atwater's deathbed apology (1995: 11).

References

Bates, E. (1998), "Private Prisons," *The Nation*, 5 January, pp. 1–5. http://prop1.org/legal/prisons/980105.htm

Brecher, J., Costello, T. and Smith, B. (2000), *Globalization from Below: The Power of Solidarity*, Boston: South End Press.

Cabral, A. (1973), *Return to the Source*, New York: African Information Service.

Canada, G. (1995), *Fish, Stick, Knife, Gun: A Personal History of Violence in America*, Boston: Beacon Press.

Castells, M. (1996), *The Rise of the Network Society*, Oxford and New York: Blackwell Publishers.

CBS (2000), "Rich Get Richer, Poor Stagnate." CBS Online, 18 January. http://www.cbsnews.com/stories/2000/01/18/national/main150545.shtml

Ceppos, J. (1997), Editorial, *The San Jose Mercury News*, 11 May.

City Project (2000), Following the Dollars: Where New York State Spends Its Prison Moneys, New York: City Project, pp 1–7.

Cockburn, A. and St. Clair, J. (1998), *Whiteout: The CIA, Drugs and the Press*, New York: Verso.

Conrad, C. and Lindquist, M. (1998), "Prosperity and inequality on the rise", *Focus*, 26(4): 1–2. http://www.jointcenter.org/focus/issues/may98.htm

Currie, E. (1998), *Crime and Punishment in America*, New York: Metropolitan Books.

Davis, A. (1998), "Masked Racism: Reflections on the Prison Industrial Complex", *Color Lines* 1(3): 1–5. http://www.tgsrm.org/PrisonIndustrialComplex.html

Dunne, J. (2002), "When will New York correct its mistake?" *The New York Times*, 10 May.

Fellner, J. and Mauer, M. (1998), Losing the Vote: The Impact of Felony Disenfranchisement Laws in the United States, Human Rights Watch Publications, October. http//www.hrw.org/reports98/vote.html

Fullilove, M., Green, L. and Fullilove, R. (1999), "Building Momentum: An Ethnographic Study of Inner-City Redevelopment", *American Journal of Public Health*, 89(6): 840–4.

Gangi, R., Schiraldi, V. and Ziedenberg, J. (1998), *New York State of Mind? Higher Education vs. Prison Funding in the Empire State, 1988–1998*, Washington DC: The Justice Policy Institute.

Gardner, G. (1995), "Prisons and Capitalism: The New York State Prison Experience", in Sbarbaro, E.P. and Keller, R.L. (eds), *Prison Crisis: Critical Readings*, New York: Harrow & Heston, pp. 16–33.

Gilmore, R.W. (1998–99), "Globalization and US Prison Growth: From Military Keynesianism to post-Keynesian Militarism", *Race & Class*, 40: 171–88.

Goldberg, E., and Evans, L. (2000), *The Prison Industrial Complex and the Global Economy*, Berkeley: The Prison Activist Resource Center.

Greenberg, C.L. (1991), *Or Does It Explode? Black Harlem in the Great Depression*, New York: Oxford University Press.

Hamid, A. (1992), "Drug Patterns of Opportunity in the Inner City: the Case of Middle Aged, Middle Income Cocaine Smokers", in Harrell, A.V. and Peterson, G.E. (eds), *Drugs, Crime, and Social Isolation,* Washington DC: Urban Institute Press.

Health and Hospitals Corporation (1991), A Summary Examination of Excess Mortality in Central Harlem and New York City, New York: Office of Strategic Planning.

Hitz, F.P. (1998), "Synopsis", CIA Inspector General's Investigation of Alleged Ties Between CIA, the Contras and Drug Trafficking. Unpublished paper. The entire two-volume report is available at www.cia.gov.

Huggins, N.I. (1995), *Voices from the Harlem Renaissance*, New York: Oxford University Press.

Jackson, J. (2001), *Harlem World: Doing Race and Class in Contemporary Black America*, Chicago: University of Chicago Press.

Johnson, J.W. (1990 [1930]), *Black Manhattan*, New York: De Capo Press.

Kilborn, P.T. (2002), "Towns with Odd Jobs Galore Turn to Inmates", *The New York Times*, 27 March.

Lee, F. (1994), "Another America", *The New York Times*, 8 September, A1.

Marable, M. (2001), "Structural Racism and American Democracy", *Souls: A Critical Journal of Black Politics, Culture and Society* 3(1): 6–24.

Mauer, M. (1997), *Intended and Unintended Consequences: State Racial Disparities in Imprisonment*, Washington DC: The Sentencing Project. www.sentenceproject.org.

Mauer, M. (1999), *Race to Incarcerate*, New York: The New Press.

Mauer, M., Potler, C. and Wolf, R. (1999), *Gender and Justice: Women, Drugs, and Sentencing Policy (#9042)*, Washington DC: The Sentencing Project.

Miller, J.G. (1996), *Search and Destroy: African-American Males in the Criminal Justice System*, Cambridge: Cambridge University Press.

Mollenkopf, J.H. and Castells, M. (eds) (1991), *Dual City: Restructuring New York*, New York: Russell Sage Foundation.

Moore, J. (1996), "Bearing the Burden: How Incarceration Weakens Inner-City Communities," *1996 Oklahoma Criminal Justice Research Consortium Journal* volume 5. http://www.doc.state.ok.us/DOCS/OCJRC/Ocjrc96/Ocjrc43.htm.

Mullings, L. (1995), "Households Headed by Women: The Politics of Race, Class and Gender", in Ginsburg, F. and Rapp, R. (eds), *Conceiving the New World Order: The Global Politics of Reproduction*, Berkeley and Los Angeles: University of California Press, pp. 122–40.

Mullings, L. and Wali, A. (2001), *Stress and Resilience: The Social Context of Reproduction in Central Harlem*, New York: Kluwer Academic/Plenum Publishers.

Mullings, L., Wali, A., McLean, D., Mitchell, J., Prince, S., Thomas, D. and Tovar, P. (2001), "Qualitative Methodologies and Community Participation in Examining Reproductive Experiences: The Harlem BirthRight Project", *Maternal and Child Health Journal* 5(2): 85–93.

New York City Housing and Vacancy Survey (1999), Central Harlem: Selected Characteristics by Year, New York City: www.census.gov/hhes/www/nychvs.html

Omi, M., and Howard W. (1995), *Racial Formation in the United States: From the 1960s to the 1980s*, New York: Routledge & Kegan Paul.

Parenti, C. (1999a), *Lockdown America: Police and Prisons in the Age of Crisis*, New York: Verso.

—— (1999b), The Prison Industrial Complex: Crisis and Control, *Corporate Watch: The Watchdog on the Web*. http://www.corpwatch.org/feature/prisons/c-parenti.html

Phinney, D. (1998), Prisons Brought Jobs and Murder to Youngstown, ABCNEWS.com. http://abcnews.go.com/sections/us/prison/prison_youngstown.html

Reiman, J. (1998), *The Rich Get Richer and the Poor Get Prison: Ideology, Class, and Criminal Justice*, Boston: Allyn & Bacon.

Roberts, D.E. (2001), "Criminal Justice and Black Families: The Collateral Damage of Over-Enforcement", *UC Davis Law Review*, 34 (929): 1005–28.

Sassen, S. (1991), *The Global City: New York, London, Tokyo*, Princeton, NJ: Princeton University Press.

Schlosser, E. (1998), "The Prison Industrial Complex", *Atlantic Monthly*, December.

Sharff, J. (1998), *King Kong on Fourth Street*, Boulder, CO: Westview Press.

Smith, N. (1997), *The New Urban Frontier: Gentrification and the Revanchist City*, New York: Routledge.

Soja, E. (1991), "Poles Apart: Urban Restructuring in New York and Los Angeles", in Mollenkopf, J.H. and Castells, M. (eds), *Dual City: Restructuring New York*, New York: Russell Sage Foundation, pp. 359–97.

Sullivan, M.L. (1991), "Crime and the Social Fabric", in Mollenkopf, J.H. and Castells, M. (eds), *Dual City: Restructuring New York*, New York: Russell Sage Foundation, pp. 225–45.

Sullivan, M.L. and Miller, B. (1999), "Adolescent Violence, State Processes, and the Local Context of Moral Panic", in Heyman, J.McC. (ed.), *States and Illegal Practices*, Oxford: Berg Publishers, pp. 261–83.

Susser, I. (1991), "The Separation of Mothers and Children", in Mollenkopf, J.H. and Castells, M. (eds), *Dual City: Restructuring New York*, New York: Russell Sage Foundation, pp. 207–25.

Taylor, M. (1994), "Gentrification in Harlem: Community, Culture and the Urban Redevelopment of the Black Ghetto", in Dennis, R. (ed.), *Research in Race and Ethnic Relations*, Greenwich: JAI Press.

—— (2002), *Harlem: Between Heaven and Hell*, Minneapolis: University of Minnesota Press.

Thomas, P. (1994), "Making Crime Pay: the Cold War of the '90s", *Wall Street Journal*, 12 May: A1.

Tonry, M. (1995), *Malign Neglect: Race, Crime, and Punishment in America*, New York: Oxford University Press.

U.S. Census Bureau (1957), County Business Patterns, 1–4, Washington DC: Office of Domestic Commerce.

—— (1997a), County Buisness Patterns, 36–41, Washington DC: Office of Domestic Commerce.
—— (1997b), Surveys of Minority– and Women–Owned Business Enterprises. http://www.census.gov/csd/mwb/Minorityp.html.
Wagner, P. (2002), "Importing Constituents: Prisoners and Political Clout in New York", *Prison Policy Initiative Report*, 22 April: 1–16. http://www.prisonpolicy.org/importing/importing/shtml.
Waldman, A. (2001), "Beneath Harlem Block's New Surface, a Dark Undertow", *The New York Times*, 19 February.
—— (2001), "On a Harlem Block, Lines That Divide and Ties That Bind", *The New York Times*, 21 February.
Waters, M. (1998), "Foreword", Webb, G., *Dark Alliance: The CIA, the Contras, and the Crack Cocaine Explosion*, New York: Seven Stories Press.
Watkins, B. and Fullilove, M. (1999), "Crack Cocaine and Harlem's Health", *Souls: A Critical Journal of Black Politics, Culture, and Society*, 1(1): 36–48.
Webb, G. (1996), "'Crack' Plague's Roots Are in Nicaraguan War", *San Jose Mercury News*, 18–20 August.
—— (1998), *Dark Alliance: The CIA, the Contras, and the Crack Cocaine Explosion*, New York: Seven Stories Press.
Wilson, W.J. (1987), *The Truly Disadvantaged: The Inner City, the Underclass, and Public Policy*, Chicago: University of Chicago Press.
Youth Law Center (1999), "And Justice For Some", in *Building Blocks for Youth*, Washington DC: www.buildingblocksforyouth.org/justice forsome
Ziedenberg, J. and Schiraldi, V. (1999), *The Punishing Decade: Prison and Jail Estimates at the Millennium*, Washington DC: The Justice Policy Institute.

Part III
Rapid, Inconsistent Expansion

–10–

Bangkok, The Bubble City

Ara Wilson

In July 1997, a sudden crisis in the banking industry in Bangkok ended three decades of boom for the national economy of Thailand. The crash quickly reverberated among the finance institutions in Kuala Lumpur, Singapore, Jakarta, Seoul, and Tokyo, producing what has became known as the "Asian economic crisis." Worldwide, the swift decline from Asian miracle to economic bust has become an exemplar of the risks of rapid global financial flows and "bubble" economies. Within Thailand, one of the common analogies applied to the crisis was a centuries-old invasion of the previous capital of Siam: not since the 1767 sacking of Ayutthya, the refrain went, has Thailand been so ravaged by outside forces. The parallel between foreign invasions of old and new capitals points to an urban quality of the economic crisis.[1] The crisis not only originated in financial institutions located in Bangkok, but significantly, in the spectacular development of the city itself, an urbanity not incidental to the particular vulnerabilities of the booming economy. In turn, the banking crisis and the remedies directed by the International Monetary Fund (I.M.F.) transformed the infrastructure and identity of the city, while the Thai government's response to the recession, including an "Amazing Thailand" campaign, reframed the economic downturn in national, and nationalist, terms.

In this chapter I outline the urban dimensions of the 1997 economic crisis. During the "boom era" (*yuk boom*), I conducted research on modern commercial venues, including the shopping malls, telecommunications, and sex establishments that became hallmarks of the new social worlds of Bangkok, and I draw on this research to sketch the long-standing mercantile character of the city and the emergence of its speculative "bubble" economy. My observations of the crisis and its aftermath derive from visits to Bangkok in 1998 and 2000, as well as from non-governmental organization (N.G.O.) reports, news media, and academic publications.

The Non-colonial City

The capital city foreigners call Bangkok was founded in 1782 and is officially named Krungthepmahanakorn, Krungthep for short.[2] In addition to being the political seat of an evolving nation-state, Krungthep (read grungtehp) existed as an important port city, a crossroads for international trade and regional migrations in a context of Western, and later Japanese, imperialist influences. The Kingdom of Thailand, which was known as Siam until after the Second World War, was never colonized by Europe. This non-colonial history shaped the evolution of the powerful capital city as a commercial city and the dominant locus of the nation.

Politically, the absence of European colonialism allowed the concentration of domestic power. For more than two centuries, the Chakri dynasty retained formal authority over the country from its seat in Bangkok. During the period of high colonialism in Asia, when British, Dutch, and French empires were remaking the port cities and terraced farms of neighboring Southeast Asian territories, Siamese rulers expanded, centralized, and modernized their governance over the country, in order to resist European colonization and consolidate power. Bangkok codified its control over northern kingdoms and hill-tribe peoples, Lao communities in the northeast, and Malays in the south. The nineteenth and twentieth century political regimes (by the 1920s a constitutional monarchy) established Bangkok's hegemony over the evolving Thai nation state (Thongchai 1994). Bangkok defined its customs, language, Buddhism, and cuisine as Thailand's national culture (with regional variations acknowledged for local texture), and envisioned its own urban modernity as the country's future. Thus, the definition of the nation-state, and the spaces of nationalism, centered on the city.[3]

The capital's power was economically predicated on the expanding farmland and shrinking forests of the countryside. The absence of colonial rule in Siam meant that family farms were not converted to landlord's plantations (except in the areas close to Bangkok). Commoner men, women, and children farmed rice on small plots (with women performing about half of the backbreaking work of wet-rice agriculture). As more rice was exported, families settled frontier areas and spent more time cultivating the cash crop than weaving, tool-making, or gathering forest goods—that is, they grew more rice by intensifying, rather than drastically reorganizing or rationalizing, their labor (Ingram 1954, Lysa 1984, Pasuk and Chris 1998). Until the recent industrial boom, the majority of the population lived on such small farms.

Whereas colonial systems radically reformulated local societies and identities elsewhere in Asia, in Siam, the market economy played a major role in cultural change. International trade, not colonialism, provided the key avenue for outside influence on Bangkok and the general population. For nearly two centuries, the economic basis for Siam, later Thailand, surrounded export trade of rice (as well as rubber, teak, and forest produce).[4] Into the twentieth century, international and interregional commerce was allocated to foreign men. Bangkok was a multicultural commercial city, comprised mostly of male immigrants organized into shifting enclaves of Chinese, Indian, Vietnamese, European, and Muslim communities,[5] with the majority coming from the 1800s–1949 diaspora from the southern coast of China. Merchant families from Chinese or Sino-Thai communities formed the powerful business class in the nineteenth and twentieth century. While Siamese men were tied to agricultural and corvee labor, Siamese women were present in Bangkok in significant numbers, often partnering with Chinese men, and running businesses of their own. Chinese and Siamese women owned property and were landlords in nineteenth century Bangkok (Wilson 1989).

The Sino-Thai commercial world, particularly after the Second World War, underwrote the modernization and growth of the economy into the 1990s. Key diasporic family businesses in rice, manufacturing, and retail from the 1940s and 1950s grew into Thailand's major banks and corporations, the architects behind Bangkok's post-1960s economic boom (Pasuk and Chris 1992: 10–27; Wilson fc). Examples include the Bulakun family (Mah Boon Krong company), which went from agribusiness to real estate holdings, including the major shopping mall, M.B.K.; the Chiaravanont family's Charoen Pokphand (C.P.), which grew from selling seed and fertilizer, chickens and eggs into an enormous and diverse regional conglomerate (and was implicated in the Clinton-era "donorgate" scandal concerning political donations from Asians); and the Chirativat family's Central Group, which began as a dry goods store to become the largest department store chain and a major manufacturer and real estate developer (Wilson fc: chapter one).

The built environment of the capital city displays multiple influences from Asia and Europe and reflects the city's economic characteristics as well as the political visions of its rulers. If the royal palace was predicated on ancient cosmologies derived from India (O'Connor 1978), the city itself was shaped by the rice trade and the businesses surrounding it. Important nodes of activity were clustered as much around docks and markets as around Buddhist temples. The port city of Bangkok did not develop according to European or American visions of urban planning, although it incorporated Western styles of architecture and public monuments.[6] Instead it evolved in a haphazard way, along canals and lanes, following traffic and trade rather than any clear governing plan. The city's later simultaneous sprawl and congestion were forged by this history. In later years, the infrastructure would prove inadequate for the dramatic increase in road traffic that accompanied the economic boom.

The centrality of Bangkok in the nation, established during the modernizing years in the era of European colonialism, continued into the twentieth century. Bangkok exemplifies the geographic rubric of the "primate city," which refers to a city at least ten times larger than the next most sizable urban area (in this case, Chiang Mai or the combined southern cities of Haat Yai-Songkla). Krungthep is the only large city in Thailand, and serves as the hub for every major institution in the country, including government, education, and religion. Progressive writers and activists have demonstrated how, for a century or more, government programs for development, modernization, and centralization have continually and consistently favored the capital over and at the expense of the provinces (for example, Pasuk 1998). Nationalist efforts to modernize and develop Thailand solidified the central place of the city in the identity of the nation and its subjects.

The Speculative City

Thailand's economy grew from the 1960s on, through a mixture of investments in manufacturing, services, and retail based in Bangkok; by the late 1980s through 1996, it was booming, at the highest rate of growth in the world. Modernization and development followed along urban, industrial, and free-market capitalist lines. Development did not mean redirecting the distribution of wealth to poorer classes or rural areas; rather the city, and its pivotal relation to the nation, enabled specific economic practices and institutions that fueled accumulation from industrial and speculative investment.

Initially, Thailand's economic growth was spurred by the U.S. presence during the Indochina wars. U.S. aid paid for roads and electricity in the countryside, shoring up the military's control over the government, media, nation, and its borders. The U.S. presence also introduced the go-go bar and produced a sex industry oriented to foreigners. It established a flow of young women from the countryside to Bangkok, in numbers that at times exceeded those of male migrants (Pasuk 1982, Truong 1990, Van Esterik 2000). All of these developments paved the way for the enormous tourist industry that took off in the 1980s, significantly enhanced by the sex trade for Western and East Asian men found in Bangkok, at the U.S. military retreat for rest and relaxation Pattaya, and other tourist sites. By the 1980s, tourism was responsible for bringing more foreign currency into the country than rice exports or manufacturing (Pasuk 1982). Tourism transformed numerous neighborhoods of Bangkok: the sleepy quarter of Banglamphu became a backpacker haven, neglected stretches of the river sprouted high-rise hotels, while new strips of go-go bars and sexually-transmitted-disease clinics appeased in several business districts. Tourism also informed Thailand's national identity, and helped Bangkok residents and Thai citizens become versed in a foreigner-oriented image of their society. The major profits from the tourist boom went to Bangkok-based Sino-Thai real estate developers (including members connected to Mah Boon Krong and Central Department Store) and foreign or multinational companies in the hospitality industry, like Sheraton Hotels.

The core of the modernizing economy was new modes of manufacturing.[7] In the 1970s, the government promoted export-oriented production in the by now famous formula of light assembly, typically in small and medium firms employing large numbers of young women workers (Nash and Fernandez-Kelly 1983). Migrants from the countryside made textiles, electronics, leather items, wood products, canned foods, jewelry, and other light goods. Often based in small shops in the greater Bangkok area, this manufacturing was key to capital accumulation and the development of the finance industry in Thailand. In a matter of fifteen years, the motor of the Thai economy shifted from agricultural exports to manufactured goods (made in or around Bangkok) (Pasuk and Chris 1998), finance and services, and tourism.

A favorite of the U.S., Thailand was well poised for an economic "take-off", which nonetheless was some decades coming. In the 1960s, a Thai economist with the U.S. Agency for International Development (US AID) wrote, "[s]ince Thailand, classified as having a non-colonial heritage, is committed to a free-enterprise system, and continues to be pro-Western, it has created an investment climate suitable for attracting private foreign industrial growth" (Trirat 1965: 53). Yet foreign investment remained limited until the late 1980s. Greater Bangkok's industrial boom was funded most of all by domestic capital—a combination of the cumulative bank savings of Thais (who saved at high rates until the height of the boom) and Sino-Thai business capital. Businesses like Central Department Store and C.P., begun as small-scale trading concerns in the earlier part of the century and still largely under Sino-Thai family control, ventured into manufacturing goods for stores in Thailand and for export.

Foreign investments did exist, particularly from within Asia.[8] Capital flows from Japan, invested simultaneously in industrial manufacturing and corporate retail (Nakagawa 1987), increased tenfold between 1985 and 1990 (Pasuk and Chris 1998: 3). Yet until the 1990s, domestic capital was the real source of the investment boom. Such local investments were rooted in ethnic and kin networks that linked banks and corporations and allowed companies easy access to cheap loans.

Thailand's economic miracle was grounded in and focused on Bangkok. As the feminist economist Pasuk Phongpaichit and coauthor Chris Baker (1998: 6) conclude, "the single outstanding theme of social change in the boom decade was the rise of the city". The "rise of the city" refers to literal spatial and demographic growth, and also to the increasing symbolic, political, and economic power of the city over the nation. From the 1960s to the 1970s, Bangkok's urban territory doubled, moving eastward in particular, along roads formed over paved-in canals. The "primacy" of the city in relation to other cities only increased as its disproportionate economic role increased: to make real money, one had to go to Bangkok. This primacy drew ever more migrants from the declining towns and farms of the provinces to work as taxi drivers, exotic dancers, factory workers and domestic help.

Between the 1960s and the 1990s, Bangkok's population increased rapidly, from close to two million to close to six million.[9] Most of the laborers in manufacturing and services were young migrants from the northeast or north. Urban economic development relied on their rural farming families to provide this migrant labor, reabsorb unemployed workers, and feed the city population. The combined patterns of male and female migration left farming communities with few young adults except during harvest time, and linked their households to metropolitan culture, consumption, and capital (see, for example, Mills 1999).

In the 1960s, in response to the growing population, and the potential for unrest among the urban poor, the government launched a widely heralded program of population control (Knodel 1987, Sternstein 1982). This effort dovetailed with public-health surveillance of the workers in the sex industry (through which the government regulated a trade that was, until 1996, officially illegal). In general, the government took steps to contain the messier manifestations of development, like the sprawling informal economy, urban population growth, and the sex trade: the ministry of public health regulated both market vendors and sex workers. These efforts aimed to inspire the confidence of international observers (including the representatives of multinational corporations, multilateral organizations, and First World governments) and to fulfill elite and official visions of urban modernity.

The primacy of Bangkok, forged by a century of policies and attitudes, generated challenges to elite visions for and control over the growing city (Korff 1990, Sternstein 1982). State agencies and various experts proposed decentralizing institutions concentrated in Bangkok. Not only were the pollutants and noises of factories unwanted in an increasingly front-office city, but also the swelling ranks of rural migrants. A host of incentives, regulations, and policies pushed factories to the periphery of the city, or preferably to new industrial estates located at some distance along the eastern and southern highways, thereby redirecting migrant flows away from Bangkok proper. At the same time, official agencies attempted to change the look of the city by relocating or dismantling long-standing markets and explicitly favoring corporate structures over old-fashioned shophouses.

The "rise of the city" manifested itself in the rapid transformation of urban space and city life. The real estate industry emerged as a major sector in the boom economy, as a significant form of investment and collateral for Sino-Thai firms like M.B.K. and C.P. as well as international concerns like Richard Ellis. The flow of capital, and boom-time profits, inspired a flurry of building. Retail, tourism, and services defined the architecture, infrastructure, and flavor of the city more than manufacturing itself did. A proliferation of office buildings, shopping malls, and high-rise apartment buildings—but not public parks or low-cost housing—remade central Bangkok. The frontiers of urbanization were gated housing estates, mega-shopping-complexes, and modern-styled shophouses at the outskirts of the city. The national bird of Thailand, the joke went, was the crane (Jacques 1999: 89).

Real estate and retail economies fashioned a city oriented around cosmopolitan consumption. No longer comprised of ethnic enclaves or distinct quarters (except for "Chinatown," the slums of the port, and an old Muslim neighborhood mostly known for refusing to make way for the expressway), the commercial character of the old port city only intensified. In post-1960s urban sprawl, malls and department stores provide major landmarks. Their names are listed on the sides of buses as sites demarcating the non-linear routes. The name of Siam Square, for example, refers to a major shopping area associated with middle-class youth (including the M.B.K. mall) and provides a shorthand for one of Bangkok's central business and shopping districts. Throughout the 1990s, a software business predicated more or less on bootlegged copies flourished, clustered particularly in the Pantip Plaza (which also specialized in the growing trade in potent Buddhist amulets) and gradually taking over more and more space in shopping complexes.

Without question manufacturing, retail, and finance capital underwrote a burgeoning consumer culture in Bangkok. Beginning with Thai and foreign elites and the Sino-Thai business class, corporate retail expanded across the income spectrum to attract lower middle-class and wage-earning families into the city's consumer orbit. At the same time, concrete shop-houses, local markets and street vendors selling to poor residents and rural migrants proliferated as well (for example, Napat 1986), keeping government regulators busy, and eliciting critical disdain from the elite arbiters of Bangkok's modernization. Broadcast nationwide over the increasing number of radios, television sets, videos, and satellite dishes, portrayals of urban consumer culture only increased the power of Bangkok in the national imagination. The emerging cultural matrix it produced was characterized by national confidence and cosmopolitan aspirations, including revamped "prosperity religions" that drew on Indian, Chinese, new-age and ascetic Buddhist traditions for a new middle-class spirituality that aimed for material well-being in this incarnation (Jackson 1999).

By the 1990s, when the Thai economy had established itself as the most lucrative emergent market worldwide, the country was compelled to open up to more international investments. Foreign capital rushed in, not so much as direct investment in business as through rapidly moving financial circuits (for example, portfolio funds). Whether from the Eurodollar market or Japanese and U.S. sources, this influx made inexpensive money available to local corporations. The result was hyper-investment, a speculative bubble of short-term loans whose worth far outstripped the likely promise of profits. In 1996, the value of short-term capital investments equaled 8 per cent of Thailand's gross domestic product, while the cumulative debt owed to international lenders amounted to half of the G.D.P. (Jacque 1999: 89). Fueled by easy capital, and invisibly subsidized by inexpensive rice farming, the manufacturing boom and the speculative economy created an urban bubble, a city increasingly organized around urban real-estate development and consumer culture.

Crisis City

In the first international commentary, the onset of the Asian economic crisis was identified as the Thai government's devaluation of the baht in July 1997, which then became a "contagion" spreading through the region and requiring "good medicine" and "therapy," to use the medical metaphors that prevailed at the time. The origins of the crisis did not lie with government indebtedness, as was the case with the debt crises in Latin

America. Instead, the crisis of debt, currency value, and capital flow originated in the private sector: it was effectively bad business debts in banking and real estate. These debts were by and large the result of non-performing loans held by wealthy entrepreneurs and leading corporations. Because the borrowers had long-standing and multilayered relations with the bank management, including marriages and ethnic ties, and because the corporations themselves were, typically, in the hands of Sino-Thai families, the Thai business world was now labeled as a prime example of "crony capitalism."

It is difficult to separate the impact of the banking crisis from that of the I.M.F.-influenced responses to it. Despite the fact that Thailand's crisis originated with private debt, the I.M.F. responded with the same remedies it has applied to public debt, proposing measures that targeted mainly government policies. Thailand accepted an I.M.F. bail-out package of U.S. $17.2 billion (amounting to the second-largest I.M.F. loan ever), which mandated conventional actions aimed at reducing inflation, renewing the government's surplus, and reforming the finance industry.[10] This formula passed the costs created by business onto ordinary Thais. The I.M.F. program socialized the crisis in numerous ways: significantly, it transformed private sector debts into public debts (through bailouts, recapitalization, a quasi-public body that took over non-performing bank loans, and so forth). It increased the sales tax (value-added tax), cut government services for the public (public spending), and reduced citizens' buying power (as the baht sank to one half of its former value). Thailand's repayments to the I.M.F. are a serious burden for the general population; by 2005, it is possible the amount of debt could add up to about a fifth of the government's budget (Focus 2000).

Critics suggest that the I.M.F.'s one-size-fits-all approach created an economic recession. The emphasis on public debts was misplaced (when private corporations, not the government, had borrowed and mismanaged money), and the emphasis on deflationary measures, while perhaps rewarding for elites, incorrectly assumed that inflation was a pressing risk. These measures did not succeed in attracting significant foreign capital—the main aim of I.M.F. strategy—nor did they dramatically increase exports (by lowering the value of the baht and thus prices), which was the hope for restoring the economy. International Monetary Fund measures also resulted in a "fire sale" of state enterprises at 37 per cent of their book value, packaged in such large bundles that they were only accessible to international bidders. Growing opposition to the sale of government agencies (like telephone services and the national airline) halted the dispersal of public assets.

In the news media, state rhetoric, N.G.O. and academic commentary, and in everyday conversations, the origin of the economic crisis was not attributed to the devaluation of the baht. Instead, the crisis was attributed to problems long brewing, inside the country, but especially outside. Using translations of English terms, people spoke of the "bubble" bursting and of what "measures" had to be taken to reestablish "liquidity." For example, during a massage, my chiropractor, a Japanese immigrant to Bangkok, animatedly dissected the non-productive base of real-estate investments and profit making in Thailand, using the Thai word, "soap bubble." Numerous observers targeted the corrupt family-based banking world and flawed macro-economic policies (such as pegging the baht to the dollar). A multi-factored explanation suggests that the crisis was produced internationally by rapid movements of international investments, and domestically by a speculative economy oriented to real estate and the urban developments associated with modern business and consumption—mainly in Bangkok—along with the vulnerabilities of export production and the hybrid family-corporate mode of business operations labeled "crony capitalism" by the West.

The Quiet City

However we analyze it, the downturn represented the country's most severe economic crisis at least since the world depression, and severely affected most Thais. A number of people—some quite prominent—committed suicide. As many as two to three million people were laid off, as manufacturing plants closed, advertising agencies lost business, services lost customers, and tourism dropped off. In 1998, up to 1,000 businesses closed each month and 50,000 workers requested job placements from state authorities. But many of the newly unemployed did not find new full-time jobs.

The reduction in public services was felt immediately. Increasing numbers of children (400,000 in 1996–7) dropped out of primary school as their families could not pay basic school fees. Scores of well-off Thai students abroad had to return home, their families no longer able to afford tuition or their government fellowships cut. The Ministry of Public Health's 2000 budget was lower than it had been in 1996, reducing support for public clinics, the main form of health care for the majority of the population. The number of those living under the poverty line increased officially by 1.5 per cent. Overall, the official measures of hardship were buffeted by small-scale survival strategies: Thais used their savings, sold assets, drew on social networks, or worked in the informal economy.

Hundreds of thousands of Bangkok dwellers returned to their homes in the provinces, particularly the northeast, where at least the rice crop did well that year. By and large, the provinces proved unable to sustain their return, however, and many again migrated to Bangkok or other urban centers.

Some people reentered work in the formal economy, but most became self-employed—doing home-based piecework, or patching together other sources of income. Working-class men took up taxi driving and more women, it was said, entered the go-go bars and sex establishments. One area doing a growth business, people noted, was car repossessions. Many turned to small-scale selling as another short-term response to unemployment. Small-scale and makeshift markets for second-hand goods or cheap consumer goods sprouted in available spaces across the city. Some who could afford the start-up fee turned to more legitimate forms of selling, such as Amway or Avon, which launched aggressive campaigns to recruit more sellers and buttress slipping sales, bringing in expertise from places seasoned in economic crisis, like Brazil (Wilson 1999). Thus for many Thais, marketing provided a major recourse, if only part time. The turn to marketing on the part of Thai men represented a shift in the identity of selling, work that was ethnically and gender coded, associated specifically with women and with the Chinese (Wilson fc). These forms of markets, moreover, had been marginalized during Bangkok's development; now, authorities looked the other way, as the government relied on the disdained informal economy to remedy problems generated by the corporate elite it had favored.

The economic crisis began in, and immediately affected, the city itself. Urban real estate foundered. As money became tight (with higher taxes and higher interest rates on loans), construction, rentals, and sales virtually halted. A favored form of investment during the boom years, real estate properties were thoroughly intertwined with bank loans, and therefore with international borrowing. Since real estate provided collateral on loans, and the majority of those loans became "non-performing," banks found themselves with swelling portfolios of unmovable properties. The real estate economy entered a recession. This downturn intensified the banking crisis and exacerbated the economic recession.

The city transformed. All over Bangkok, construction of office buildings, condos, shopping malls, and the elevated train system stopped. Vacancy signs proliferated. Depopulation, coupled with massive repossessions of cars, finally ameliorated the notorious traffic conditions in the city, long considered among the worst in the world. With construction halted, thousands of residents departed for their rural communities; hotels and go-go bars emptied as tourism declined: the city became quiet.

Urban space changed in other ways. For example, entrepreneurs offered "virtual offices," providing an address and telephone answering service in order to present the semblance of physical space in prestigious business districts without the expense of an actual office. The increase of small-scale vendors converted public and private spaces into impromptu markets: in front of a large mega-store, in M.B.K. shopping mall's first floor (in the empty space where a movie theater had been), on building steps, in public parks.

Amazing Bangkok

The Thai government adopted several strategies of its own to address the crisis, including public relations campaigns. Some aimed at bolstering Thailand's economic image internationally, "restoring confidence" through, for example, creating banking facilities "to build up Bangkok's image as a regional financial center" (Jacques 1999: 88). Others had domestic goals, to bolster morale and guide people's reactions toward desired ends. These drew on, but redefined, the urban-centered visions of Thai nationalism and culture.

Thailand has been representing itself through tourist marketing for nearly four decades. During the crisis, the Tourist Authority of Thailand (T.A.T.) launched its "Amazing Thailand" campaign (Figure 10.1). While the Thai government attempted to prevent the fire sale of public assets and corporate stock, T.A.T.'s "Amazing Thailand" sale effectively transformed the country into a nation-wide duty-free shopping mall of exotic cultural items and inexpensive luxury manufactures for tourists (see Van Esterik 2000: 3). The collaged imagery of this campaign collapsed different ethnic handicraft and elite consumables into a picture of "comparable advantage" for foreign consumers. A magazine advertisement featured a multi-armed Shiva-like image (not particularly a Thai symbol) bearing crafts and consumer goods in each of her many hands. These images found their way onto widely distributed posters, notebooks, and other forms.

The T.A.T.'s tourist rhetoric has long influenced Thai people's portrayals of Bangkok and the country to foreigners, just as tourist imagery has come to decorate goods aimed at, or at least sold to, the domestic market. In the case of the Amazing Thailand campaign, these effects were even more pronounced. When it launched the campaign, the government

Figure 10.1 Amazing Thailand campaign: map of central Bangkok. Photograph by Ara Wilson.

gave notice that "Amazing" was a slogan that could be appropriated by the Thai public. (Such official permission flags the fact that the U.S. has forced Thailand to become more compliant with its intellectual property laws, particularly regarding software and pharmaceuticals.) With state encouragement, the label "Amazing" has proliferated (Figure 10.2). Bangkok has an Amazing beauty salon and Amazing Thai silk. During a visit in 2000, a hand-scrawled sign on a neighborhood stall read, "Amazing coffee." Tropical shirts had the words Amazing Thailand embedded in the floral design. And the sex industry had joined the fray, for example in this new spin on the standard advertisement:

Figure 10.2 Amazing Thailand campaign: Cyber Café. Photograph by Ara Wilson.

> The Amazing traditional Thai massage
> special enjoy with oil and body massage
> direct service in your own room or hotel
> just call 24 hours.

The Amazing trope also lent itself to satire. An NGO dedicated to grassroots politics used "Amazing Poverty" on the cover of its newsletter. Sarcastic humor about the Amazing crisis was pervasive. Yet for the most part, the marketing pitch aimed at foreign shoppers was picked up locally as a nationalist slogan whose English made it transnationally legible.

The nationalism of Amazing Thailand joined with the collective critique of external causes of the economic crisis. Overall, the focal point for the experience of the recession was the I.M.F., whose austerity measures and top-down dosage of "good medicine" were noticeably resented and widely criticized. In everyday life in Thailand, the emergent shorthand for the current problems faced by Thai people and the nation was "I.M.F." The period was dubbed "I.M.F. time," and signs all over invoked the three English letters as a new modifier (Figure 10.3). An N.G.O. leader designed a handkerchief for the sex work advocacy organization, Empower, which read "I.M.F. Can't Make Me Cry." Posters reading "Stop I.M.F." meant cheaper prices in restaurants and stores. My sense is that, the trenchant critiques of I.M.F. practices aside, in these discourses the Fund was

Figure 10.3 "I.M.F Time." One of many signs invoking the three English letters.

a metaphor for the impact of the global economy, or globalization in general, and in a more veiled way, for the U.S., long an unassailable ally of the country. (Criticisms of the U.S. role in generating an enormous and world-famous sex industry for foreigners, or of U.S. customers of the trade, for example, were always relatively muted.)

The Thai government remained circumspect in its criticisms of the I.M.F., its important lender. It launched campaigns to mollify and modify the public, including a comparatively small employment-generating program and larger marketing programs, replete with broadcast slogans declaring, "everyone is affected." A public relations campaign announced, "Thais Buy Thai," and "Thais Help Thais," as well as "Thais Help the

Nation." A new Thai political party formed, Thai Love Thai (Thai rak Thai). Ordinary citizens responded by donating cash and gold to the national cause. These efforts were part of a revamped "economic nationalism" (Kasian 2002) that used discourses about consumption and "traditional" culture to mobilize the citizenry.

Just as markets indexed everyday survival strategies, buying and consuming also indexed significant features of the crisis. A longstanding problem for Thailand's economy was the consumption of imported goods. The drain on foreign reserves particularly characterized the urban consumption of elites and professionals, and youth, in Bangkok. For some time, the purchase of imported consumer goods in particular had been targeted as a problem in the imbalance between exports and imports and the trade deficit. With the crisis, the government launched a campaign urging Thais not to buy imported goods, such as foreign wine, fruit, or clothes, broadcasting its "Thais buy Thai" campaign on television, radio, billboards, buses, and as a slogan printed on notebooks. For the most part, the elite consumer goods on the tabooed list were products associated with women—clothes and perfume, invoked through name brands like Gucci—not industrial goods, or cars, or masculine consumer items such as whiskey. At least briefly, trendy young women sported home-made items like a beaded bag or macramé vest, a style that conveniently fit with a revival of Western 1960s and 1970s fashions.

At the same time that imported luxuries were seen as a problem, overall consumption served as an indicator of the economy's health. Even with the devalued currency and thus low prices, exports disappointed. The resurgence of domestic purchasing allowed finance ministers and the I.M.F. to declare that the economy was recovering: as many observers noted, "the crucial factor driving growth in 1999 was domestic demand" (Focus 2000), particularly on the part of wealthy consumers who most benefited from the I.M.F.'s strategies (like income tax reductions). The "Thais help Thais" concept was picked up by businesses, which posted special low-priced lists and menus (in Thai) under that slogan. Further abetting the return to consumption was the proliferation of the low-level selling of petty commodities—toys, American second-hand blue jeans, and homemade bags—creating a cumulative effect of domestic buying on the national economy. Thus, formal and impromptu markets played an important role in providing an income for many while spurring signs of economic growth.

The government's nationalist campaigns invoked Thai tradition and identity, often overlapping with, and folding into, earlier campaigns to preserve and promote Thai culture.[11] The private sector joined the effort.

Corporations like Siam Cement ran campaigns to bolster Thai culture, defined by such traits as discipline and deference to parents (Pasuk and Chris 1998: 178). Corporate and state promotions of Amazing Thai culture dovetailed, pre- and post-crisis, with both nationalist solidarity and economic instrumentality. At the same time, foreign economists and policy experts, whose usual frameworks evacuate cultural contexts, began to wax sentimental about Thailand's pragmatic Buddhist culture, seeing in it the social salve for capitalist crisis. As one international finance expert wrote, "Thailand's ability to weather this crisis hinges upon its socio-political reservoir of patience . . . Buddhist societies have a long tradition of resilience to adversity" (Jacque 1999: 98). Amazing Thai Buddhism.

Perhaps Buddhism and a socio-political reservoir of patience shaped Thais' ability to weather the economic storm. Post-crisis, advocates of doctrinal Buddhism, who had long criticized the superstitious "prosperity religions," were revitalized (Jackson 1999). But it is also possible that, because rural communities took in so many of the displaced urban workers; because women picked up where reduced social services left off; and because of possibilities in the informal economy, Thailand did not see the same social unrest as did other countries affected by the Asian economic "meltdown". In Indonesia, ethnic Chinese populations became vulnerable to collective rage from groups of ethnic Malay, and their persons and property were attacked. The nationalist interpretation of the crisis did not resolve this rage (see, for example, Budianta 2000). Thailand has long been known for much more peaceful relations between Thais and Chinese, both categories being more complex than the terms suggest (Bao 1998), even as Chineseness is equally associated with urbanity, business, and capital. The Chinese are generally not perceived as outside the Thai nation proper, and have become an ethnicity within the Thai nationality. During the boom years, Sino-Chinese identity became more valorized, at times the choice figure representing Thailand's modernity in soap operas and movies (Ong 2000, Pasuk and Chris 1998: 172–6, Reynolds 1996). In Thailand, there were no similar assaults on Chinese-Thai people or stores.

If Thai reactions to the crisis took an ethnic form focused on boundaries between Thais and others, it was against the Burmese who already occupied an unpopular position as ancient enemies and eighteenth-century pillagers of the historic Siamese capital city. The numbers of workers and refugees from Myanmar had increased over the prior decade. Official and popular hostility towards them became more intolerant and explicit, and Burmese in Bangkok were increasingly arrested and deported. After the crisis, migrant workers were repatriated back to their home countries. In 1999 and 2000, the Thai government stepped up deportation in response to

Burmese activism, after a siege of the Burmese Embassy in Bangkok (to protest the Myanmar regime) was followed by a more radical (or fringe) takeover of a provincial hospital in Ratchaburi. The pressure on Burmese in Bangkok intensified as the city prepared to host the 2000 United Nations Conference on Trade and Development (Human Rights Watch 2000) (It continues today as part of the government's severe crackdown on methanphetamines, trafficked from Burma. *The New York Times*, 8 April, 2002). The common analogy between Burma's 1767 destruction of Ayutthya and the destructive invasion by the IMF and global capital of the Thai economy indirectly but at times pointedly informed popular concern over Burmese border crossing into Thailand.[12] Such ethnic, national, and border anxieties reflect Thailand's enduring urban nationalism: the ways that the city serves as a metonym for the nation, and also, absent formal colonialism, the ways Thai nationalism has been directed as much to threats from neighboring Asian regimes as to those from Europe or the U.S.

The Recuperating City

The dominant public image of Thai identity forged during the boom years centered on Bangkok, and was firmly affixed to the notion of Thailand's ascending position on the international stage. The economic crisis presented, therefore, a material and also representational crisis, a challenge to the identities of the modern city, nation, and citizen. During the boom, economic citizenship meant participating in and contributing to the modernizing economy, a goal most visibly realized by working and consuming in the capital city. A cluster of prosperity religions decentered middle-class spiritual practice from Buddhist temples and the monkhood (Jackson 2002). High-flying executives and managers, "flexible citizens" (Ong 2000) versed in cosmopolitan cultures, became symbols of Bangkok and Thailand's future.

When boom turned to bust, government and dominant discourses enlisted the collective, as distinct from the urban, citizenry. These campaigns marshaled nationalist conceptions of Thai culture that combined urban elite traditions with images of peasant culture (images codified in Bangkok and shaped by international tourism). They presented a nation united in the face of external post-colonial forces of globalization and the West. Official responses to the economic crisis in Asia conflated the citizen with business and government, and the capital with the nation: everyone is affected, so Thais help Thais. The future of Bangkok business is equated with the future of the nation, which in turn is equated with the future of its subjects. The official Thai government response to the crisis presented the suffering and consequences of the crisis as shared nationwide, by all Thais, in a horizontal model of hardship. Many observers of the Asian economic crisis have noted that state responses intensified nationalist rhetoric, perhaps most famously in Malaysia and Indonesia (see, for example, Budianta 2000). Discourses in Thailand shared a critique of the I.M.F., and constructed a sentimental nationalism of mutual affection, identification, and aid. This nationalism changed the place of the city in signifying the nation, presenting sovereignty and suffering as shared by the country as a whole: not Amazing Bangkok, but Amazing Thailand.

To a great extent, this response to the crisis has been successful in shaping a sense of shared suffering. The sense of the economic bust as a national crisis presented a version of equality of sorts among a citizenry united in a collective problem, even as they were left to face it for the most part on their own in conjunction with friends and families. (While employment-generating projects received about 13 million baht from the government, key banks and companies received at least a 300 billion baht bail-out in 1998.) The presentation of the problem as one of economic sovereignty, then, while useful in criticizing the powers and policies of the I.M.F. and other multilateral agencies, collectivized a problem generated by and through economic and social inequalities, and obscured possible critique.

Although Ayutthya fell under Burma's assault, the reign of Bangkok over the territory of Thailand has survived the threat of European colonization, Japanese occupation, communist overthrow, and now, I.M.F. intervention. Just as earlier external threats constructed Bangkok as the metonym and center of the nation (Thongchai 1994), the campaign of "Thais help Thais" and blaming of the I.M.F. rendered a vision of horizontal hardship hegemonic. At the same time, rising critiques from industrial workers, N.G.O.s, and progressive intellectuals have provided trenchant interpretations of the vertical and uneven nature of the bubble economy and ensuing crisis (Kasian 2002). Labor unrest, such as a lengthy and publicized dispute with Thai Melon, marked the rejection of corporate triage. Farmers threatened rebellions and articulated the flaws with government policies that had favored Bangkok while exploiting the rural safety net and food supply. There have been protests against the World Trade Organization. In these ways, responses to Bangkok's hegemony and the unchecked operations of the global economy it facilitated have galvanized networks of protest that speak to, but extend beyond, Amazing Krungthep.

Notes

1. This chapter draws on research in Thailand spanning 1988 to 2000, including fieldwork from 1993 to 1994, the height of the economic boom. This research investigated the impact of capitalist development and globalization on sex/gender meanings in Thailand by studying various manifestations of the market economy, including department stores, Avon, and the sex industry (for example, Wilson, fc). My account of the economic crisis derives from observations made on trips in July to August 1998 and December 2000 (funded by a Seed Grant from The Ohio State University), from conversations with Thai NGO workers and ordinary citizens, and from textual sources. I would like to thank Jane Schneider for the invitation to present and publish this material and for helpful editing of this piece.
2. Bangkok or Krungthep's official name is actually much longer, a paragraph long, the recitation of which was turned into the lyric of a pop song. For a good overview of research on Bangkok, see Askew, *Interpreting Bangkok* (1994).
3. Thongchai Winichakul (1994) provides a critical history of the centralizing control of Bangkok over neighboring regions during the era of European colonialism, noting that the official focus on external threats (Burma, southern uprisings, or Europe) masked its own colonizing role: "what should be a history of regional hegemonism turns out to be a glorious anticolonial history performed by the Siamese elite" (Winichakal 1994: 148).
4. The Siamese state earned money directly from the rice trade through tariffs on exports, but also indirectly (and most lucratively) from extracting money from immigrant communities through a residence tax and fees on the opium houses, brothels, and gambling dens that serviced them.
5. A majority of ethnic Chinese resided around Sampeng lane and Yaowarat road, an area referred to in English as "Chinatown." Built over the former Vietnamese quarter, a point called Pahurat was home to South Asian men, and remains known for its textile markets. The Europeans, small in number but great in influence, concentrated themselves along the major Charoenkrung road that ran along the river.
6. Some Chakri kings emulated various features of the European city—the avenue Rajadamneun aspired to the Champs-Elysées, for example. European-styled architecture became favored for office buildings,

palaces, shops, and homes, supplanting a taste for Chinese styles and classic Siamese architectural forms. For the development of the city from the eighteenth to the early twentieth century, see Askew (1994, 2002); Hamilton (2001); Lysa (1984); O'Connor (1978); Sternstein (1982); Wilson (1989).

7. In addition to light manufacturing, chemical and oil businesses were also important areas of manufacturing and foreign investment in Thailand.
8. Beginning in the 1970s, relatively small amounts of U.S. capital were invested in petroleum, electronic components, and consumer goods. Capital from Japan soon exceeded that from the U.S., and most of the foreign direct investment in Thailand came from Asia, including from its newly industrialized countries (N.I.C.). In the 1990s, money began being invested more in finance and construction. See, for example, Nimfa et al., (1997) and Pasuk and Chris (1998).
9. Bangkok's 1960 population is tallied at 1,703,346 (Akin 1975); for 1990, the count was 5,716,779 million, 10 per cent of the national population of 55.5 million (Thailand 1992). These numbers are probably less than the actual city population at the time.
10. The Fund's measures involved stabilizing exchange rates, increasing interest rates, limiting government spending, advancing economic liberalization, and modifying the finance sector. For a conventional account of the IMF package, see Jacques (1999). For critical accounts from within Thailand, see Focus (2000), Kasian (2002) and Pasuk and Chris (1998).
11. What counts as Thai tradition is one part derived from a selective version of historical Thai peasant society (from the window between being freed from strict feudal control and being oriented to urban markets and wage labor), and one part derived from the values and aesthetics of the urban, "Indianized" Thai aristocracy.
12. The historic Burmese invasion informed the interpretations of Burmese migrants and more metaphorically, of global capital and the IMF. Following the destruction of Ayutthya, a Sino-Thai ruler named Thaksin established a new capital city and dynasty in the area of the town of Bangkok. Interestingly, Thaksin is also the name of a Sino-Thai telecommunications tycoon (I worked for one of his corporation's subsidiaries, a cable television concern) who was elected Prime Minister in 2001 as head of the Thais Love Thai party (see Wilson fc: chapter four).

References

(Thai authors are listed by given (first) name, following Thai convention.)

Akin Rabibadana (1975), *Bangkok Slum: Aspects of Social Organization*. Ph.D. Dissertation, Southeast Asia Program, Cornell University.

Askew, M. (1994), *Interpreting Bangkok: The Urban Question in Thai Studies,* Bangkok: Chulalongkorn University Press.

—— (2002), *Bangkok: Place, Practice, and Representation*, London: Routledge.

Bao, J. (1998), "Same Bed, Different Dreams: Ethnicized Sexuality and Gender among Elderly Chinese Immigrants in Bangkok" *positions* 4(2): 475–502.

Budianta, M. (2000), "Discourse of Cultural Identity in Indonesia during the 1997–1998 Monetary Crisis", *Inter-Asia Cultural Studies*, 1(1): 109–28.

Hamilton, A. (2000), "Wonderful, Terrible: Everyday Life in Bangkok", Bridge, G. and Watson, S. (eds), *A Companion to the City*, Oxford: Blackwell, pp. 460–71.

Harvey, D. (1989), *The Condition of PostModernity*, Oxford: Basil Blackwell.

Human Rights Watch (2000), Press release. http://www.hrw.org/press/2000/05/thailand0506.htm (March 2001).

Ingram, J.C. (1954), *Economic Change in Thailand Since 1850*, Stanford CA: Stanford University Press.

Jackson, P.A. (1999), "Royal Spirits, Chinese Gods, and Magic Monks: Thailand's Boom-time Religions of Prosperity", *South East Asia Research*, 7(3): 245–320.

Jacque, L.L (1999), "The Asian Financial Crisis: Lessons from Thailand", *The Fletcher Forum of World Affairs*, 23(1): 87–99.

Kasian Tejapira (2002), "Post-Crisis Economic Impasse and Political Recovery in Thailand: The Resurgence of Economic Nationalism", *Critical Asian Studies*, 34(3): 323–56.

Knodel, J. (1987), *Thailand's Reproductive Revolution: Rapid Fertility Decline in a Third World Setting*, Madison: University of Wisconsin.

Korff, R. (1989), *Bangkok and Modernity,* Bangkok: Chulalongkorn University Social Research Institute (CUSRI).

Lysa, H. (1984), *Thailand in the Nineteenth Century,* Singapore: Institute of Southeast Asian Studies.

Mills, M. (1999), *Thai Women in the Global Work Force*, New Brunswick: Rutgers University Press.

Nakagawa, T. (1987), "Asian Retailing Revolution and Japanese Companies: The Thailand Case." International Economic Conflict Discussion Paper no. 34.

Napat Sirisambhand and Szanton, C. (1986), *Thailand's Street Food Vending: The Sellers and Consumers of "Traditional Fast Foods"*, Bangkok: Women's Studies Programme, Social Research Institute, Chulalongkorn University.

Nash, J. and Fernandez-Kelly, P. (eds) (1983), *Women, Men, and the International Division of Labor*, Albany, NY: State University of New York Press.

Nimfa B. Ogena, Kusol Soonthorndhada, Kriengsak Rojnkureesatien, Jirakit Bumtomglarp (1997), *Globalization with Equity: Policies for Growth in Thailand*, Nakhon Pathom, Thailand: Institute for Population and Social Research, Mahidol University.

O'Connor, R.A. (1978), *Urbanism and Religion: Community, Hierarchy and Sanctity in Urban Thai Buddhist Temples*. Ph.D. dissertation, Cornell University.

Ong, A. (1999), *Flexible Citizens: The Cultural Logics of Transnationality*, Durham: Duke University Press.

Pasuk Phongpaichit (1980), *From Peasant Girl to Bangkok Masseuse*, Geneva: I.L.O. Report.

Pasuk Phongpaichit and Baker, C. (1998), *Thailand's Boom and Bust*, Chiang Mai: Silkworm Books.

Reynolds, C. (1996), "Tycoons and Warlords: Modern Thai Social Formations and Chinese Historical Romance", in Reid, A. (with assistance of Rodgers, K.A.) (ed.), *Sojourners and Settlers: Histories of Southeast Asia and the Chinese*, Honolulu: University of Hawai'i Press, pp. 115–47.

Sternstein, L. (1982), *Bangkok Portrait*, Bangkok: Bangkok Metropolitan Organization, Committee on the Rattanakosin Bicentennial.

Thailand (Royal Thai Government) National Identity Office (1992), Thailand in the 90s Bangkok: National Identity Office, Office of the Prime Minister, Royal Thai Government.

Thongchai Winichakul (1994), *Siam Mapped: A History of the Geo-Body of a Nation*, Honolulu: University of Hawai'i Press.

Truong, T. (1990), *Sex, Money and Morality: Prostitution and tourism in South-East Asia*, London/NJ: Zed Books.

Thorbek, S. (1987), *Voices from the City: Women of Bangkok*, London: Zed Books.

Trirat Promsiri (1965), *Thailand's Transition: A Study of the New Approach of Developing Countries*, Bangkok: Prae Pittaya.

Van Esterik, P. (2000), *Materializing Thailand*, Oxford and New York: Berg.

Whittaker, A. (1999), "Women and Capitalist Tranformation in a North-eastern Thai Village", in Jackson, P.A. and Cook, N.M. (eds), *Genders and Sexualities in Modern Thailand*, Chiang Mai: Silkworm Books, pp. 43–62.

Wilson, A. (Fc), *The Intimate Economies of Bangkok: Tomboys, Tycoons, and Avon Ladies in the Global City*, Berkeley: University of California Press.

—— (1999), "The Empire of Direct Sales and the Making of Thai Entrepreneurs", *Critique of Anthropology* 19(4): 401–22.

Wilson, C.O. (1989), "Bangkok in 1883: An Economic and Social Profile", *Journal of the Siam Society* 77(2): 49–58.

–11–

Contemporary Ho Chi Minh City in Numerous Contradictions: Reform Policy, Foreign Capital and the Working Class[1]

Suhong Chae

> The Diamond Plaza, the Cathedral and the Thong Nhat Palace form a triangle, each making (marking) its respective historical period. The Roman style cathedral belongs to the early days of the French colonial period, the Thong Nhat Palace (formerly Independence Palace) to the days of the American-backed regime, and the Diamond Plaza to today's Vietnam". (Nguyen Khac Vien and Huu Ngoc 1998: 255–56)

> After 40 years of war (1939–1979), Vietnam has found itself in position of having to face many of the contradictions of today's world. The situation therefore is all the more complicated. In Vietnam, Saigon is the place where (which) concentrates the most numerous (of the) contradictions. (Nguyen Khac Vien and Huu Ngoc: 1998: 191)

As you explore downtown Ho Chi Minh (H.C.M.) City, you cannot miss the three buildings mentioned above, each representing three crucial periods of Vietnamese history. What struck me most during my fieldwork (1998–2000) was that the Diamond Plaza, the most expensive skyscraper in the city, built mainly with foreign capital and technology in the late 1990s, towers over the other two buildings—the Cathedral and Thong Nhat Palace—which symbolize the two imperial powers that the Vietnamese people fought to expel during their modern history.[2] This might be why the Vietnamese intellectual, Nguyen Khac Vien, has defined Saigon as "the locus of the most numerous contradictions."

It is not a new phenomenon that a Third World city is experiencing an intensified linkage to economically advanced foreign capital and its transnational operations. What makes the H.C.M. City case distinctive is that the local gatekeepers of global forces show self-contradictory ideologies and roles in "the transition from socialism to capitalism." For example, the socialist state of Vietnam, famous for its strong anti-imperialism, has desperately lured foreign capital to stabilize its economy. Moreover, the state has ironically restored its power through the market economy and dependence on foreign capital.[3] The majority of the working class seem to prefer economic liberalization to the poverty that the inefficient socialist planned economy created, even though they are increasingly caught up in capitalist discipline. Not surprisingly, the role of socialist trade unions, formerly the transmission belt between the state and the workers (see Pravda and Ruble eds. 1986), has become ambiguous and self-contradictory.

This chapter seeks to outline the various contradictions that the rapidly transforming H.C.M. City has faced in the process of socialist reform since the mid-1980s. Toward this end, I will first explain the historical background of the reform policy. Second, I will describe the change of H.C.M. City in general and then of a specific industrial area. Third, based on my fieldwork experience, I will discuss how the working class both deals with and resists the capitalist transition and foreign capital, with consequences for the future of the city.

Postwar Economy and the Construction of Socialist Vietnam

The current social economic situation of H.C.M. City is the product of three mutually related factors: the Vietnamese war, the failure of socialist transformation, and the reform policy—the latter intended to heal a country wounded by the Vietnamese war and re-wounded by the socialist transformation.

It is well known how Vietnam was affected by the drastic war. Staggering numbers suggest how many lives were destroyed—"fifteen million tons of munitions (deployed) during 1964–72, twice the amount used in all of Europe and Asia during World War II" (Kolko 1997: 2), ten million refugees, one million widows, 880,000 orphans, 250,000 drug addicts and 300,000 prostitutes (Marr and White 1988: 3). Especially in H.C.M. City, the economic center of the south, the war brought more than physical destruction. With its end, the sudden dislocation of an "assisted" economy destabilized most of the southern people, who had become accustomed to the extravagant commodities provided by the American-financed Commercial Import System (or C.I.P.) and by the GIs.[4] Left in its wake were some newly created industrial bases and a highly unproductive and over-urbanized population.[5] The industrial facilities in the pan-Saigon area, including Bien Hoa city, had depended almost totally on foreign raw materials, technology and military demands, and were suddenly disadvantaged by the war's end (Nguyen Khac Vien and Huu Ngoc 1998: 156).

In the devastating postwar situation, the Vietnamese government and party were too optimistic about the reconstruction toward socialist ideals and the unification of the two long-separated regions. Without taking practical measures to mitigate the economic shock suffered by the southern people, the new Communist regime set about rearranging the overpopulated H.C.M. City and transforming its capitalistic relations of production. On the one hand, city residents were encouraged to migrate to the mountainous areas in the central region under a program of developing New Economic Zones, or they were told to go back home to the Mekong delta. On the other hand, the regime sought to nationalize the industrial sector as well as to collectivize rural areas. Trade union demands led to 1,500 capitalist enterprises being converted into 650 state-owned enterprises (S.O.E.s) with 130,000 employees (Nguyen Khac Vien 1980: 7). In this process, ethnic Chinese business owners were severely squeezed.

The nationalization process provoked reactions against its overconfident Maoist style of social-economic transformation. As the southern peasants were reluctant and actually resisted joining the cooperatives, agricultural productivity dropped and the price of food, already inflated, soared. Wealthy merchants in the city and rural areas seized the opportunity to speculate on staples and hoarded gold in collusion with corrupt communist cadres (Beresford 1988: 107). Both inflation and speculation dealt a serious blow to the working class in the city, who had to find a way to eke out a scanty livelihood.

The socialist regime interpreted this turmoil more in terms of the reactionary activities of the propertied class than as a structural legacy of a deeply rooted colonialism and the subsequent war economy. Its more radical follow-up measures targeted what the leaders called "compradore bourgeois or capitalists", 70 per cent of whom were ethnic Chinese (Vo Nhan Tri 1990: 59–72). There is an understandable historical background to the ethnic policies of the socialist regime. From the time when Saigon was colonized by the Nguyen dynasty 300 years ago, ethnic Chinese exercised commercial power in the greater-Saigon area. Following the Tay Son rebellion (1778–1802), which was supported by the southern peasants, the Chinese were forced to settle in the current Cholon[6] area (Q. 5). From there they controlled three-fourths of the economy of the city, dominating all the domestic wholesale trade, 80 per cent of industry, 70 per cent of foreign trade and half of retail trade with the cooperation of the French colonial administration and the former southern regime (Nguyen

Khac Vien 1980: 267). When 670 families were classified as "enemies of the people" in the late 1970s, 117 Chinese families were included in the 159 families who had their holdings confiscated (Vo Nhan Tri 1988: 77–8). This brought about an exodus of 300,000 Chinese (1978–9) accompanied by diplomatic discord with China surrounding the Kampuchea resolution.

The Background of the Reform Policy and its Effects

The dilemma of the new socialist regime was that the radical transformation of relations of production did not bring about an increase of productivity in the south. In the agricultural sector, especially in the Mekong delta—the main food provider to the city—peasants' resistance against collectivization became ferocious. They refused to harvest crops, fed rice to pigs, slaughtered livestock, and deserted the land, which resulted in a serious blow to state procurement of agricultural products (Vo Nhan Tri 1990: 72–85). Yet the unrest was an expectable consequence of the government's decision to set a low price for agricultural products and levy unrealistic quotas. In the industrial sector, many enterprises operated at only 30–50 per cent of capacity because of the lack of raw materials, parts, and energy as well as poor management skills (Vo Nhan Tri 1988: 82). In the commercial sector, wage earners, including public servants, suffered from the lack of consumer goods and endeavored to survive through illicit trading, contributing to corruption. Ironically, the new relations of production reinvigorated the old, although now illegal, capitalistic practices rather than eradicating them.

The resulting predicaments led to a series of reform policies, enhanced by the international circumstances of the 1980s when almost all of the socialist countries overhauled and modified their economies. In Vietnam, reform was nurtured by the historic sixth Plenum of the Party Central Committee which recognized "objective laws" beyond "revolutionary ardor" (quoted in Marr and White 1988: 4). And yet, the party had to take a few steps to see a positive outcome. The Fifth Congress of 1982 recognized the category of "family economy", allowing families to appropriate a private surplus after "negotiating with the state," although reclassifying this as part of the socialist relations of production (Vo Nhan Tri 1988: 84). Stimulated by the astonishing increase of productivity, particularly in agriculture, the sixth Party Congress in 1986 under the leadership of pioneering reformer, Nguyen Van Linh, finally declared the renovation (*Doi Moi*) of core socialist policies, including central planning, state price controls, collectivization and egalitarian wages.

There is no doubt that the recognition of private economic activity in the late 1980s enlivened H.C.M. City, the economic center of the south. Food surpluses, for example, began to flow in, animating various kinds of commercial activities in the markets. However, the national economy as a whole still suffered from low labor productivity, high production costs and poor quality of commodities, which produced a rampant inflation (around 1,000 per cent per year by early 1988) and set a limitation on further growth (Marr and White 1988: 5). It wasn't until the door opened to foreign capital in the 1990s that privatization and the re-introduction of a market economy actually enhanced the standard of living in H.C.M. City.

Foreign Investment and the Change of a City

The impact of foreign investment has been substantial in H.C.M. City. Every year for the last ten years, three to four billion U.S. dollars, which is more than half of the total foreign investment in Vietnam, has gravitated here and to neighboring Dong Nai and Ba Ria-Vung Tau provinces. This foreign capital has played an important role in high annual economic growth (around 10 per cent per year on average in the 1990s) and significantly transformed the appearance of the city and its lifestyles. Most of all, rapid economic growth has contributed to enhancing, however unevenly, the average annual income per person, bringing it up to 800–1,000 U.S. dollars by the end of the 1990s.[7] This has further boosted the city as the central consumption market in the country.

The social economic changes of H.C.M. City cannot be understood just with the quantitative records. First of all, we need to look at the characteristics of the foreign capital invested. Most of it has gone into the "unproductive" or luxurious commercial sector and into the labor-intensive industrial sector. In the downtown, foreign capital was chiefly invested in the construction of large commercial and office buildings and hotels—not in improving the city's infrastructure, its transportation, communication, banking and information networks.[8] To the extent that these have been improved, it is to provide conveniences for foreign and local businessmen and the powerful, rather than to enhance the living conditions of ordinary people in the long run. In the industrial sector, Hong Kong, Korean, Taiwanese, Singaporean and Japanese investors pay mostly for old machines imported from their home countries to process raw materials also imported from or through these home countries. It is questionable what the Vietnamese can get besides the low wages, taxes, rents and the capitalist management skills for labor intensive industry. This exploitative aspect of foreign capital can be witnessed in many Third World countries, being characteristic of capitalist accumulation. What makes the Vietnamese case peculiar is that an ostensibly socialist state justifies such neocolonial arrangements—the very arrangements it forcefully negated until the mid-1980s.

In addition, we need to pay attention to the fact that a considerable proportion of foreign capital is being invested by the very people who were once ostracized by the socialist government. It is a bewildering phenomenon that the government now ardently welcomes the return of "Viet Kieu" (Vietnamese abroad), including "Hoa" (ethnic Chinese) whom they earlier defined as "compradore" capitalists and/or reactionaries. According to local newspapers, about 2.6 million Viet Kieu(s) were living in 75 foreign countries as of 1999 including 450,000–500,000 boat people and 400,000 people who were sent to foreign countries by the Orderly Departure Program (Vietnamese Agriculture No. 15. 1999). The state estimates that Viet Kieu(s) control U.S.$20 billion a year and emphasizes that the government will not need to beg for foreign capital if they invest 10–15 per cent of their money in Vietnam. Not betraying the state's hopes, Viet Kieu(s) have sent more than U.S.$700 million a year legally and illegally to help their relatives, as well as for investments in Vietnam, mostly in H.C.M. City (Cho and Sung 1997: 68). The influence of the Viet Kieu(s)' money is demonstrated by the economic boom of the city around the Lunar New Year when 80,000–240,000 of them visit Vietnam. Among the Viet Kieu, the ethnic Chinese have been notably expanding their business territories in the city in cooperation with relatives who have already regained the dominant commercial influence since the reform policy was initiated.

The general processes of the capitalist transformation of H.C.M. City, accelerated by the increase in foreign influence, have produced an array of problems: rapidly increasing inequality, speculative investment in real estate, corruption, waves of migration from the rural areas, an exploding informal economy, and questions of urban sustainability. I will briefly illustrate some of these processes for the city in general, and for an industrializing district (Quan or Q.) called Thu Duc in particular.

Uneven Development of the City after the Reform Policy

H.C.M. is a mega-city with the population of more than 5 million. The population would probably far exceed this number if we considered the unreliability of official statistics,[9] the rapidly expanding informal sector, and the waning effectiveness of residence regulation. With less than 10 per cent of Vietnam's total population (around 75 million–78 million in the late 1990s), the city is estimated to control around 40 per cent of money in circulation in the country (Nguyen Khac Vien and Huu Ngoc 1998: 216). It is not too much to say that the impressive economic performance of Vietnam after the open door policy owes a great deal to the development of this city.

The rapid annual economic growth of the 1990s has dramatically transformed the appearance of H.C.M. City as well as the life of its residents. People in colorful T-shirts ride motorbikes[10] while new buildings rise almost daily in the downtown. Bicycles and *xich lo* (pedicabs) are disappearing. Even though there are still many street people including pickpockets, street vendors and beggars who keep an eye on foreigners, tourists are no longer warned to watch even their hats and glasses as they were in the beginning of the open door policy when every commodity was scarce and valuable. It is unbelievable how quickly bars, cafés, restaurants, night clubs and karaokes have mushroomed along the streets renamed for Vietnamese revolutionary heroes. As far as consumption levels are concerned, H.C.M. City has begun to escape from the dearth of consumer goods and markets characteristic of massive socialist transformation following the war (1975–85).

However, the (re-)emergence of a consumer market in the former Saigon is only one aspect of the scenery of this rapidly changing city. Like other cities in the Third World, the development of H.C.M. has been astonishingly uneven between and within the districts. Most of the political economic power is concentrated in the core districts (Q.1 and Q.5) along the Saigon River that have been developed since the French colonial period. These districts, collectively known as the "Saigon-Cholon" area, comprise large hotels, both large-scale modern supermarkets and traditional market places, foreign trading offices and banks, and local administrative offices. Big construction projects and commercial activities are mainly executed in the core area, which provides easier access to the social networks of powerful players in the market[11] such as foreign companies, local bureaucrats (Q.1) and wealthy local merchants (Q. 5).

At some distance from the core are the industrial areas that surround the city. Despite differences in degree, the districts comprising the industrial areas share basic morphological characteristics: factories mixed with pre-existing rural villages, small shops, and cafés. Thu Duc and Nha Be districts make good examples. They are located to the north-east and the south of the downtown respectively; the Saigon River divides the downtown and the two districts. In both districts, the creation of E.P.Z.s (export processing zones) and I.Z.s (industrial zones) has led to the construction of massive industrial and assembly plants (see Figure 11.1). The people in the districts are overwhelmingly workers in these labor intensive factories as well as peasants, peddlers and small merchants, whose access to political-economic power is extremely limited. Under the socialist regime, Vietnamese workers have exercised greater political and economic influence than did workers in other developing countries. However, not only has their standard of living remained relatively low but the political economic support of the state is also declining.

Other districts (Q.10, Q. Tan Binh, Q. Binh Thanh, Q. Phu Nhuan, for example), display characteristics intermediary between the core and the industrial areas. Foreign and locally owned factories of various size are scattered throughout, mixed with private commercial, residential, and (to a shrinking degree now) agricultural spaces. This kind of disordered mixture is rather typical in every district, even though the core area is more organized for large-scale administrative and commercial activities whereas industrial complexes in some districts are more neatly separated from residential areas. In other words, uneven development and class

Figure 11.1 Teddy bear factory, Export Processing Zone, Ho Chi Minh City. Photograph by Suhong Chae.

differentiation can be seen within each district as well as between the districts. It is not difficult to find small shanties in the shadows of sleek high rises and commercial buildings, even in the center of downtown, such as on Nugyen Thi Minh Khai Street of District One.

This uneven development of H.C.M. City both within and between districts began to emerge in the Socialist period. During this period, too, control over the service sector in the central districts became a source of upward mobility, with consequent further differentiation. Today, most of the large companies in the industrial sector are state-owned or in the hands of foreign capital, while domestic private capital is concentrated in the safer and more lucrative service sector. It is increasingly the case that the core of the city produces and reproduces class differences and inequality more rapidly than any other area given its better access to both domestic and foreign capital and the control that its merchants exercise over the formal and informal service sector.

Especially critical to social change in contemporary H.C.M. City are thus global (or foreign or transnational) capital, on the one hand, and the emergence of a domestic petite bourgeoisie on the other hand. Global capital, predominantly from Hong Kong, Singapore, Taiwan, Japan and Korea, has dominated the large-scale construction and service sectors in the core of the city as well as the labor-intensive industries in the industrial areas, whether independently or in cooperation with state-owned companies. At the same time, private capital, which is primarily controlled by revitalized domestic Chinese merchants, dominates small and medium-size service functions in the core area, also accelerating class differentiation. The whole process makes us understand why Kolko (1997) lamented that those who sacrificed their lives for the liberation and socialism would be screaming.

The Reform Policy and the Transformation of Thu Duc

Now, we will explore how working-class people have faced new problems in the light of the reform, massive investment of foreign capital and consequent uneven development by focusing on the industrial district called Thu Duc. Located between H.C.M. downtown (Sagion-Cholon) and Bien Hoa City in Dong Nai Province, Thu Duc (T.D.) can be divided into two parts according to geological features: lowlands (10,000 ha). and highlands (5,000 ha).[12] Watered by the Saigon and Dong Nai Rivers, the lowlands are used as rice and vegetable fields. In contrast, the highlands are mostly for industrial, residential and commercial use. Prior to 1975, the area was a part of the military ring protecting the downtown as well as a food provider to both the southern army and the guerrillas. In addition, there were some small- and medium-size factories, mostly owned by the ethnic Chinese.

For the past 35 years, T.D. has undergone massive transformations in its social, political and economic structures and in population as a result of three significant transitions: the construction of socialism or "hard reform" (1975–85), the onset of the (soft) reform policy (1986–90) and the influx of foreign capital (since the 1990s). After the postwar unification, the socialist government designated the area for two specialized functions. First, the lowlands were reorganized as a vegetable provider to the city. Through the government sponsored "Green Ring Movement (Vanh Dai Xanh),"[13] a significant number of rice fields and deserted lands were transformed into vegetable gardens to replace the vegetables formerly imported from the southern mountainous areas such as Da Lat and Bao Loc. Second, the highlands were intensively industrialized to solve the country's scarcity of consumer goods. However, because of a lack of capital and raw materials, the main effect of this industrialization drive was to expand the already existing factories in Phouc Long, Linh Trung and the area along the Highway Number One.

The onset of the reform policy (1986) resulted in the government taking another position concerning T.D. First, the rapid expansion of population in the city, through both high birth rates and migration, required that more land be used for residential areas. Thus, the government set up a project to transform parts of the lowland fields, raising the ground level for construction. Two lowland areas just across from the downtown were included in this plan, but only the An Phu area was successfully reclaimed because of financial difficulty. Unfortunately, the construction plan could not fulfill its original purpose because the An Phu area became too expensive and inaccessible for ordinary people. Instead, the plan ignited an epidemic of private construction led by relatively wealthy H.C.M. City residents who built spacious suburban houses with orchards. At the same time, the reform policy accelerated the expansion of industrial construction into Binh Chieu, adjacent to Dong Nai and Binh Duong provinces, while small private brick factories flourished around Long Binh village on the Dong Nai River. In the end, the whole process of construction and industrialization only produced more crowded and deteriorated residential quarters and the expansion of slums along the Saigon River. The children of peasants who lost fields in the process and the immigrants from other rural areas had to look desperately for both jobs and a place to live.

Finally, the appearance of foreign capital in the first part of 1990s extraordinarily intensified the changes triggered by the reform policy. The central industrial areas such as Linh Trung and Phuc Long were expanded to have one E.P.Z. and a few I.Z.s full of joint-ventures and independent multinational enterprises. Other areas such as Binh Chieu also gained an E.P.Z. and some industrial compounds. Now this area is full of factories producing mainly textiles, garments, shoes, bags, utensils, toys, plastic goods, and assembling electronic products—all combining large quantities of very low-waged labor with surprisingly small quantities of capital. Simultaneously, the construction of luxurious houses, villas, a golf course and a theme park has turned a small part of T.D. into a bedroom community and entertainment center for rich foreign businessmen. With the construction boom, a lot of people jumped on the bandwagon of speculative investment in real estate until the Asian financial crisis of the late 1990s "put a damper on the fever".[14]

The economic stimulation brought on by foreign capital has not resulted in "modernization" (*hien dai hoa*) as the government had promoted and expected. Quite apart from the poor who live in the Thu Thien slum[15] and in illegally built residential areas, the majority of the people in T.D. still suffer from a high level of unemployment, low wages in the multinational factories, and unstable jobs such as temporary construction work, street vending and low wage service work. Besides the deepening unevenness and disparity in social economic structure within the district, there is little general improvement of infrastructure in and between the villages. For example, although the main roads connected to the Highway Number One[16] and industrial complexes, all of them crucial to industrial transportation, have been expanded and paved, most of the small roads are still unpaved and remain as alleys. Furthermore, many roads are still equipped with old sewerage facilities built by the French colonial government and often flood during the rainy season. Living in a city with a miserable public transportation system, people must take dangerous motorbikes on slippery roads. Other public facilities such as schools, hospitals and various district administrative offices remain mostly unchanged or meagerly renovated despite increasing foreign investment in the industrial areas.

A notable exception to this bleak picture of underinvestment is in areas where small local enterprises are active. For example, the local market places in the villages that were blighted and barely survived as black markets during the postwar reform era are rapidly revitalizing with various commodities and commercial activities. By the same token, as the private ownership of real estate becomes more secure in practice, if not in law, individual efforts to renovate and raise the value of houses, commercial buildings and land are gradually changing the appearances of the villages in the area. In short, the improvement in living standards in this industrial district is realized mainly through individual effort and as a privatization process. In such circumstances, only a small number of people, in particular local merchants, landlords and bureaucrats who have access to the political and economic resources of the district, have the potential for improving their lives. Working-class families, underpaid in the new industries and losing the benefits provided by the socialist state such as housing and social insurance, are falling behind.

Despite facing these social economic problems, curiously enough, there has so far been no sign of large-scale protest or major reactions from the working class in the area. Why did and does this happen? To address this question, I will briefly examine how the working class has responded to the change in work and household economy after the massive influx of foreign investment.

Culture, Resistance and Capitalist Discipline in the Early Period of Foreign Investment

One day a boy asked his father about "Collective Mastership" (*lam chu tap the*). The father explained that "Collective Mastership" comprises four elements: party, government, trade union and people. Then the boy asked what party, government, trade union and people are. The father answered "I am giving you an order, so I am the party. Your mother takes care of you and your brother, so she is the government. Your grandmother always protects you, so she is the trade union. And you and your brother are the people." The next day, his teacher asked him to describe family life in the evening. He said "Last night, I saw the party embrace the government, the trade union doze off and the people wet their beds." He got a perfect score.[17]

When foreign companies first set about managing joint ventures with state-owned enterprises in Thu Duc between 1993 and 1995, there was considerable tension between foreign management and Vietnamese workers, which culminated in frequent strikes. Problems of cultural difference, nationalist antagonism and limited communication on the shop floor generated conflict, as they still now do. Besides these general problems, there was a specifically Vietnamese issue that resulted in friction.

Significantly, the workers who had been accustomed to different relations of (and in) production were suddenly subjected to capitalistic discipline in which the foreign factory managers had full discretion to make use of their labor as they saw fit within the contracted working hours. Although not satisfied, the workers endured this discipline, in the hope that the foreign companies would compensate their harder work with a bonus at the end of the year as the previously existing (state-owned) companies had done. When they found out that the distribution of profit was totally different under the new factory regime, they became furious. The managers of foreign companies argued that they could not afford a bonus because they had not made any significant profits. Others argued that under the contract profits were not supposed to be distributed as bonuses and should be used for accumulation.

The workers desperately needed the bonus to cover what they called their "thirteenth month salary", a form of socialist distribution and sharing of annual profits especially in the state-owned companies. As the Vietnamese Lunar New Year (Tet) drew near, they had to buy special foods, visit relatives in their hometowns, and give lucky money (*ly xi*) to their children. Tet is so meaningful that the T.D. native workers would spend two to three times their monthly salary to fulfill their kinship obligations, including ancestor worship and the support of their parents. Immigrant workers from north and central Vietnam even saved money for several years in "piggy banks"[18] so that they could take the train for three to ten days to visit their parents back home. In short, as capitalist discipline challenged the workers' concept not only of work but also of the proper way of sharing and maintaining social ties, they resisted, hoping to restore what they thought was culturally meaningful. Responding to the strikes, many of the foreign companies began to offer a Tet bonus.

In the early period of foreign investment, foreign capital, the Vietnamese government, trade unions and workers were all perplexed by the clash of different ways of thinking, as the Tet bonus episode shows. The circumstances have changed considerably since then. The government and trade unions found ways to avoid conflictual situations by negotiating labor laws[19] that could be imposed on both the foreign management and the Vietnamese workers. The foreign managers also learned to respect the indigenous culture, realizing that in doing so they could actually discipline the workers more effectively. Older workers, both in and transferred from the state-owned factories, became used to the new concepts and rules of work, catching up with the young workers in the foreign and private companies who were subject to capitalist discipline from the beginning. Overall the changes indicate how rapidly capitalist relations of production are penetrating the industrial areas of H.C.M. City. The social, political and economic changes brought on by rapid capitalist transformation created a new context for response and resistance on the part of working people. It will be helpful to examine the dynamics of household economy to understand how the working class adapts, responds to and resists the imposed changes of the new context.

Material Conditions, Social Networks and Resistance

The workers' material conditions in T.D. are uneven according to many variables including family property, the number of dependents, marital status, and the conditions of work. New immigrants from other provinces, arriving in the 1990s, tend to live a harsher life than the T.D. natives because of their problems finding housing and meeting settlement expenses. The workers in the state-owned factories suffer from low productivity and consequent erratic work schedules whereas the workers in private and foreign companies are more worried about lay-offs. Despite these differences, the workers in T.D. have much in common.

The average monthly wage of a factory worker is 0.7 million–1.3 million Dong (U.S.$47–87). Average household income is around 1.5–2.5 million Dong (U.S.$100–167),[20] which is almost equivalent to the minimum living expenses for a household with three to four people. In other words, one household needs at least two workers who have stable jobs in a factory, or one worker and one or two other family members with temporary or lower income jobs, such as street vendor, temporary construction worker or service worker at a café or restaurant. The income earned by wage laboring in the factory is so crucial to the reproduction of the household economy that many daughters in the factories of T.D. do not marry, being obliged to support their parents. When the daughters are married, under normal circumstances they can manage a household for some time with only supplementary income from their husband. However, once they have two children, a married couple cannot pay for their entire living expenses without extra income, because of the high cost of baby formula and education. In sum, one worker's income is both indispensable and insufficient for the reproduction of the working-class household.

There are various kinds of situations and expenses that aggravate the financial problems of a working-class family. First of all, they themselves have to deal with emergency situations such as the medical problems of unemployed family members and housing (including rent hikes and house repairs), because the state's support for medical insurance and housing are now becoming nominal and of extremely low quality at best. Under socialist policy, most working-class families had members who worked for state-owned companies and were at least guaranteed medical treatment, educational fees and housing, even though the quality of assistance might have been lower than today's privatized care (see Han 1998). They can no longer enjoy these benefits. Secondly, the expenses associated with maintaining ties with relatives and friends are not minimal for working class families. For example, in 1999 factory workers would spend an average of 50,000–200,000 V.N.D. (U.S.$3–13) a month for wedding gifts for their relatives and fellow workers. Even though these expenses are part of a system of "prolonged balanced reciprocity" (Sahlins 1972: 191–6), they are obviously a large burden on a tight household budget, especially during the wedding season from October to March. In addition, to maintain necessary social relationships, workers need to spend considerable amounts of money for other ceremonies such as ancestor worship, birthday parties and the annual celebration of Tet. Lastly, burgeoning consumer markets are a temptation hard to overcome. A variety of consumer goods including clothing, foods and electric home appliances, formally not widely available in the distribution system of the state, are now in the market. Refrigerators and motorcycles in this subtropical country with a poor public transportation system are considered now almost necessities and have become the objects of saving for the working-class family. Even though many companies provide buses to transport workers from the villages in the district and other districts, the workers feel under pressure to buy motorcycles for personal and family mobility.

Under the circumstances, a working-class family easily reaches a financial crisis. There are primarily two ways to prepare for and resolve financial problems. One way is to utilize social networks including kinship. Workers can ask favors of relatives and acquaintances in the neighborhood. Around two-thirds of the T.D. population[21] are natives whose families have lived in the area for generations and who have well-developed social networks. Even new immigrants who arrived in the 1990s usually had relatives who helped them to settle in and find jobs. The social networks not only assist the workers financially but are also a source of information and recommendations. However, the mutual assistance among relatives and friends has limits because they are likely to share the same straightened circumstances.

Another and more active way to cushion financial crises is to join a traditional "informal credit union or mutual saving club" called Hui. Hui is so popular among the workers that there are numerous groups and organizers (called Chu Hui) in any given factory.[22] People actually belong to more than one Hui at the same time, but we can explain the logic of the situation by looking at one. Each Hui has around twenty to thirty members. Each member contributes about 50,000–100,000 V.N.D. (U.S.$3.3–6.6) every two weeks. Each Hui is organized in a cycle. The cycle is the number of members times the period for contribution. If there are thirty members, each contributing once every two weeks (usually on paydays), then the cycle is 60 weeks. The art or science of the Hui is based on the rule that a member can collect the holdings of one Hui only once in a cycle. But they cannot collect all the holdings; during the cycle the size of "the pot" therefore increases. Especially at first—at the beginning of the cycle—the person who asks for the least amount of money gets what they ask for, and the remainder stays in the pot. So if the Hui is collecting, for example, 30 (members) × 3 (U.S.$), or U.S.$90, in the first collection, the person who gets it will very likely be the one who asks for much less than 90. But you have to keep contributing for the whole cycle. In the process, Hui functions as a way for workers to both save and obtain relatively large sums of money at a time. Because of people's deep-rooted distrust and the inefficiency of the formal banking system, Hui is very important and popular among factory workers.

The strong social ties between relatives, friends and members of Hui organizations have, as with pooling associations elsewhere, provided not only mechanisms to manage the unstable household economy but also the grounds for active solidarity among the workers. This has been especially evident during times of wage cuts and layoffs. Six strikes taking place in the old Thu Duc in 1998 (out of a total of thirty-eight in H.C.M. City) and five strikes in 1999 (out of a total of twenty-five in H.C.M. City) are examples. One can ask if the strikes, already minor given the conditions in many of the factories in T.D., would even have occurred had it not been for the Hui cushion.

The unstable economic life in T.D. and the compensatory social organizations like Hui can be a source of internal fission and antagonism as well as solidarity and resistance, however. For example, the high level of unemployment (10–20 per cent) and the expanding industrial reserve army in the 1990s have intensified competition among workers. At the same time, many of the Hui organizers engage in loan sharking, exacting a high rate of interest (10–40 per cent) and creating hostility among fellow workers. As the Chu Hui(s) gain control of U.S.$10,000 to 20,000, the workers suffer from heavy debts. In addition, the Hui mechanism itself can also contribute to the acceleration of class differentiation among the ordinary members because the longer you can wait to ask for your collection from the pot in a Hui cycle, the larger the total pot probably is. This favors the more financially secure and better off members; indeed it is a mechanism for transferring some amount of money to better off members. In other words, the Hui(s) transfer funds from households with low or variable income, such as single wage earners, to more secure and stable households, such as those with multiple wage earners.

The other important variable that has mitigated the political potential of the working class in this area is Vietnam's "corporatist" political structure between state, trade union, management and the working class, considered by many a source of political stability (see Chan 1993: 61, Norlund 1997, White, Howell and Shang 1996). However, the political structure and the trade union's role as a "transmission belt" have been rapidly changing as capitalist relations of production permeate the factories. How the workers will ultimately respond to the structural changes introduced by foreign capital and new state policy remains to be seen.

Conclusion

I have surveyed the dynamics of change in H.C.M. City in general and Thu Duc in particular in terms of two mutually related factors: growing foreign influence and privatization. There is much evidence that the city will continue to change according to these two factors. The influential power of foreign capital was more than proved by the Asian economic crisis of the late 1990s, when a sudden decrease in foreign investment undermined economic growth in the city, creating a recession. It seems unlikely, indeed virtually impossible, that the Vietnamese government will reverse the pro-privatization policy, however, at least as long as the remaining state-owned companies continue to drain national wealth.[23] In fact, the socialist government is more anxious about the slow tempo of privatization, including the creation of a stock market (Co Phan Hoa), than about the negative results of privatization.

The most noteworthy consequence of the changes in the city is the implausible juxtaposition of the "numerous contradictions" and political stability (Nguyen Khac Vien and Huu Ngoc 1998: 191). First, the city has witnessed rapid class differentiation and growing inequality. The children of prosperous merchants and high officials appear in the downtown discotheques every night, arriving in expensive cars and ordering $200 whiskies. Meanwhile, 300 residents on the island of Ba Sang in T.D. manage to live with 300,000 V.N.D. (U.S.$20) of monthly household income.[24] Such contrasts become increasingly common as the uneven development of the city accelerates. Nor can the trade unions be counted on to win better working and living conditions for the working class. As more workers fall under capitalistic relations of production, the trade unions are losing their ability to influence the decision-making process of the companies. In this process, it is questionable how the socialist state can maintain support from the workers and unions. Finally, the discrepancy between the dominant ideologies of the socialist state and the social and economic realities of the city creates a number of self-contradictory realities and discourses. The construction of socialism through privatization and "strong trade unions" cooperating with their companies are just a few of the contradictions.

At this moment it is not easy to predict what changes will occur, or when, or how. It is however clear that the future of the city depends upon how these contradictions are, or are not, resolved.

Notes

1. The research on which this article is based was sponsored by the Social Science Research Council and the Wenner-Gren Foundation. I would like to thank Gerald Sider, Jane Schneider and Hy Van Luong for their helpful comments.
2. The Diamond Plaza was built by a joint venture of Korean and Vietnamese steel companies. The building is located on Le Duan street and cost U.S.$92 million.
3. Many reports suggest that the "soft" reform socialism of 1986–9 stabilized the Vietnamese state (for example, Fforde and Vylder 1996: 258). According to Nguyen Khac Vien (1998: 189–90), the government "has won the bet because it has provided efficiency," an example being the successful prohibition of firecrackers during the lunar New Year.
4. The southern people expended 114 per cent of G.D.P. between 1960–74, most of it on consumption, presumably because of the influx of G.I. spending (Beresford 1988: 98–9).
5. In 1976, after many left the cities, it was estimated that 30.5 per cent of the southern people were urbanized, mostly in Da Nang and Saigon (Beresford 1988). In some places, the population density was more than 28,000 people/km^2 (Nguyen Khac Vien and Huu Ngoc 1998: 160).
6. "Cholon" means big market in Chinese.
7. The official statistics from the Vietnamese government are not so consistent and show some differences with those of foreign sources.

According to research of the U.N.D.P. and World Bank, G.D.P. per person in Vietnam was $103 ($165 in the urban areas, $85 in the rural areas) in 1994. In comparison, the World Almanac gives an estimate of $230. In 1999, the official G.D.P. per person in Vietnam was $374 (Korean Trade-Investment Promoting Agency, internet data).

8. For example, in 1999, the city still used many roads and sewage facilities built by the French colonial government. In the rainy season, roads flooded often. Public transportation was terrible. There were only 2,837 buses in this megacity: one seat on a bus for every 1,000 people. Thus only 2 per cent of the people used the public transportation system, relying instead on dangerous motorbikes. This gave H.C.M. City the highest traffic accident rate in the world. Telephone distribution covered only 10 per cent of residents and it took at least one year after application to get telephone service. In the primitive communication infrastructure, there were but 22,000 Internet subscribers, most of them foreign or associated with large domestic companies (*Saigon Gai Phong*, 11 November 1999; *Saigon Marketing*, 31 July 1999).
9. For example, the official population of H.C.M. City in 1994 was 4.63 million and 4.8 million in 1995 while KOTRA (Korean Trade-investment Promotion Agency) estimated it to be 5 million in 1994 and 7 million in 1995.
10. Honda Dream, made in Japan, is the most popular motorbike and costs U.S.$2,500–3,000. Even though some privileged youth have this brand, it is not affordable to the majority of people. It is common to purchase lower priced brands (U.S.$1,500–2,000) or used ones (500–1,500 U.S.D.). Some people, including most of the XE OM (commercial motorbike) drivers, still use the old cycles produced in the 1960s.
11. As one Vietnamese sociologist expressed it, “with power and access to the market you can change your life, without that you can’t get rich” (Drakakis-Smith 2000: 3).
12. Thu Duc is now divided into three districts: districts 2, 9 and Thu Duc. However, what people usually mean by Thu Duc—and the meaning adopted in this essay—is the old Thu Duc area, including the two newly separated districts.
13. The Green Ring Movement was also initiated in the rural districts surrounding other cities, for example Go Vap, Binh Chanh and Hoc Mon, all of them situated in the former Gia Dinh province. According to the local officials of the time, besides the Green Ring, there were several other government-led movements, for example the

V.A.C. or garden (*voun*)—pond (*ao*)—cage (*chuong*) movement, which encouraged efficient management of the family economy. The concept was one of raising poultry on fields or gardens, throwing the residue of animal feed into ponds stocked with fish, and using animal dung as manure. Clearly, food production was vital to central planning after liberation.

14. Some people received a private loan and participated in the speculation, especially in An Phu area, but suffered from debts as the Asian financial crisis resulted in the reduction of foreign investment and fall in the price of land.
15. The Thu Thiem slum is just across the Saigon river. The native poor and the immigrants working as *xich lo* (pedicab) and *xe om* (commercial motorcycle) drivers, temporary construction workers, and street vendors live in the slum areas formed along the river. The slum areas are notorious for drug addiction and crime.
16. A national highway connecting the north, center and south.
17. Intellectuals in the north tell this joke which, however sarcastic, shows the primary problem of the political structure in the socialist Vietnam.
18. Typical piggy banks (*hop dung tien*) are in the shape of round ceramic bottles. In many television dramas, a family member breaks the piggy bank with a small hammer to meet a financial exigency.
19. The new labor law was established in January 1994 and became effective from June 1995.
20. This calculation is based on my research in thirty multinational corporations in H.C.M. City and a year-and-a-half of fieldwork (1998–2000) in a joint venture. The number is similar to the one reported by a local newspaper, *Saigon Gai Phong* (16 October 2000). According to the article, in the Asian-invested textile sector, workers earned, on average, 0.7–1 million Dong (U.S.$47-67) per month.
21. I could not find any statistics on the ratio of native to immigrant populations in Thu Duc. However, the district and factory administrators whom I interviewed estimated that one-third of the district population were immigrants who had moved to the area in the second half of twentieth century and identified themselves as such. This was also the case in the textile factory I studied.
22. It has also been an important way for small merchants to raise funds. Hui created a major social problem in H.C.M. City, however, as some Hui groups went bankrupt. The bankruptcy caused by a famous female singer's swindle in 1993 amounted to U.S.$5 million. Even today, the government is challenged by problems related to Hui

activity, in particular bankruptcy, loan sharking, and violence (see Leshkowich 2000).

23. The number of state-owned companies in the industrial sector is still around 50 per cent. According to a World Bank report, private companies create one job per $800 of investment whereas the state-owned companies spend $18,000 to create one job. In 1997, the state-owned companies actually lost 1.4 trillion V.N.D., including their tax exemption (www.kotra.or.kr/main/country).
24. I visited this island during my fieldwork. Working at private and state-owned brick factories, the residents earn 300,000–500,000 V.N.D. (20–33 U.S.D.) a month. They have electricity only three hours a day because their community cannot afford full coverage, which costs 100,000 V.N.D. (U.S.$7) daily. The communist secretary of the island estimated that the government needed to spend 2 million V.N.D. (U.S.$133) per year to alleviate the poverty.

References

Beresford, M. (1988), "Issues in Economic Unification: Overcoming the Legacy of Separation in Postwar Vietnam", in Marr, D.G. and White, C.P. (eds), *Dilemmas in Socialist Vietnam*, Ithaca: Cornell University Southeast Asia Program, pp. 95–110.

Chan, A. (1993), "Revolution or Corporatism? Workers and Trade Unions in Post-Mao China", *The Australian Journal of Chinese Affairs*, 29: 1–40.

Cho, Y.B. and Sung, B.H. (1997), *Here in Vietnam*, Seoul: Shin Woo.

Drakakis-Smith, D. (2000), *Third World Cities*, London and New York: Routledge.

Duiker, W.J. (1995), *Vietnam: Revolution in Transition*, Boulder: Westview Press.

Fford, A. and Vylder, S. (1996), *From Plan to Market: The Economic Transition in Vietnam*, Boulder CO: Westview Press.

Han, D.H. (1997), "Rural Reform and Welfare in Vietnam", *The Journal of Rural Society*, 8: 161–85.

Kolko, G (1997), *Vietnam: Anatomy of a Peace*, London and New York: Routledge.

Le Manh Hung (chief author) (1999), *Vietnam Socio-economy: the Period 1996–1998 and Forecast for the Year 2000*, Hanoi: Statistical Publishing House.

Leshkowich, A.M. (2000), *Tight Woven Threads: Gender, Kinship and "Secret Agency" among Cloth and Clothing Traders in Ho Chi Minh*

City's Ben Thanh Market. PhD Dissertation, Department of Anthropology, Harvard University.

Marr, D.G. and White, C.O. (eds) (1988), *Postwar Vietnam: Dilemmas in Socialist Development*, Ithaca: Cornell University Southeast Asia Program.

Nguyen Khac Vien (1980), *Vietnam Five Years After,* Hanoi: FLPH.

Nguyen Khac Vien and Huu Ngoc (eds) (1998), *From Saigon to Ho Chi Minh City: A Path of 300 Years*, Ho Chi Minh City: The Gioi Publishers.

Norlund, I. (1997), Democracy and Trade Unions in Vietnam: Riding a Honda in Slow Speed. Paper presented to the 49th meeting of American Association of Asian Studies, Chicago.

Pravda, A. and Ruble, B. (eds) (1986), *Trade Unions in Communist States*, Boston: Allen & Unwin.

Sahlins, M. (1972), *Stone Age Economics*, Chicago: Aldine.

Smith, D.A. (1996), "Going South: Global Restructuring and Garment Production in Three East Asian Cases," *Asian Perspectives*, 20(2): 211–41.

Vo Nhan Tri (1988), "Party Policies and Economics Performance: The Second and Third Five Year Plans Examined", in Marr, D.G. and White, C.P. (eds), *Dilemmas in Socialist Vietnam*, Ithaca: Cornell University Southeast Asia Program, pp. 77–90.

—— (1990), *Vietnam's Economic Policy Since 1975*, Singapore: Institute of Southeast Asian Studies.

Walzer, M. (1992), The Civil Society Argument. In Mouffe, C. (ed.), *Dimension of Radical Democracy: Pluralism, Citizenship, Community*, Verso: London, pp. 90–7.

White G., Howell, J. and Shang, X. (eds) (1996), *In Search of Civil Society: Market Reform and Social Change in Contemporary China*, Oxford: Clarendon Press.

Part IV
Reconstruction and Recovery

–12–

Belfast: Urban Space, "Policing" and Sectarian Polarization

Dominic Bryan

Territorial divisions have always defined the city of Belfast in Northern Ireland. But from 1969, widespread political violence led to large population movements, leaving the city more polarized than ever. Even the peace process in the late 1990s does not appear to have reduced segregation; indeed tension at interface areas is arguably worse than ever. The management of this polarization is a struggle for ordinary people and policy makers alike. Whilst Belfast goes through changes common to many cities around the world those changes have specific local ramifications. In this chapter I want to explore the "policing" of boundaries and interfaces in Belfast, its effect on people and on the built environment. By "policing" I am not simply referring to the activities of the institution of the police but to the practices and beliefs of communities that continue to divide urban space. I then want to look at ways that projects and policies are attempting to overcome these difficulties in the light of actual and potential investment in the city.

By 1967 the civil rights movement had started to hold demonstrations that penetrated the centers of the cities and towns of Northern Ireland, centers viewed as Protestant. The movement demanded fairer allocation of housing and jobs for Catholics from Protestant-controlled government, local authorities and employers, as well as an end to gerrymandering of votes at elections. Small groups of fundamentalist Protestant protestors stood in the town centers and the Royal Ulster Constabulary (R.U.C.), a predominantly Protestant police force, kept the sides apart. Political tension increased and violent clashes, of increasing ferocity, developed between police and civil rights demonstrators. The conflict inevitably and increasingly became understood in ethnic terms (Feldman 1991: 22). Areas of north and west Belfast and the Bogside in Derry became the site of confrontations between the police and Catholics and between Protestants and Catholics. In August 1969, with the R.U.C. demoralized and discredited, the British Army was introduced onto the streets, in the first place to protect Catholics. Paramilitary groups on both sides started to "police" and "protect" their areas. The period known as "the Troubles" had begun and issues of civil rights came secondary to those of nationality (see Bew, Gibbon and Patterson 1995: 145–91). Violence increased and between 1969 and 1976 approximately 15,000 families in Belfast were forced to relocate, around 12 per cent of the population (Boal and Murray 1977).

Belfast has a long history of residential ethnic divisions based on whether members of a community are Protestant or Catholic, showing allegiance to Britain or Ireland respectively. During times of relative peace ethnic segregation was still the norm with territory marked out and "policed" by the flying of flags, the holding of commemorations, and by the normal forms of "telling" the other (Burton 1978: 37–67). But during times of violence the boundaries were further inscribed through crowd invasions, pogroms and sectarian murders. The boundaries then became more clearly marked by vacant housing that no one dared occupy, by cleared waste ground, and, in recent years, by purposefully built walls separating communities (Murtagh 2002: 45–64).

It is possible to characterize the divisions in Belfast as having a form distinct from divisions common in most cities. Belfast has been described as "located in the middle of an Irish British interface zone, and a very untidy interface zone it is" (Boal, Murray and Poole 1976: 121). Boal suggests Belfast is a *polarized* city as opposed to simply a divided city. A crucial element of his description is that governing of parts of the city takes place without consensus. "Simple service delivery questions and planning decisions regarding the use of space are transformed into conflicts" (Boal 1994: 31). He argues that polarized cities such as Jerusalem, Brussels and Montréal, in being the focal point of conflict between two national groups, suffer from a severity of division that goes beyond divisions widely observed in north America and Europe. In other cities socio-economic division may exist in ethnically homogenous or in ethnically heterogeneous environments, but in polarized cities ethno-nationalism offers the possibility of a strategy of separatism.

> In a polarised city, such group identity is reinforced through ethno-nationalist expressions in the urban landscape. These can include symbolic buildings linked to, or hosting, opposition political parties; administrative centers of pseudo-state activity or murals or other graphic expressions of resistance and territoriality. (Bollens 1999:35)

A Brief History

Belfast, more than any other city in Ireland, was shaped by the industrial revolution, much like the cities of Manchester and Liverpool in England and very like Glasgow in Scotland. It was a relatively insignificant town in the eighteenth century, notable for being close to the rapidly expanding linen industry. It was a predominantly Presbyterian town and home to some of the radicals who took part in the uprising of the United Irishmen against the British Crown in 1798. At the start of the nineteenth century the cotton industry fluctuated but Belfast grew in the boom periods. The linen industry prospered. The population of Belfast was 20,000 in 1801 but 70,000 by 1841. In 1786, 722 ships passed through the harbor but by 1820 the number was up to 2,423 (Bardon and Burnet 1996: 37–43). Conditions in the city were very poor. By the 1840s very high infant mortality meant that average life expectancy was nine years (Bardon and Burnet 1996: 60). There was growing employment but many jobs were low paid and physically demanding. By the second half of the nineteenth century Belfast was established as an industrial city. It was a great linen producer, had a growing ship building industry, boasted the largest rope factory in the world, and as a result also developed a substantial engineering industry. In 1861 its population was up to 121,000 and by 1901 it was 350,000. Between 1891 and 1901 alone the population increased by 93,000. Low-rental housing built up around the industries. In 1888 Belfast received a royal charter and became a city (Boal 1995: 13–14, Bardon and Burnett 1996: 64–8).

Early in the nineteenth century there was not much to indicate the sectarian divisions that were to become a feature of Belfast. In 1811 Catholics made up 4,000 of a population of 30,000 (Bardon and Burnet 1996: 46). As fears over Catholic emancipation grew, however, so did tensions. In 1832, after the December election, four people died in riots. In 1845 the potato crops failed and thousands of people, predominantly, but not only, Catholics, poured into the city, the Catholics mainly settling in poor districts to the west. Residence within the city was increasingly definable in sectarian terms and according to social class.

From the 1830s through to 1970 the Catholics made up between a quarter to a third of Belfast's population. As the overall population increased the sectarian boundaries might become blurred, but political events, such as elections and campaigns for Home Rule for Ireland, and tensions over parades and commemorations, often led to rioting and pogroms. This is particularly true of the Protestant Orange parades on the

Twelfth of July, anniversary of the Battle of the Boyne. Major riots took place in the city in 1857, 1863, 1864, 1872 and 1886 (Boyd 1969, Budge and O'Leary 1973). The riots in 1864 between Protestant "ship carpenters" and Catholic "navvies" were of particular ferocity and riots in 1886 saw over fifty people killed (Wright 1996: 476–509). On each occasion Catholics were evicted from Protestant areas and Protestants from Catholic areas and it was also not uncommon for expulsions of Catholics to take place at predominantly Protestant work places. Ethnic exclusivity in housing or work was periodically reinforced.

From the 1870s onwards parades in Belfast became larger and more frequent, whereas events of an Irish nationalist character were excluded from the city center. Protestants dominated policing until 1865 when the local force was amalgamated with the Royal Irish Constabulary. As such, by the 1880s, although senior officers were Protestant the force was relatively evenly balanced. During the 1886 riots many Protestants accused the government of packing the force with Catholics (Weitzer 1995: 29–30). Control of the city both in terms of urban space, housing, local politics, and employment was contested through a complex network of class relationships (Patterson 1980) but Belfast was, symbolically and politically, a Protestant city.

The partition of Ireland in 1920 placed the Protestant community through the Ulster Unionist Party (U.U.P.) in a dominant position in the new northern quasi-state. The new police force, the Royal Ulster Constabulary (R.U.C.), was dominated by Protestants, heavily armed and backed by repressive emergency legislation. Unionist politics was driven by fears of the new Catholic state in the south and the existence of a military threat from the I.R.A. The Catholics of the north were thus depicted as the enemy within. Nationalist events were restricted and Irish Republican commemorations banned. Sectarian disturbances were still common and in 1935 riots in the Docks area of Belfast left seven Protestants and three Catholics dead and 430 Catholics and sixty-four Protestants forcibly evicted from their homes (Hepburn 1990). After the Second World War community relations seem to have improved, possibly in part due to the lack of a credible nationalist campaign in the north.

In the 1950s Belfast's linen industry went into decline, followed by the shipbuilding industry a decade later. Unemployment became consistently higher than in the rest of Britain. Slum housing led to urban redevelopment on the edges of the city and the population of the center of the city started to fall. From a high of nearly 450,000 after the Second World War, by 1971 it had dropped to 350,000 and has since dropped to 280,000. Belfast's greater urban area stands at around 480,000 (Boal 1995: 22–3).

Boal has estimated that at the turn of the century around 59 per cent of the population lived in segregated streets (defined as a street where more than 90 per cent of the households are all Catholic or all Protestant). He believes that although there were periods when this percentage declined slightly, such as in the 1940s and 1950s, every period of conflict dramatically increased segregation. By the mid-1960s, 68 per cent lived in segregated streets, 78 per cent by the mid-1980s (Boal 1995: 27). In the 1990s, thirty-five of Belfast's fifty-one local council wards contained either a 90 per cent Catholic or 90 per cent Protestant population (Bollens 1999: 59). Segregation is particularly marked in the public housing sector. Displays of bunting and flags, the building of Orange arches and the holding of parades demarcated Protestant areas around the Twelfth of July whilst displays of Irish Tricolors mark Catholic areas, particularly around commemorations of the Easter Rising.

For most of its modern history Belfast has been segregated although this segregation has not always been marked by violence. It is a city in which the Protestant community dominated politically and, to a varying extent, economically. The center of the city is full of statues and buildings that symbolize this. And until recently Irish nationalism has been either suppressed or pushed into the margins of west Belfast and other Catholic enclaves.

"Policing" the Boundaries

Throughout the Troubles, a set of micro and macro political practices acted to exacerbate and institutionalize polarization in Belfast. The civil rights marches in principle were demanding rights within the state of Northern Ireland. In practice they were questioning the hegemonic position of Unionism. This was not only true in the wider political sense but also in a symbolic, territorial, sense. The civil rights demonstrations took routes where, for over forty years, only the Protestant Orange Order had marched. Albeit that the territory under question was the center of Belfast, Derry and other towns, this nevertheless created a new political dynamic. Soon transgressions led to pogroms with the police failing, sometimes deliberately, to protect Catholics. From 1969 onwards the Catholic working-class communities practiced resistance to the state by forming what became known as no go areas. That resistance shifted from being one of political street protest under the civil rights banner to armed resistance by the Provisional Irish Republican Army (I.R.A.). At the same time the British state introduced the army to support regular policing duties and disbanded various elements of the R.U.C. The Protestant community, particularly in urban working-class areas, lost confidence in the role of the state in policing and formed local defense organizations that patrolled territory. By 1972 these organizations were amalgamated into the Ulster Defense Association (U.D.A.) joining the older existing loyalist paramilitary group, the Ulster Volunteer Force (U.V.F.).

At first, the boundaries between Protestant and Catholic areas were marked by space with housing no one would live in and by police and army checkpoints with armored vehicles and barbed (razor) wire. Ritual practices such as parading took on added meanings in the new political context. Whilst parades by the Orange Order, Black Institution, and Apprentice Boys of Derry, generically termed the loyal orders, are perceived as "traditional," they can be shown to have altered significantly after 1969 (Bryan 2000). Most parades do not cross ethnic territorial boundaries but a significant few do. In the 1950s and 1960s they were tolerated within Catholic areas perhaps through a sense of powerlessness in that community but also because the parades themselves were less assertive. By the 1970s the local marching bands that are hired by the Orange lodges were playing music, carrying names and flags that reflected loyalist paramilitary groups. Added to which these parades brought with them large numbers of security forces. In the 1980s and 1990s, as the R.U.C. became less willing to facilitate such displays, confrontations developed between participants and the police. This in turn created attitudes towards the R.U.C. in Protestant areas that at times have been like those in Catholic areas. Since 1992 opposition to loyal order parades has been more concerted and organized with the development in some Catholic areas of "residents' groups" that, by their very nature, attempt to define "their" territory, communicating that they do not want the loyal order parades passing through (Jarman and Bryan 1996, 1998).

In many respects, however, it is just as important to look at the ritual events that remain inside the boundaries. Jarman (1992, 1993, 1997a, 1998, 2001) and also De Rosa (1998) have mapped the synergism between annual commemorative parades, local marching bands, the painting of wall murals, the painting of curb stones, and local plaques of remembrance. Paramilitary displays at republican and loyalist funerals have also played an important role. O'Reilly has similarly looked at the use of Irish language that in Catholic areas is deployed for street names, on shop and pub signs and on murals (O'Reilly 1998: 43–62). Although the rituals, the murals and the signage give messages to "the other," they are more about talking to "their own" community; indeed most wall murals are not painted at boundary edges but within housing estates.

> The centrality of macroterritorial concepts such as "united Ireland" or a "British Ulster" and their complex interplay with microterritorial constructs such as the community, the neighbourhood, the street, and the parade route reinforces the manner in which geography serves to posit history as a cultural object. (Feldman 1991:27)

The power of these events and practices is in part due to the role of state and paramilitary interventions since the late 1960s when working class areas of Belfast and Derry became mapped by violence (Fay, Morrisey and Smyth 1998). The years 1971 to 1976 saw particularly high levels of violence (in 1972 there were 497 deaths) with civilians (not security forces or paramilitaries) making up more than half those killed (Smyth 2000: 118–35). The worst affected areas have been to the west and north of Belfast and Derry. Loyalist violence was marked by the frequent random killing of Catholics, the most well known gang being the notorious Shankill Butchers (Dillon 1990). Attacks on mixed marriage households in Protestant areas were also common. In the Catholic areas of west Belfast violence was a part of the forms of *resistance* directed towards the state (Sluka 1995: 71–102). From low level street disturbances to paramilitary attacks on the R.U.C. and British Army, violence helped define Catholic areas. Quite simply, for many youth, if you saw a police or army vehicle you picked up a stone and threw it. The security forces responded, often with violence, overtly and covertly. In August 1971 security forces interned over 300 people without trial. Up until the 1998 peace agreement, security operations to uncover arms or arrest suspects remained common place. A range of surveillance techniques have been deployed at a host of fortified military bases and police stations. There were even notorious army listening posts on the tops of high-rise flats in west Belfast. Most of us living in Belfast in the 1980s and 1990s were accustomed to the constant noise from army helicopters above our heads 24 hours a day.

Just as the rituals and symbols are not only about reinforcing boundaries but also about control within communities, violence works within as well as across the territories. The paramilitaries "police" their own areas. The republican paramilitaries have killed 381 Catholics (compared to 316 Catholics killed by the security forces) and loyalists have killed 207 Protestants (Smyth 2000: 125). Punishment beatings are used by all paramilitary forces both to control their organization and to deal with "anti-social" elements within their respective communities (Knox and Monaghan 2000). In addition, rival paramilitary groups within areas compete for control. There have been periodic confrontations between the Irish National Liberation Army (I.N.L.A.) and the I.R.A., for example, and since the summer of 2000 feuds between the U.V.F. and U.D.A. have resulted in a number of murders (Persic and Bloomer n/d).

Two further elements should be considered when exploring the urban interfaces: the commercial center and social class. As the I.R.A. mounted a concerted car bombing campaign in the center of Belfast from 1970, security strategies developed to create what became known as a "ring of steel." Cars were often stopped and checked entering the city center, security men boarded buses to check for bombs, and security barriers were installed on certain roads to allow areas to be sealed off (see Figure 12.1). This process was effectively added to by the building of the Westlink road that cuts between west and north Belfast and the center, offering six crossing points that could be strategically held by the security forces (Jarman 1993: 116). The east of the center is bounded by the River Lagan over which there are three crossing points.

It is vitally important to recognize the role played by social class in the way people experience territorial polarization and violence. Middle-class areas with privately owned houses have seen less of the conflict and are more likely to have a mixed residency. This is most obvious in the

Figure 12.1 Security barrier, Springfield Road, West Belfast. Photograph courtesy of Neil Jarman.

university and Malone Road area of south Belfast but is also true of areas of north, east and west Belfast. People's experiences of a sense of "place" are "local and multiple" (Rodman 1992: 643); their experiences of the conflict also vary widely. The Troubles have been considerably more intense for the working classes (Fay, Morrisey and Smyth 1999).

Interfaces

People who live in interface areas understand a complex set of local rules. Knowledge of the geography has been a matter of life and death yet it is also a way of living a normal life. Anyone living in Belfast for any length of time will soon learn where the interfaces are, even those that are not immediately obvious. Some interface areas have remained simply as cleared ground or empty and derelict housing, perhaps marked by graffiti or flags on the street lights. The response by government to these areas has been twofold. Either a structure ironically called a "peace wall" is erected or attempts are made to introduce commercial buildings in the form of small industrial estates. Interface areas may also be marked by roads and barriers. The Short Strand area in east Belfast is a small Catholic enclave with wide roads on three sides and relatively low fencing. Next door is Cluan Place, a tiny Protestant cul-de-sac, consisting of twenty modern town houses, ten of them burned out or boarded up. It is surrounded on three sides with a thirty-foot high fence offering protection against flying missiles such as bottles, stones and petrol bombs.

North Belfast has the highest concentration of interfaces. Some, such as Limestone Road, consist of ugly, hastily built high fencing with interspersed doorways. Others, such as at Clifton Park Avenue, are relatively new and are not quite as ominous in appearance. Clifton Park Avenue runs right through a "peace wall" that has no gates, only a large clear area with empty housing. The "peace wall" between the Shankill and Springfield Road does have gates, some that are open unless tension is high when they can be closed automatically from a police station, and others that are never open except to allow a parade through (see Figure 12.2).

As noted above, interfaces are not always so obviously physically marked. I live in a street full of semi-detached privately owned houses in north Belfast. The area is "mixed" yet probably locally defined as Catholic. At election time Sinn Féin (political wing of the I.R.A.) and the Social and Democratic Labour Party (S.D.L.P.) canvass in our street. Thirty yards along the road a left-hand turn takes you down to the Shore Road. This junction does not show any signs of being an interface, I

Figure 12.2 "Peace Wall," North Belfast. Photograph courtesy of Neil Jarman.

suspect because the houses on both sides are privately owned, and I have never seen any trouble at it. But it is an interface and the Ulster Unionist Party (U.U.P.) and the Progressive Unionist Party (P.U.P.—political wing of the U.V.F.) canvass in this street. The street takes you down to the Mount Vernon estate with low- and high-rise flats which are U.V.F. controlled, with a large mural making sure everyone is aware of this. Walking in towards the city along the Shore Road, an economically depressed part of the city, there is a lamppost on which fly two loyalist paramilitary flags, one of the U.V.F., one of the U.D.A., marking the boundary between Mount Vernon and Tigers Bay. Tigers Bay is controlled by the U.D.A. Crossing this interface is unproblematic in spite of ongoing conflict between these two loyalist groups. However, during the summer of 2000 in the west of the city a serious feud developed between the U.V.F. in the upper part of the Shankill and the U.D.A. This was sparked by a parade organized by the U.D.A. passing a U.V.F. bar. The violence became so serious that families were again forced out of their homes and British soldiers were brought back onto the streets of Belfast. Some taxi firms from the upper part of the Shankill preferred to go to the city center via the republican controlled Springfield and Falls Road rather than through the U.D.A. controlled area.

Research in north Belfast provides a vivid portrait of the problems. A community enquiry in 1996/97 (Jarman 1997b), conducted after major civil disturbances in the summer of 1996, highlighted levels of intimidation felt in all communities and a lack of understanding between them. This report noted the desire amongst people to live in mixed communities although others have shown that segregation provides a sense of security (Murtagh 1994: 5). A recent report looking at the north Belfast communities of the Ardoyne, viewed as Catholic, and upper Ardoyne viewed as Protestant, showed how people living in both undertake avoidance strategies, motivated by fear. It found that around a quarter of people had moved to their present homes due to insecurity or intimidation in other areas. Over three-quarters of both communities would not shop in "the other" community. Only 17 per cent of men and 3.8 per cent of women "would walk through an area dominated by the other religious/ethnic group at night" (Shirlow 2000).

Peace Building

From 1970 onwards Belfast has seen a series of attempts at regeneration that have involved "redevelopment, population relocation, major infrastructural investment in transportation and communication, compensatory social programs, city center and riverside development" (Gaffikin and Morrissey 1999: 229, Murtagh 2002: 62). This has only been led in part by the city council, as under the centralized form of government through the Troubles, responsibility for housing was devolved to the Northern Ireland Housing Executive (N.I.H.E.) and much of the planning lay with the Department of the Environment (Ellis and McKay 2000: 49, Murtagh 2002: 52–9). Regeneration has also been encouraged since 1988 through *Making Belfast Work* and *Belfast Action Teams* with a brief to increase economic development, increase employment and improve the quality of life for residents (Bollens 1999: 68–9, Ellis and McKay 2000: 52). In addition there has been large scale investment from the European Union as part of the Special Support Programme for Peace and Reconciliation. The scheme aims to "enhance creatively the environs of sectarian interface areas" and "actively involve local residents, especially the most socially excluded, in the design and implementation of projects." Funding has been directed through a range of partnership boards on which sit local council members and key individuals from statutory and community bodies (Murtagh 2002: 143–4). In both Belfast and Derry those boards have run "city vision" processes in an attempt to imagine unified cities on which planning might be based (Hughes et al. 1998, Ellis and McKay 2000: 53, Murtagh 2002: 143–8).

These developments have been closely associated with the peace process that culminated in the signing of the "Good Friday" or "Belfast" Agreement in 1998. A number of attempts at an overall settlement had been tried but the timing and structure of the present agreement appears to give it more chance of succeeding than its predecessors. Conflict management and conflict resolution have taken place at a number of levels including working at an overall political settlement; developing political, social and economic strategies within particular areas; developing legal and educational strategies to combat sectarianism and inequality and thus improve community relations; developing more local political institutions stressing "partnership"; and encouraging localized community enhancement projects. However, one of the more striking features since the cease-fires in 1994 has been ongoing "low-level" sectarian violence and major disputes over parades resulting in civil disturbances and increased segregation in some areas (Jarman 1997b, Bryan 2001). In other words, the broadly consociational peace agreement has not, as yet, reduced polarization. Indeed, evidence suggests that it may be increasing. The N.I.H.E., which is generally seen as having worked well to develop public housing, has tried to promote integrated housing areas but these have been expensive failures (Bollens 1999: 103). Whilst officially the Housing Executive is "color-blind" in terms of its housing distribution policies, this does not necessarily insure equality of outcome and in effect has merely reinforced existing boundaries (Bollens 1999: 94–119).

Apparently, whilst many people maintain an ideal of living in mixed communities (Hadden et al. 1996), the peace lines in interface areas make them feel more secure (Murtagh 1994, Bollens 1999: 72, Jarman and O'Halloran 2000: 10, Murtagh 2002: 49–50). Some argue that this is an illusion, however. For although peacelines "were constructed to provide psychological security, living along a peaceline presents a direct threat, imposes restriction on movement, and creates and reinforces a deteriorated quality of environment" (Bollens 1999: 77). Communities in interface areas suffer higher levels of social and economic disadvantage (Jarman and O'Halloran 2000: 10, Murtagh 2002: 49–52). Studies have shown stone throwing and general violence to be common at interface areas (Murtagh 1994, Templegrove 1996). Yet, even if long-term improved community relations might demand that local territories be broken down there are, to date, few signs in north or west Belfast that this is happening.

The interface communities and their boundaries are "policed" by a range of groups with different interests. Public bodies involved in planning such as the N.I.H.E. and the Department of the Environment have effectively sustained boundaries, even marked them through housing policy and the development of the built environment. Although some have claimed that there has been a conspiracy to foster divisions through policy implementation, Murtagh argues that the evidence suggests otherwise (Murtagh 2002: 165–7). The R.U.C., now the Police Service of Northern Ireland (P.S.N.I.), pays special attention to interface areas and is in control of the range of gates at the "peace lines". Interfaces are also "policed" by paramilitaries in the sense that they help mark territories and act to "police" people within them even to the extent of developing alternative justice systems.

An extraordinary level of community work has developed around the interfaces that, in effect, also attempts to manage the polarized relationships. It is estimated that there are 5,500 voluntary organizations, community groups and charitable bodies in Northern Ireland, one organization for every 270 residents (Ellis and McKay 2000: 51). A number of these groups have necessarily played a role in "policing" territory. In one particular project community workers in a number of communities in north Belfast were issued mobile phones with the idea that they would react to events by mobilizing key people and perhaps avoid major police intervention. In some areas this system developed into a form of "neighborhood watch" (Jarman 1999:32). By 2000 the network had increased from ten interface areas to twenty-five and the project has been replicated in other parts of Belfast (Jarman and O'Halloran 2000: 15).

New Visions or "Lipstick on the Gorilla?"

> In one sense Belfast is a proud product of increased globalisation as it built some of the greatest ships in the world at a time when structurally the British economy within the empire was predominant. It is now in a marginal position. As such, . . . places like West and North Belfast are weak areas in a weak region of what has been a relatively weak European economy. (Gaffikin and Morrissey 1999: 227)

I have painted a comparatively bleak picture of Belfast as a polarized city. Yet, as anthropologists have consistently shown, relationships between the ethnic communities are complex, with people sharing common values and a strong sense of decency in relationships with neighbors (Harris 1972, Leyton 1974, Donnan and McFarlane 1983, 1986). A dynamic view of the conflict in Northern Ireland does provide some reasons for optimism. Belfast has clearly changed markedly over the last twenty years. In the

1980s urban policies offered highly attractive financial incentives to selected large corporations in part to re-invent the city (Murtagh 2002: 25). In the 1990s large-scale capital projects, aimed in part at tourism, have been funded, most notably the Waterfront Hall, Odessey Center, and new Hilton Hotel. Not five minutes walk from Cluan Place and Short Strand, they are part of the important redevelopment of the Lagan River area, a site for the expansion of upscale housing. The commercial center of Belfast has become more successful with large multi-national retail firms moving into new shopping complexes, although there is evidence that even such large complexes as Castle Court are becoming defined as Protestant or Catholic (Urban Institute 1998: 18). This of course has been at the cost of local firms and has tied Belfast more closely to the networks of global corporations.

There has also been an attempt to open the city centers to all communities and develop a common civic culture for Belfast. Historically, Irish nationalism has been particularly marginalized, yet Sinn Féin has been allowed to hold events in the city center since 1993 and there is also now an annual, though controversial, St. Patrick's Day parade (Jarman and Bryan 1998: 69–84). Alongside this have been bids to re-imagine the city through the holding of entertainment and sporting events that are open to all communities and by having *city vision* processes undertaken by a partnership board in Belfast. These processes are "designed to foster an inspiring and imaginative approach to developing cities" (Gaffikin and Morrissey 1999: x) and have looked to empower citizens. The Belfast City Vision for 2025, which involved contacting all households in the city, called for a city "that belonged to its people," "addressing our divisions honestly," a city that will "overcome sectarian stress, the legacy of violence, physical blight and population shifts," "moving beyond respectful tolerance of each other to a more common civic identity" (www.belfastvision.com). During 2002, under the banner *Imagine Belfast 2008*, the city also made a bid to be named as European capital of culture for 2008. Organizers claim that it will show that the people of Belfast still possess "the pioneering spirit and innovative talent that first made this small region synonymous with progress" (www.imaginebelfast2008.com). The bid was not successful.

The question remains, however, as to how the initiatives discussed above might impinge upon polarization. Do injections of global capital or cultural projects help create a less divided city? As in other cities, processes of gentrification have been taking place. Redevelopment in one of the oldest working-class areas of the city, Sandy Row, in south Belfast is presently causing tension, not least because this area is seen as a heartland for loyalism. Maybe this will be a good development, necessarily destroying sectarian enclaves. The history of Belfast, however, shows that movements of population often create more conflict both in developing urban areas and in satellite towns. In addition, many of the jobs created in the central areas of Belfast are relatively low paid and low skilled. A large project like the Waterfront Hall continues to be subsidized by the ratepayers of Belfast whilst the main beneficiaries are arguably the large hotel chains that demand low labor costs.

Equally problematic are attempts at a common cultural vision for Belfast. One civil rights activist and left-wing commentator recently warned of "the insatiable appetite of mainstream commentators for developments which, however implausibly, can be projected as evidence that peace and reconciliation are magically at hand, without need of unsettling change" (Eamon McCann—*The Sunday Tribune* 14 January 2001). Neill has been most critical in noting that "re-imaging the city in the eyes of Belfast's residents and investors has been a distraction from dealing with real and deeply felt ethnic tensions. It risks being lipstick on the gorilla" (Neill 1995: 69).

Bollens (1999), adapting Benvenisti (1986), has identified urban policy strategies for dealing with polarization. He describes as *neutral* those policies that address ethnic conflict at an individual level, employing technical criteria for allocating resources with no reference to ethnic identity, power inequalities and political exclusion (p. 23). Strategies of *equity* give "primacy to certain ethnic subgroups in the population in order to decrease historic and contemporary inter-group inequalities" (p. 25). Unlike the first approach this assumes conditions of ethnic conflict in the urban environment. The *resolver* strategy goes further in attempting to deal with root causes including issues of sovereignty. "In this way, it seeks to link urban peace-building to national peace-making" (p. 27). So for example issues within particular ethnic groups "are linked to the lack of representation of those groups at the decision-making table" (pp. 27–8). These three strategies are distinct from the *partisan* strategies that would have previously underpinned polarization within Belfast. Bollens suggests that the strategies can facilitate or impede peaceful inter-group coexistence depending upon control over land and economic resources; upon access to services and the political or policy making process; and upon the maintenance of group identity (1999: 31–7).

A recent report on housing suggested the following:

> The Housing Executive does not believe that North Belfast is yet at the stage where the existing boundaries between communities could be radically altered.

In fact this issue, we believe, is beyond the ability of any agency to deliver. (Northern Ireland Housing Executive 2000: 13)

Very few of the projects under-way in Belfast would meet the *resolver* criteria; rather most seek to manage the polarization through strategies of equity. The range of interests involved in "policing" territory in Belfast is heterogeneous and multi-layered. In this context the influx of global capital has complex effects and it remains difficult to map a policy route to reduce divisions in the city. Besides, *resolver* strategies are most difficult when the majority of people in interface areas feel safer with a *status quo* of polarization.

It is difficult to ignore the reality that recent investments of capital in Belfast redevelopment, and recent projects promoting peace and reconciliation, have been accompanied by an *increase* in interface disturbances. The political, territorial, and sectarian divisions of the city do not exist outside the forces of globalization, with their consequences for employment, gentrification, dislocation, and pressure on housing. Although rightly seen as part of the solution to Northern Ireland's difficulties, these new initiatives at the same time threaten the present definition of territories. In 2003, five years after the signing of the Good Friday Agreement, conflict at the interfaces appears more prevalent than ever.

References

Bardon, J. and Burnett, D. (1996), *Belfast: A Pocket History*, Belfast: Blackstaff Press.

Benvenisti, M.S (1986) *Conflicts and Contradictions*, New York: Villard Books.

Bew, P., Gibbon, P. and Patterson, H. (1995), *Northern Ireland 1921–1994: Political Forces and Social Classes,* London: Serif.

Boal, F.W. (1994), "Encapsulation: Urban Dimensions of National Conflict", in Dunn, S. (ed.), *Managing Divided Cities,* Keele: Ryburn Publishing.

—— (1995), *Shaping a City: Belfast in the late Twentieth Century,* Belfast: Institute of Irish Studies

Boal, F.W. and Murray, R.C. (1977), "A City in Conflict", *Geographical Magazine*, 44: 364–71.

Boal, F.W., Greer, J., Hughes, J., Knox, C., and Murray, R.C. (1976), "Belfast: The Urban encapsulation of a National Conflict", in Clarke, S.E. and Obler, J.L. (eds), *Urban Ethnic Conflict: A Comparative*

Perspective, Chapel Hill, University of North Carolina: Institute for Research in Social Science, pp. 77–131.

Bollens, S.A. (1999), *Urban peace Building in Divided Societies: Belfast and Johannesburg*, Colorado: Westview Press.

Bryan, D. (1999), "The Right to March: Parading a Loyal Protestant Identity in Northern Ireland", in Allen, T. and Eade, J. (eds), *Divided Europeans: Understanding Ethnicities in Conflict,* Amsterdam: Kluwer International, pp. 173–99.

—— (2000), *Orange Parades: The Politics of Ritual, Tradition and Control*, London: Pluto Press.

—— (2001), "Parade disputes and the peace process in Northern Ireland", *Peace Review*, 13(1): 43–51.

Boyd, A. (1969), *Holy War in Belfast*, Tralee: Anvil Press

Budge, I. and O'Leary, C. (1973), *Belfast: Approach to the Crisis,* London: Mcmillan

Burton, F. (1978), *The Politics of Legitimacy: Struggle in a Belfast Community*, London: Routledge Kegan Paul.

Cebulla, A. and Smith, J. (1995), "Industrial Collapse and Post-Fordist Overdetermination of Belfast", in Shirlow, P. (ed.), *Development Ireland: Contemporary Issues,* London: Pluto Press.

De Rosa, C. (1998), "Playing Nationalism", in Buckley, A. (ed.), *Symbols in Northern Ireland*, Belfast: Institute of Irish Studies.

Dillon, M. (1990), *The Shankill Butchers: A Case Study of Mass Murder*, London: Arrow Books.

Hastings, D. and McFarlane, G. (1983), "Informal Social Organisation", in Darby, J. (ed.), *Northern Ireland: The Background to the Conflict,* Belfast: Appletree Press.

—— (1986), "Social Anthropology and the Sectarian Divide in Northern Ireland", in *The Sectarian Divide in Northern Ireland Today,* Royal Anthropological Institute of Great Britain and Ireland, Occasional Paper. no. 41.

Ellis, G. and McKay, S. (2000), "City Management Profile: Belfast", *Cities*, 17(1): 47–54.

Fay, M.T., Morrissey, M. and Smyth, M. (1998), *Mapping Troubles-Related Deaths in Northern Ireland 1969–1998,* Derry: INCORE.

—— (1999), *Northern Ireland's Troubles: The Human Costs,* London: Pluto Press.

Feldman, A. (1991), *Formations of Violence: The Narrative of the Body and Political Terror in Northern Ireland,* Chicago: University of Chicago Press.

Gaffikin, F. and Morrissey, M. (1999), *City Visions: Imagining Place, Enfranchising People,* London: Pluto Press.

Hadden, T., Boal, F. and Irwin, C. (1996), Survey supplement to *Fortnight* magazine. December 1996.

Harris, R. (1972), *Prejudice and Tolerance in Ulster*, Manchester: Manchester University Press.

Hepburn, A.C. (1990), "The Belfast Riots of 1935", *Social History*, 15: 75–96.

Hughes, J., Knox, C., Murray, M. and Greer, J. (1998), *Partnership Governance in Northern Ireland,* Dublin: Oak Tree Press.

Jarman, N. (1992), "Troubles Images", *Critique of Anthropology,* 12(2): 133–65.

—— (1993), "Intersecting Belfast", in Bender, B. (ed.), *Landscape: Politics and Perspectives*, Oxford: Berg.

—— (1997a), *Material Conflicts: Parades and Visual Displays in Northern Ireland*, Oxford: Berg.

—— (1997b), (ed.) *On the Edge: Community Perspectives on the Civil Disturbances*, Belfast: Community Development Center, North Belfast.

—— (1998), "Painting Landscapes: The Place of Murals in the Symbolic Construction of Urban Space", in Buckley, A. (ed.), *Symbols in Northern Ireland,* Belfast: Institute of Irish Studies.

—— (1999), *Drawing Back from the Edge: Community Based Responses to Violence in North Belfast,* Belfast: Community Development Center, North Belfast.

—— (2001), "Fragments et Strates: decryptage de la geographie sectaire de Belfast", "Fragments & Layers: Uncovering the Sectarian Geography of Belfast", in Bromberger, C. and Morel, A. (eds), *Limites floues, frontieres vives: des variations culturelles en France et en Europe*, Paris: Editions de la Maison des Sciences de l'Homme.

Jarman, N. and Bryan, D. (1996), *Parade and Protest: A Discussion of Parading Disputes in Northern Ireland,* Coleraine: Centre for the Study of Conflict.

—— (1998), *From Riots to Rights: Nationalist Parades in the North of Ireland,* Coleraine: Center for the Study of Conflict.

Jarman, N. and O'Halloran, C. (2000), *Peacelines or Battlefiends: Responding to Violence in interface Areas,* Belfast: Community Development Centre, North Belfast.

Knox, C. and Monaghan, R. (2000), "Informal Criminal Justice Systems in Northern Ireland", Report to the Economic and Social Research Council. Belfast: University of Ulster.

Leyton, E. (1974), "Opposition and Integration in Ulster", *Man* (N.S.) 9 (2): 185–92.

Murtagh, B. (1994), *Ethnic Space and the Challenge to Land Use Planning: A Study of Belfast's Peace Lines,* Center for Policy Research. Paper 7. Jordonstown: University of Ulster.
—— (2002), *The Politics of Territory: Policy and Segregation in Northern Ireland*, Hampshire: Palgrave.
Neill, W.J.V. (1995), "Lipstick on the Gorilla: Conflict Management, Urban Development and Image Making in Belfast", in Neill, W., Fitzimmonds, D. and Murtagh, B. (eds), *Reimagaing the Pariah City, Urban Development in Belfast and Detroit,* Aldershot: Avebury.
—— (1999), "Whose City? Can a Place Vision for Belfast Avoid the Issue of Identity?" *European Planning Studies* 7(3): 269–81.
Northern Ireland Housing Executive (2000), *The North Belfast Housing Strategy: Tackling Housing Need*, Belfast: Northern Ireland Housing Executive.
O'Reilly, C. (1998), "The Irish Language as Symbol: Visual Representations of Irish in Northern Ireland", in Buckley, A. (ed.*), Symbols in Northern Ireland,* Belfast: Institute of Irish Studies.
Patterson, H. (1980), "Class Conflict and Sectarianism in Belfast", Belfast: Blackstaff Press.
Persic, C. and Bloomer, S. (n/d) *The Feud and the Fury: The Response of the Community to the Shankill Feud, August 2000*, Belfast: Springfield Intercommunity Development Project.
Poole, M. (1971), "Riot displacement in 1969", *Fortnight*, 34: 17.
Rodmen, M. (1992), "Empowering Place: Multilocality and Multivocality", *American Anthropologist*, 94: 640–56.
Shirlow, P. (2000), *Fear, Mobility and Living in the Ardoyne and Upper Ardoyne Communities*, Report by the Mapping the Spaces of Fear Research Team at the University of Ulster. http://cain.ulst.ac.uk/issues/community/surveyxs.htm
Sluka, J. (1995), "Domination, Resistance and Political Culture in Northern Ireland's Catholic Ghettos", *Critique of Anthropology*, 15(1): 71–102.
Smyth, M. (2000), "The Human Consequences of Armed Conflict: Constructing 'Victimhood' in the Context of Northern Ireland's Troubles", in Cox, M., Guelke, A. and Stephen, F. (eds), *A Farewell to Arms? From "Long War" to Long Peace in Northern Ireland*, Manchester: Manchester University Press.
Urban Institute (1998), *Belfast Vision,* Report by the Urban Institute in Belfast.
Wright, F. (1996), *Two Lands on One Soil: Ulster Politics Before Home Rule*, Dublin: Gill & McMillan.

–13–

"Healing the Wounds of the War": Placing the War-displaced in Postwar Beirut

Aseel Sawalha

Before the Lebanese civil war (1975–91), Um Karim, her husband and four children, lived in their ancestral Druze village in the mountains overlooking Beirut. As a result of the war, Maronite Christian and Druze militiamen fought each other for control of such mountain villages, forcing their residents to flee, a great many of them to Beirut. Reconstituting their lives in Ayn Al-Mreisi, a neighborhood in the city's (Muslim) western zone, Um Karim and her family exemplify the ongoing struggles of one category of "war-displaced" in the city—the category of formerly rural people who became committed urbanites during the War. Their tale is one of repeated dislocation and ongoing struggle for stability in the face of violence—both the violence of war and, I argue, the violence of the postwar "reconstruction".

Before the war, Beirut was Lebanon's center of banking, commerce, and tourism whose *laissez-faire* economy encouraged the florescence of educational and cultural institutions, a thriving publishing industry, and an effervescent nightlife. Renowned as the "Paris" or "jewel" of the Middle East, it occupied a unique position in the Arab world. The civil war changed everything, leading in the first years to the creation of a militarized "green line," a 10 mile "no man's land" with few gates, dividing a largely Christian eastern zone from a largely Muslim western zone, and closing off part of the center. Office buildings were converted to military bases, businesses relocated to the suburbs, and Beirutis of long standing were forced to evacuate. As the war progressed, and ceasefires were repeatedly negotiated, implemented and then broken by the various warring factions and the military machines of Israel and Syria, the state collapsed and the city became a center of regional and international arms dealing, drug smuggling and money laundering—an icon of destruction.

Additional long-time residents, many from the middle classes, went into exile in neighboring Arab countries, France, the U.S., or Africa, seeking security within the Lebanese diasporas of other times.

By the end of the war, much of Beirut's transport, communications and electrical infrastructure had been destroyed, its industrial capacity obliterated, and the city center—the heart of Lebanese commerce—lay in ruins. One quarter of all housing units and many historic mosques, churches, and other buildings were damaged or demolished, some of them bulldozed to facilitate the movement of military hardware or for heliports. Half of the population had temporarily or permanently left their homes (Charif 1994, Faour 1991, Trendel 1992). Ironically, though, it was this level of exodus and destruction that enabled the rural war-displaced like Um Karim and her family to survive. Back in the village, they had earned their living as farmers. In the city, the husband found work as a taxi driver, in a vegetable market, and then as a member of one of the war militias until he was killed in a street battle. Um Karim, now a household head needing to provide for her children, was helped by militiamen and charitable organizations.

Um Karim's ongoing quest for housing illustrates the complexity of displacement in war-torn Beirut. Upon arrival in the Ayn Al-Mreisi neighborhood, she and her family shared a two-bedroom apartment with relatives for nine months. They were able to move into an adjacent apartment in the same building when its owners, a Christian family, left for east Beirut, entrusting the keys to Um Karim's host so as to protect the space from squatters until their hoped-for return. After living in this apartment for five years, in the summer of 1982, during the Israeli invasion of Beirut, Um Karim by then a widow was displaced a third time. A charitable organization helped her find a vacant room in an abandoned hotel in the destroyed city center where she shared a bathroom and cooking facilities with many other "refugee" families.

The insecurity and violence experienced by families like Um Karim's did not abate with the end of the war in 1991, despite the determination of the postwar "government of national unity" to heal the wounds and return Lebanon to normality. On the contrary, a major reconstruction project initiated to rebuild the city center displaced them yet again. Moreover, whereas during the war these families found ways—often informal or illegal—to put together a livelihood in the city, and to help shore up a fragile urbanity, the new, postwar process of displacement has relegated them to utter social and economic marginality.

Rebuilding Beirut is a national government priority. Indeed, the Ministry of Planning signaled as much in the early years of the war, creating a Council for Development and Reconstruction in 1977. Two postwar leaders, Rafiq Hariri and Elias Hrawi, respectively the prime minister and president as of 1992, immediately committed resources to restoring infrastructure and clearing debris. Then, in 1994, Hariri, with a well-capitalized background in the construction industry, founded Solidere, a public-private Lebanese company dedicated to the development of 6 million square feet of land in Beirut's Central Business District (B.C.D.). Among its tasks was to negotiate property rights among owners, tenants, leaseholders, and squatters in light of the many layers of displacement affecting formerly rural and urban Beirutis for twenty years. War-displaced residents of the center and surrounding neighborhoods were offered modest compensation packages, administered through a government program, to relocate.

Although hailed by the government and private investors as a project of national reconciliation, rejuvenation and unity, Solidere was immediately criticized by various Lebanese intellectuals and planners as draconian and insensitive, leading to various modifications in the overall plan. Yet even the critics do not speak for formerly rural urbanites like Um Karim whose third city "home" lay in the path of Solidere's bulldozers. After lengthy negotiations with representatives of the company, and with the Lebanese Central Fund for the Displaced, she was evicted in 1996, receiving U.S.$5,000 as compensation. The money served for a down-payment on a small apartment in a squatters' suburb of south Beirut. Whether this can be called home or not is up in the air, given that the building was illegally built on land owned by the government. Having earlier found shelter in the abandoned buildings of the ruined city center, Um Karim has experienced the end of the war not as a time of peace and hoped for security, but rather as what might be described as a "postwar state of emergency."

This essay is an ethnographic account of the lives and struggles of families like Um Karim's who occupy a "liminal position" in the politics of Beirut's postwar reconstruction. Focusing on one neighborhood, Ayn Mreisi, I explore the discursive strategies deployed by state institutions, real estate developers (both regional and international), critical intellectuals, and Beirut's prewar residents as they seek to exclude the war-displaced from the future plans of the city. How have they sought to disqualify these people from access to urban space? What strategies and means of negotiation have the displaced used, in turn, to resist expulsion, hang on to housing, retain their urban foothold?

The Research Site

As preparation for studying the effects of postwar reconstruction on the daily lives of residents in Beirut, I visited the city in the summer of 1995, choosing Zqaq el-Blat as a research site. A lively multi-ethnic and multi-religious neighborhood, and one of the oldest, it was adjacent to the downtown area. Commercial and residential buildings stood next to each other, old men hovered over backgammon boards in front of shops and women sat on the balconies overlooking the narrow streets and alleys where children played. At the time I arrived, the neighborhood was populated by a mix of pre-war property owners and tenants—Beirutis who saw themselves as the original residents of the city—and families who had been displaced from homes in other parts of the city and country during the sixteen years of civil conflict. I assumed I had found the ideal neighborhood for my fieldwork but upon returning to Beirut six months later, Zqaq el-Blat was almost gone. In that short period of time, the residents had been evacuated and most of the buildings demolished. The few structures that remained stood covered in dust, their windows shattered, pitifully evocative of another time as if props on a long-abandoned movie set. The once-vibrant sounds of music, the chattering of neighbors, the play of children had given way to the jarring noise of construction equipment, laying the foundation for the highway that now encircles the Solidere area, cutting it off from the rest of the city.

Hence my decision to locate in Ayn Al-Mreisi, just west of the downtown area. Similar to Zqaq al-Blat, Ayn Al-Mreisi was considered one of the oldest neighborhoods of Beirut, and was inhabited by people of varied ethnic, religious and socio-economic background. Whereas Zqaq al-Blat was eliminated, however, Ayn Al-Mreisi faces the Mediterranean and has become a magnet for investors speculating on houses and buildings in anticipation of the completion of the Solidere project. I found local owners and tenants debating amongst themselves whether to sell to these investors and outsiders, wait until the prices rose yet higher, or hold onto their rights to property, thus preserving the neighborhood. Displaced families, having no rights of tenancy or ownership over the spaces they had been occupying, were negotiating for compensation and looking for alternative places to live. Throughout Beirut, most of the apartments and spaces occupied by the displaced were in a state of decay; the owners were either absentee or they shunned maintaining their properties for "squatters". Nor were the displaced willing to fix up places that they were not sure they could keep. Toward the end of the essay, I present two case studies from Ayn Al-Mreisi illustrating the scramble for housing that accompanied the Solidere redevelopment initiatives in the late 1990s.

Solidere and its Critics

As it was initially conceived, the Solidere plan for downtown Beirut called for building a man-made island, a "petite Manhattan" connected by bridges to the old city. The planners sketched two tall towers evoking New York's World Trade Center and a boulevard wider than the Champs Élysées in Paris. At work, here, was a kind of deep fantasy expressing what most residents of Beirut feel: the desire to forget (Makiya 1996: 16). For both the government and Solidere, the stated goal was to restore Beirut to its pre-war role as Lebanon's premier center for banking and financial services, commerce and tourism, with as much dispatch as possible.

Almost from the outset, debates surrounded the institution of Solidere and its approach to planning. What should be the respective roles of the company and the state, what macro-economic model should inform the master plan, what balance should be struck between office buildings, commercial and entertainment emporia, hotels, arts centers, public parks, memorials, a waterfront esplanade? What about residential space in the new Central District? Was there a danger in having one company monopolize the reconstruction effort, especially a globally oriented company whose New York-inspired vision meant obliterating many historic buildings and ignoring Beirut's Lebanese surroundings? Did the emphasis on the Central Business District presage neglect of the rest of the city? Would the downtown and waterfront evolve as a "ghetto of prosperity" in the midst of a crumbling Third World city, perhaps even inaccessible without a private car? If so the center would cease to integrate people from varied walks of life. Many individuals and groups, drawn into critical discussions of the Solidere project, expressed concern for the future identity of their city. Given the tragedy of recent strife, an especially challenging question was how the future urban fabric would integrate the interests and honor the histories of its many ethnic, class and religious constituencies.

In response to this lively engagement, Solidere modified its plans, (less to promote social solidarity, however, than to commit to the historic preservation of some 300 buildings), promoting the new scheme under the label, "Beirut an Ancient City for the Future." Significantly, neither the planners, nor their critics, nor the revised plan gave voice to the war-displaced, above all those like Um Karim whose prewar roots were rural.

On the contrary, the reconstruction effort evicted such people from their hard-won urban niches, repossessing their houses and disrupting their social and political networks. Lacking a socio-economic component to replace the wartime informal economy, its main effect was to deepen their insecurity and poverty, and to funnel them toward illegal settlements on Beirut's periphery. In defense, the planners hold up the compensation system as a source of fair rewards for those who are newly displaced.

The Compensation System

After the permanent cease-fire in November 1990, the Lebanese government established two temporary agencies—the Ministry of the Displaced and the Central Fund for the Displaced—to handle the overwhelming challenge of people who had lost their homes. According to the Ministry:

> 9000 families had been displaced, with an average of 5.7 persons in each family. 18,000 homes were completely destroyed, and many seriously damaged. 45,000 families illegally occupied the homes of other families. 12,000 families lived in dwellings not designated for human habitation, such as commercial buildings, industrial centers, and buildings liable to collapse. (The Ministry of the Displaced, Lebanon 1996: 9)

The Ministry further offered a specific definition for "war-displaced," called *muhajarin*, which it put to use in reports, studies, plans, and surveys:

> The displaced person is any individual, Lebanese or non-Lebanese national who lives on the Lebanese soil and has been affected by the war and hindered by its consequences from enjoying his or her full legal and civil rights to the house and properties from which he or she was displaced. (The Ministry of the Displaced, Lebanon 1996: 5)

Placing such persons was a foremost priority of the postwar government, which authorized the Ministry and the Fund to negotiate between them, their political representatives (the Amal Movement and Hizballha, two political parties representing the Shiite Muslim communities in West Beirut), and property owners, investors and developers such as Solidere. The interests of the state, the developers, investors, and property owners were widely divergent, yet they shared the view that areas and buildings occupied by displaced families needed to be cleared to "heal the wounds of the war," allow city residents to forget the agony of past emergencies, and help Beirut become "normal" again. After extensive deliberations with all parties, a consensus was reached: "Qualified" displaced persons were to be paid cash compensation for evacuating the public and private properties they had been occupying since the war.

Intellectuals, some political groups and the displaced themselves criticized this solution, arguing that the state should offer alternative housing in government-managed housing projects, or provide construction materials for people to rebuild their homes in their prewar places of residence. To the war-displaced, the circumstances of the war gave them the right to occupy empty buildings, including private homes in the relatively safe areas of the city, since they were unable to access their legal homes. In the postwar era, it was the responsibility of the state, the developers, and the property owners, who stood to benefit from retrieving the contested properties, to make alternatives available. According to sociologist Nabil Beyhum, in the absence of alternatives, "the project will not bring the end of displacement. On the contrary it could provoke more displacement" (Beyhum 1994: 21–2). There was also criticism of the government for assigning absolute authority and a special police force to Solidere to carry out the downtown evictions (see Corm 1996, Salam 1998, Tabet 1996).

As many commentators realized, paying cash compensations to the displaced in no way ensured that they would return to their prewar homes. Of various ethnic and religious background (Maronite Christian, Greek Orthodox, Sunni Muslim, Shiite Muslim[1] and Druze), the majority came from rural areas that lacked basic services and employment opportunities. Former residents of Shiite south Lebanon were especially thwarted, because many of their villages were at the time still occupied by Israel; in fact the Israeli army was forcing yet more Shiites to leave.[2] In addition to these obstacles, the displaced had adopted an urban affinity and lifestyle during the war. Indeed, a whole generation had been born and raised in the city, their identities and socio-economic networks shaped by the urban context. For all of these reasons, many of the displaced, after receiving cash compensation, simply moved to areas surrounding Beirut, thereby creating new illegal situations. An official at the Ministry of the Displaced describes the southern suburb where the majority have settled (Um Karim among them) as an "urban massacre".

> They are constructing buildings without following the city's codes of urban planning. In these areas, there are no parking spaces, no sewage system, and not a single tree. We begged the city several times to enforce the rules there, but no one cares [*la hayata li man tunadi*].

If they do not guarantee the eventual return of the war displaced to their prewar locations, all of the solutions point toward their removal from the city proper. Neither the public and private planners nor their critics have called for incorporating them into the plan for the downtown area and its surroundings. Perhaps this is not surprising. The postwar reconstruction represents a second great moment of modernity for Beirut, following its earlier Paris-inspired transformation under the Ottomans. To the modernizing urban planners, whatever their position on Solidere, the war-displaced lack urban culture and civility; they disturb the social order of the city by making it grubby, dirty, and backward. Reconstruction means cleaning and organizing disordered spaces, repressing illegality, imposing aesthetic "standards" on what has become "unsightly." As we will see, a lively public discourse on the war-displaced reinforces this enthusiasm for the modern, and the power relations underlying it, in many ways.

Discourses of Exclusion

According to the definition of *muhajarin* used by the Ministry of the Displaced, most of Beirut's residents qualify; they are able to present persuasive arguments or evidence showing that they were uprooted or relocated at least once during the war.[3] As we have seen, numerous Beirutis fled Lebanon for neighboring countries or abroad; others moved about within the country or moved from one neighborhood to another within Beirut. Whatever the circumstances, the word *muhajarin* frames the war-displaced as victims. Something was done to them, they did not themselves chose to move. And because they are not agents of their own movement, they should not be viewed as the cause of problems.

Governmental agencies, political groups supporting the displaced, the displaced themselves, and journalists all use the word *muhajarin*. Yet its definition is vague and open to manipulation. Moreover, another, more widespread and popular label for the war-displaced is the word *muhtalin*, meaning occupiers—people who continue to occupy spaces they do not "legally" own or lease. In using this term, owners of illegally occupied properties and long-term residents of the city reconfigure the displaced as usurpers and outsiders—and as blameworthy actors with full agency. The victims in this scenario are property owners who find themselves at the mercy of "occupiers". By this definition, the displaced are a constant reminder of wartime instability and unpredictability—aliens who endanger the postwar return to normality.

Lebanese social scientist Khalil Abu Rjeileh distinguishes between the "real displaced" and the occupiers. For him, many of those who file claims for compensation at the Ministry of the Displaced are opportunistic *muhtalin*. Proof lies in their ownership of homes other than the ones they are illegally occupying. When asked why people would occupy a house if they already owned another one, Abu Rjeileh said:

> Real displaced persons fled to Beirut from rural areas during the war. They stayed in schools and public buildings. Most of them evacuated these places soon after the war. They had self-respect and appreciated private property. Thus, they won't take over the property of others. The "occupiers" who filed claims as displaced persons were in fact wartime militia members, who forced people out of their homes and occupied them during the war.[4]

In Abu Rjeileh's analysis the "real displaced," as victims of the war and as persons who respect private property, have a legitimate right to use "empty" buildings owned by the state, although not privately owned commercial and residential spaces. The officials of Solidere are considerably less tolerant. To them, evicting the displaced, whether inauthentic or "real," is intrinsic to the process of "cleansing" the city of its wartime tragedies so that it can be rebuilt as a city for the future. Public discourse, circulating through gossip, private conversation and the media, also sidesteps the distinction between "real" victims of wartime uprooting and opportunistic squatters. Indeed, whereas Abu Rjeileh assigns legitimacy to the war-displaced with rural origins, these once agrarian people—Um Karim and her family among them—are particular targets of stigma and exclusion.

In *The Suspended City*, for example, Wadah Shararah describes the displaced population in Beirut as temporary residents of the city who impose their "authentic rural culture" on the urban environment without integrating into the city's rational social life. They hinder Beirut's urban heritage by "ruralizing" it, he argues, even violating civic life through the use of violence (Shararah 1985: 13–15). Similarly, some of the criticisms of the cash compensation solution are based on the idea that the war-displaced were unable to make wise decisions about spending money, and did not care about the country or its national economy. They were ignorant of what was good for themselves and the city. One consultant I interviewed declared the compensation system a waste. According to him:

> The displaced are limited socially, education-wise, and culturally. They managed to get a good amount of money, both legally and illegally. They did not buy houses or land, and did not invest (the compensations) in establishing businesses. Many of them spent the money on marrying a second wife, buying gold, expensive cars, and mobile phones. Unfortunately the money was spent

> on dead items. If they started a commercial business, in two years their money might have doubled and this would have revived the economy of the country. Marrying a second wife, and buying gold or cars is a waste of the money.

Concern for the war-displaced goes beyond attempting to interpret this complex problem. Many wartime political parties, influential personalities, and leaders use the issue of displacement to seek economic and political gains. In 1996, for example, some candidates for the parliament offered selected displaced families help in obtaining their compensation in exchange for votes. Others used their connections with officials at governmental institutions to get late applications accepted. Politicians on all sides accused one another of giving money intended for the "real displaced" to followers who were not deserving. According to Randa, a municipal employee:

> Three months before the parliamentary elections, we received a memo informing us that people will come to file for disbursements for home repairs. This was not publicly announced. It was done by word of mouth among (Prime Minister) Hariri supporters. We issued checks for the first few hundred applicants. Later on, when everyone in Beirut knew about it, the municipality postponed any further payments until further notice.

Randa, who processed many of the applications, believed that the prime minister was engaged in bribery but when she asked for an explanation, her supervisor informed her that the municipality as well as Hariri benefited from the deal. "Hariri paid money and gained votes, and the municipality distributed it and collected thousands of overdue fees from city residents who had not paid for the last twenty years." This was because, before accepting the applications for home repairs, the municipality asked for proof that the applicants were no longer in arrears. Meanwhile, a member of parliament, Najah Wakim, accused Prime Minister Hariri and the minister of the displaced of diverting U.S.$800 million from compensation payments for the "real" displaced into unrelated construction projects (highways, a "sports city," and the airport); into funding evictions for Solidere; and into underwriting electoral campaigns and mobilizing votes among their clientele (Wakim: 1998: 122–3). Although never substantiated, the accusation added to the climate of rumors and uncertainty characteristic of the postwar era.

From the end of the war in 1991, the Lebanese television media and newspapers addressed the issue of displacement on a daily basis. In response to the continued concerns among the public, and influenced by developers, investors and the state, they presented the displaced as an obstacle that needed to be removed in order to put an end to the war's emergencies. The image of the violent intruder, the outsider to urban "culture", was continually reiterated, as illustrated by these newspaper excerpts:

> Evacuations of the displaced did not pass peacefully: Confrontations and hostilities took place. (*Al-Anwar*, 10 October 1996: 7)

> Is Al-Mreije turning into a new Wadi Abu Jmil? The number of the building occupiers is doubling. There is chaos in registering the names. 750 families became 2500, and some of them are living in cardboard tents. (*Al-Nahar*, 25 June 1996: 8)

> Three civilians and fourteen policemen were injured in the Qintari confrontations. The residents are asking to stop the explosives in the Vinecia Tunnel. The Central Fund for the Displaced promised to solve the problem (*Al-Nahar*, 28 January 1997: 12)

In 1996, the media also picked up on a government official blaming a displaced family for their own deaths. A building occupied by displaced families collapsed when Solidere blasted an adjacent structure with dynamite and a family of six who had been waiting for the promised compensation was killed. According to the official, "While the head of the family was bargaining for higher compensation, the house collapsed and killed his wife and children. They refused to take the compensation suggested by Solidere; they wanted more."

The media excerpts cited above suggest that the displaced abused both the state and Solidere by forging claims for greater compensation than they deserved. Stories were told in both the media and informal conversation about some displaced persons receiving huge amounts of money based solely on clientelism and connections. There were rumors of families acquiring close to $100,000 in compensation. These stories, regardless of their dubious authority and despite their negative connotation, raised people's expectations regarding the compensation system, leading many families to consider themselves unfairly paid.

In the end, confusion, uncertainty and an aura of secrecy surrounded the compensation process, making it illusory and chaotic. In one neighborhood, Wadi Abu-Jmil, Solidere faced an especially serious challenge. Because it was the last on the program for evictions, the political parties and groups in the neighborhood, apprised of the process in other neighborhoods, were well prepared. Many of them conducted their own surveys of the number of displaced families, presenting numbers different from those arrived at by the Central Fund and Solidere. An employee of Solidere claimed that the company was being "milked," as the new numbers were three times what was estimated in the initial survey. In Wadi Abu Jmil, the political parties also urged the displaced not to abandon the occupied properties without first getting their compensation.[5] "We knew that some of these families had never lived there," the Solidere employee stated, "but we did not want to use violence; that might lead to political conflicts. We did not want to start another war."

Mentioning a neighborhood like Wadi Abu Jmil became shorthand for corruption and unfairness in the distribution of money. Wadi Abu Jmil was mockingly called "the valley of gold," *Wadi al-dahab*, referring to the questionable and excessive payments. A similar example was Hay Lif. According to the government's initial survey, there were only sixty-five displaced families in this Beirut neighborhood, but by the time the eviction process was begun, 300 families had to be paid.[6] After that, Hay Lif was dubbed "Bank Lif".

Belonging in Beirut: Self-definition

In *Purity and Exile*, Liisa Malki discusses the systematic invisibility of refugees in the literature on nations and nationalism, for the mere fact that refugees are not yet classified as part of the nation. "They are not seen as representatives of any particular local culture and they have lost a kind of imagined cultural authority to stand for 'their kind' or for the imagined whole of which they are or were part" (Malki 1997: 7). The war-displaced of Beirut are similarly without a legitimate place in the existing postwar hierarchies but live "betwixt and between" (Turner 1967: 97).

It is worth mentioning here that although many displaced families lived in the same locations for as many as 20 years, they did not attach themselves to these places, or to others they experienced throughout their quest for refuge. Property owners, although they may have lived outside of the country during the entire war (often entrusting their homes to servants) had the support of the state and could return to reclaim their property without question. This did not mean that the displaced were passive, however. Just as the returning owners believed they had the legal right to evict "occupiers," the war-displaced felt legitimate in seeking the maximum compensation possible for relocating. Claims to legitimacy influenced the negotiation process for both.

During the postwar era of reconstruction, the displaced lived in a continuing "state of emergency," their uncertainty expressed in the familiar refrain, "let us wait and see." In order to accommodate this uncertainty, the present was silenced, ignored, and put on hold. At the same time, claims to space, and to the right to belong in Beirut, drew upon their prewar and wartime experiences and memories. After all, they had been the defenders and protectors of the city, unlike the legal residents who fled, abandoning it "when it needed them the most." In the words of displaced persons I knew in Ayn Al-Mreisi, "we paid the price of these places with our blood and nerves," or "we lived in these places for 20 years. Our children are urbanized. They know only Beirut as home." Through such phrases they sought to counter the accusation of being outsiders, illegal occupiers, and a burden on the city.

In narrating their experiences, the war-displaced made note of a number of sites, in particular, their villages of origin, prewar homes if they had them in other parts of the city, various places of refuge where they had been sheltered over the past two decades, and the homes they illegally occupy in the present. Their narratives generally seemed fond of the villages of origin for their close and intimate social relations, but at the same time rejected the government's plan to return them there—a nostalgia without a desire to return. They gave the following reasons. First, villages lacked such urban amenities as jobs, education for their children and health services. Second, many had left their villages after enduring massacres and threats; in such cases they feared or resented the idea of going back. Third, although some maintained contacts with rural relatives who stayed behind, and often returned for special occasions (holidays, elections, funerals and anniversaries), on the whole the war-displaced no longer enjoyed village-centered socio-economic and political networks.

Unlike many Beirut dwellers who associated wartime spaces and experiences with violence and impairment, the displaced spoke approvingly about the civil war period when economic resources were available to them, they were involved in political groups and parties and, most importantly, they felt they belonged.

Compared to the past, the present confronted them with economic instability, a lack of services, conflict among family members, and the sense of being disoriented or lost. Collecting what information they could from government employees, private sector workers, the gossip and rumors of other displaced, and people affiliated with the political parties, they struggled to obtain just compensation and construct a legitimate identity. Two case studies drawn from Ayn al-Mreisi illustrate what they were up against.

Who Owns this Apartment: Sahar

For many of the war-displaced, their current places of residence might be the only "home" they have known. Sons and daughters who grew up in illegal spaces continued to live in such spaces after they married. Often displaced persons "illegally" purchased or leased office space, a share in an apartment, or a room in a hotel from other displaced persons in a kind of real estate black market. Paying for such spaces during the war, when there was no state or owner to buy anything from, naturally fostered claims to ownership, against which other claims would be asserted.

One such ambiguous "owner" was Sahar, whom I met in 1996 when she was staying with her in-laws in Beirut. Having recently returned from three years in Saudi Arabia, she was locked out of the apartment she once "owned". Sahar's family had moved to Ayn al-Mreisi from East Beirut at the beginning of the war when she was eight years old. After growing up there, she married Ahmed, a displaced person living in the neighborhood. They managed to "buy" an apartment from another displaced family nearby:

> We did not have enough money, so I sold my gold—the dowry—to buy our apartment. We renovated it, replaced the windows, painted the walls, and connected the apartment to electricity from a neighboring generator.[7] We lived there for six years; then my husband got a job in Saudi Arabia. We left the keys with my in-laws.

According to the original owner of the apartment, Sahar and her husband were illegal occupiers yet she viewed the property as hers, based on her memories and experiences. She had paid for it with her dowry, renovated it, and this was where she had married and given birth. Hearing about the compensation system while out of the country, she asked her in-laws to file on her behalf. "One day, we received a phone call from my in-laws informing us that the property owner had broken into our apartment and thrown our furniture and belongings out. I flew back to Beirut immediately," she said. The owner later claimed to have put an eviction notice under the door.

Officials at the Ministry of the Displaced informed Sahar that she did not have the status of a "real displaced family;" she and her husband had been uprooted while they were still children, before marriage, making them ineligible. Sahar disagreed on the grounds that both her displacement and her marriage occurred during the war, and she supported her argument with a list of people of similar background who had received compensation. She neglected to mention, however, that the people on her list had not departed to live in another country. Later the Ministry informed her that her three years in Saudi Arabia was the real reason for her being turned down. Ironically, the original owner lived in France throughout the war. Although Sahar and her in-laws not only followed the postwar legal procedures to the letter in filing with the Ministry of the Displaced, but also pursued political channels, she lost her right to her home. Sahar is convinced that the Ministry ignored her application because the original owner had access to influential people and connections enabling him to obtain the court-ordered eviction illegally.

Sahar's case exemplifies how words such as displaced or occupiers, legal or illegal, and family or home become contested and reinterpreted in Beirut, leading to great uncertainty and unpredictability in people's daily lives and efforts to plan for the future. From her we also learn what it means to be simultaneously caught up in the intricate circles of bureaucracy, family issues and the practicalities of daily life. She had to leave her husband in Saudi Arabia and return to Beirut to rescue her furniture and try to collect compensation. She had to prove her eligibility for compensation before the officials at the Ministry of the Displaced and the property owner. At the same time she had to negotiate new relationships and a new division of labor with her in-laws who allowed her to stay, with her children, in their small, one-bedroom apartment. Her mother-in-law and one (of two) sisters-in-law looked after her children during her interminable visits to the Ministry; in return the mother in-law expected to receive some of the forthcoming compensation. In Sahar's words:

> I do not know what to do with my furniture. Now it is all piled up on a balcony at my in-laws, exposed to the sun and humidity. I cannot live with my in-laws for a long time. Their apartment is too small. In addition they themselves have received an eviction notice. They do not know where they will end up.

From Sectarian Patronage to Bureaucratic Trap: Ali

Notwithstanding the push toward modernity in postwar Beirut, the specialization and division of functions among state institutions, developers and investors, and local religious and political groups was not at all clear. A considerable overlap in responsibilities and personnel between the public and private sectors meant that a single individual could hold a governmental position, own construction companies, and at the same time be a former militia commander turned political or religious leader. It was partly because of this confusion of roles that when Beirutis needed to access resources, they "ran around in circles."

Ali, a Shiite from a village in South Lebanon, moved with his family to Beirut in 1979 when he was 15 years old. During the war, he joined various political groups and militias, securing his family's daily needs through the militia leaders who controlled his neighborhood. Facing eviction after the war he was, however, unsure how to proceed—which institution or authority to contact in order to receive his due.

I met Ali while he was waiting for his compensation from the Central Fund for the Displaced. In the aftermath of the war, the re-establishment of the state had given the Lebanese hope that the days of reliance on neighborhood strongmen and militia leaders were behind them. Based on this optimistic premise, Ali had filed his claim with the Fund without the mediation of political or religious groups, political or sectarian patrons.[8] "Now that there is a legitimate state, we do not have to seek sectarian connections and alliances," he told me.

Soon, though, Ali encountered obstacles, leading him to suspect that he had not asked the "right people" for help. The wartime militias and associated mafias, rather than being eclipsed by the state, now operated within it, he concluded.

> When I heard about the compensation, I tried to file on my own. I went to the ministry several times. I stood in line for hours. Before seeing any of the officials at the Ministry, I heard from other refugees that we had to collect signatures from the Central Fund for the Displaced, the *Mukhtar*[9] of the village that we come from, and the *Mukhtar* of the neighborhood in Beirut [where he now lived]. I collected all the necessary documents and signatures and came back. When I made it to the official at the Ministry, he asked me to go back for more documents and official signatures. These state officials would not pay attention to any application if it did not come through an influential person.
>
> Now we [the displaced] do not know the "rules of the new game" of how, where, and who can provide us with services and support. After the war the logic of things changed. During the war, I used to ask the (militia) leader to find me an apartment, or find me a job. After the war, the politicians sensed that we are not completely dependent upon them as before. But they are trying to keep us under their control. They want us to be like sheep that they own. They want us to realize that we cannot get anything without their intervention. Unfortunately, the government is afraid of the political and religious leaders; it listens to them but not to us. They are the government and the opposition at the same time. What can I tell you? "If your enemy is the judge, to whom can you complain?"

Eventually, the compensation came through, although not until Ali, alarmed by rumors of a budget shortfall in the Ministry of the Displaced, sought help from a patron. As he tells the story:

> Finally, my cousin [who is a displaced] told me that he knew someone who is influential at the Ministry and can mediate on my behalf. The help was on the condition that I use the compensation money to buy an apartment in a housing project managed by the mediator and his brother.

Like many of the displaced, Ali and his family would have to move from a neighborhood, Ayn Al-Mreisi, close to Beirut's central district where they had lived for 17 years. The compensation he received, Ali complained, "would not buy me a wall in that neighborhood." Yet he considered himself lucky to be buying a (two-bedroom) apartment in a building in which "influential" people (*nas wasleen*)—the mediator and his brother—owned more than half the units. Should the government 10 years hence decide to incorporate that area into its urban plan, he would be protected from yet another displacement. When I asked Ali why he did not move back to his village of origin, he responded: "Who is going to feed my family? My work is here in Beirut and my village is far from here. In addition, the compensation money is not enough for me to buy land and build a house in the village." A troublesome detail is that the apartment was yet to be built. The compensation was paid as a first installment on a dwelling he had so far only seen on a map. What would have happened, he wondered, had he kept the money and looked for housing elsewhere?

> Now that it is summertime, I sent my wife and children to stay with my mother in the village. I am staying temporarily with friends and relatives in Beirut. Sometimes, I sleep at construction sites and get paid as a night guard. The serious problems will start when school begins [in the fall]. Who is going to host my three children in the city? I do not want to think about it right now!

Ali's case is but a miniscule example of the complexity of negotiating for housing in postwar Beirut. Most of the war-displaced were unsure how much money, if any, they would be paid, when they would receive it, or where to go after being evicted from their wartime niches. All too often, to obtain what was owed them they had to obligate themselves to others—relatives and political patrons, mainly—and this undermined their ability to plan, creating more uncertainty in the present and unpredictability for the future. Should they return to their villages of origin? Should they buy or rent places in the city? Should they use all the compensation money for alternative housing or was it wiser to set aside some of it to meet more urgent needs? Each dilemma enmeshed them in a multi-layered web in which the state, the politicians, and their kin were all entangled.

Conclusion: the Right to a Home

> No one shall be subjected to arbitrary interference with his privacy, family, home, or correspondence, or to attack upon his honor and reputation. Everyone has the right to the protection of the law against such interference or attacks. (Universal Declaration of Human Rights, Article 12)

According to this Article of the Universal Declaration of Human Rights, the Lebanese state and its institutions (the Ministry of the Displaced, the Central Fund for the Displaced), as well as the private developers and the public-private company Solidere, all violated the rights of Beirut's war-displaced to a decent home, privacy and reputation. In effect they created more displacement, as their projects for reconstruction generated a series of "postwar emergencies." Even some of the non-displaced, the legal tenants and owners, were forced to move from downtown Beirut into the surrounding areas and suburbs. Complicated power relationships affected the struggle over urban sites, for although the state and the developers controlled who had access to the newly designed and constructed areas, the displaced population strategically manipulated its prewar and wartime experiences to get something, too.

Developers and investors presented their projects as a means to modernize and thereby improve city life. The implementation of urban planning laws and regulations to "upgrade" and "order" space was high on their agenda. This implied making space available to new users while depriving marginal and powerless groups, specifically the war-displaced, of their urban foothold. Their official rhetoric, amplified by public discourse and the media, rendered these groups undeserving: they were not sufficiently urbane; they belonged back in the countryside where they came from. Yet one of the unanticipated consequences of the civil war in Lebanon was to give thousands of villagers, uprooted from their homes, a deepening urban identity—as deep as that of some "native" Beirutis who spent the war years abroad. Rather than return to their villages, the war-displaced, evicted under the conditions of postwar reconstruction, have relocated to squatter suburbs on the city's periphery. In other words, the launching of a vast project for modern reconstruction has reproduced the very symptoms it was designed to eliminate: informality, illegality, visual blight, patched together services. Its rhetoric to the contrary, top-down planning produces social and political ruptures; it cannot "heal the wounds of war"

Notes

1. Displaced Shiite Muslims from south Lebanon constitute a large percentage of those receiving compensation.
2. The Israeli army withdrew from large areas of south Lebanon in 2000.
3. Beirut had earlier become a refuge for thousands of Palestinians forced out of their villages and towns as a result of the creation of the state of Israel in Palestine. Yet although Palestinians who lived in refugee camps in Beirut were displaced during the Lebanese civil war, they were excluded from the Ministry's compensation programs for the displaced.
4. Significantly, perhaps, the minister of the displaced, Walid Junblat was the leader of the Druze militia (the Progressive Socialist Party). Many Christians accuse this militia of forcing Christians from their villages in Mount Lebanon.
5. Of the political parties, it was mostly Hizballah and the Amal Movement that presented themselves as defendants and representatives of the displaced.
6. From an interview with an official at the Ministry of the Displaced.
7. Until recently, the state did not provide electricity to residential areas. It was the responsibility of each house to provide its own. Enterprising people bought generators and provided electricity to their neighbors, charging them on a monthly or weekly basis.
8. See Johnson (1986) for more details on patron-client relationships in Beirut.
9. A *mukhtar* is a neighborhood-level authority, appointed by the state, who is responsible for registering births and deaths and issuing proof of residence.

References

Beyhum, N. (1994), "Population Displacement in the Metropolitan District of Beirut: Are the Displacements Over?" in Shami, S. (ed.), *Population Displacement and Resettlement:Development and Conflict in the Middle East*, New York: Center for Migration Studies.

Charif, H. (1994), "Regional Development and Integration", in Collings, D. (ed.), *Peace for Lebanon? From War to Reconstruction*, Boulder and London: Lynne Rienner Publishers.

Corm, G. (1996), *Reconstruction and Public Interest: Postwar Economy and Politics*, Beirut: Dar al-Jadid. (In Arabic).

Faour, A. (1991), *Beirut, 1975–1990: Demographic, Social and Economic Transformations*, Beirut: Geographic Institute. (In Arabic.)

Johnson, M. (1986), *Class and Client in Beirut: The Sunni Muslim Community and the Lebanese State, 1840–1985*, London and Atlantic Highlands NJ: Ithaca Press.

Makdisi, S. (1997), "Laying Claim to Beirut: Urban Narrative and Spatial Identity in the Age of Solidere", *Critical Inquiry*, 23: 661–705.

Makiya, K. (1996), "Forgetting Beirut", *New Perspectives Quarterly*, 13 (Summer): 16.

Maliki, L. (1997), *Purity and Exile: Violence, Memory, and National Cosmology Among the Hutu Refugees in Tanzania*, Chicago: Chicago University Press.

Mitchell, T. (1988), *Colonising Egypt*, Cairo: The American University in Cairo Press.

Percy, C. (1995), "United Debates Participation in the Economic Recovery of Lebanon", *Mediterranean Quarterly; A Journal of Global Issues*, 6 (2): 1–16.

Salam, A. (1998), "The Role of Government in Shaping the Built Environment", in Hashem Sarkis and Peter Row (eds), *Projecting Beirut: Episodes in the Construction and Reconstruction of a Modern City*, Munich: Prestel, pp. 122–33. (In Arabic.)

Shararah, W. (1985), *The Suspended City*, Beirut: Dar al-Matbouat al-Sharqeyyeh. (In Arabic.)

Tabet, J. (1996), *Reconstruction and Public Interest: Tradition and Modernity, the City of War and the Memory of the Future*, Beirut: Dar al-Jadid. (In Arabic.)

Trendle, G. (1992), "Between a Rock and Another Place: The Displaced and Politics of Return", in *The Lebanon Report*, 3 (October): 10–11.

Turner, V. (1967), *The Forest of Symbols: Aspects of Ndembu Ritual*, Ithaca, NY: Cornell University Press.

Wakim, N. (1999), *The Black Hands*, Beirut: Dar Al-Nahar. (In Arabic.)

–14–

Wounded Palermo[1]

Jane Schneider and *Peter Schneider*

Palermo is a city in transformation. Its historic center, formerly neglected, abandoned by many, and a shabby symbol of degradation and decay, has sprung to life with noisy projects of recuperation. Among the refurbished buildings is the Teatro Massimo, the third largest opera house in Europe after Paris and Vienna. Reopened in 1997 after twenty-three years of haunting silence during which pigeons nested in the rafters and water leaked through the roof, this structure is at the ceremonial center of the renewal. In June, 1999, it served as the stage for Hillary Clinton's address to an international audience on the topic of "civil society". In December 2000 it hosted the opening ceremony of the United Nations Convention against Transnational Organized Crime, with speakers from Kofi Annan, to the Presidents of Italy and Poland, to Pino Arlacchi, then United Nations Under Secretary for Drug Control and Crime Prevention, praising what they called the "Palermo Renaissance." Like the transformed Massimo, the city that was once the "capital of the Mafia" now offers itself to the world as the "capital of the anti-Mafia," its people having suppressed, according to official rhetoric, a "crime-friendly culture" of indifference and cynicism in favor of a "law-abiding culture" of civic pride.

Integral to this reversal of images is Palermo's liberation from the "long 1980s"—the years 1978 to 1992 during which its streets were bloodied by exceptional and unprecedented violence. At the outset of these years, the Corleonesi, a group of notoriously aggressive Mafiosi whose leaders originated in the town of Corleone, an hour's drive into the mountains, waged a takeover of the established Mafia "families" of the city. The aggressors' strategy, on occasion imitated by their enemies, included murdering public officials—police and Carabinieri officers, magistrates and political leaders. As the center of gravity for these events, Palermo (population around 700,000) lost 100 or more persons annually to assassination, not counting disappearances (LoDato 2000: 18, Santino 1988: 238).

Underlying this exceptional violence was the Mafia's assumption of a strategic role in global heroin trafficking; responding to the violence was a massive police and judicial repression accompanied by a citizens' anti-Mafia social movement. This essay looks beyond drug trafficking to another aspect of organized crime in urban settings: its integral relationship to the industries of real estate and construction. Examined from this perspective, Palermo's recovery from the drug mafia is more complex and perhaps less promising than the city's anti-Mafia promoters would have us believe.

The "Sack" of Palermo

More than other cities of Western Europe—certainly more than other Italian cities—Palermo was damaged by its rush into modernism after the Second World War. Sadly distorted because unregulated and undercapitalized, and further warped by the aggressive involvement of Mafiosi in real estate speculation and construction, the modernist transformation of the 1950s through the mid-1980s is now referred to by many as the *scempio* or "sack" of the city. The years 1957 to 1963 were the high point in private construction, followed in the 1970s and 1980s by a greater emphasis on public works (see Chubb 1982: 132, 150–1). Overall the rhythm reflected the rapid urbanization of Sicily after the Second World War, as a land reform and resultant mechanization of agriculture created a massive peasant exodus, and as rural landlords—owners of vast latifundia—moved their investments into urban real estate. In the same period, an expanding national welfare state made cities attractive as a source of public employment. Palermo, which in 1946 became the capital of the new, autonomous Region of Sicily, grew from a citizenry of 503,000 in 1951 to 709,000 in 1981, an increase of 41 per cent. Although an urban plan, mandated by the Regional Government, was developed in 1962, it did not deter the willful acts of large and small investors, hoping to profit from the resulting demand.

Uniquely unhappy events further distorted the postwar construction boom. Bombed by the allied forces in 1943, the city's historic center lost its moorings. More severely damaged than any other southern Italian city, 70,000 rooms were lost, leaving nearly 150,000 people condemned to live in crowded slums, shantytowns and even caves (Chubb 1982: 129). Opulent *palazzi* were severely affected, so much so that their noble owners, rattled by the pending land reform, abandoned them to roof leaks and water damage. Vandals removed architectural embellishments from their empty carcasses—statues, columns, fountains, even the plumbing. Built with a double-walled technique in which crushed stone fills a wide space between interior and exterior walls enhancing insulation, many of them began to crumble. The city administration, ever opportunistic, collected the rubble as landfill, dumping it along the coast. If an earlier wave of development had not already reoriented the city away from its beautiful waterfront, the unsightly piles of junk on the beach would perform the coup de grace.

Bombing raids also affected popular neighborhoods of the historic center. Here precarious buildings, at risk of falling, were either demolished or stabilized by a dense crisscrossing of long wooden beams at the level of the upper stories, propping them up against facing structures while cutting out light below (see Figure 14.1). Walking the narrow streets, one

Figure 14.1 Precarious buildings, historic center. Photograph by Jane Schneider.

still enters the shadows of these overhead "bridges". All told the raids weakened or leveled any number of testimonies to a rich architectural history, leading observers to evoke "Beirut" when describing the result. Ferns sprout from abandoned stone balconies like "pale-green moustaches," writes one such observer, and because there is no preservation, everything "is either ruining or mutating from mineral to vegetable" (Eberstat 1991: 67). Meanwhile, vibrant informal uses of space proliferated. Immigrants from Africa and Asia moved into the condemned buildings; cloisters and courtyards were turned into parking lots, depots for construction materials and stolen goods, or artisans' noisy workshops; and empty quarters of all kinds lent themselves to prostitution and the retail sale of drugs (see Cannarozzo 1996, Lo Piccolo 1996).

More serious than the destruction was the political decision to turn away from restoration in favor of building a "new Palermo," at first concentrated at the northern end, beyond an Art Nouveau neighborhood of nineteenth-century expansion, then in other peripheral zones to the west and south. Here the built environment spread over, and obliterated, if sometimes oddly and in patches, orchards, villas, and hamlets. Aristocratic landowners were, apparently, as eager to sell their orchards as to sell their latifundia and this fact accelerated the cementification of what was formerly green. The traces include abandoned and crumbling villas totally suffocated by surrounding apartment houses several times their height; villas restored like movie sets for wedding receptions that are, however, hemmed in by incongruous high-rises; and single trees or rows of trees, proud survivors of the orgy of clearing.

Former hamlets are today the commercial centers of the new suburbs. Modest owners of the houses and commercial buildings that line their main streets have eagerly sold out to speculative investors who either super-elevate or demolish and begin anew. The resulting mix of shapes and styles overlays a past of architectural coherence. At the same time, the automobile, multiplying in tandem with the suburban population, has turned these once sleepy village streets into quagmires of congestion.

Nor is this the worst of the "sack" or *scempio.* The thinking of the time was that if the buildings in the historic center continued to succumb to neglect and disasters, so be it: eventually they could be leveled to create space for a thoroughly modern, New York-inspired downtown. City investments in outlying public housing and infrastructure, including a multiple-lane ring road, enticed private housing developers to the outskirts—often in advance of the promised lines for gas and water, electricity and transportation and the provisioning of services like schools (Chubb 1982: 151–6). In 1968, an earthquake in the Belice Valley south of Palermo shook the old center one more time. Subsequent decisions replicated the established pattern: the city would cover more orchards with tracts of public housing and relocate center-city residents rather than attempt to repair their compromised buildings. Numbering 125,000 in 1951, the population of the historic center fell to less than 40,000 over the next thirty years (Cole 1997: 30).

Hence peripheral Palermo's vast expanses of high-rise condominium and rental slabs, laid out in block after monotonous block, distinguished from their Eastern European equivalents mainly by the profusion of cacti and geraniums that overflow the balconies. Some of the slabs have penetrated the historic center, lighting upon spaces that happened to be cheaply available. Wherever one encounters them, they seem shabby, both for their flaking and chipping cement surfaces and because a heavy reliance on iron rods and railings for support and decoration has produced, over the years, the stains of spreading rust.

Some blame the *scempio* partly on "the times," recollecting from personal experience how gripping modernism seemed. Given Palermo's pattern of postwar growth, a large proportion of the consumers of new housing were formerly rural people encouraged by the land reform, or by work stints in northern Europe, to dream of escaping from "backwardness"—to imagine becoming, in their terms, *evoluto* or modern. Easy credit, co-mingled with migrants' remittances, facilitated their project. Anyone wanting to purchase an apartment could get away with a down payment of less than three million *lire* (about $2000), with the builder negotiating a bank loan for the difference. For employees of the Regional Government, low-cost loans were a standard benefit (Chubb 1982: 129). In such an atmosphere, even native Palermitans formed the idea that anything old was unworthy, unless perhaps it were really old, with the patina of antiquity. When, in 1960, Palermo's one and only "skyscraper" was completed—an office tower in the middle of what was once the Art Nouveau quarter—these modernists raced with excitement to see its crowning red light go on for the very first time. In retrospect, they confess, Prague would have been a better model than New York.

But blaming what happened on the power of style—on the desire to be modern—only goes so far. Narratives of the construction boom are far more likely to point to the corrupt *intreccio* or "tangle" between political, economic, and mafia interests. Christian Democratic politicians owed their success in local and regional elections to votes that were mobilized by Mafiosi, particularly those who had their roots in the zones of urban expansion. Formerly agriculturalists, Mafiosi in these zones flooded into activities associated with construction—hauling materials, pouring cement, speculating on land, building apartments for family, friends, and profit. Their role and the role of the politicians in mutilating the postwar development of Palermo cannot be over-stated.

Multiply this by the money that circulated during the "long 1980s," when Palermo was the hub of the global heroin traffic. Clandestine refineries, moving into high gear in 1978, were situated in the city, as well as along the western coast, in the mountain town of San Giuseppe Jato, and on a property in the Palermo suburb of Ciaculli (Pezzino 1995: 300–1). Over the next few years, between 4 and 5 tons of pure heroin were produced each year in Sicily, worth 600 million dollars in annual profits and meeting roughly 30 per cent of U.S. demand (Paoli 1997: 317–18).

The golden age of narco-trafficking did not last long for Sicilian Mafiosi. Both the anti-Mafia operations of the mid-1980s, the growing popularity and availability of Andean cocaine, and the global trend toward processing drugs closer to their point of production, relegated them to a minor and less lucrative role. Nevertheless, the moment of accumulation enabled the Corleonesi faction to capitalize several new construction firms, broaching their postwar ambition of directing the construction sector of the Palermo, and regional, economy (Centorrino 1986: 89–90). Not only did these firms pursue the usual interventions—bribes to politicians, rigged bidding, collusion between firms that entered false bids or withdrew from the competition to "fix" the outcome, intimidation of inspectors. From about 1985, they also laid claim to the ground floor and top floor apartments of the buildings being built. More seriously, according to the Direzione Italiana Antimafia (D.I.A.) evidence, public works became a privileged locus for reinvesting drug profits, the goal being "complete control and the substantial internal conditioning of the entrepreneurial world" in this sector (D.I.A., quoted in Paoli 1997: 319).

In the past, each Mafia "family" or *cosca* had been free to impose kickbacks on contractors working within its territory, but now the Corleonesi sought exclusive claims over these relations regardless of place, engaging Angelo Siino, a wealthy businessman from of San Giuseppe Jato, as coordinator. Siino (described in the press as the Mafia's "Minister of Public Works") articulated the bosses with local coalitions of businessmen, politicians and public officials whose hands were on the system of parceling out bids at auction. Classically, the *cosca* of the territory where the work was being done received 2 to 3 percent and was permitted to determine the subcontractors, the suppliers, and the pick-up work force—if necessary backing its requests with letters of extortion or menacing fires. By "piloting" which companies would win, in what order, and under what terms, Siino spread the rewards as even-handedly as possible, enhancing the Mafia's reputation for "taking care of its people." And this at the very same time that the Corleonesi were lurching into a spiral of terror that would disgust even some of their own (Paoli 1997: 320–1). Although these trends enhanced employment in the construction sector, it was at the price of an increasingly disturbing web of illegal activity and violence.

What is it about Construction?

The construction industry and the industries supplying construction materials together account for a greatly disproportionate share of the Palermo economy—33 per cent of the industrial work force in the 1970s compared with 10 per cent in Milan. Made up of myriad firms employing between 25 and 30 workers or less, this sector also provided the city's "major source of wealth," the more so as national government moneys became available for public housing (Chubb 1982: 131). As late as 1999, a glossy brochure put out by City Hall to attract investment capital indicated that 48.2 percent of the 14,201 firms registered with the Palermo Chamber of Commerce were in the construction sector, more than all other forms of manufacturing activity combined.

Also to the point is the almost predictable "organic permeability" of this industry to organized crime. Consisting of numerous branches (commercial, highway, industrial, pipelines, housing, monuments), divided between public works and private projects, and employing a broad mix of skilled and unskilled workers, it is perhaps best characterized as an economic sector rather than an industry as such (Kelly 1999: 76–7). Robert Kelly, addressing the question why "criminal pathologies are endemic" to construction in New York City, makes the following useful observation:

> . . . the construction industry is fragile because it is so atypical. Construction work more than most other types of industrial work depends on weather, coordination and integration of dozens of subcontractors, specialized crafts, and groups of laborers. Site clearance, demolition, and excavation must be done; concrete poured; superstructures raised; plumbing installed; carpentry and electrical work carried out; telephone wiring and elevator installation completed—all in a predetermined order and often unchangeable sequence . . . A racketeer with influence or control over supplies, union officials, or building inspectors can exacerbate or reduce the fragility; the racketeer thus has many opportunities to extract money from the industry's participants. At the same time, the contractors who themselves are often victims or potential victims of gangsters do not hesitate to exploit those gangsters for their own greedy

> designs or to ensure some degree of stability in an otherwise capricious work environment. Consequently, it is not unusual for a builder/contractor to seek out racketeers who can eliminate competition, quiet labor unrest, or skirt the maze of regulations that fills the construction landscape. (Kelly 1999: 90–1)

The Palermo experience points to another ingredient, as well. Heavily capitalized construction firms—American, Italian, Saudi Arabian, German, Japanese, to name a few—bid on contracts the world over. By the same token, construction components are increasingly modular; transportable from place to place (see Linder 1994). And yet, by its very nature, the building business is grounded—dependent for profit and promise on local contractors and subcontractors, on local materials, and on the local and regional administration of laws governing transportation, public housing, zoning, contract bidding, taxation, credit and finance (Harvey 1989: 65ff). This, plus the dependence of the industry on local labor, or labor that has immigrated into the area, constitutes a rich terrain for mediating clientelistic relationships—for industry representatives and friends to deliver the votes of construction workers and suppliers to compliant municipal and regional politicians, in turn prepared to look the other way when the "maze of regulations" is violated. In many places, the story of the expansion of organized crime in recent decades, and of the very recent attempts to suppress it, is also a story of municipal authorities transforming the built environment.

The Construction Industry and the Left

Nothing better illustrates political corruption in the Palermo construction industry than the participation of the Left, including the Communist Left, in some of the wheeling and dealing. This is because, in rural Sicily, the Communist Party had earned the reputation of being almost alone in opposing the Mafia. Defending peasants in the their struggle for land at the end of the Second World War, several Communist leaders had suffered reprisals from Mafiosi defending landowners. Nearly fifty Communist, Socialist, and peasant leaders had, indeed, been martyred between the end of the war and the mid-1960s. All the more telling, then, that the Left should soften its anti-Mafia rigor in the urban context.

Palermo was bursting with newcomers in the 1960s and 1970s, many of whom found employment in the building trades, which all of the unions, including the Communist union, competed to organize. Most employees of the region's largest construction companies—in particular four large Catania-based firms whose owners had been knighted by the state and were known, therefore, as the "Knights of Labor" (Cavalieri di Lavoro)—joined the Communist union, the C.G.I.L. Reciprocally, the union defined these companies as "progressive" and cooperated with their owners in the maintenance of labor peace. The owners have since been indicted for collusion with the Mafia. Perhaps more seriously, in the 1970s, the Communists organized several cooperative building firms known as "red cooperatives" that benefited from the city, regional, and national government practice of parceling out public works contracts to competing firms in proportion to the electoral success of the parties with which they were affiliated. Dependent on rigged bidding, this practice was of course illegal, as were the rigged auctions through which the red coops, along with many other firms, obtained sub-contracts from the largest companies.

In the 1980s, both external and internal critics of the Communist Party and union were becoming a vocal presence in the anti-Mafia movement. Significantly, none of the critics thought that the leaders profited, personally, from corruption; rather, they believed them to be motivated by the need to create employment for a rapidly expanding peasant-to-worker constituency, and by a desire to be involved in the provision of public housing. And yet the criticism stung, putting older generation Leftists on the defensive. Until the late 1970s, the Sicilian Communist Party nurtured a political culture premised on a model of society in which dramatically unequal social classes confronted one another across discrete boundaries. According to the resulting morality of struggle, solidarity within the class on the bottom took precedence over individually negotiated ties of patronage between members of this class and their class superiors -- ties that were heavily stigmatized. Inevitably, Communist Party stalwarts resented the exposure of clientelistic practices in the red coops and union; after all, the votes of the members of these organizations were already assured. At the same time, they expressed nostalgia for a simpler time, when it was clear who held the moral high ground with regard to anti-Mafia.

Defenders of the Left's anti-Mafia credentials like to remind their critics that until the late 1970s, the Communist Party funded the Palermo daily, *L'Ora*, famous for exposing the scandals behind savage construction. Under a courageous editor, Vittorio Nisticò, reporters wrote stories on the city's delay in approving an urban plan, on its failure to guarantee adequate space for services and recreation amidst the spreading concrete jungle, on specific instances of corruption involving Christian Democratic officials in City Hall and Mafioso contractors and suppliers who were their friends. Defenders are also quick to insist that the damage done by the C.G.I.L. and the red coops pales in comparison to the "sack of Palermo," organized by the Mafia-sponsored contractors allied with the Christian Democrats. In self-defense, one Communist leader has stated, in words widely quoted by friends and enemies alike: "Well, we cannot analyse the blood of everyone we do business with."

The Rognoni–La Torre Law

Having sketched the *intreccio* between the Mafia, the Palermo real estate and construction industries, and various political forces (including the ostensibly oppositional red coops and Communist union), we turn to the difficulties encountered by the anti-Mafia process—both its criminal justice and social movement aspects—in the city's recovery from the *scempio*. Two initiatives will be considered: an effort to recycle mafia properties and a new urban plan.

In 1982, in the wake of the assassinations of the anti-Mafia coordinator and prefect of Palermo, Carlo Alberto dalla Chiesa, and Pio La Torre, Sicilian Communist leader, the national parliament passed the Rognoni–La Torre law. Among other things, it obligates the state to sequester and confiscate the illegally acquired assets of persons convicted of organized criminal activity, and turn them to "socially useful" purposes such as spaces for social services, recreational centers, *bocci* courts, meeting places for civic groups. Convicted Mafiosi are likely to have a portfolio of properties: apartments or apartment buildings, land parcels, businesses and stocks. An office of confiscations in the regional branch of the Ministry of Finance must record for each asset whether or not it was purchased with "dirty" money; its market value; and the progress, or lack thereof, in rendering it "free" for subsequent use. According to the law, "free" means emptied of current tenants or users. The list of Palermo properties confiscated as of 1999 totaled 213, of which eighty-eight were two-to-four room apartments; fifty-six were small plots of land.

As many as ten to twelve years might pass between the act of sequester and the final confiscation. Just for starters, Mafiosi cleverly mislead the authorities by signing over what they own to others—usually their wives. The Finance Guard, the police branch of the Ministry, often has difficulty locating sequestered residences, let alone assessing their value. An unwelcome presence in many neighborhoods, its agents encounter local *omertà* upon asking directions to courtyards or byways not on their maps. In Italy as a whole, assets worth $3.4 billion were seized from organized crime figures between 1990 and 1997, compared with only $240 million that were actually confiscated (Jamieson 2000: 113).

Nor are confiscated properties necessarily desirable. Because being a Mafioso does not guarantee solvency, particularly in light of lawyers' fees and bad gambles in real estate or drugs, many of the assets are encumbered with debt. Most important, the parcels of land and apartments are frequently tenanted, usually with relatives or clients of the owner. Although the state is obliged to help all legal tenants of an affected building find another residence, the tenants, given sixty days notice, often balk. Add to this the possibility that the former owner may feel vengeful toward a successor. Between deterioration, debts, and the threat of retaliation, the state has accumulated properties that no one wants. As of 1999, the city of Palermo had rejected about a third of the real estate offered to it by the Finance Ministry—a rejection rate so high that the prefect complained, after which a few more properties were taken on as a "moral obligation."

Consider, finally, the situation of employees in businesses affected by the law. In one case, the tenants of a store, upon learning that they had to relocate because their landlord was a front for a Mafia leader, wrote to the President of Italy. "We are victims (who) must lose our clientele built up piece by piece over 20 years, lay off two employees, and give up an activity that our son and our partners' son expected to inherit" (*Giornale di Sicilia*, 25 August 1999). Court-appointed administrators are charged with keeping companies running until their eventual disposition, most probably to a workers' cooperative. Although by law, anyone with a criminal record is to be purged in the interim, this does not usually happen. Instead, the administrators, in the interest of the firm's viability, alter as little as possible. When one large construction company was seized, the workers struck, declaring the action a threat to their well-being. Reluctance to pursue any charges of corruption in this case is a telling indication of the Mafia's entanglements and the difficult road ahead.

The End of an Era: Between Old and New Economies

Integral to the anti-Mafia process in Palermo has been the reversal of the *scempio,* evident in a large-scale project for the restoration of the historic center of which the Teatro Massimo is emblematic, and in the more tortured effort to develop an urban plan for the future of the entire city. The most controversial feature of the new master plan is its assumption that the city is overbuilt, will not grow in population, and must therefore consolidate and curate what it has. As the anti-Mafia voices behind this vision argue, a portion of the cement already laid down stands empty and, in addition, more spaces will open up through the on-going recuperation of the historic center. It should not be necessary to keep on building. Sealing their argument against additional construction is a staggering datum: national standards of urbanism dictate that a city of Palermo's size should have 12,600,000 cubic meters devoted to "services"—schools, parking, public amenities, parks and gardens—amounting to approximately 18 cubic meters per person. In Palermo, such services are allotted only 2,485,000 cubic meters, which is 3.55 cubic meters per capita.[2]

The planners' proposal for closing this gap is to consider outlying parklands as part of the formula, inflating the cubic meters of "service space" per person to 15.5. These, and any other green expanses, including all agricultural holdings still in the city limits, should be defined as no longer potentially buildable under any circumstances. The residual agrarian properties need not be expropriated; they can continue to be cultivated by private owners. But the plan interdicts these owners from selling them for development. In the planners' words, "if we block expansion, we can dedicate energy and resources to 'constructing' the 'already constructed' . . . to curating the riches we already have." One might even imagine demolishing a few things "because they are offensive to a civic asset" (a panorama, for example. Cervellati 1995: 68–70).

In keeping with the new urban plan's rigid commitment to a greener, less cement-strewn Palermo is the application of the anti-Mafia policy of *spaccatura,* severing corrupt relationships, to the building sector. North Italian and foreign contractors are to be favored over locals for public contracts. There is also a new law requiring companies bidding on contracts to present a certificate from the Prefecture that they are not under investigation or indictment. And the city has set up a "committee for securing public order" to discuss and act upon reports of the police and Carabinieri engaged in on-site monitoring of construction projects. The parties to a project, sub-contractors included, must sign "protocols" of commitment to transparency and legality.[3]

Perhaps not surprisingly, the new urban plan is intensely controversial. To the greener constituencies of the anti-Mafia movement, it encapsulates the most progressive concepts of urban planning—decentralization, conservation of nature, "sustainable development," quality of life, and values of neighborhood and community participation. Others, including anti-Mafia activists whose political formation has been more red than green, see it as utopian—an unrealistic and arbitrary attempt to impose values, sub-divisions, and transportation practices that are alien to local life. The fiercest polemics reflect uncertainty about the role to be played in the new Palermo of the construction industry—the industry that has defined the city, its urbanscape as well as its economy, since the Second

World War. After all, "constructing the already constructed," restoring what is there while not moving on, means shedding a substantial number of construction jobs.

In 1996 we conducted a series of interviews with working-class people, approached through our study of four middle schools located in poor neighborhoods. Because their children were in attendance in these schools —not drop-outs or truants as happens quite often—and because the schools are heavily involved in anti-Mafia educational projects, the persons we interviewed were generally not hostile to the anti-Mafia process. This makes their response to our questions regarding Sicily's future all the more significant. Regardless of the neighborhood, and quite without our anticipating it, the interviews revealed the overwhelming impact of the construction industry on the livelihoods of postwar working-class families.

In more than half the families we met, the men worked, or had worked, in trades associated with building, either as wage earners or small-scale contractors, or a combination of both. Moreover, a majority of families had given expression to their "evolving" urban identity through the handiwork of the man or men of the household. In the boom years,

Figure 14.2 Demonstration to "save 500 jobs; this too is to struggle against the Mafia." Photograph by Jane Schneider.

construction workers of all kinds remodeled, expanded, or totally rebuilt their own and their relatives' apartments, ignoring the building codes as necessary. Interviewees proudly showed us roof-top terraces turned into extra rooms, reconstructed archways and windows, extensive floor and wall tiling. Some told of tapping into gas and electrical lines before these services were provided by the city.

To most of the interviewees, Palermo is in an economic crisis due to the abrupt slowdown of construction, which they associated with the anti-Mafia prosecutions or, to quote one, "hysteria" about legality. Several said, without our prompting, "the Mafia gave us work, and now the anti-Mafia has taken this work away."[4] According to one man, thanks to the politicians and the Mafia, "there used to be a lifting crane every 20 meters well into the 1980s, but now the cranes have vanished because all of their owners are in jail." An ironworker experiencing a three quarters reduction in his work claimed the same for any craftsman (woodworker, tile layer, plumber, electrician)—connected to the building trades. The halt in construction, in the view of still others, was having a giant domino effect, construction being the first link in a long chain. The chain now broken, even fishmongers suffered, as customers could no longer afford to dine in restaurants that purchased fish. In other words, "if the masons don't work, neither does anyone else" (see Figure 14.2).

The "Spectacle" of Competition for Global Capital

Hillary Clinton was present in Palermo in June 1999 to serve as the keynote speaker for a four-day conference on "Educating for Legality," sponsored by Civitas, an international N.G.O. concerned with civic education against crime and corruption. Delegations of educators came from all over the world. In addition to Sandra Feldman, president of the American Federation of Teachers, and the above mentioned Arlacchi, speakers included Baltasar Garzon Real, the Spanish magistrate who pressed human rights charges against Pinochet; Otto Schily, German Minister of the Interior; and Wole Soyinka, Nobel Prize winning Nigerian writer. Several key figures in the anti-Mafia establishment of Palermo also participated: the mayor Leoluca Orlando, the education commissioner Alessandra Siragusa, and the Archbishop Cardinal Pappalardo.

Clinton complimented the people of Palermo on the restoration of the theater from whose stage she was speaking, and on the recuperation of their city from a time of disorder and violence. Order, she suggested, rests on a "three legged stool," one leg the government, a second the economy, and a third the civil society. By the latter she meant the social space outside of economy and government from which citizens generate initiatives for moral, cultural, and political reform. Neither she, nor anyone else at the conference, had much to say about the "economy" leg, the most wobbly of the three, having been shattered by an unfortunate coincidence of the collapse of the Mafia economy with the decline of the welfare state. In the 1990s, as a consequence of the financial reforms undertaken by Italy to become a full partner in the European Monetary Union, funds to the southern provinces were cut and the Cassa per il Mezzogiorno, the massive development agency of the postwar decades, dismantled. A report in the Financial section of *La Repubblica* (21 June 1999) correlated rising unemployment in the South and Sicily with the consequent declining level of public investment, which fell from 4.3 per cent of G.N.P. in 1980 to 1.3 per cent in 1998. The issue now is what kind of investment (private and public) will take the *Cassa*'s place.

Penn Kemble, attending the conference as acting director of the United States Information Agency, was reassuring. To his surprise, he said, Palermo was full of pleasant rather than stressed and fearful faces. It had created a model for the "reconquest of democracy" that could be exported to other places. Acknowledging that if people lack material benefits, the Mafia might come back, he offered this panacea: "international finance" will make capital flow in response to the new climate. Capital must "be able to make profits, certainly, but above all it must find conditions of security and trust . . . economic progress is not determined by large investments, but by political and cultural changes that create fertile terrain. And today, I see no reason why American investors would not want to contribute to the economic growth of Palermo" (*Giornale di Sicilia*, 15 June 1999). Roy Godson, Georgetown University political scientist and director of another participating organization, the National Strategy Information Center in Washington DC, further assured the people of Palermo that their good example in "educating for legality" would translate into broader benefits. "Your city represents a model in the world for the struggle against the 'octopus.' . . . Naturally, much remains to be done but the mentality is changing." Palermo's best resource, he added, "which is certainly a great richness, is called tourism." Significantly, the 98,369 foreign tourists hosted by Palermo in 1993 climbed to 220,263 in 1999, and the number continues to grow (Lo Dato 2000: 18).

But competing for tourists can be a chimera, as development specialists are quick to point out; the more so in a place where many amenities have been ruined and must be reconstituted. So other alternatives must also be considered—for example, the Dublin model, which emphasizes education to enhance the qualifications of the labor force, attracting jobs related to information processing. Fitting this pattern are the several Italian and foreign companies currently expected to create "call centers" in Palermo (La Dato 2000: 18). Unfortunately, however, Palermo's school system suffers from the panoply of ills that currently accompany educational stratification in cities around the world (see Schneider and Schneider 2003: 277–9, 288).

And yet, the momentum to present a new Palermo continues, as illustrated by the United Nations Convention Against Organized Crime in December of 2000. On that occasion, Kofi Annan depicted a global division of good against bad—"civil society" in international combat with criminals, drug dealers, and other "forces of evil." The President of Poland called for a "global war" of "civilization and order" against "violence and lawlessness." There could have been no better opening for the Orlando administration to position Palermo in the vanguard of the good. "We once exported the disease," the mayor told the delegates during the opening ceremony; "now we export the therapy." Nor was this so far-fetched. The city lavishly hosted its guests, some 2000 delegates from 115 countries, cordoning off many miles of roadway to enable their circulation, and lining the venues of the multiple events—debates on the proposed treaty and related protocols, simultaneous scholarly symposia, a performance of Beethoven's Ninth Symphony conducted by Zubin Mehta—with thousands of cyclamins and poinsettias. Green lawns were rolled out along the newly restored waterfront and, to the amazement of everyone, also on the Piazza Magione, a bombed-out wasteland in the historic center still showing scars from the Second World War. So beautiful was the presentation, one almost overlooked the thousands of police, Carabinieri, soldiers and guards (10,000, according to the press) deployed at every angle, arms at the ready.

Of very great interest was the relationship between culture and economy presented to the world by those who would package the Palermo experience as a model. Their frequently repeated narrative emphasized how in the early postwar years, Italy had followed the prescription of the Left for fighting the Mafia: develop the underdeveloped South through massive state investment (the Cassa per il Mezzogiorno). This, however, had made the problem worse. Money ended up in the wrong hands, above all in the coffers of the corrupt politicians and bosses who used it to wreak havoc. Now, a different solution was being tried and this one appeared to be working: create a "culture of lawfulness" in anticipation of building an "economy of legality." Admittedly, this economy has yet to crystallize, but perhaps it is on the horizon: in October of 2000, Moody's Investor Service gave the city of Palermo an Aa3 rating—the same rating as Italy as a whole and San Francisco. In the words of Orlando, "Sicilian society today finds itself in a position to put to fruit—from an economic point of view—the cultural changes that have marked these last few years." National and European Union financing will continue to support improvements in transportation, schools, infrastructure, and historic preservation, with tourism and perhaps information processing defined as sectors for growth. Moody's warns, however, that "despite these positive signals, the city's weak local economy is still of some concern as GDP per capita remains low and, at 29 per cent, the unemployment rate remains high . . ." (Moody's Communique 2000: 64).

Because estimates of unemployment are based on persons registered at local unemployment offices, they exclude the many who have become discouraged and dropped out of the labor force. At the same time, however, participation in the informal economy is not reported in the official statistics. These two lacunae—there are others as well—actually mean that there are no accurate statistics on unemployment. The approximate estimates are nevertheless disturbing. *The Economist* (26 June 1993) reported teenage joblessness at 50.4 per cent for south Italian boys, and 68.2 per cent for girls, compared with 15.1 per cent and 27 per cent, respectively, in the north. In the course of our research, we heard the figure "from 25 to 40 per cent unemployed" for Palermo overall, the "official" rate having climbed from 25.5 to 35 per cent between 1981 and 1991 (the last census). In its "dossier" for the year 2000, ranking all the provinces of Italy on various economic and quality-of-life indicators, the newspaper *Il Sole-24 Ore* assigned the Province of Palermo the rank of 100th out of 103 on the employment scale, stating that 28 per cent of the workforce was in search of work (11 December 2000). With 48 per cent of its businesses failing for every 1,000 registered, Palermo Province ranked 96th out of 103 on business health.

Global narcotics trafficking, vastly expanding in the 1980s and 1990s, has had devastating consequences for many cities or parts thereof. In Palermo, illnesses and death associated with drug use have been less significant than the noxious effects of a great expansion of illegal money in circulation. Violent encounters between Mafiosi competing for this money; assaults on state officials charged with repressing the traffic; and the artificial inflation, hence inevitable contraction, of the construction sector through political corruption and the hyper-investment of narco-dollars are indicative. Recovery from these wounds should, we believe, include the idea of publically funded "work substitution" schemes, equivalent to the crop substitution programs proposed for rural areas of heroin and coca cultivation.

Put somewhat differently, it is not enough to imagine that programs of "cultural re-education" can translate into infusions of private capital in time to intercept yet another generation of unemployed youth from participating in organized crime. There is also the question, raised by this book, of whether private corporate investment will nourish opportunities for hanging-out "street people" or whether, on the contrary, it might further displace this constituency, if for no other reason than to "aestheticize" the streets. As is the case in other wounded cities, what seems to be needed is a revitalized collective vision for the urban polity as a whole.

Notes

1. An expanded development of the arguments in this chapter can be found in Schneider and Schneider (2003).
2. By the same token, already in the 1960s, zones of new construction in Palermo were reaching a density of 21 cubic meters per square meter, in contrast to the national norm of 3.5 cubic meters per square meter in urban areas (see Chubb 1982: 134).
3. Of course, no one considers these adequate, and proposals have been floated to develop elaborate computer programs to monitor projects (*La Repubblica*, 5 June 1999).
4. Revisiting some of the families in 1999, we heard the refrain again ("when there was the Mafia, there was construction," "the Mafia *dava da mangiare*" (put food on the table). Note was also made of television reports of a pick-up of out-migration by Sicilians, and of the government's over-generous approach to foreigners—described as "taking our jobs" or "working for too little pay." Gypsies, who "don't know how to live in apartments and expect handouts," were another target.

References

Cannarozzo, T. (1996), "Riqualificazione e ricupero del centro storico", In Cannarozzo, T. (ed.), *Palermo tra memoria e futuro: riqualificazione e ricupero del centro storico,* Palermo: Publisicula Editrice, pp. 23–71.

Centorrino, M. (1986), *L'economia mafiosa*, Saverio Manelli: Rubbetino Editore.

Cervellati, P.L. (1995), *Palermo: le città nella città*, Palermo: Sellerio Editore.

Chubb, J. (1982), *Patronage, Power, and Poverty in Southern Italy; A Tale of Two Cities*, Cambridge MA: M. I. T. Press.

Cole, J. (1997), *The New Racism in Europe: A Sicilian Ethnography*, Cambridge: Cambridge University Press.

Eberstadt, F. (1991), "Annals of Place: The Palace and the City", *The New Yorker*, 41–84 passim.

Harvey, D. (1989), *The Urban Experience*, Baltimore, MD: The Johns Hopkins University Press.

Kelly, R.J. (1999), *The Upperworld and the Underworld: Case Studies of Racketeering and Business Infiltrations in the United States*, New York: Kluwer Academic/Plenum Publishers.

Linder, M. (1994), *Projecting Capitalism: A History of the Internationalization of the Construction Industry*, Westport CT: Greenwood Press.

Lo Dato, E. (2000), Palermo's Cultural Revolution and the Renewal Project of the City Administration, Symposium on the Role of Civil Society: "Creating a Culture of Lawfulness"; The Palermo, Sicily Renaissance, Palermo: City of Palermo.

Lo Picolo, F. (1996), "The Historical Center of Palermo", in Cannarozzo, T. (ed.), *Palermo tra memoria e futuro; riqualificazione e recupero del centro storico,* Palermo: Publisicula Editrice, pp. 71–91.

Paoli, L. (1997), *The Pledge to Secrecy: Culture, Structure and Action of Mafia Associations*, Ph.D. dissertation, European University Institute, Florence.

Pezzino, P. (ed.) (1995), *Mafia: industria della violenza. Scritti e documenti inediti sulla mafia dalle origini ai giorni nostri*, Florence: La Nuova Italia.

Santino, U. (1988), "The Financial Mafia: The Illegal Accumulation of Wealth and the Financial-Industrial Complex", *Contemporary Crises*, 12: 203–43.

Schneider, J. and Schneider, P. (2003), *Reversible Destiny: Mafia, Antimafia and the Struggle for Palermo*, Berkeley CA: University of California Press.

Epilogue: Baghdad, 2003[1]

Jane Schneider and *Ida Susser*

Thinking about wounded cities requires that we engage in a breathless game of catch-up with challenging world events. As the introduction to this volume notes, the attack on New York City in September of 2001 jarred us to reconsider a project that was already under way. Now, with the manuscript in production, the pre-emptive U.S. war on Iraq demands that we acknowledge affronts to urban life under the new conditions of twenty-first century military expansion.

The invasion of Iraq opened with a campaign of terrifying, explosive fireworks aimed at urban centers, most spectacularly Baghdad. It is difficult, however, to assess the damages from the aerial assaults. Although independent sources indicate more than 2,000 civilians lost,[2] the invaders have not released estimates of Iraqi deaths from direct or errant hits, nor clear descriptions of the impact on electrical grids, water-filtration plants, garbage- and sewage-disposal systems, transportation networks, and so forth—the underlying anatomy that makes a city possible from the point of view of basic health and safety. The bombs were, in any case, a prelude to subsequent developments. From south to north, Iraqi cities soon trembled under the weight and startling appearance of fighting tanks. A bloom of debris, including unexploded ordinance, put residents of these cities, especially children, at risk of death or maiming. Armor-piercing shells, whose depleted uranium tips release radio-active dust upon burning, are a particular hazard amidst the litter. And then came the post-invasion anarchy and crisis. Throughout the second half of the twentieth century, the names of certain cities—above all Hiroshima and Dresden—evoked the unbelievably destructive power of bombardment from the sky. Hearing these names one thought of a massively high toll in human life and the reduction of the built environment, its architectural and historical patrimony, to a moonscape. In contrast, in the dawning years of the twenty-first century, cities in the crosshairs of U.S.-led warfare may well index a different kind of destruction, the kind generated by the breakdown of civil order. The following reflection on Baghdad concerns less the bombs and tanks than the *time of chaos* that has been their aftermath.

Because the Middle East has the world's longest history of urbanization, many of its cities are not only palimpsests of urban development; their museums and libraries and educational institutions are world repositories of human achievement related to city life. Baghdad is no exception. Built by an Abbasid caliph in the eighth century, in the heart of the already urbanized Tigris-Euphrates valley on a line between Damascus, rival center of the Ummayads, and Isfahan in Persia, it was the capital of the medieval Muslim world. Paper, introduced from China, became a local manufacture, supporting the translation of Greek and Latin texts into Arabic. In touch with all of the civilizations of the time, Baghdad became a rich commercial and cultural center, renowned for its flourishing intellectual life and tradition of poetry.

In the thirteenth century, Mongol invaders destroyed the medieval city, burning books and libraries and demolishing Abbasid monuments. The Ottomans, subsequent invaders, made Baghdad the capital of an important province of their Empire in 1638. Each conquest unleashed processes of destruction and reconstruction, leaving the footprints of new mosques, markets, palaces, and defensive structures, built to ward off rival conquerors and Bedouin tribesmen. In the nineteenth century, British merchants, travelers and officials visited and surveyed the territories that would become Iraq, aware of their potential oil resources and geo-political position on the route to India. Western visitors also noted Baghdad's multiplicity of coexisting ethnic and religious groups; amidst the domes and minarets of both branches of Islam there were several synagogues and churches.

The Ottoman alliance with Germany during the First World War helped motivate the British to invade the lands they called Mesopotamia; they then obtained a mandate from the League of Nations to govern these lands when the Ottoman Empire fell. Various Iraqi constituencies mobilized against this Western intrusion but they were countered by Britain's installation of a puppet king, invitation to Western companies to develop oil fields, and reassertion of military occupation at the time of the Second World War. In 1958, Iraq became an independent republic, overthrowing its philo-British monarchy (although the Iraqi Oil Company, a creation of the British, was not nationalized until 1972). Ten years later, the first regime of national independence was undone by a Baathist Party coup, in turn an opening for the political contestations that brought Saddam Hussein to power in 1979.

Throughout these troubled times, Baghdad was acquiring a modern face. During the British mandate, projects of electrification, waterworks, public health and flood control accelerated the transformation of many of the older neighborhoods into blocks of flats. Light industries—textiles, tobacco, brick-making, tanning, brewing, milling—multiplied, drawing labor from the countryside. An agrarian reform following independence sent more rural migrants streaming into the city, stimulating public and private construction, and contributing to a growth in population from 140,000 in 1900 to over five million today. The concentration of impoverished newcomers in peripheral neighborhoods—the neighborhood of al-Sha'b, renamed "Saddam City" under Hussein, for example—provoked much official hand-wringing over the need for slum reform. Conversely, oil wealth paid for high living in the wealthy neighborhood of al-Mansour (targeted for bombing during the U.S. invasion because of intelligence reports that Hussein had been there), and paid, as well, for a succession of opulent new palaces, monuments, and mosques.

Sadly, the time of chaos following the U.S. invasion of Baghdad has irrevocably damaged the city's heritage. Yes, the bombs missed the golden domed mosques, but looters and thieves robbed the National Museum of treasured artifacts, both Islamic and pre-Islamic, just as they pilloried unsecured archaeological sites in the Mesopotamian heartland of civilization. Looters stole from and set fires in the National Library and Archives, an unparalleled storehouse of Ottoman documents, some two million volumes of which are now gone. The Library of the Korans at the Ministry of Religious Endowment was sacked as well. The pillaging of antiquities has happened before, in the wake of the Gulf War of 1991 and in earlier centuries, but this time it was exacerbated by the disappearance of policing authority, the proliferation of demobilized yet armed former militaries, and an international antiquities market rendered "hot" by globalization. The scale and scope of the plunder are unprecedented, while the occupying forces, despite advance warning, apparently lacked the preparation and commitment to bring it under control. The loss of national treasures and, more than this, the treasures of civilization writ large, has compromised the city's bequest to us all, not to mention its citizens' connection with their past.

In the past, Baghdad was the capital of both a repressive state and a welfare state. Imagining its future, one has to ask if it will again be capable, in the manner of Bangkok after the Asian financial crisis, of asserting claims on the rest of the country and on foreigners. Will it also be required, because of U.S. hegemony, to categorically privatize industries and forgo public investment in health and education? Such long-run questions are intriguing but almost beside the point. The preceding chapters are a brief for treating more immediate processes of the time of chaos as highly consequential, threatening a "depreciation or degradation of life" that is not merely "transitional".

At first glance, there seems something temporary or reparable about the orgy of looting that followed the appearance of the bombs and tanks in Baghdad. Companies around the world are eager for contracts to replace the furniture and supplies, the plumbing and equipment, of schools, hospitals, banks, government buildings, universities. The loss of polio and measles vaccines, which vanished when hospital refrigeration systems succumbed to gratuitous vandalism, might also be considered a momentary tragedy that can be overcome. More complicated is the vandalism that has interfered with repairs to the electricity, water, sewage, and telephone communications networks, all affected if not destroyed by the bombing. Interrupted repairs threaten public health and guarantee weeks of darkened streets, a boon to further lawlessness, car-jacking and violence.

More to the point, such extraordinary destruction renders institutions non-functional, affecting thousands of livelihoods. Over and above the disruptions of school and work, healthcare, dispute settlement, and governance, there is to consider the ripple effects of public servants and others having no money to spend. As several of the chapters in this volume illustrate, in conditions of economic collapse more-or-less organized criminal groups begin to transcend simple predatory acts of theft and kidnapping, pursuing extortion and racketeering on a more permanent basis. They menace violence, corrupt authorities, and protect themselves from prosecution and, needing lucrative revenue streams to purchase arms and pay bribes, members of such groups gravitate toward trafficking in (morally or legally) proscribed commodities. Economic collapse also produces waves of additional participants in trafficking, drawn from sectors of the population no longer making a living. This is why the sale of drugs and munitions gained a foothold in the poorer neighborhoods of U.S. inner cities and why it is regaining a dominant presence in Afghanistan today. Elsewhere, traffics in child laborers, coerced sex workers, or antiquities have mattered more. Whatever the commodity, its commerce may become the basis of a political-economy—perhaps more viable than the "official" political-economy—subjecting citizens to the misery of insecurity for decades to come. As Afghanistan suggests, the bombing is only the beginning of the story.

Even in the short run, insecurity leaves many scars. The chapter on Mexico City offers a vivid picture of what it means to endure a crime wave in which, contrary to more common crimes of passion or bar-room brawls, the victims are anonymous to the perpetrators. Inadequate and corrupt policing compel dependence on vigilantes who render the city less, not more, safe. Coining the phrase "the wear and tear of crisis" as well as the striking leitmotif, "the depreciation of life," Lomnitz notes the sacrifice of a young generation, the compromise of amiability, and the disproportionate distribution of these burdens across social groups. The technocratic rhetoric of officialdom, according to which such problems are transitory, their social costs to be erased by eventual economic growth, does not convince him. The chapters on U.S. cities (New York and Philadelphia), and on Kingston, closely examine communities where the hardships are compounded not only by crime but by intense criminalization and over-incarceration, at great cost to families and community life.

In Beirut the neighborhood strongmen operate like patrons as well as police, procuring food, employment, and housing for favored clients. Like "mafias," they also sway the official bodies set up to compensate victims for wartime losses. The compensation packages rarely accommodate the complexities of people's varied situations and are unobtainable without a patron's intervention. Citizens believe them to be grossly unfair and are bitter as a result. Then there is Medellín, a more extreme case, with its shifting bands of assassins, extortionists, and others armed in the self-defense of businesses and neighborhoods. One can rather easily hire a gun to kill, kidnap, or send a message; the state is helpless or collusive or, through its engagement of paramilitary forces to repress disorder, an active contributor to the mayhem. In the shanty towns that ring the city, residents afflicted by the violence of drug trafficking are now doubly harmed by a terrorizing "war on drugs."

Post-crisis Bangkok witnessed the invasive spread of informal markets into every imaginable public and cultural space, as men and women, suddenly cut loose with no income, turned to street vending as a way to cope. In other cities, insecurity along with disinvestment has meant abandoning public spaces and cultural offerings, possibly even schools and places of work. With public disinvestment, several U.S. cities have seen whole neighborhoods gradually degenerate into wastelands. In Siberia the disappearance of public transportation left a growing void that people fear to enter. Better to stay home, they believe, isolating themselves in their "icy coffins," than undertake a daunting journey through terrain rendered unfamiliar by emptiness and bandits. Humphrey describes how these citizens have elaborated the concept of "moral harm" to capture what they are going through, meaning by it the interruption of normal decencies and obligations—from taking a shower, to cooking for a son, to being able to be there for a relative who is dying.

Both as individuals, and as members of mutually supportive families and networks, citizens accumulate memories of the devastating effects of fear and uncertainty on their everyday lives. Belfast may represent a special case because of the hardening over many decades of sectarian strife, the raw material for grinding a set of discrete lenses through which to view future quarrels. Should memories be predominantly unhappy in Baghdad, and should they become politicized, a massive and costly investment of the world community in peace-making and peace-keeping will be required at some future time.

As this book has suggested, many wounded cities, uncertain of where to turn to put themselves back together, have nodded in the direction of international tourism. Sustained by oil revenues in the past, and having lost treasures more than once to the rapacity or negligence of invaders, Baghdad has at best a shallow history in this regard. There is also to note that the tourism "fix" may have run its course. Insecurities fostered by the attacks on the World Trade Center, and by pre-emptive warfare, have begun to tarnish the glamorous side of globalization and with this the commodification of cities. So too have new epidemic diseases and possible bioterrorism, especially in light of growing awareness that disinvestment in state services has weakened the public health systems of many countries. No wonder that we already see a steep decline in global transit, whether for business or pleasure, a worldwide rash of airline bankruptcies, and growing malaise among service workers in the pampering trades: hairdressers, taxi drivers, artisanal producers of "authentic" commodities and so forth. All told, attracting tourists, visitors, and shoppers may no longer be the salve for urban wounds that it once appeared —a very recent and disillusioning reality that must be affecting several of the cities in this volume.

The preceding chapters teach that the reconstruction of cities can create new waves of turmoil and suffering. Beirut's postwar rebuilding has intensified struggles for urban space and identity between those who left and those who stayed during the Civil War. In Palermo the shells of buildings bombed by the U.S. and the British at the end of the Second World War were left to decay as the Mafia and allied politicians "sacked" the historic center and over-built the periphery. Baghdad's recuperation has so far been entrusted to gargantuan U.S. engineering and construction firms closely identified with the political factions that supported the war against Iraq and more broadly with America's "military-industrial complex." Together with the other contractors and sub-contractors lining up to rebuild roads and railroads, electrical utilities and hydraulic works, ports and airports and oil fields, these corporations would seem to have replaced the glitzy logo-emblazoned companies of global tourism and shopping as the driving wedge of globalization. What will their stance be toward the privatization of public assets? And toward the corrupting influence of organized crime? The citizens of Baghdad (like the citizens of New York) will have to struggle for a reconstruction effort that is sensitive to their histories and memories and, as well, responsive to their material and moral needs, and longings for security.

Hope, we believe, is not naïve. On February 15, 2003, the largest worldwide demonstrations ever known took place in protest against the U.S. proposed war on Iraq. This visually stunning movement across the globe could never have been imagined a few years ago and powerfully illuminates the possibility of a world organized to further global justice. In the U.S. itself, 160 cities voted for anti-war resolutions. Following the invasion, and in spite of the climate of repression fostered by passage of the Patriot Act widening government surveillance and curtailing civil liberties, we see the U.S. edging back from the brink of unilateralism toward an engagement with the United Nations, in an effort to better restore the demolished civil orders of the cities it has (so smartly) bombed. We trust that this volume will provide some understanding of the crucial choices to be made, above all in constituting cities as healthy "bodies politic," in which, despite globalizing pressures, there is broad, collective participation in constructing the future.

Notes

1. This essay is written from the general perspective of concerned citizens of the world, neither of whom is a specialist on Iraq. We are fortunate that Samira Haj, who is a specialist, generously agreed to review an earlier draft. Her comments were of great help and are much appreciated although we, of course, are responsible for any remaining errors and gaps in understanding.
2. See http://www.iraqbodycount.net/background.htm and http://www.itszone.co.uk/zone0/links/wwe_iraq_bodyclock_about.html.